ABRAHAM LINCOLN AND THE

FORGE OF NATIONAL MEMORY

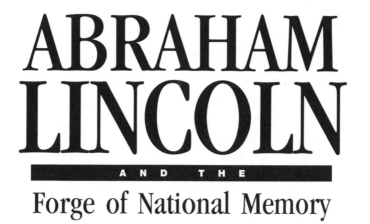

ABRAHAM LINCOLN

AND THE

Forge of National Memory

BARRY SCHWARTZ

THE UNIVERSITY OF CHICAGO PRESS

CHICAGO AND LONDON

BARRY SCHWARTZ is professor of sociology at the University of Georgia. His books include *Vertical Classification: A Study of Structuralism and the Sociology of Knowledge* and *George Washington: The Making of an American Symbol.*

The University of Chicago Press, Chicago 60637
The University of Chicago Press, Ltd., London
© 2000 by The University of Chicago
All rights reserved. Published 2000
Printed in the United States of America

09 08 07 06 05 04 03 02 01 00   1 2 3 4 5

ISBN: 0-226-74197-4 (cloth)

Library of Congress Cataloging-in-Publication Data

Schwartz, Barry, 1938–
   Abraham Lincoln and the forge of national memory / Barry
      Schwartz.
      p. cm.
   Includes bibliographical references (p.) and index.
   ISBN 0-226-74197-4 (cloth : alk. paper)
   1. Lincoln, Abraham, 1809–1865. 2. Presidents—United
States—Biography. 3. Lincoln, Abraham, 1809–1865—Public
opinion. 4. Lincoln, Abraham, 1809–1865—Influence.
5. National characteristics, American. 6. Social psychology—
United States. 7. Memory—Social aspects—United States.
8. Public opinion—United States.   I. Title.

E457.2 .S38 2000
973.7′092—dc21
[B]
                                                  99-462226

to Jay

Contents

PART THREE

Twentieth Century: Symbolizing Unity

Preface

Moments after President John F. Kennedy was buried in Arlington National Cemetery, a black limousine pulled up to the Lincoln Memorial. The two people inside sat silently for ten minutes, gazing at the memorial and thinking about the image inside. Scanning the past for images to make sense of their grief, Bobby and Jackie Kennedy had found Abraham Lincoln.

Scanning similar scenes of dedication and reverence, contemporary scholars and commentators are finding hegemony. Even in the grip of private distress, they say, people support the system by constructing heroes in its image and revering them. Is this what Bobby and Jackie were doing? Supporting the system? Or was the system, with its depth in time, tradition, and memories, supporting them?

Recent analyses of the American past help us think about and answer this question. Much of that work conceives collective memory as a "ruling idea" concealing oppression, sustaining "false consciousness," and satisfying the needs of a money-making "heritage industry." Collective memory is in every case a "social construction" soothing the soreness of the day.

To focus solely on memory's constructed side is to deny the past's significance as a model for coming to terms with the present. What better way to trash the past than to define it as a mere disguise for present interests and balm for present troubles? Believing all realities to be socially "constructed," a generation of scholars has depreciated collective memory by dwelling on how people differ, individually and collectively, in their interpretations of events and by studying how these differences are influenced by elite programmers. The first strategy relativizes the past by linking it to competing interests and points of view; the second strategy degrades the past by revealing the profane motives and means by which it is preserved and commemorated. By day's end, the past—or what is known of it through history and commemoration—is fairly well annihilated.

Constructionist research is at bottom admirable and necessary, for it emphasizes historical developments—the harmful exploits of Columbus, the erosion of native American societies, the consequences of the oppression of blacks, Asians, and Hispanics—hitherto ignored. The problem with the research is its inconsistency. As constructionists present the nation's sins as matters of indisputable fact, they present the nation's virtues as "myths," "metanarratives," and "inventions" concocted by a privileged majority determined to secure its domination over minorities. Conductors of this research are positivist on the matter of the vices of American history, constructionist on its virtues.

"As long as one does not call his own position into question but regards it as absolute, while interpreting his opponents' ideas as a mere function of the social positions they occupy, the decisive step [toward a thoroughgoing sociological analysis] has not yet been taken." Karl Mannheim's observation (1936, 77) on the sociology of knowledge applies directly to its rapidly growing branch, the sociology of memory. Every image of the past, ours and theirs, virtuous and vicious, is a construction, uninterpretable outside its selective, narrative framing; yet the materials going into the image consist of facts (assertions of varying reliability and generalizability), whose interpretation is constrained by rules of evidence. True, the careful gathering and interpretation of facts are undertaken within biased perceptual frames, but this bias is what makes events knowable in the first place. Given the mind's limits, selective emphasis is a condition of, not an impediment to, knowing. Thus, the "frequent *rethinking* of the past" (italics in original) is as necessary as it is normal (Lukacs 1994, 34–35) but must involve, beyond recognition of one's own biases, the submission of all propositions, whatever their source, to verification.

My concept of collective memory is biased toward Max Weber's concept of meaning. Culture solves the problem of meaning, I believe, by providing perspectives explaining otherwise enigmatic, stressful, and disorganizing happenings. An intrinsic part of culture, collective memory works in tandem with these perspectives—science, politics, religion, art, common sense—to interpret experience. Collective memory works by subsuming individual experiences under cultural schemes that make them comprehensible and, therefore, meaningful.

The future use of sociology will involve an understanding of collective memory as a framework of meaning—not as merely a tool for challenging and maintaining power. This book cannot turn away from the politics of memory but must embed it within meaning-defining frames. Although new generations always recognize the inadequacy of earlier generations' frameworks of memory, it is the very need for revision—the necessity of a meaningful past to make present experience cognitively, emotionally, and morally comprehensible—that I take as my point of departure.

Modern society sustains a minimum of memories common to all its members, and many American heroes could serve as vehicles to explore these. Abraham Lincoln is the most appropriate case because in the early decades of the twentieth century—the era during which the United States was rapidly becoming an industrial, urban society—he personified the substance of America's sense of itself. Since America's self-conception has always been based on the ideals of liberty, equality, individualism, populism, and laissez-faire (Lipset 1996), Lincoln's life, by exemplifying these ideals through self-reliance and belief in the dignity of the common man, has always lent itself to his country's political discourse. Garry Wills (1992) has, in fact, argued that Lincoln was more than a character in America's story; he single-handedly redefined its plot and laid the foundation of a new society by propagating new ideals of equality and justice. For Wills, the story of Lincoln nourishes America's moral identity by reiterating the nation's history and traditional values, shaping the moral character of its citizens, and orienting the way they interpret and engage the world. Given Wills's claim, we must determine whether the abrupt elevation of Lincoln's reputation at the turn of the century resulted from new biographical information or deep changes in American culture transcending Lincoln himself. Understanding Lincoln's transformation from a controversial president to a national deity helps to clarify how Americans of that time gained a sense of historical continuity that seems to be less evident today.

The task of explaining the vicissitudes of Abraham Lincoln's reputation must be divided into two parts. In the first part, this book, Lincoln's image is traced from April 14, 1865, the day of his assassination, through the Progressive era, to May 30, 1922, dedication day for his national memorial in Washington, D.C. In the second part, a half-completed book, Lincoln's reputation will be traced from its peak during the Great Depression and World War II to its dramatic decline during the last four decades of the century. These two works must be kept separate because each deals with a different aspect of collective memory. The present work, set in a newly industrialized America, connects the politics of memory to the resentments, achievements, and aspirations of the Progressive era. It also focuses on the authority of the past and the rapidly growing prestige of the presidency. The future work, focusing largely on the last third of the twentieth century, a period in which presidential authority has diminished, documents the erosion of the past as a frame of political and moral reference.

Since individuals engage the past as they adapt to changing environments, every turning point in American history has led to a revised Lincoln image. We need to know, however, why this image's continuities are as distinctive as its vicissitudes, how change and continuity frame as well as reflect new political realities, how existing conceptions of Lincoln restrain efforts to produce new conceptions, how diversity in his image's details upholds consensus in fundamentals, and how Lincoln in remembrance has affirmed fundamental aspects of American identity.

Acknowledgments

I began this project in 1987 while a Fellow at the Center for Advanced Study in the Behavioral Sciences, Stanford, California. After working on Lincoln periodically for the next five years, I regained focus at the National Humanities Center in Research Triangle Park, North Carolina, during 1992–93. In summer 1993 I spent a Smithsonian Institution Senior Fellowship on the project in Washington, D.C., then an academic quarter free of teaching made possible by a University of Georgia Humanities Center Fellowship.

In addition to this institutional support, for which I am most grateful, I have benefited from the critical eyes of colleagues. For Howard Schuman's multiple readings and extended commentary I am most obligated. His reactions have been a source of constant insight and challenge. I also owe special thanks to Michael Schudson, whose comments on my very first draft, covering 1865 to the present, convinced me to split the project into two parts. To say special thanks to Howard Schuman and Michael Schudson is to say a great deal, for Gary Fine, Alan Woolfolk, and Steven G. Hague, former Director of the Abraham Lincoln Library and Museum, Harrogate, Tennessee, also read earlier drafts of this work, and each returned extensive and pointed suggestions for improving it. I spent many hours exploiting their help. These colleagues, as well as a still anonymous University of Chicago Press reviewer, were indispensable to me; I am proud to be indebted to each of them.

My wife, Janet, too, is a colleague, but I thank her separately for her proofreading help. An old-fashioned English teacher who can parse any English sentence, she hates two things: the passive voice and sentences beginning with or including "it is." I can only say I have done my best.

Two Faces of Collective Memory

After the 1955 Montgomery, Alabama, bus boycott, civil rights demonstrations spread across the South, intensifying during the spring and summer of 1963. President John Kennedy, although drawn into the conflict against his will, acted decisively in major confrontations with Southern governors. Tensions peaked in Birmingham, where police turned dogs and fire hoses against young demonstrators. Against this background, U.S. Representative Fred Schwengel of Iowa rose to deliver the 1963 commencement address at Lincoln Memorial University in Harrogate, Tennessee.

Mr. Lincoln, against a thousand and one indignities that we commit against our own tradition of freedom, against the shame of white citizens councils and dogs set on school children, we have, like a great cry in the wilderness, the immortal ring of your name.

We turn, Mr. Lincoln, in our guilt and our self-disgrace to you. We hold you up against the horizon before the whole of living mankind. We say to all the world—to all the world—we say this:

We say: No, Birmingham in the year of our Lord 1963 is not the American tradition. Nor is a Little Rock of yesterday. Nor is the disgrace of the inadequate schools for the Negroes and whites in the District of Columbia— in the shadow of the Capitol Building that symbolizes the ideals you loved

1

so devotedly. No, Mr. Lincoln, with a piteous cry out of the depth of the American conscience, we proclaim here and throughout the land with all the sincerity of a free people, right out of the marrow of our bones, we declare, we pledge that—not Birmingham, not Little Rock, not Faubus, nor Wallace, not "Bull" Conner, but here in you, Mr. Lincoln, is the true genius of the American people. . . . Our authoritative position, Mr. Lincoln, is the position you left us. (Schwengel 1963, 10173)

Lincoln's Position

Despite Representative Schwengel's accolades, which seemed reasonable to most Americans in 1963, Abraham Lincoln was no civil rights champion.[1] He was a Whig who believed in emancipation followed by colonization (deportation) of all former slaves and free blacks. No aspect of Lincoln's life, however, was more distorted during the peak of the civil rights movement than his position on race relations, and Martin Luther King Jr. knew this when he asked President Kennedy to issue a "Second Emancipation Proclamation" making segregation illegal. King knew that the Great Emancipator had not been the Great Integrator; that Lincoln, influenced by his ideal, Henry Clay, supposed that the Declaration of Independence entitled blacks to the protection of life and property, but not to the right to vote, petition, or serve on juries—and certainly not to social and cultural equality. In 1856, Lincoln joined the antislavery Republican Party and adopted its policy that "all the unoccupied territory of the United States, and such as they may hereafter acquire, shall be reserved for the white Caucasian race—a thing which cannot be except by the exclusion of slavery" (Durden 1965, 364–65). If slavery crossed its present borders, Lincoln said, black workers would be everywhere, "as every white laborer will have occasion to regret when he is elbowed from his plow or his anvil by slave niggers" (Lincoln 1953–55, 3:78). Lincoln believed that democracy gave every white man the right to enrich himself through hard work, but this right would mean nothing without restrictions on slavery—and without homestead legislation, protective tariffs, and federally supported internal improvements (including a nationwide railroad system), all opposed by the Southern Democratic slave power.

In the middle decades of the nineteenth century, few whites felt more sympathy for the plight of blacks or treated them more decently and respectfully than did Abraham Lincoln. Few white politicians opposed slavery more insistently than Lincoln. But this opposition says little by today's standards, and while the racist culture in which Lincoln was reared can be discounted by standardizing his attitudes against the prevailing mode, Representative Schwengel, eager to convince himself that racial integration is intrinsic to America's heritage, conceived Lincoln's attitudes to be more progressive than they were.

Lincoln's political speeches opposed equality for blacks, as did the audiences to whom he spoke. Debating Stephen Douglas during the 1858 Illinois senatorial campaign, Lincoln's greatest fear was that his opposition to slavery's extension might be mistaken for a radical view favoring racial equality. He explained: "I will say then that I am not, nor ever have been in favor of bringing about in any way the social and political equality of the white and black races . . . and I will say in addition to this that there is a physical difference between the white and black races which I believe will for ever forbid the two races living together on terms of social and political equality" (Lincoln 1953–55, 3:145–46). Lincoln's antislavery supporters did not believe he made this statement in order to win their votes. He had made many similar statements in the past and had supported policies consistent with them. In 1858, the year he debated Douglas, a black abolitionist named H. Ford Douglass asked Lincoln to sign a petition asserting the right of blacks to testify in court. Lincoln refused (Zilversmit 1971, 65–67). On June 26, 1857, Lincoln referred to whites' attitude toward racial "amalgamation" (intermarriage) as one of "natural [as opposed to culturally learned] disgust" (Lincoln 1953–55, 2:405). Three months earlier, he had objected to the Supreme Court's Dred Scott decision, which denied the states power to grant citizenship to blacks. But he was arguing in principle, not substance: "If the State of Illinois had that power, I would be opposed to the exercise of it" (3:179). Three years earlier, in 1854, he contemplated a society in which whites and blacks were socially equal. "My own feelings," he said, "would never admit this" (2:256). In 1840, he attacked presidential candidate Martin Van Buren for voting in New York to extend the right of suffrage to free blacks (1:210).

In his 1861 Inaugural Address, Lincoln promised never to interfere with slavery where it existed and, shortly afterward, embraced a proposed amendment to the Constitution guaranteeing that the federal government would never interfere with slavery. Lincoln thought this guarantee to be implicit in the Constitution but declared, "I have no objection to its being made express and irrevocable" (Lincoln 1953–55, 4:270). Even when war began, he returned escaped slaves to their masters and reprimanded field officers who sheltered them. Lincoln represented a constituency largely indifferent to slavery itself but fearful that millions of freed slaves would migrate to the North, lowering profits and wages and taking over jobs.

That many Northerners supported Lincoln's antislavery position because he opposed integrating blacks into society is evidenced in the 1860 New York City election results: thirty-two thousand people voted for Lincoln, but only sixteen hundred voted for the black suffrage amendment on the same ballot (Litwack 1961, 271). When "Honest Abe" said he opposed racial mixing, his supporters believed him. In 1864, Lincoln ran for reelection and won almost 80 percent of the soldier vote. Most of these men, according to James McPherson's analysis (1994b), favored emancipation, but not because they opposed the principle of slavery. In an army containing four Democrats for every six Republicans, emancipation seemed a good way to weaken Confederate war-making powers, abolish the institution that had split the Union, and protect free labor from slave labor competition.

Lincoln had promised that emancipation would not lower the wages of free labor, and if emancipated slaves were deported, as planned, "enhanced wages to white labor is mathematically certain" (Lincoln 1953–55, 5:535).[2] His deportation projects failed, but he continued to speak against making blacks equal members of society. Given the contribution of African Americans to Union victory, he favored voting rights for selected blacks in the reconstructed state of Louisiana but did nothing to secure these rights. Many present-day admirers, taking Lincoln's personal preference on this particular issue as evidence, assume that his friendly statements on racial justice reflected his true sentiments, while his earlier black-baiting arose from political necessity.[3] Many others, admirers and critics alike, assume that Lincoln's call for separation and colonization reflected his true feelings, while his public recognition of black rights and interests was induced by irresistible pressures from within his own party—forces that grew stronger as military victory approached (Sinkler 1971). A successful war enhanced the abolitionist powers Lincoln had resisted throughout his presidency.

As Southern authorities formalized the Jim Crow system in the late nineteenth century, with Northern popular approval, they claimed they were doing what Lincoln would have done. Lincoln never advocated formal segregation in Illinois because segregation was already a fact of life, but if twentieth-century segregationists were referring to what Lincoln would have done under circumstances comparable to theirs, they may have been right (Schwartz 1997). Most Americans probably thought so, for at the dedication of the Lincoln Memorial on May 30, 1922, Union army veterans, dressed in their blue uniforms, stood beside gray-clad Confederate army veterans. President Warren Harding noted in his address that Abraham Lincoln would have been thrilled to know that "the states of the Southland joined sincerely in honoring him." Chief Justice and former president William Howard Taft, the second speaker, emphasized Harding's point. The Lincoln Memorial, Taft said, marked the final restoration of "brotherly love" between North and South (*New York Age,* June 10, 1922, 2). However, nothing was said about brotherly love between blacks and whites. The U.S. Congress, with the full support of its Southern members, had built the Lincoln Memorial to celebrate regional, not racial, reconciliation.

Remembering Lincoln

That Representative Fred Schwengel, speaking in June 1963, convincingly portrayed Lincoln as a civil rights prophet—two months before Martin Luther King Jr. delivered his "I Have a Dream" speech at the Lincoln Memorial—demonstrates the malleability of the past and justifies Maurice Halbwachs's claim that "collective memory is essentially a reconstruction of the past [that] adapts the image of historical facts to the beliefs and spiritual needs of the present" (1941, 7). Schwengel's remarks on the District of Columbia's schools and his allusion to Lincoln (whose children attended the finest private schools) as a champion of public education reinforce Halbwachs's point.

Schwengel never thought his conception of Abraham Lincoln might project the ideas of his own generation; he considered Lincoln a fixed and cherished memory, and he was not entirely wrong. Social memories, as aspects of culture, do more than "express" social reality; they shape reality by articulating ideals and generating the motivation to realize them. Representative Schwengel seemed to know this intuitively. Defining the civil rights struggle as one episode in the continuous narrative of American history, he held up Lincoln as a model by which American society could judge itself. Schwengel conceived Lincoln's image not as a mirror of his contemporaries' experience but as a model for shaping that experience and making it morally intelligible—"an extrapersonal mechanism," as Clifford Geertz would say, "for the perception, understanding, and judgement of the world" (1973b, 216).

Lincoln's 1863 emancipation policy must be distinguished from 1963 efforts to integrate blacks into contemporary society, but if Schwengel's remaking of Abraham Lincoln required some invention and exaggeration, the historical record also justified it. Lincoln's role in the record of black history certainly cannot be reduced to his enthusiasm for colonization. Although he and his supporters saw no necessary connection between freeing slaves and assimilating them as equals, racial equality is inferable from emancipation, and this inference became clearer to more people in 1963 than it had ever been previously. Historically, Lincoln's Emancipation Proclamation was the first step toward a racially integrated society. Representative Schwengel's commencement address does more, therefore, than invent history; it valuates history by lifting the morally significant elements of Lincoln's life above the mundane. If Lincoln's historical role had been different and less decisive, his place in American memory would not now be what it is, and Schwengel's address would have been pointless.

Considering Lincoln's image as a mere projection of present problems is as wrong as taking it to be a literal account of his life and character. That the American people have conceived Lincoln in their own image, seen that image harden over the years, and come to revere what they have themselves created is only part of the truth. Americans have invoked Lincoln so often because the ideals he symbolized contrast with the realities they face, and his example remains recognizable because beliefs about him have outlived changes in society. Nothing, then, could be more vacuous than to characterize Lincoln as a mythical construction. A myth, to abstract from Henry Murray's definition, "manifestly consists of the essential features of an important, more or less natural/preternatural [extraordinary] situation or event" (1962, 8). But how far can we reconstruct an event before losing sight of what is "essential" about it?

The story of Lincoln may be defined as a reconstruction in at least four senses. It may have been (1) invented out of thin air, bearing no relation to known biographical facts; (2) patterned on established facts, some of which are exaggerated, muted, or altered in sequence; (3) patterned after established facts without exaggeration, but so selectively as to distort reality; (4) patterned consciously or unconsciously after subjective attitudes erroneously inferred from Lincoln's conduct. How, then, are we to regard Lincoln? Is he an invention? An exaggeration? A selective perception? An inference imperfectly drawn? And what are we to make of the significance of his image? Is he a model *of* society or a model *for* society (Geertz 1973c, 93–94)? A mirror or a lamp for the present? A reflection of the concerns of the day or a pattern for understanding and dealing with them? And how variable has this image been? Is it conceived anew by each generation, or does it remain consistent across the years?

These questions admit of no realistic answers. To conceive of collective memory as a mirror of reality is to conceive a fiction, for if, independently of historical evidence, our changing understanding of the past uniquely parallels changes in our society, then the only relevant reality would be the present, and the very concept of collective memory would be meaningless. To conceive the meaning of the past as fixed and steady is likewise meaningless, since any event must appear differently as perceptual circumstances change.

During the 135 years since Abraham Lincoln's death, his reputation has alternately risen and fallen (Schwartz 1998). It rose abruptly after his April 1865 assassination, but he did not become a national idol until the first two decades of the twentieth century. These pivotal years, 1901–20, were distinguished not only by Theodore Roosevelt's presidency and the Progressive movement, but also by America's rise to global power. Since so much of the Lincoln we know today emerged from this period, we need to find out how Lincoln appeared to nineteenth-century Americans, how his image changed during the early twentieth century, and, in each era, what ideological issues his image articulated.

These questions differ from those Merrill Peterson explored in *Abraham Lincoln in American Memory* (1994), a superbly detailed account of Lincoln's reputation from 1865 to 1994. Peterson's work organizes Lincoln's biographies and commemorative symbols around five images: Savior of the Union, Emancipator, Man of the People, Self-Made Man, and First American. In these images he finds Lincoln's public memory (distinguishable from the historical record) and traces it through the twentieth century. As a chronicler of biography, poetry, statuary, paintings, monuments, and ritual, Peterson is expansive and complete, but he is silent about how these symbols operate as vehicles of conception. To say, as he does, that memory "restages the past and manipulates it for ongoing public purposes" (35) ignores important questions. Who does the manipulating? Why do they choose Lincoln as their tool? Does the public understanding of

Lincoln differ from the manipulators'? Which parts of Lincoln's life are selected for the purposes of manipulating the public? Which aspect of "ongoing public purposes" does biographical selection affect? What relation do these purposes bear to the exploited biography? In particular, why did Lincoln as Self-Made Man and Man of the People so long dominate Lincoln as Emancipator? What does the answer tell us about American culture and the power of the Lincoln image?

Exploring the social roots of Abraham Lincoln's reputation shows how collective memory reflects and frames the American experience. My study, however, seeks to encompass, not enlarge, Peterson's work. Peterson's *history* of commemoration has asked the *what* of Lincoln's reputation; my work, a study of the *sociology* of commemoration, deals with the *how* and *why*. In James McPherson's words, Peterson "does not offer an explicit answer to the big question: Why does Lincoln's image loom so large over our cultural landscape?" (1994a, 7). We cannot deal with Abraham Lincoln in collective memory, however, until we know more about collective memory itself. What are the principal components of collective memory? How do we know it when we see it? Providing a clear definition will move us a step closer to answering McPherson's question.

The Meaning of Collective Memory

Personal and Institutional Remembrance

"Society is not the work of individuals that compose it at a given state of history, nor is it a given place. It is a complex of ideas and sentiments, of ways of seeing and feeling, a certain intellectual and moral framework distinctive of the entire group" (Durkheim [1925] 1973, 277). Collective memory is part of society's "intellectual and moral framework."

Collective memory refers simultaneously to what is in the minds of individuals and to emergent conceptions of the past crystallized into symbolic structures.[4] Individual acts of recall and recognition take place in "mnemonic communities" passing on "mnemonic traditions" to its members through "mnemonic socialization" (Zerubavel 1997), but these individual memories, although deeply rooted in social experience, do not function in the same way as collective memory. Howard Schuman notes in this respect that collective memory is not like individual memory at all; it is more similar to public opinion, because both memory and opinion have an individual aspect or meaning yet transcend the individual level. Collective memory, thus, cannot be reduced to an aggregate of individual memories.[5]

Collective memory affects what individuals think about the past but transcends the individuals because it is constituted by what Alfred Kroeber called "superpersonal" properties ([1923] 1963, 62), which include narratives, pictorial objects, monuments and shrines, place-names, and observances that are accumulated and transmitted across generations. At this level, collective memory embraces not only events occurring during the lifetime of a population but also events occurring before any member of a population was born. Words referring to individuals' remembering and forgetting, in this sense, are metaphors. "Remembered" events occurring before an individual's birth are stored not in the mind but in museums, libraries, and schools; history books and biographies; monuments, statues, paintings, and relics. They are recalled not through neural passageways but by call number and computer command, by invocation, pilgrimage, and commemorative ritual.

Distinctions between personal and institution-based memory have never been absolute. Many people alive during the Civil War may have remembered their personal experiences but nothing about the war itself. Later, they attributed to their own memory what they learned from history books and family members. Likewise, millions of Americans remembered Lincoln's assassination firsthand, but their memories were determined mainly by the way newspapers, clergymen, teachers, and politicians defined the event. Even those participating directly in the war learned about the conflict in the same indirect way they learned about previous historical events.

To define collective memory, even after years of fairly intensive research, would be prematurely restrictive, for definitions should conform to reality, and much about reality remains to be discovered. Yet a tentative, superpersonal[6] conception may be proposed: collective memory is based on two sources of belief about the past—*history* and *commemoration*. Collective memory is a representation of the past embodied in *both* historical evidence and commemorative symbolism.

History and Commemoration

Commemoration mobilizes symbols to awaken ideas and feelings about the past. The word *commemoration* derives from Latin: *com* (together) + *memorare* (to remember)—to remember together. Commemorative processes, remembering together, occur at every level of social life—family, occupational association, community, and society—but their dynamics are most visible at the societal level. By marking events believed to be most deserving of remembrance, commemoration becomes society's moral memory. Commemoration makes society conscious of itself as it affirms its members' mutual affinity and identity.

Commemorable events are always important to society; however, their significance may sometimes be negative. Negative commemoration, the marking of events weighing on the present generation as sources of shame and dishonor, has arisen during the late twentieth century in connection with society's recognition of minorities and expression of regret for the historical wrongs these groups have suffered. Subsumed under the new commemorative politics of regret (Olick 1999) are new shrines, monuments, and museums marking the era of slavery, maltreatment of minorities, and unpopular war. That earlier monuments were heroic, however, does not mean they symbolized uniform admiration. It means—and this is crucial to understanding Lincoln's image—that negative sentiments were rarely expressed in major commemorative or historical forms.

Commemorative symbolism and historical facts must be adequately distinguished. History, according to Maurice Halbwachs ([1950] 1980), is "situated external to and above groups" and develops independently of their problems and concerns. Once established, history remains stable—its stream of facts and demarcations "fixed once and for all." History is objectively conceived, sustained by evidence and unaffected by the social context in which its practitioners work. In contrast, collective memory, the way ordinary people conceive the past, reflects immediate interests and concerns. Collective memories vanish, Halbwachs explains, when they cease to be relevant to current experience (80–81).

Only in modern societies does history challenge collective memory. In traditional societies there is no history. The early Christians, to take an example from Halbwachs's *Legendary Topography of the Gospels in the Holy Land* ([1941] 1992), had no conception of "historical preoccupations such as we think of them. . . . Their memories were tied to rites of commemoration and adoration, to ceremonies, feasts, and processions" (222). Since collective memory is the "repository of tradition," history must start "when tradition ends and the social memory is fading or breaking up" ([1950] 1980, 78; see also Plumb 1970; Yerushalmi 1982; and Lukacs 1994).

Following Halbwachs, Pierre Nora (1996) sees history and collective memory existing in separate and opposed realms. Collective memory is composed of its *lieux de mémoire* (sites of memory),[7] which include not only geographical places symbolizing the past but also flags and anthems, monuments and shrines, sanctuaries and ruins, statues and busts, portraits and history paintings, coins and medallions, holidays and rituals. "Literature, film, and popular visual imagery in such popular media as postcards, cartoons, and posters"—these, too, are important *lieux de mémoire* (Sherman 1994, 186).

During the last half-century, *lieux de mémoire*, "fleeting incursions of the sacred into a disenchanted world," have been overwhelmed by deconstructive history. "If we still dwelled among our memories, there would be no need to consecrate sites embodying them" (Nora 1996, 7). Assuming that the very commemorative activities affirming commitment to the past are nostalgic symptoms of its diminution, Nora's sharp distinction between history and collective memory, like Halbwachs's before him, has seduced readers into asserting unwittingly, and often despite themselves, that what is not historical must be "invented" or "constructed"—a position transforming the study of collective memory into a kind of cynical muckraking.

Reduced to commemoration, collective memory becomes, for Halbwachs and Nora, a distorted version of history. They cannot see, let alone examine, collective memory as the reciprocal working of history and commemoration. History disenchants the past, commemoration and its sites sanctify it; history makes the past an object of analysis, commemoration makes it an object of commitment. History is a system of "referential symbols" representing known facts about past events and their sequence; commemoration is a system of "condensation symbols" (Sapir 1930, 492–93) expressing the moral sentiments these events inspire. History, like science, investigates the world by producing models of its permanence and change. Commemoration, like ideology, promotes commitment to the world by symbolizing its values and aspirations (Durkheim [1890] 1973; Geertz 1973b).[8] Commemoration is not to be understood as inferior history; nor, for that matter, is history to be understood as an antidote to commemoration.

Commemoration and history perform work so different that we confound both by assessing them in terms of one another's techniques and achievements, but they are highly interdependent. History always reflects the ideals and sentiments that commemoration expresses; commemoration is always rooted in historical knowledge and can only be intellectually compelling when it symbolizes values whose past existence history documents. The making of monuments, shrines, paintings, and statues, the naming of places and observance of anniversaries connected with the life of a historical figure, become more meaningful if the virtues and achievements they celebrate are factually confirmed. Just so, history is morally compelling when it documents extraordinary events, for the chief function of commemoration is to select out of the welter of history the events that are politically and morally most significant. Many historians take an interest in events in the first place because they have been commemoratively distinguished.[9]

America's knowledge of Abraham Lincoln is preserved by the systematic recording and explaining of his experiences and accomplishments, but the elements of Lincoln's life story are evaluated differently:[10] some of his accomplishments, such as his work as a railroad attorney, are ignored or treated indifferently; others, such as his decisions to wage war and to abolish slavery, are commemorated, that is, invested with extraordinary moral significance and assigned a distinct place in society's conception of him. So far as commemoration selects and lifts out of Lincoln's biographical record the episodes embodying fundamental values, Americans commemorating an event in Lincoln's life connect themselves to it, identify with it, and exercise their sense of who they are collectively in terms of it. Commemoration transforms historical facts about Lincoln into objects of attachment by defining their meaning and explaining how people should feel about them.

To distinguish between Abraham Lincoln's commemoration and biography is only the first step in understanding his place in American memory. The next necessary step is to make explicit the theories to be employed in explaining commemorative symbolism and biographical writings. Since interpretations of the past can discredit or confirm the status quo, legitimate or resist oppression, promote or undermine interests, the making of commemorative symbols and assertion of biographical and historical facts are, in important respects, political acts. How far this assertion should be relied on to explore Abraham Lincoln's case will be evident as we appreciate the merits and inadequacies of the politics of memory theory.

Two Theories of Collective Memory

The Politics of Memory

Present understandings of commemoration and history are conditioned by changes that have occurred in American society during the last third of the twentieth century. Richard Terdiman has observed that "[a]ny revolution, any rapid alteration in the givens of the present places a society's connection with its history under pressure" (1993, 3). As that pressure grows, a "memory crisis"—defined as a significant weakening of the present's connection with the past— ensues. Since the past frames present existence, the complete detachment of past and present is theoretically as well as empirically impossible; however, in some instances the rupture of the tissue of memory is so severe that it becomes an object of special inquiry. Hence the unprecedented explosion of collective memory research during the last two decades of this century.

The memory crisis of late-twentieth-century America accompanies the nation's new postindustrial economy, expanding multinational commercial relations, growing mass media, and diffusion of power from traditionally privileged to traditionally marginal populations. Fuller inclusion of minorities into the social mainstream and lessened tolerance of inequalities induce criticism of conventional interpretations of history, recognition of past immorality, and greater sensitivity to the way historians have written the powerless out of the historical record.

Whether it is desirable for individuals to live in connection with the past, whether revisionist understandings of past events are more valid than traditional accounts, whether textbooks should be modified to include more about the experience of American minorities, whether ethnic groups should be encouraged to cultivate their own heritage or subordinate it to the unifying memories of the nation— these are issues on which most of us have opinions, but they are not sociological issues. Sociological issues concern the conditions under which one version of the past rather than another dominates, how versions of the past change, what factors limit revision and afford history and commemoration their autonomy. At the core of these issues reside the realities of power.

Power and Remembrance In the theory of the politics of memory, pronouncements about the past, whether in the form of historical

or commemorative statements, are placed against a background of
political struggle.[11] No perspective that reduces social experience to
politics can be very true to reality, yet the theory of the politics of
memory is no straw man whose shortcomings make alternatives look
more convincing. Indeed, no perspective on collective memory would
be more difficult to discredit; no perspective has done more to align
collective memory study to the conditions of a new kind of society,
one where the minorities and the powerless enjoy more dignity and
rights than ever before.

The theoretical coherence of the politics of memory, the clarity
of its concepts, and the boldness with which these enter into propositions about reality make it a good point of departure for developing
knowledge of how collective memory works. If this theory is not relevant to the Progressive era, the focal setting of this project, no theory
can be. The Progressive era was above all a period of political fer-
ment, of suspicion of plutocracy and political bosses, a time for rou-
tinized muckraking and reexamination of the assumptions underlying popular conceptions of government. No one knew exactly what
to do about the corporate giants that had given the nation such pro-
ductive power, but many were up in arms against them. For the first
time, exploitation of workers in mines, sweatshops, and factories
provoked widespread reform activity. As traditional relationships between the state and the individual eroded, Americans required new
ways of understanding the past. Just as political and economic conflict was pivotal to the thinking of the great progressive historians
Charles Beard, Frederick Jackson Turner, and Vernon Parrington (see
Hofstadter 1969), so it shaped the content of the era's commemorative symbolism.

Research on the politics of memory (ably summarized in Zelizer
1995 and Olick and Robbins 1998) is exemplified in many fine
works, including that of Eric Hobsbawm and Terence Ranger (1983,
263–308) on the invention of public rituals and spectacles as modes
of social control during Europe's democratic revolutions and John
Bodnar (1992) on official and vernacular memories in the United
States. These two works are exemplary because they articulate so
clearly the constructionist position that this book seeks to qualify.

For Hobsbawm and Ranger, the void left by the decline of traditional political structures has led to invented traditions that symbolize societal cohesion, legitimize new institutions, statuses, and relations of authority, and inculcate new beliefs and values. These social
forms are "invented" in the sense of being deliberately designed and

produced with a view to sustaining order. Tradition, commonly defined as a conception or practice unwittingly transmitted across generations, becomes a conscious strategy adopted by political regimes
to reinforce their authority (see also Handler and Linnekin 1984;
Alonso 1988; Gillis 1994; and Zerubavel 1995).

The richest and most coherent application of this approach to
American studies is John Bodnar's *Remaking America* (1992). Bodnar develops the agenda of the politics of memory by distinguishing
between "official memory"—state-sponsored commemorations of
familiar national events, including the American Revolution and
the Civil War; and "vernacular memory"—ethnic, local, and regional
communities' recollection of subnational pasts. Official and vernacular memories erode one another, but the battle is uneven: commemorative resources have always been controlled by the dominant class
(Protestant middle-class businessmen of the nineteenth century; professionals, editors, and government officials of the twentieth), whose
official "programmers" are "disciplining authorities" seeking to promote loyalty to the state and its leaders. The great narratives and
symbols of official memory, from the best-selling high school history
texts to Fourth of July celebrations and the Washington Monument,
are means by which America's elite class beguiles and imposes its
own values on the rest of society and preserves the institutions in
which it has a personal stake. Do planners and organizers of the ethnic past play a similar role? Are they "disciplining authorities" who
promote loyalty to the ethnic community and obedience to its leaders? No; they are too busy defending their culture against the state.
Only the custodians of the national past seek hegemony.[12]

Bodnar's approach, emphasizing the profane motives that go into
the preservation and commemoration of the past, is ideologically
driven, for it is never applied to memories cherished by minorities.
Bodnar offers no account of what Charles Maier (1993, 142–49)
calls the American "Holocaust industry," no account of the political
wrangling associated with memorials to African American heroes or
inflated Native American claims. The theory of the politics of memory, given its affinity for postmodernism, multiculturalism, and hegemony theory,[13] focuses on the social construction of the *official* past
because the retention of state hegemony depends on control over the
way that past is represented (Tuchman and Fortin 1989; Baigell
1993; Gillis 1994; Boyarin 1994).

If social change is conceived in terms of the redistribution of
power, the theory of the politics of memory is also a theory of "the

history of memory," or, more precisely, a theory of how political changes revise understandings of the past. The most systematic studies in this tradition show how memories of particular *subjects* change across generations. Thus, James Loewen (1995) explains how the claims of newly empowered minorities transformed Christopher Columbus from a major hero in 1892 to a villainous murderer and thief in 1992. Lyn Spillman's comparative study (1997) reveals late-nineteenth-century Australia and America celebrating their national centennials as English-speaking republics governed by beneficent, native-born white men. One hundred years later, both countries, adapting to a newly inclusive political situation, articulated their identities through symbols of egalitarian democracy. At the end of the Civil War, according to Thomas Connelly (1977), Southern newspapers criticized Robert E. Lee for having lost the war by throwing his army into Union cannon fire at Gettysburg. In 1870, Lee died, reaction to Reconstruction set in, and individual and institutional sponsors interested in Lee's reputation (including General Jubal Early and Washington College [now Washington and Lee College]) transformed him into the perfect commander whose losses resulted from the faults of other officers. Gary Fine (1996) shows Warren Harding to have been the most popular political figure in the United States while he was alive; shortly after his death, his political supporters abandoned him, and he became the personification of all America's failed presidents. And so it goes (see, for example, Peterson 1960; Kammen 1978, 1991; Loveland 1971; Pelikan 1985; Schwartz 1991; Friedlander 1992; Koonz 1994; Zerubavel 1995; Ducharme and Fine 1995; and Olick and Levy 1997; see especially Ben-Yehuda 1995). Images of past events and their participants change as time passes and political actors replace one another.

Conceiving the past as a political fact, made and remade in the service of new power arrangements, leads to an atemporal concept of collective memory, one that makes the past precarious, its contents hostage to the political conditions of the present. All events, including progressive challenges to the status quo, are insidious efforts to deepen the oppression of the powerless. This claim has become monotonous. True, the past is always transmitted through lines of authority. The American Revolution, the Civil War, and the two world wars were defined for us by adults while we were still children and adolescents; we did not determine for ourselves what to make of them. This defining does not mean that our instructors were consciously or unconsciously manipulating us. It does not mean that officials planned commemorative celebrations in order to get us to do their bidding or to make us loyal to a political system against which we would have otherwise rebelled. Collective memory is in truth an effective weapon in contemporary power struggles, but the battlefield image of society, taken alone, distorts understanding of collective memory's sources and functions, leaving out, as it does, the cultural realm within which the politics of memory is situated. Not until this cultural realm is explored can we grasp Lincoln's part in the forging of national memory.

Memory as a Cultural System

The politics of memory produces little understanding of collective memory as such—only of its causes and consequences. How the past is symbolized and how it functions as a mediator of meaning are questions that go to the heart of collective memory, but they have been skirted. Now is the time to engage them.

It has been said that humans, because of their psychological constitution, cannot live without attachment to some object that transcends and survives them, that there is a human craving for meaning that appears to have the force of instinct, and that people are "congenitally compelled to impose a meaningful order upon reality" (Berger 1967, 22). This need for incorporation into something that transfigures individual existence may or may not be based on genetic realities, but it is basic to an understanding of what collective memory is. Ever since Max Weber designated "the problem of meaning" as the key problem of human culture, different investigators have shown, in different ways, how symbolic frameworks enable us to make sense of the world. Connecting past events to one another and to the events of the present, collective memory is part of culture's meaning-making apparatus. How this apparatus works is, to say the least, problematic; that we depend on it as part of the nature of things is certain. How collective memory establishes an image of the world so compelling as to render meaningful its deepest perplexities remains to be investigated.

Efforts to work through this problem must build on Clifford Geertz's semiotic interpretation of culture. Geertz's inquiries into selected articulations of culture—"Ideology as a Cultural System" (1973b), "Religion as a Cultural System" (1973c), "Art as a Cultural System" (1983a), and "Common Sense as a Cultural System" (1983c)—define culture as an organization of symbolic patterns on which people rely to make sense of their experience. Articulating a symbolic pattern of commemoration, memory becomes a meaning-conferring cultural system.

Modeling Collective memory, like all cultural systems, is a pattern of "inherited conceptions expressed in symbolic forms by means of which men communicate, perpetuate, and develop their knowledge about and attitudes toward life" (Geertz 1973c, 89). Since collective memory is never a simple act of power but a symbolic filter through which experience—political and otherwise—is apprehended, it

> consists of the construction and manipulation of symbol systems, which are employed as models of other systems, physical, organic, social, psychological, and so forth, in such a way that the structure of these other systems . . . is, as we say, "understood." Thinking, conceptualization, formulation, comprehension, understanding [and memory] consists not of ghostly happenings in the head but of a matching of the states and processes of symbolic models against the states and processes of the wider world. (Geertz 1973b, 214)

Understanding memory, then, is a matter of knowing not only why the past is interpreted but also how it is interpreted.

The past is matched to the present as a model *of* society and a model *for* society. As a model *of* society, collective memory reflects past events in terms of the needs, interests, fears, and aspirations of the present. As a model *for* society, collective memory performs two functions: it embodies a *template* that organizes and animates behavior and a *frame* within which people locate and find meaning for their present experience. Collective memory affects social reality by *reflecting, shaping,* and *framing* it.[14]

Collective memory reflects reality by interpreting the past in terms of images appropriate and relevant to the present; it shapes reality by providing people with a program in terms of which their present lines of conduct can be formulated and enacted; it frames reality through standards in terms of which the effectiveness and moral qualities of their conduct can be discerned.

The distinction between memory as a model *of* and a model *for* social reality is an analytic, not an empirical, one: both aspects are realized in every act of remembrance. Memories must express current problems before they can program ways to deal with them, for we cannot be oriented by a past in which we fail to see ourselves. This is what Charles Horton Cooley—one of Lincoln's great admirers—meant when he observed: "the function of the great and famous man is to be a symbol, and the real question in our minds is not so much, What are you? as, What can I believe that you are? How far can I use you as a symbol in the development of my instinctive tendency?" ([1902] 1964, 341). On the other hand, the programming and framing functions of memory are what make its reflexive function significant, for we have no reason to look for ourselves in a past that does not already orient our lives. In Cooley's words: "The mind, having energy, must work, and requires a guide, a form of thought, to facilitate its working. . . . Therefore, we feed our characters, while they are forming, upon the vision of admired models" (312).[15]

Memory at once reflects, programs, and frames the present; yet these multiple functions remain peripheral to our knowledge. Sociological literature is filled with rich accounts of how collective memory symbolically encodes and reproduces class conflicts, interest structures, and mentalities, but it contains little information about (and few concepts to describe) memory as an entity in itself—an ordered system of symbols that makes experience, including political experience, meaningful. Humanistic literature, by contrast, is filled with artistic, musical, poetic, and biographical works that sustain the past as an object of reverence and emulation; but an analytic account of this material—one that provides reference points for description, comparison, and generalization—does not exist.

My account does not start from scratch. References to the orienting power of collective memory have appeared in Mannheim's commentary on vivid historical events persisting as points of contemporary reference ([1928] 1952, 309–12), Cooley's analysis of emulation of past heroes ([1902] 1964, 293–316), and Mead's assertion that the "present can only be known and interpreted in the past which it involves" (1938, 94; see also Maines, Sugrue, and Katovich 1983, 163–64). More recent references appear in Shils's conception of tradition as a constituent of present actions (1981) and Heilman's ethnography of faithful Jews invoking the past as a means of reforming and completing ("traditionalizing") the present (1982, 62–63; see also Nisbet 1966). The most current statements include Bellah et al. on "communities of memory" (1985), Lowenthal on the past as a source of identity (1985, 41–49) and heritage[16] (1996), Rusen on traditional memories as "indispensable elements of orientation" in historical consciousness (1989, 44), Schuman and Rieger's research (1992) on the uses of past wars (Vietnam and World War II) as historical analogies supporting or opposing the Persian Gulf War, Olick's research (1999) showing collective memory and collective goals to be encased in the same irreducible "profile" of political meaning, Schudson's understandings (1994, 1997) of the ubiquity of the past in present political situations, Yael Zerubavel's analysis (1995) of commemorative stories as paradigms affecting self-conceptions and conduct, and Eviatar Zerubavel's treatment (1997) of individuals identifying themselves with the enduring memories of their communities.

Each of these writers recognizes, but none explains, the past as a program for the present. None explains why we evoke collective memory when we do, what we expect collective memory to achieve, and how it functions. None shows precisely how depth in time, tradition, and memory affects the way people interpret what is happening to them. None offers a conception of the symbolic structures that connect the political roots of collective memory to its political functions. None distinguishes the principal modes in which we think about the past: whether we invoke the past in order to define ourselves by difference or resemblance, or whether we invoke the past in order to connect ourselves to it and think of our experiences as short episodes in a long narrative. None explains the conditions under which the past is invoked unwittingly rather than deliberately, solemnly rather than cynically, broadly rather than narrowly. Above all, none describes the mechanisms sustaining the content of collective memory across time—even as political structures drastically change.

Evidence

Collective memory's qualities can be discerned once historical and commemorative data are assembled and aligned. The *history* of Abraham Lincoln's life can be charted through analysis of historiographic studies, biographies, and textbooks. The *commemoration* of Lincoln's life can be charted through analysis of eulogies and other hagiographies, monuments, shrines, statues, state portraits, history paintings, prints, and centennial, sesquicentennial, and annual birthday observances.

Historical and commemorative objects representing Lincoln are produced by people with a stake in a positive interpretation. Lincoln's reputational entrepreneurs included Republican and progressive leaders, but their enterprise was but part of a larger one. The many people who had occasion to interpret Lincoln, from clergymen, poets, artists, and municipal orators to students giving a report to their classmates, participated in the maintenance and evolution of his reputation (Fine 1996, 1162).

Knowing the past from the subject's viewpoint, however, raises difficult questions. Observers, given the limitations of their own experience, cannot know the world as their subjects do. And even if they could know it, they would be obliged to transcend it, for to assume the role of a subject causes observers to become trapped within the very perspective they seek to understand. The way to resolve this dilemma is not to imagine ourselves as Lincoln's contemporaries (Democrats, Southerners, progressive reformers, conservative businessmen, immigrants, African Americans, socialists, or suffragists) and then witness and report our own thoughts, but to search out and assemble the symbolic forms, including words, pictorial images, and institutional observances, in terms of which people exploited Lincoln to represent themselves to one another (for detail on this process, see Geertz 1983c). Procedurally, this means tracing the flow of Lincoln discourse and the symbolic devices people used to represent and communicate their understandings. The visual and literary forms articulating Lincoln's image and the role they played in the life of the persons using them—these are my data. Knowing the meaning of Lincoln's memory means knowing what different groups of Americans were up to—what they intended to accomplish for themselves and for one another—when they invoked it.

My documentation provides contestable accounts of Abraham Lincoln's image because it reveals the impressions of Lincoln that a small number of people wrote down, drew, painted, or carved for others to read or see. It does not provide an even partially representative sample of what people believed, how intensely they felt about Lincoln, or how these beliefs and feelings were distributed across the population. And if the symbolic forms of a generation are part of the context in which its members have thought about him, the question of why and how their thoughts arose remains to be answered.

Commemorative patterns warrant speculation about this question. They show reputational enterprise interacting with the public's knowledge and taste. Some reputational entrepreneurs shared that taste; some exploited it, dealing mainly with features of Lincoln's life that would interest a mass audience. Others believed their efforts would be of no significance if they did not somehow affect as well as reflect public conceptions. Lincoln's image-makers, then, did their work with a definite audience in mind, while those who financed their efforts, such as publishers, printmakers, and municipal councils, were confident of the audience's interest in what they had to say. In a literal sense, therefore, portrayals of Lincoln are more than idiosyncratic representations of their creators' interests and biases;[17] they are collective representations—images that existed in the mind of the entrepreneur because they first existed in certain segments of the society. There is, of course, no exact correspondence between the image-maker's intent and how the image is received. After four years of war and more than a million deaths and injuries, the public's acceptance of positive portrayals of Abraham Lincoln was problematic. Lincoln's sympathetic interpreters have always reflected the people's conceptions of him imperfectly and have had less influence than they hoped. Because their portrayals reflected at least part of the collective view of the man, however, they can be used to estimate how certain elements of the population conceived him and how these conceptions changed over time. Depictions of Lincoln cannot typify the full range of conceptions of him, but they provide ways of coming into contact with and understanding them.

That these commemorative depictions are objective—super-personal—is evident, since it was common access to a collective symbolic structure, existing outside the mind, that allowed entrepreneurs to produce, and audiences to understand, the iconic, verbal, and ritual objects on which this book is based. These objects have not been randomly sampled, but they have been seen, read, or heard by a large percentage of the American population in succeeding generations. I wish to know what these objects meant by restoring them to the context in which they appeared. I wish to know what it was in the repetitive display of commemorative words and pictures that actually got said and understood as one generation, with its unique aspirations, fears, values, and concerns, succeeded another.

In his April 1865 funeral eulogy, Ralph Waldo Emerson said that Lincoln had "the pulse of twenty million throbbing in his heart, the thought of their minds articulated by his tongue" ([1865] 1990, 33). Emerson's "twenty million" consisted of the Northern white population. This book shows how well Lincoln measured the nation's pulse as its population diversified and grew to one hundred million by the turn of the century. The pulse of the nation was not always discernible in Lincoln. It was not discernible in August 1864—three months before his reelection, when the disastrous military situation caused every state to turn against the president and prompted him to write a farewell letter, whose envelope his cabinet signed, urging his successor to preserve the Union. The pulse of the nation was not discernible in him on the day of his death, when he faced the divisive question of whether to allow the South to go its own way or to impose upon it the law and customs of the rest of the land. No position Lincoln could have taken on this issue would have prevented part of the country from turning against him. Only when Lincoln died, only when his own heart stopped beating, did the pulse of twenty million throb in it.

Lincoln was not the only president commemorated at the turn of the century, but no president makes the dynamics of commemoration more visible. Following America's conception of Lincoln from his death to the dedication of his memorial tells us about the nation's self-conception during a critical phase of its history.

From Martyr to Idol

Assassination transformed Abraham Lincoln from a controversial president into an emblem of Northern society. Chapter 1 of this book shows how extraordinary funeral rites elevated Lincoln's political status even as many people continued to condemn his wartime policies and reconstruction plans. The contrast between what people actually believed about Lincoln and how they felt and acted in response to his death makes problematic the meaning of his commemoration. Comparing Lincoln to James Garfield, William McKinley, and John Kennedy, who were also assassinated in office, demonstrates the contingent power of nineteenth-century mourning rites. Sudden death in the context of crisis elevated Lincoln's stature. Mourning ritual, however, *created* rather than *reflected* first impressions of his presidential greatness.

That no single group of admirers controlled Lincoln's image is evident in chapter 2, which traces Lincoln's reputation from the time of his death to the beginning of the twentieth century. As the excitement following his funeral died down, old animosities returned. Many Americans—the vast majority when white Southerners are included—questioned Lincoln's merits. Opposing these critics, many organizations, including the Republican Party, veterans' groups, and Lincoln's personal acquaintances, created a literal cult of commemorative biography, poetry, statuary, painting, monuments, shrines, and ritual observance. Few Northerners openly disparaged this cult, but most were unwilling to embrace it.

Not until the early twentieth century, when the generation resentful of Lincoln died out and America became a more democratic urban industrial nation, did Abraham Lincoln replace George Washington as America's idol. Chapter 3 documents the surging of Lincoln's reputation and the enlargement of his symbolic role during the Progressive era. In its advancement of electoral democracy and definition of new ideals of human welfare, the Progressive reform movement adopted Lincoln as its dominant historical symbol. Commemorative rites for the 1909 centennial of Lincoln's birth, like those commemorating his 1865 death, swelled his reputation amid an upsurge of national feeling.

Chapter 4 shows how progressive ideals were communicated in the form of a national "man of the people" mythology that departed from the facts of Lincoln's life. Notwithstanding countless stories about his poverty and commonness, Lincoln was reared in a solidly middle-class rural family. Not only was his objective situation middle class; he was subjectively committed to middle-class culture, with its emphasis on refinement, rationality, achievement, and paternalistic governance. He entered state politics as a Whig, deeply distrusted Jacksonian democracy, married a genteel woman who appreciated his intellect and manner, sent his son to Phillips Exeter Academy and Harvard, and enjoyed a life of upper-middle-class comfort. Abraham Lincoln was not known as a rail-splitting man of the frontier until his presidential campaign managers made him one. The "people's president" image, sharpened by nineteenth-century biographers, was magnified during the first two decades of the twentieth century in the context of a new relationship between the individual and the state. Every sector of the society, including socialists, conservatives, women, African Americans, immigrants, and Southerners, developed their own variations on the progressive Lincoln—the president accessible to all, embracing all. Thus, in chapter 5, Lincoln the war president becomes Lincoln the economic reformer, champion of labor and women's rights, friend of the black man, welcomer of the foreigner, lover of the South. Abraham Lincoln was pressed into the service of integrating as well as democratizing America.

Sometimes, conceptions of the past powerfully organize collective experience, communicate serious problems, and mobilize remedial action. Chapter 6 shows how local and federal agencies invoked Lincoln's image to clarify the purpose of World War I, to legitimate preparations for it, and then to orient, inspire, and console the people who fought it. In a crisis, people depend on symbolic forms to reinforce old conceptions and learn new ones; commemorative forms assume significance because they clarify national purpose, the meaning of sacrifice, the rights and obligations of citizenship. Rationalizing the experience of World War I, Lincoln's image was a better model for reality than during any preceding period.

Lincoln's most ardent supporters always saw something majestic in him, and their impression crystallized during the Progressive era and the Great War. This new appreciation of Lincoln's epic qualities is explained in chapter 7 by three case studies—the debate over the George Grey Barnard and Augustus Saint-Gaudens statues of Lincoln, the "restoration" of Abraham Lincoln's log cabin birthplace and the making of a marble temple to commemorate it, and the controversies over the design of the Lincoln Memorial. These studies of the two Lincolns—the folk hero and the epic hero—define the tension within the American heroic vision itself.

Examining Abraham Lincoln's reputation across two generations leads to a revision, not rejection, of the theory of the politics of memory, and this revision is summarized in the concluding chapter. Political structures shape our understanding of the past, observes Michael Schudson; "[b]ut this is half the truth, at best, and a particularly cynical half-truth, at that" (1989b, 113). The Lincoln case enables us to capture the other half of the truth. Lincoln's image in the late nineteenth and early twentieth centuries makes no sense unless the nature of politics itself is recast. Existing approaches to the politics of memory conceive power as a medium of oppression and resistance. Lincoln, however, symbolized the benevolent administration of power; his image inspired and energized rather than intimidated and pacified, illuminated rather than manipulated public concerns and interests. Lincoln's case also shows changes in collective memory being appended to its continuities in such a way as to sustain rather than replace traditional ideals.

What are the lineaments of commemorative persistence and change? How, precisely, does commemoration lead to new patterns of perception and remembrance and new conceptions of national destiny while affirming old ones? And how does the dualism work? We turn to these questions now.

PART ONE

Nineteenth Century:
Symbolizing Nationhood

Death and Commemoration

When a man contributes something of vast importance to a nation—solves some problem, achieves some triumph of fateful consequence—he is set above others and revered. Leader-centered theories of social order and change, notably psychoanalytic theory (Freud [1913] 1950, [1921] 1960, [1939] 1970) and charisma theory (Weber 1968), make this reaction intelligible. But when people honor the very man whose competence and value to society they have long questioned, and continue to question, a puzzle emerges whose solution requires a different kind of theory. The esteem suddenly shown Abraham Lincoln after his assassination is a prominent instance of such a puzzle, and Emile Durkheim's theory of ritual is the most promising key to its solution.

Applying Durkheim's insights to an event such as the assassination of Lincoln is not in itself a novel exercise. Many analyses of secular symbolism and state rituals have already made effective use of Durkheim's work. Lloyd Warner's account (1959) of the Yankee City Tricentennial, Edward Shils and Michael Young's study (1975) of the coronation of Elizabeth II, Mona Ozouf's treatment (1976) of the festivals of the French Revolution, Jeffrey Alexander's collection (1988) of topical essays based on Durkheim's analysis of culture and ritual, David Kertzer's wide-ranging thesis (1988) on ritual and its central role in modern political affairs—all these efforts show ritual to be a vehicle for the politics of memory. The present chapter generalizes this tradition further by subsuming under it a new kind of case. The case of Lincoln's death is unique because it lends itself to Durkheimian analysis while denying assumptions that Durkheim and even his most recent interpreters take for granted. They hold that society creates sacred things out of ordinary ones by projecting upon them "the principal aspirations that move it, as well as the means of satisfying them" (Durkheim [1915] 1965, 243). By embodying society's cherished ideals, mundane objects and undistinguished people come to be respected or revered. However, this study shows how Lincoln became an object of intense mourning while most people held him in mixed or low regard. It is one of many cases in which positive rituals are enacted despite negative beliefs about a political actor yet act back upon and modify those beliefs.

Because Lincoln had led the nation through a long and grievous civil war, his assassination led to elaborate funeral rites and an outpouring of public commentary. The commentary, however, provided no new information about him at all. Transforming ambivalent ideas into unified positive sentiment, the funeral rites were creative not in the sense of reconstructing Lincoln but in the sense of generating an emotional context within which people felt differently about what they knew about him. In the previous chapter we distinguished commemoration's emotional lineaments from the analytic concerns of history. That Lincoln died violently at the hands of an enemy intensified the significance of his funeral rites causing emotion to dominate reaction to his death,[1] and this emotional transformation affected future commemoration of Abraham Lincoln's life.

Since later generations know how Lincoln's life ended and how its commemoration began, the meaning of his presidency appears different to them than it did to his contemporaries. Waging civil war to save the Union, persevering in war despite heavy casualties and repeated defeats, emancipating four million slaves, pressing a determined enemy to the bitter end—all these events are contextualized in hindsight by Lincoln's assassination and majestic funeral. Much has been written recently about ritual temporarily promoting national belonging, collective identity, and collective memory (Berezin 1997; Falasca-Zimponi 1997; Spillman 1997). Lincoln's funeral ritual as a unifying symbol for new generations can be seen as we begin our analysis.

A Remarkable Transformation

When Abraham Lincoln awoke on the last day of his life, almost everyone could find something about him to dislike. Less than six months earlier, in November 1864, he had won reelection with 54 percent of the Northern vote, but only after pivotal victories on the battlefield changed the minds of thousands who had thought the war unwinnable.[2] Even when he was renominated, political opponents denied him acclamation, and many believed his reelection reflected dislike of challenger George McClellan rather than endorsement of Lincoln himself (Carr 1907; Oates 1977, 436). By winter's end in 1865, the war was almost over, but widespread dislike of Lincoln remained. Supporters of the war remembered his indecisiveness in fighting the South, and they now opposed his lenient postwar policy. Opponents of the war were untroubled by secession, sympathized with the South, or believed for other reasons that the war's costs exceeded its benefits, and they continued to resent what Lincoln had done to the country. The exact proportion of the population holding these negative attitudes is unknown, but since so many American newspapers expressed them (Randall 1957, 298–99; Donald [1947] 1989, 60), even as the fighting entered its last month, we can assume that that proportion must have been significant. Democratic newspapers, like Democratic voters, were most critical. Lincoln's friends regarded his March 4, 1865, Inaugural Address promising "malice toward none, with charity for all" (delivered six weeks before he died) as a fitting speech, but the *Chicago Times* saw it as more "slipshod," "loose jointed," and "puerile" than his administration. "Was there ever such a coming out of the little end of the horn? Was ever a nation, once great, so belittled?" (March 6, 1865).

Lincoln realized that his address was "not immediately popular" (1953–55, 8:356) and steeled himself for the full weight of public reaction. The *Buffalo Courier* told its readers that Lincoln's "exhortation to finish a war the limits and nature of which are not even hinted at" summarized his entire presidency (quoted in *Detroit Free Press*, March 11, 1865). Although Lincoln had failed to use his inauguration to justify the war to its opponents, he had succeeded in convincing them that he was a radical concerned mainly with the well-being of black people. His speech, according to the *New York World*, amounted to a "prose parody of John Brown's Hymn" that "mocked the nation in its calamity" (March 6, 1865, 6).[3] On April 11—four days before his death—Lincoln delivered a major address defending his plan for Louisiana's reentry into the Union. He prepared his speech carefully but was "very anxious" and then "extremely disappointed" about its reception (Oates 1977, 61). His words were too vague about general reconciliation and too clear about black rights to satisfy the antiwar Democrats. The war's supporters, on the other hand, saw behind his words a renunciation of the fruits of their victory, and they were furious. After sending hundreds of thousands of men to their deaths, Lincoln, they believed, wanted to treat the enemy as if there had been no war at all (*New York World,* April 13, 1865, 4; see also Randall 1957, 6).

Martyrdom

Unfriendly feelings toward Lincoln during the war's last month were not universal, but they were extensive and made dramatic the contrast between his reputation in life and in death. Only in death, as David Donald put it, "did Lincoln win universal applause" ([1947] 1989, 167). Hostility toward Lincoln at the time he died need not be overestimated to appreciate the magnitude of this opinion shift. "Even taking into account all of those contemporaries who did recognize greatness in Lincoln," Don Fehrenbacher points out, "one finds a remarkable contrast between his reputation while still alive and his subsequent historical stature" (1987, 175). Lincoln's contemporaries expressed this same conviction. "Had he not been stricken down," John Egar explained, Lincoln "would not have passed into history with the same nimbus of glory that now surrounds his memory" (1865, 14).

The "nimbus of glory" to which Reverend Egar referred was bright, but not blinding. Horace Greeley surmised in an editorial several days after Lincoln's death "that Mr. Lincoln's reputation will stand higher with posterity than with the mass of his contemporaries—that distance, whether in time or space, while dwarfing and obscuring so many, must place him in a fairer light—that future generations will deem him undervalued by those for and with whom he labored" (*New York Tribune,* April 19, 1865, 4). Likewise, Reverend George Briggs declared in his funeral eulogy that Lincoln would be "hailed in the coming time . . . with a truer, deeper homage than he wins today" (1865, 28). George Templeton Strong also believed Lincoln to be lacking in too many ways to merit the respect of his own generation. "But his weaknesses are on the surface," Strong added, "and his name will be of high account fifty years hence" ([1865] 1952, 3:580). Greeley's, Briggs's, and Strong's statements are important because they assess explicitly the public's opinion of Lincoln.

Although Lincoln's murder did not cause his generation to idolize him, it made him more prominent than any previous nineteenth-century president. No other public reputation, in fact, has risen in America so dramatically in so short a time. Yet the reason for this change is unclear. Most people gain new insights into another after he or she dies: they appreciate achievements and character traits they had not appreciated before and forget faults they had previously criticized. Likewise, many critics discovered admirable qualities in the same Lincoln they had once maligned, and they were sincere when they publicly conceded the discovery. None of the things said about Lincoln in oratory or in print, however, revealed any virtues that were not known by his supporters before he died. Nor did friendly commentaries ignore faults for which his opponents had previously held him accountable. Criticisms were certainly stated more gently and with more qualification after his death than before, but they were stated nonetheless. If Lincoln had been judged solely by what people believed about his policies and statesmanship, he would have been regarded as a good man who did his best but not the best man for the times, let alone a great man.

The "Great Calamity" (Lincoln's assassination), however, was not primarily an occasion for clarifying the merits of what Lincoln did and did not do as president. Above all else, his assassination was an occasion for ritual acts of national affirmation and national communion. The symbolic power of these rituals elevated Lincoln to a new and higher plane. When observers describe the explosion of affection for the murdered president, it is more to these rituals than to the people's subjective mood that they refer. Nowhere are such rituals described more clearly than in Emile Durkheim's *Elementary Forms of the Religious Life* ([1915] 1965).

Durkheim discovered that the "aptitude of society for setting itself up as a god or for creating gods" is most apparent during social upheavals. At these critical moments, the flow of information increases and contact among people becomes more frequent. With attention focused on a common object, interactions become concentrated, and "the very fact of the concentration acts as an exceptionally powerful stimulant. When [people] are once come together, a sort of electricity is formed by their collecting which quickly transports them to an extraordinary degree of exaltation." Many events can produce this effect. The periodic gathering of dispersed groups; changes in the structure of society, including revolutionary changes—any occasion that assembles people for some social purpose is a potential source of collective excitement. In particular, although mourning differs from other rituals, including rituals of joy, "there is one feature in which it resembles them: it, too, is made up out of collective ceremonies which produce a state of effervescence among those who take part in them. The sentiments aroused are different; but the arousal is the same." Out of these ceremonies and these states of moral arousal comes the idea that there is a sacred world apart from the profane world of everyday life, and in this sacred world ordinary men are transformed into extraordinary beings (244–47, 250, 445). The public response to Abraham Lincoln's assassination in the Northern states is a case in point.[4] It will be traced through (1) an account of the excitement and ritual attending Lincoln's death; (2) an estimate of what people actually thought about Lincoln before and after he was assassinated; and (3) an analysis of the ultimate object of Lincoln's funeral rites—the new power of the American state—and of how Lincoln's prestige benefited from its celebration. "The state is invisible," said Michael Walzer. It must be "personified before it can be seen, symbolized before it can be loved, imagined before it can be conceived" (1967, 191). Just so, Lincoln's death symbolized and made imaginable a critical new phase in America's political development. This analysis defines the realm of political rituals and symbols as constitutive elements of national memory.[5]

Day of Indignation

On April 9, 1865, Robert E. Lee surrendered. When people heard the news, they ran into the streets and celebrated. Businesses closed. Speeches, demonstrations, and fireworks abounded. Four years of carnage were over; the North was euphoric. Freshness of feeling fed upon itself and was invigorated by the upcoming Easter holiday. From death to life, from defeat to victory—resurrection—the time was perfect for consolation as well as celebration. At the peak of this euphoria and anticipation—Good Friday, April 14—Abraham Lincoln was shot.

Within hours of the report of his death the next day, crowds formed again in public places throughout the country. Everyone was trying to find out what had happened in Washington. Was Lincoln actually killed by a Southerner? Was the secretary of state killed? His son? The secretary of war? The cabinet? General Grant? Has the war been resumed? Who is the new president, and what will he do? These were the kinds of questions that flew through the air on that Saturday, and the people asking them were in turmoil.

Throughout the nation, officials responded to Lincoln's death by drafting proclamations of grief and condolence along with instructions for public mourning. Federal and state officials were doing this at the New York Customs House when an immense crowd began to form around them. The scene must be examined closely—not because it represents the way all or even a majority of people reacted on this Day of Indignation, but because it reveals the kind of sentiments Lincoln's death evoked.

Eight men spoke from the Customs House balcony. One of them, Major General Benjamin Butler, a perceptive demagogue, understood the passions of the people and knew how to exploit them. His radical views on Reconstruction were known to many, and the reaction to his arrival at the Customs House showed that the crowd's mood did not consist of grief alone. A *New York Times* correspondent reported that upon Butler's appearance, "a loud shout was heard, and a great rush was seen in the street. Cheer upon cheer rent the air, and for a moment it seemed as if the people had forgotten their grief and were remembering only the great victories of the republic." As General Butler advanced to speak, "cries of 'Butler, Butler' arose from the street, assuming mighty proportions, and growing finally to a hurricane of applause" (April 16, 1865, 8).

Benjamin Butler raised both arms. The assemblage hushed. He began. Just a few days earlier, he recalled, throngs of happy people gathered at this spot to celebrate the Confederacy's surrender. Now, suddenly, they have gathered again to share their grief. The intensity of the previous joy makes Lincoln's death all the more shattering. Yet the occasion is not without its consolations, for it ends all arguments over postwar policy. "With a blind hatred characteristic of the rebellion, they have struck down the most forgiving, gracious, lenient, kind-hearted friend the rebels had." From the crowd below arose booming rejoinders: "That's so," cried one man. "True to the letter," yelled another; then applause, abruptly subsiding as Butler continued: "If the rebels can do a deed like this to the kind, good, generous, tender-hearted ruler, whose every thought was purity, whose every desire a yearning for forgiveness and peace, what shall be done to them in high places who guided the assassin's knife?" In one voice the multitude answered, "Hang them! Hang them!" The scene had by now become "most exciting." No single voice was heard, only the chorus shouting in unison for vengeance.

The turning point had come. "Lincoln drove out of the manifest rebellion all its life and strength," said Butler, but Lincoln was no more. It remained to "crush out the spirit of treason" once and for all. To this proposal the crowd assented with cheers, and these became louder and more enthusiastic when Butler revealed the government's new policy. "I know the new President and can tell you that he is determined to treat this rebellion as you want to have it treated." Prolonged applause followed. Lincoln's policy, it is true, called for reconciliation, with minimum penalty for the Confederate leadership. But Lincoln was the first victim of his own mistake. If he had not overestimated the nobility of his enemy, Butler explained, he could have saved himself. Conclusion: treat the Confederacy in ways it can understand. "Retribution, retribution, swift, unerring, terrible and just, must and will be visited on the perpetrators of this great and terrible crime." The general stepped back, then turned and retired to the sound of thunderous applause (*New York Times,* April 16, 1865, 8).

The other speakers' words resembled Butler's. Some spoke a little more favorably about Lincoln, others less so; some were more or less expansive than others in their condemnation of the Confederacy. All speakers converged on the antinomy between the gentle, well-meaning president and the vicious, malignant enemy. As the Confederacy's corruption highlighted the president's purity, the two images drew force from one another. Taken separately, these images justified vengeance; taken together, they demanded it.

Everyone who walked the streets on this bleak Saturday knew that vengeance was in the air. D. L. Hunt of Rochester, New York, was overheard saying that Lincoln should have been assassinated four years earlier; a resentful crowd surrounded him at once, but a policeman saved his life by arresting him. In New York City, a man "quite likely insane" who expressed pleasure at the president's death was pulled off the street by a sympathetic dry goods company employee just before the crowd reached him. Another "blasphemer and insulter" of the president was attacked and knocked down, but managed to escape his assailants. Lincoln sympathizers were on the lookout for anti-Lincoln sentiments, sensitive to the slightest nuance of disrespect. Known Confederate sympathizers were fair game. Eight men confronted former president John Tyler's widow in her home and demanded she turn over to them the Confederate flag displayed in her parlor (*New York Times*, April 16, 1865, 5, 8; April 18, 1865, 2).

The climate of indignation transcended politics. New York City was a Democratic stronghold, but its courts administered stiff penalties for public expressions of disrespect. "Old Abe, the son of a _____, is dead, and he ought to have been killed long ago," declared George Wells on a public street; he was sent to the penitentiary for six months for inciting riot. John Gallagher and Thomas Adams, in two separate incidents, said the same thing and received the same sentence (*New York Times*, April 18, 1865, 5; April 19, 1865, 2). "The sacred thing," said Emile Durkheim, "is *par excellence* that which the profane should not touch, and cannot touch with impunity" ([1915] 1965, 55). The memory of Abraham Lincoln fit this definition. In New York and other Democratic cities, Lincoln's memory, now intertwined with the offended dignity of his office, was more sacred than Lincoln himself.

Outraged people filled the public squares and buildings everywhere. As soon as news of the president's death reached San Francisco, "the public wrath began to kindle; soon it burst forth into a consuming conflagration, threatening the destruction of everything treasonable in its path," including that city's pro-Confederation newspaper (*Daily Alta California*, April 16, 1865). General McDowell, the military commander of the city, sympathized with the mob and addressed it approvingly. By turning against the treasonous press, he said, "you have but anticipated me and have perhaps saved me some trouble." The editor of the San Francisco *Daily Alta California* believed there was good reason for public excitement. Treacherous murder "was more than human nature could stand," enough to "heat the blood and madden the brain of the most cool and phlegmatic" (April 16, 1865).

The mood was the same in Boston, where a succession of clergymen addressed city residents in a large public meeting. Reverend Kirk described the assassination as the last of a long series of acts trying God's patience. Each act reminded him of a "harper tuning up the screws of his instrument, turning little by little until the last screw was turned at 10 o'clock last night [the time President Lincoln was shot], and now the nation is in tune for God's work. [Great applause.]

Now we are ready. God of Battles, lead us on; slavery and treason shall die. [Great applause]" (*Boston Daily Advertiser,* April 17, 1865, 1).

In Boston, as in other cities, speakers addressed aroused audiences whose ideals and feelings they shared. Sentiments provoked by the speaker's words in such situations "come back to him, but enlarged and amplified, and to this degree they strengthen his own sentiment. . . . It is no longer a simple individual who speaks; it is a group incarnate and personified" (Durkheim [1915] 1965, 241). Sometimes collective passions became so intense as to prevent any utterance, in which case the group was incarnated and personified by fervent silence. Emotion-choked Colonel James Garfield became momentarily speechless on the New York Customs House balcony. Elsewhere in the city, D. D. Field rose to advise his fellow lawyers of the next day's memorial ceremonies, but "he seemed for a few moments overcome with emotion and was unable to speak." On the same day, Rabbi Adler tried to address his Sabbath congregation "but was so overcome by his feelings that he was compelled to desist" (*New York Times,* April 16, 1865, 4–5, 8). In San Francisco, Rabbi Cohn, receiving word of Lincoln's death just as he was about to deliver his Saturday sermon, "was so overcome that, bursting into tears, he sank almost senseless." Wondrously, he recovered to express eloquent words of love for "our reverend President, the twice anointed High Priest in the sanctuary of our Republic" (*Daily Alta California,* April 16, 1865, 1). Faltering, freezing, then arising with force and eloquence, Rabbi Cohn embodied the complex emotions—the paralysis and the passionate energy—of the entire society.

People who met in the streets on Saturday would meet again the next day, Easter Sunday, in the churches. This year, the Easter attendance was greater than ever before. New York's churches, for example, were filled to capacity long before the hour of service, and many had to turn people away. Each church expressed in its own way the continuity of America's political and religious life. Bishop Potter of New York instructed priests to dedicate to the country the standard Catholic prayer for persons under affliction, replacing the words "him" and "his" with "us" and "our"; after the joyous Easter service, the church was to be draped in black. In at least one of the Jewish services, the Kaddish, a prayer for dead family members, was recited, literally adopting Lincoln into the family of the people. Protestant services, conducted from altars draped in black, were likewise emotionally charged. "There was great excitement" among the congregants of one church, "many being moved to tears"; and if the typical Sunday sermon sometimes failed to interest churchgoers, this day's sermon was "listened to with profound attention" (*New York Times*, April 16, 1865, 5, 8; April 17, 1865, 1, 8).

Funeral Journey

During the next several days, people had a chance to settle down, contemplate what had happened, and prepare for April 19, the official day of mourning. On this day, the churches reopened and filled again. State and city governments conducted their own ceremonies. Solemn processions, unprecedented in size and scope of participation, marked the day in every Midwestern and northeastern city and town. In San Francisco, the memorial observance was "the greatest demonstration ever made on the Pacific Coast" (*Daily Alta California,* April 19–20, 1865). The most significant scene, however, was enacted in Washington, D.C.

After Lincoln's official funeral was concluded at the Capitol building, his body was removed to the train station, in the presence of a massive crowd. From the station it began the journey to Oak Ridge Cemetery in Springfield, Illinois. The planners of this journey belonged for the most part to the Republican Party, but the public reaction, although benefiting the party, was unanticipated. Party interests and enterprise were parts of the story but cannot fully explain what happened. As originally conceived, the journey was to be formal and dignified (Lewis 1929). The train would retrace most of the route Lincoln took to assume the presidency in February 1861, and his body would be displayed at major cities along the way. There was no reason to believe this meticulously contrived procession would spontaneously turn into the most striking state ritual that Americans had ever witnessed or would ever witness again. Not everyone could take part in this ritual, but everyone knew from newspapers and word of mouth what was happening along its route.

The funeral procession's first major stop was Baltimore, where four years earlier to the day rebel sympathizers had attacked Massachusetts troops on their way south. Sympathetic spectators packed Baltimore now. Taken to the Exchange Building in a glass-covered hearse, the dead president's coffin was opened for a few hours, and he was viewed by more than ten thousand people before resuming his journey. Up to Pennsylvania the funeral train ran, slowing as it passed one town, stopping at another to receive flowers from local women. In the capital, Harrisburg, the coffin was again removed, and ten thousand waited through a violent rainstorm to view the president's body. The rain continued through the night and into the next morning, when fifteen thousand more people came to see the reopened coffin. They passed through the capitol building quietly, in dread anticipation of what they were to see. They moved forward one step at a time, stood on tiptoe. One observer recorded what must have been the impression of all: "The appearance of the illustrious statesman and martyr was strikingly sublime in the repose of death. The countenance still preserved the expression it bore in life, though changed in hue, the lips firmly set but half smiling. . . . The beard was shaven close save a tuft on the chin." The form in the mahogany coffin, it is true, was "a mere shell, an effigy, a sculpture. . . . All that made this flesh vital is gone forever" (*Pennsylvania Daily Telegraph,* April 24, 1865, 1). No one who saw Lincoln that day would forget it.

The next day the train headed east, and as it approached Philadelphia something new occurred: crowds formed along the tracks, miles before the terminal. In sight of 500,000 people, a procession escorted the coffin to Independence Hall, where it was placed next to the Liberty Bell. Not even a sizeable minority would get to see the president, for the lines leading to the catafalque were never less than three miles long. The lucky ones who reached the hall were prodded by sentries to prevent long stays in front of the coffin. Many women fainted and had to be carried away. Some visitors broke into tears and refused to move. Throughout the day it was the same: tens of thousands of viewers haltingly moved by. Outside, the bells of the city rang and guns went off every minute. The crowds were constantly on the edge of riot, and of the thousands of combat veterans assigned to keep order, 150 collapsed from exhaustion (*Evening Star* [Washington, D.C.], April 24, 1865, 1; *New York Times,* April 24, 1865, 8).

New York's turnout was even greater. In the presidential election held six months earlier, New York City had rejected Lincoln by a margin of two to one. Now it embraced him. A procession of 160,000 people led the hearse, itself pulled by sixteen gray horses, to City Hall. The deterioration of the sacred body robbed some viewers of their "melancholic pleasure," but most were too stunned to care about it. Three weeks ago the war had ended. Today the war president lay dead in a black suit and white gloves. The city shut down as hundreds of thousands of people poured into its streets, most of them content to get a glimpse of the departing hearse and coffin, as the viewing of the man himself was almost beyond possibility because of the crowds (*New York Times,* April 26, 1865, 1).

So it went: from New York to Albany and Buffalo, then to Cleveland and Columbus. In small towns and villages in between, crowds formed and grew. The church bells of Richmond, Indiana, rang tumultuously as the lead locomotive passed through at two o'clock in the morning. Minutes later, the funeral train itself rolled under the evergreen arch into a depot draped and wrapped in mourning regalia and lit by hundreds of lamps. Twelve thousand people stood transfixed, their eyes on the car bearing Lincoln's body, as if not believing what they were seeing.

The procession was like an ancient "royal progress"—the series of stops and appearances that stamped provincial territory with signs of the king's sway and affirmed the people's connection to him and his throne (Geertz 1983b). In America in 1865 thrones were out of fashion, but the state still sought ways to affirm itself as an instrument of the nation, justify its claims on the people, acknowledge their sacrifices, sustain their devotion. The people, in turn, sought visible markers of the invisible Union to which they had attached themselves. Thus the funeral train moved on, creating a union of its own, bringing together at places along its way more people than had ever been brought together before. Leaving Richmond behind, the train gathered speed, then slowed as it approached Centerville, where by 3:25 A.M. two thousand people were standing by bonfires on both sides of the track; then Cambridge, at 4:15 A.M.; and, ten minutes later, Dublin, to which farmers and their families had traveled twenty miles in the night chill to watch Lincoln's train slow down.

Meanwhile, the people of Indianapolis were descending on their own train depot. By six o'clock in the morning it was packed. When the train arrived at seven, rain was falling, but nobody seemed to know it. People wanting to see the president came in streetcars that bore slogans showing what was on their minds. On car number 10: "Sorrow for the Dead; Justice for the Living; Punishment for Traitors." Car number 13: "Fear Not, Abraham; I Am Thy Shield; Thy Reward Shall Be Exceedingly Great." Car number 20: "Thou Art Gone and Friend and Foe Alike Appreciate Thee Now" (*Indianapolis Daily Journal,* May 1, 1865, 4).

The players were new; the scenes, old. Two and a half centuries earlier, Elizabeth I, in royal progress, carried to the "periphery" of society "the charisma that the center had fashioned for her." But she always carried that "charisma" back to London, making the city "the capital of Britain's political imagination as it was of its government" (Geertz 1983b, 128–29). Lincoln's procession, too, originated in the capital and affirmed its dignity. But Lincoln would never return to it; his train was carrying him home. As the train moved along its route, the geographical coordinates of center and periphery became blurred. The seat of America's government remained where it was, but the capital of its political imagination (to use Clifford Geertz's term) was shifting to the west.

Late at night the funeral train set out from Indianapolis for Chicago, passing Whitestown at one in the morning, where a hundred people had gathered around a single bonfire; then into Thornton at 2:10, Stockwell at 2:50 . . . Truly, the land was taking possession of Lincoln. Here a pantomime, there a dirge, tableau, or stage effects; elsewhere just silence, men and women lowering their heads as the train slowed down or momentarily stopped.

Approaching Chicago, the funeral train was never beyond the sound of booming guns. Then it entered Chicago itself. No less than 80 percent of the city's people, according to one estimate, engaged in or watched the procession. The coffin, as before, was lifted from the funeral car, but this time it was placed on Lincoln's native soil. Around it young women in white walked in solemn ritual, then followed as it entered the city and was placed in state at the courthouse. Chicago had given Lincoln only a modest majority in the previous election. Before his generals won their important victories in fall 1864, the entire state of Illinois opposed him. Now everything had changed. Arguments over Lincoln's policies continued; but now one saw his hearse wheel into view, heard the tramping feet of its escort, smelled its horses, tasted its dust, gazed at its coffin, and later saw Lincoln inside it. Here was no longer a president to praise or criticize. Here was a talisman on which people could gaze and thereby see themselves as a nation. All day and all night the people passed by the open coffin. The next day they saw it closed and returned to the waiting train. Now remained only the journey to Springfield. The fallen president was carried there and viewed for twenty-four hours; then, at last, he was entombed (*Chicago Tribune*, May 2, 3, 4, 1865).

Ritual and Belief

Assassination does not uniformly create sacred symbols, but Abraham Lincoln's funeral made him one. The assassinations of James

Garfield and William McKinley caused national uproars, but the mourning bore no resemblance, in breadth of participation or emotional intensity, to that for Lincoln. Not in the act of assassination but in the reaction it produced is where we seek the basis of Lincoln's transformation.

The causal link assumed by this argument—the link between ritual and belief—is interactive. Each individual's reaction to the assassination was determined not only by how he or she felt about Lincoln but also by how others felt about him. Whenever one "ventured a word of remark or inquiry" about the assassination, Reverend H. Harbaugh observed, it was with the hope "that the one addressed might be able to express and interpret for him his own feeling" (1865, 5). One person's attitude affected others' words and conduct as well as his own. "Every sentiment," as Durkheim would put it, "finds a place without resistance in all the minds, which are very open to outside impressions; each re-echoes the others, and is re-echoed by the others. The initial impulse thus proceeds, growing as it goes, as an avalanche grows in its advance" ([1915] 1965, 387). Accordingly, as individuals enter into close relations with one another, a new climate of belief and feeling emerges. To account for the impressions he receives and the emotion he feels in the "close relations" of national crises and solemn assemblies, the individual "attributes to the things with which he is in most direct contact properties which they have not, exceptional powers and virtues which the objects of every-day experience do not possess" (469). Lincoln, an ordinary man, thus turned into a heroic man.

Northerners, attached to Lincoln during the heat of war, exaggerated his virtues in their intense reaction to his death: such is the inference to which the thread of Durkheim's argument leads. But such an argument proceeds by logic, not empirical demonstration. To assess this argument's validity, beliefs must be observed independently of ritual conduct. What people *thought* about Lincoln after he died must be separated from what they *did* after he died; otherwise, no persuasive claim can be made about the relation between the two.

Public figures expressed uniformly positive impressions of Lincoln, although public pressures affected what they said. For many months following the assassination, no publisher would have dared to print harsh opinions of the president, even though many people continued to hold them. The number of these people should not be underestimated. Assassination changed many negative opinions about Lincoln's policies, but one cannot assume that it converted

most or even a majority of his critics. Amid the most positive statements on Lincoln are hints about the darker side of his public image,
clues to continuing differences of opinion about him as a man and
as a president. The terms in which Lincoln was praised in death bear
clear traces of the terms in which he was criticized in life.

Among people who wrote publicly about Lincoln in the spring
of 1865 were political representatives addressing state, county, and
local constituencies; newspaper editors and commentators addressing
subscribers; poets and essayists addressing a narrower audience of
educated readers; and clergymen addressing their still narrower audience of religious congregants. All reflected the public's opinion of
Lincoln; however, some articulated it better than others.

Since political representatives spoke about Lincoln in ceremonial
contexts, their statements were the most formulaic, typically including brief remarks about Lincoln's moral character, his service to the
nation in a troubled time, and his heinous murder, then extending
consolation to his family and support to his successor. Friendly newspaper editors followed no design, but they covered the same ground
as did the politicians. Unfriendly editors paid their respects, too. They
acknowledged their differences with the late president but no longer
dwelled on his faults. All condemned his murderer.[6] Poetic statements
expressed public opinion least accurately. These sought to portray in
compelling language the emotional reaction to the man and his death.
On controversial points of presidential policy and conduct, however,
the poems were silent.[7]

In contrast to politicians, journalists, and poets, the nation's
clergymen prepared their statements on Lincoln for audiences that
were small in number, homogeneous in religion and race, and similar
in class and ethnicity. Having attended personally to wartime suffering, the clergymen subscribed to and reacted to community opinion
about the "war president." Their eulogies on Lincoln, drafted in sermon format and generally delivered in the privacy of the church, were
therefore longer and more detailed than other public statements.
Some eulogies were replete with praise of Lincoln; some regretted his
death begrudgingly, a few (Parry 1961) delighted in it. Most portrayed Lincoln sympathetically, but with qualifications: they not only
mentioned but also revealed and assessed the nature of his mistakes.
Of the several sources of postmortem commentary, the religious eulogies were, ironically, the least eulogistical and portrayed the broadest
range of opinion. These documents provide no infallible index of the
people's attitudes, but they give insight into conceptions of Lincoln

during the weeks following his death, and they show how religious and political ideals structured these conceptions.[8]

The first wave of eulogies appeared on Easter Sunday—an appropriate day for Protestant America to reaffirm belief in divine intervention (Hay 1969b). Indeed, "one most noticeable feature" of the assassination, explained Reverend Cheever of New York, was "that God should have caused it to take place close to the end of the week, so that the sermons of today may the better instruct the nation in the appropriate moral" (*New York Times,* April 17, 1865, 8). Within this religious context, the clergymen worked their Easter Sunday sermons around two main themes: the character of the Confederacy and the character of Lincoln—in that order of significance.

Despite the mournfulness of the day, many eulogists seemed to agree more on the South's vices than on Lincoln's virtues. John Wilkes Booth, however, did not dominate their statements. Although he was known to be the assassin, his role was discounted. The Confederacy itself was responsible. The assassination plot was of a piece with other Confederate atrocities: deliberately starving prisoners, shooting wounded men, mutilating corpses and making their bones into trinkets, spreading pestilence, burning towns and villages. Denunciations of the South, calls for vengeance against its people and the hanging of its leaders—all the hatred that Northern politicians and military officers expressed on the day Lincoln died was exceeded in the Easter Sunday sermons and those given on the Wednesday of his funeral. Intent on justifying retaliation, the Protestant clergymen explained that forgiveness is an obligation of individuals; justice, an obligation of governments. From the spontaneous applause, they knew that their congregants agreed.

As the slave power's moral shortcomings strengthened Lincoln's merit in comparison, its aristocratic roots highlighted what he shared with the people. The motives driving Lincoln to do what he did throughout the war arose from his plebeian background. He pursued the war not only for the people but also with the people. The people understood Lincoln to be one of their own, and in this understanding their relation to the state became intimate. This is what the clergymen meant when they designated Lincoln "the people's president" and "the perfect type of American democracy" (see, for example, Coddington 1865, 6).

Even Lincoln's strongest supporters, however, reflected in their eulogies the people's doubts about him. Lincoln really did *not* wish to become a dictator, they said. He really was *not* an atheist. He

was *not* a teller of vulgar stories. He did *not* regularly visit houses of
Satan—theaters—even though he was shot in one. Openly defensive
statements such as these reveal that many were still unsure what kind
of man Lincoln was. Misgivings about him were also evident in ac-
knowledgments of his unpopularity. Many Americans "were not, indeed, always pleased with his deeds" (Boardman 1865, 5). Even his
assassination, traumatic as it was, failed to reverse entirely these negative attitudes. If Lincoln's murder epitomized the themes of death
and martyrdom in America's "civil religion," as Robert Bellah (1970)
has observed,[9] it did so in an ambivalent way. In the eyes of admirers,
Lincoln was the "Prince of Martyrs," the man who died for his cause;
but since so many repudiated this cause, Lincoln's relation to American civil religion was not the same in 1865 as it is today. For many
contemporaries, his death showed what was wrong, not right, with
his presidency.

Most Easter sermons described Lincoln as too forgiving, too com-
passionate toward the South—the victim of his own leniency. This
irony—that a Southerner murdered the man who wished to protect
the South against the vengefulness of its enemies—was not lost on
the eulogists, and it led the friendliest among them to portray Lincoln
as the embodiment of Christian mercy. Eulogists drew upon the Old
Testament more often than the New, however, and its most compelling lesson, the Exodus, placed Lincoln in a less favorable light: "God
permitted the meek and gentle Moses to live only until he could ascend to the top of Pisgah, and look upon the promised land . . . then
took him away, that He might raise up in his stead a mighty man of
valor as the captain of that great host to settle them in their inheritance. So perhaps it is now . . . that to another may be intrusted the
weighty task of bringing order out of the chaos which was left in its
track" (Hoffman 1865, 9).

Just as God had removed Moses and replaced him with Joshua,
so He removed the meek and lenient Abraham Lincoln and replaced
him with the determined Andrew Johnson. The idea of removal and
replacement was prominent because Lincoln's assassination was seen
an essential part of God's plan. People throughout the North were
told, and believed, that God "permitted" the murder because He
needed "a sharper cutting instrument" (Barr 1865, 10), "a man of
sterner mood than the late President" (Robbins 1865, 13) to effect
the righteous punishment of the Confederacy. Thus, "Mr. Lincoln's
continuance in office would not have been so favorable to God's plan
as his removal" (Hall 1865, 10).

The president had to die because he was about to negate his wartime successes with ill-advised postwar policies. "Possibly, had he survived," Reverend Frank Robbins of Philadelphia speculated, "his disposition would have inclined him to a too lenient policy toward the leaders of this atrocious rebellion" (1865, 13). Lincoln's successor, Andrew Johnson, had made harsh public statements about the South's leaders ("I would arrest them; I would try them; I would convict them, and I would hang them" [*American and Commercial Advertiser* (Baltimore), April 18, 1865, 1]), but Lincoln seemed to rule out retaliation of any kind. Thankfully, the assassin's bullet made him, in Reverend Andrew Stone's words, "safe from all these possibilities of error, frailties, and failures" (1865, 349). By dying as he did, Lincoln not only preserved his own reputation but also revealed to the Union the best course for Reconstruction. "Who shall dare deny," asked Reverend George Hepworth, "that Lincoln dead may yet do more for America than Lincoln living?" (1865, 120). Such was the fallen leader's greatest service: his place in the nation's posterity resulted not so much from what he did to others as in what others did to him. His fame depended on his death.

The Easter Sunday sermons and official funeral eulogies described Lincoln as an anomalous figure; their praise was qualified and hedged. After the military victory, "friends [of Lincoln] were *firmer* friends. The doubtful and hesitating were *more* confident and cordial. Enemies were *becoming* friends" (Hitchcock 1865, 5). Yet it was "impossible to say how much better or how much worse others would have done" in Lincoln's place (Fowler 1865, 22, 16, 24; see also McClintock 1865, 9–10).

On June 1, 1865, a month after Lincoln was placed in his tomb, President Johnson proclaimed a National Day of Fasting and Humiliation. On this day, everyone had to search his or her heart and contemplate the world's darkness. The clergy's ruminations yielded a veritable treasure trove of evil. The first wave of eulogies, delivered in April, had been concerned solely with Lincoln, his assassination, and the Confederacy. The June eulogies were full of general grievances and peeves. Speakers seasoned their accounts of Southern treason by condemning universalism, humanism, socialism, and individualism; by disparaging Jews, Jesuits, Freemasons, Odd Fellows, and death penalty opponents; by railing against commercialism, alcoholic beverages, and theater attendance. Since these evils were causes, parts, or consequences of the rebellion, the Confederacy and its supporters were agents of the world's manifold corruption (Allen 1865; Bingham 1865; Gurley 1865; Harbaugh 1865).

Thus conceived, the Confederacy was the framework within

which Lincoln's character crystallized. Lincoln's most conspicuous traits, in June as in April, were forgiveness and magnanimity, but the public's attitude toward him on this account remained ambivalent. Forgiveness of one's enemies is a cardinal tenet of Christianity, and most clergymen, like Reverend Thomas Chase, trusted "that in all the councils of our rulers such mercy will be ever exhibited as is worthy of a Christian people and enlightened age" (1865, 25). Lincoln realized this ideal. No aspect of his personal life or his policy—neither his humble background nor his dedication to union and emancipation—was more frequently praised. Nothing Lincoln said was quoted more often than "With malice toward none, with charity for all . . ."

At the same time, many could not help but feel that his leniency was morally wrong. His forgiving of treason implied the forgetting of the hundreds of thousands who had died at his command. Lincoln's own reasoning on this issue was abstract and puzzling. The people of the South, he claimed, had never really left the Union in the first place. What, then, was to be made of the grief and devastation they had inflicted? And if the war was really the work of a handful of slaveholders, then why did he refuse at least to punish them? In the days following the assassination, clergymen criticized Lincoln's policies directly; beginning in June, they criticized them more often by innuendo, summarizing the uncomplimentary remarks of others rather than expressing their own disapproval. Lincoln's refusal to punish treason, however, provoked undisguised outrage: "The brave soldier, who tore himself away from a young family, that he might sustain the laws of his country, but who, in an hour of tenderness and home-sickness, is tempted to desert, is returned and tried, condemned and shot! But the arch-traitors, whose rebellion against the nation made it necessary for him to go into the service, are to be regarded as guilty of no crime!" (Harbaugh 1865, 16). In truth, Lincoln's forgiveness "sometimes overcame the demands of justice" (Briggs 1865, 24).[10]

The Obligation to Mourn

To overemphasize the critical tone of the Lincoln eulogies would be to misrepresent their content. Unflattering remarks appeared at the margins, not the core, of these statements. Yet the remarks were always clear enough to be understood. Lincoln's contemporaries, after all, had always known him as a president more vigorously attacked than defended. On the other hand, the key to understanding Lincoln's public image is not the eulogies themselves, but the relationship between their content and the funeral rites.

The scope and intensity of Lincoln's funeral rites were out of all proportion to what people actually believed about Lincoln himself. This contrast is our primary concern. Even if affection for Lincoln had been greater, even if his funeral rites had been simpler, the contrast would remain. The Lincoln rites give the impression of an extraordinary man, flawless and beloved by all. The things said about Lincoln give the impression of a mediocre man, flawed and more an object of sympathy than reverence. Between the rites that commemorate Lincoln and the beliefs about him is a significant inconsistency.

Without ritual, belief would be less comprehensible and moving. Ritual dramatizes belief and unifies people around it. For many years these assumptions were commonplace in anthropological as well as sociological research. Beliefs and rituals, ideas and actions, always develop together, A. R. Radcliffe-Brown thought; and "in this development it is action or the need of action that controls belief rather than the other way about" ([1952] 1968, 160). But if ritual action controls belief, then what are we to make of the present case, in which spectacular ceremony was dedicated to a man whose achievements and personal qualities were thought by so many to be unspectacular?

Public mourning, whose function is the affirmation of unity, requires no assumptions about the superior merit of the deceased. Abraham Lincoln was no unifying symbol before April 1865. He was not mourned because he was a unifying symbol; rather, he became a unifying symbol because he was mourned. The act of mourning, as Emile Durkheim conceived it, "is not a natural movement of private feelings wounded by cruel loss; it is a duty imposed by the group" ([1915] 1965, 443). In more contemporary language, mourning is produced in conformity with "feeling rules" that indicate what sort of affect is to be displayed on a given occasion. Public mourning, then, is "surface acting," a deliberate attempt by people to put themselves in harmony with the emotional demands of a situation. However, people commonly undertake the kind of "emotion work" that public mourning requires by "deep acting"—deliberately invoking in themselves the appropriate emotions (Hochschild 1979). In both cases—the first, in which the grief is enacted but not felt; and the second, in which it is felt because it must be enacted—the sentiment is induced by the occasion.

That mourning for Lincoln was a "duty imposed by the group"

is evident in many aspects of his funeral. Representative Robert Schenck despised Lincoln, considering him a vulgar "baboon" who prosecuted the war ineffectually. Assigned to the Ohio delegation aboard Lincoln's funeral train, Schenck knew "this journey is going to be a labor"; but he recognized his obligation, even if others did not recognize theirs. Despite "a shameful falling off of the congressional delegation," he wrote his daughters, "it seems my duty to continue through" (Peskin 1977, 28).

Everywhere there was talk of a community "doing its duty" and "doing itself honor" through mourning ritual. Everywhere, invidious distinctions were drawn. Chicago's officials bragged that the per capita turnout in their city for the arrival of Lincoln's body exceeded that of any other city. In New York, a civic-minded attorney called on the Superior Circuit Court's chief judge to adjourn for a period exceeding the state's prescribed mourning period (*New York Times,* April 18, 1865, 2). Overconformity to funerary custom, the lawyer assumed, expresses moral superiority.

Overconforming to the mourning rules of their society, women played the primary role in establishing the affective tone of Lincoln's funeral. Traditionally responsible both for the physical care of the dead and for ritually expressing their family's and their community's grief, women appeared in disproportionate numbers to view Lincoln's remains, and they surpassed men in the frequency of fainting and expression of emotion generally (see, for example, *New York Times,* April 25, 1865, 2).

It is also true, however, as Representative Schenck's letter indicated, that funerary customs were often neglected and the feeling rules violated. Everywhere there were people who declared publicly their delight at Lincoln's death, or who expressly refused to mourn it. Everywhere there were people who simply did not join in, who "failed entirely to show their grief for the nation's loss" (*Chicago Tribune,* May 2, 1865, 4).

Grief over Lincoln diminished whenever the funeral form eroded along the route of his train, as often happened. Lincoln's death was everywhere treated solemnly, but after four years of wartime shortages and Spartan existence, a state funeral proved to be an exciting break from the routine. As Lincoln's funeral train pulled into Lancaster, Pennsylvania, the crowd was electrified by rumors that General Grant was aboard, and its aspect abruptly changed from grief and mourning to excitement and expectation (*New York Times,* April 23, 1865, 1). Later, in New York City, newspapers made disdainful reference to the frisky demeanor of many who waited to witness the funeral procession or to see the president's body. Demonstrations of lightheartedness and other disorders (including the activity of pickpockets, arrested in great numbers) occurred with increasing frequency from the first to the third day of Lincoln's presence. After his body was carried from the city, a *New York Times* editorial criticized the Arrangements Committee for having the funeral last so long, asserting that the prolongation of mourning rites dissipated the grief they were designed to express (April 25, 1865, 4). The newspaper had a good point. Officials in Buffalo had arranged and conducted their own funeral for Lincoln—empty coffin and all—that attracted a large number of people and was genuinely moving. A few days later came word that the funeral train would actually pass through the city and that Lincoln's remains would be available for public viewing. The city was delighted at the news, but with its citizens' emotions having already been spent in the symbolic observance, Buffalo gave Lincoln the most proper, most self-composed reception of all—a reception "more nearly a failure," according to Representative Schenck, "than in any city we have stopped in" (Kunhardt 1965; Peskin 1977, 28). Thus the range of emotions expressed during the fourteen-day funeral journey resulted not only from thoughts about Lincoln but also from the dynamics of the rites themselves.

"The Country Is Eternal"

By participating in Lincoln's funeral procession, the millions of people who disliked him could mourn his death. In doing so, they recognized society's claim to their devotion. For any group to allow members to ignore a death that diminishes it "would be equivalent to proclaiming that it does not hold the place in their hearts which is due it; it would be denying itself. A family which allows one of its members to die without being wept for shows by that very fact that it lacks moral unity and cohesion: it abdicates, it renounces its existence" (Durkheim [1915] 1965, 445–46).

If a group dutifully affirms itself by mourning a member's death, the duty becomes greater, the affirmation more imperative, when the deceased is an elected leader who dies at the hand of an enemy. "The assassin's bullet that was aimed at [Lincoln] was aimed at the authority, the honor and the life of the nation, and against the authority and majesty of God" (Barr 1865, 4). This symbolic burden made

Lincoln's murder "the crime of the age" (7), the climax of all crimes (Gurley 1865, 14), "the fearful apex of crime," comparable to the assassinations of Julius Caesar, William of Orange, and Henry IV of France (Harbaugh 1865, 7).

Since Lincoln's assassin sought to destroy the nation, the theme of national survival was conspicuous in every eulogy: "Never was the government so strong—never was one country more secure" (Howlett 1865, 7). Lincoln's funeral demonstrated this strength and security. The essential dualism of the mourning rites—the moral obligation to express grief and the political need to display power—was resolved by a ritual division of labor. People *attending* Lincoln's state funeral expressed the nation's grief; people *conducting* the funeral expressed the nation's strength. Bearers, guards, and escorts for Lincoln's body showed no feeling as they performed their duty. In every city, from Baltimore to Springfield, the funeral's sequence of movements was stylized and almost mechanically executed. Into each terminal the train glided slowly, quietly, then stopped. No wails of grief, but utter silence—punctuated by honor guards snapping to attention—prevailed through the removal of the coffin from train to carriage. From train station to city hall or capitol building, every movement was known beforehand and performed in unison by defined groups of officials, guards, and escorts.

Orderliness, precision, structure, self-possession, and decorum (as opposed to unbounded, paralyzing grief) are evident in the photographs and prints of the funeral procession. In New York, formless crowds standing on sidewalks and at windows watched disciplined rows of marching men escorting Lincoln's hearse down Broadway. The procession in Columbus, Ohio, was stylized along similar lines, as can be seen in figure 1.1. After leaving the capitol building, with its elaborately decorated entrance, Lincoln's hearse passed a long, straight line of sentries extending to the street. The hearse was surrounded by an honor guard and preceded by cavalry and infantry marching in perfect unison. Mounted officers followed it and escorted the carriage bearing Lincoln's family and friends. The disciplined procession, in contrast to the unorganized spectators, conveys the impression of impassive suffering—an impression evident from the very beginning of the funeral journey in Washington:

To-night, reviewing the day's proceedings, all hearts are full both of sorrow and joy. We have shown to-day the neatest and most soldierly troops, the most veteran of veteran levies, the most splendid military equipment,

Figure 1.1. *Funeral of Abraham Lincoln,* Columbus, Ohio, 1865 print. Photograph courtesy of the Lincoln Museum, Fort Wayne, Indiana (3711).

representing every arm of the service, a galaxy of the most illustrious faces ever known in a single nation, and a civilian display which was not more suggestive of the spirit of our nationality than it was overwhelming, reliant, temperate, and respectful. The day of panic has gone by. We live in a more cheerful sunlight. We regret that man, but we feel that the country is eternal. (*New York World,* April 20, 1865, 1)

"We feel that the country is eternal." Such is the feeling that Lincoln's funeral was designed to promote. Its "influence for the good will be tremendous," said one Harrisburg, Pennsylvania, observer. The remains of the slain president exhibited the enormity of treason, but the mighty grief of the people "illustrated the real strength of the government" (*Harrisburg Daily Telegraph,* April 24, 1865, 2).

These funeral rites exerted "influence for the good" by erasing Lincoln's individuality and replacing it with manifestations of the power of the state. Like the ancient English kings, the American president has two bodies—the visible "body natural," which is subject to all the infirmities of the world, including mortality; and the invisible "body politic," immune to death, eternal, constituted in the name of and for the benefit of the people (see, for example, Metcalf and Huntington 1991, 168–88).

In English law, the king's death is defined as his "demise" (literally, "transfer") to capture the sense of his replacement rather than disappearance. This symbolic separation of the role from the role player cannot be precisely applied to the American presidency, where the real separation of man and office is taken for granted. The president's tenure, unlike the king's, is temporary and dependent on the consent of the people rather than on divine right. The invisibility of the state, however, not the formal status of its president, makes the concept of "two bodies" relevant to the American case. The president, while alive, embodies the state in his appearance and actions. Death reverses this. Through funereal symbols of state power, the otherwise invisible body politic becomes visible and tangible, while the body natural disappears. Lincoln's body was thus "recycled" in the service of society. John Wilkes Booth's crime, designed to destroy the state, instead brought about the formation of rituals and ritual symbols that affirmed its indestructibility. Lincoln could be universally mourned without being universally admired because the celebration of America's integrity was the ultimate object of his funeral.

Mourning and Nationhood

In every city through which the funeral procession passed, memorable displays of symbolism amplified the presence of the state. The power of the national government, in truth, had not been apparent for very long. Its dominance over the provincial regimes to the south was problematic until the war's conclusion, and the Lincoln funeral was the very first occasion for the ritual display of its newly won power. The procession in Springfield, Illinois, climaxed this display. In other cities, the president's body was led from train station to city hall or capitol and back by local representatives; in Springfield, it was led to the tomb by representatives of the nation.

Eight divisions of men, each led by a marshal and his aides, accompanied the president's body to its tomb. In the First Division were the most fearsome defenders of the state: cavalrymen, dragoons, and artillerymen; in the Second were infantry officers and enlisted men, with side arms. The Third Division consisted of the hearse itself, led by officiating clergymen and a military honor guard, surrounded by military pallbearers, and followed by family and friends. Marching in the Fourth Division were "civil [federal] authorities of the United States according to their relative ranks," foreign ministers, and civil authorities of states and territories "according to their dignity" (*Daily Illinois State Journal,* May 5, 1865, 1).

The last four divisions of the Springfield procession, made up of local citizens, were symbolically inferior to the first four. In the Fifth Division were municipal leaders from Springfield and neighboring cities. The Sixth Division comprised Springfield commissioners; delegations from nearby universities, churches, and political bodies; and, finally, lawyers, physicians, and journalists. In the Seventh Division paraded the fraternal organizations: Masons, Odd Fellows, the Catholic Institute, the Fenian Brotherhood. The Eighth Division was the last and biggest, consisting of the white citizens at large followed by the black citizens. Thus, the order of the procession reproduced the graded orders of the society. From the Eighth to the First Division was a progression from individuals and their local organizations through the authorities of the city and state to the representatives and powers of the nation.

In one respect, Springfield's cortege resembled that of other cities: it affirmed the nation's moral unity and new greatness. The salience of the rituals, more than anything else, made for their great cultural power. Wherever Lincoln was placed in state, the funeral's significance was realized in the sheer detail of its coverage. Newspapers told where the lead train, funeral locomotive, and funeral car were built, where and when they had been decorated, and by whom— adding a comment on the tastefulness of the job and words of congratulation to all workers. Removal of the coffin from the car to a municipal or state building involved hundreds of people, whose names and roles were duly listed. The soldiers that guarded the body in state were all named. The artisans who built the hearse, the men who decorated the parade route or the rotunda with funerary symbols, the morticians who attended to the condition of the body and its vestments—all were named. In many cities, the newspapers devoted more than a full page to the decoration of commercial and government buildings and private residences, giving the building's address and the name of the superintendent or owner. These practices, which would be considered boring today, were important to readers in 1865. Through these news accounts, the people who honored the remains of the late president immortalized themselves, wrote themselves into a story whose plot transcended their own lives. The sudden ascent of Abraham Lincoln's reputation must be understood in this context.

Lincoln's image changed after his assassination not only because he was the object for whose sake elaborate state rituals were enacted but also because of the people's perception of the rituals themselves. Every newspaper account of the funeral observance, regardless of the city in which it took place, tried to characterize the collective spirit it evoked. Everywhere, the funeral train's arrival was novel and unique, a sacred visitation never to be recaptured. In Harrisburg, Lincoln's funeral passage was "the most solemn, the most sacred and the most sublime spectacle ever witnessed" (*Pennsylvania Daily Telegraph,* April 24, 1865, 1). The expression of feeling was unprecedented. "Oh, it is grand, sublimely grand and godlike," a resident of Columbus, Ohio, said, "to see a great people thus bowing down and worshiping the great dead" (*Chicago Tribune,* April 30, 1865, 3). The progression through Indiana was "a glorious record" for the state "to treasure up in her heart of hearts" (*Indianapolis Daily Journal,* May 3, 1865, 1). A Chicago reporter contemplated "the rich treasures we have inherited through the assassination" (*Chicago Tribune,* April 30, 1865, 3). Participants and observers alike were conscious of the way the funeral looked to outsiders, especially foreigners. "Probably few noticed them [foreigners]," said one correspondent, "without considering whether the sight of this tremendous crowd in one city might not lead toward a more adequate conception of our real national strength and unity" (*New York Times,* April 26, 1865, 1). Before this correspondent attributed the impression of strength and unity to foreigners, however, he must have first felt it himself. And this feeling takes us directly to the political and social context that determined what the funeral meant.

The Lincoln funeral marked not only the end of a war but also a change in America's self-conception. The heroes of the Civil War had performed feats equaling anything accomplished in the nation's past, and their president stood above them all.[11] Because Lincoln had forged the unification of the United States with blood and steel, Carl Degler (1992) was right to designate him "the American Bismarck." Yet there is a difference: Bismarck created a nation; Lincoln created nothing. Lincoln was the Savior, not the Father, of the Union. He sustained what George Washington had established; hence the frequent pairing of their images. "The names of Washington and Lincoln may now be sounded together in perfect accord," Reverend Harbaugh believed (1865, 25). For Reverend Edward Cutter, "Springfield and Mount Vernon will henceforth be kindred shrines" (1865, 13). The connection was both verbally and iconically represented. When Lincoln lay in state in the U.S. Capitol Rotunda, every statue was covered but one—George Washington's. Elsewhere on the funeral journey, a statue or bust of Washington looked down upon

Lincoln's coffin, or a life-size portrait of Washington stood beside it, or a slogan linked their two names.

Taken literally, the comparisons make no sense, for in 1865 Americans imagined these two men differently. Before Lincoln was assassinated, few saw in him anything that reminded them of Washington. During the Civil War, as during his own lifetime, Washington was an idol on whose virtues all Americans agreed. Lincoln was a president whose policies and personality, even in the flush of military victory, had alienated as many people as they had attracted. This is why the observers who matched Lincoln and Washington never declared their reasoning, never wrote more than a line or so to the effect that Lincoln completed the task Washington had begun.

The essential meaning of the Washington–Lincoln comparisons is grasped by realizing that Washington's elevation was part of the *rage militaire* [war fever] that propelled the colonies into revolutionary struggle (Schwartz 1983) while Lincoln's elevation was part of the *rage funéraire* [mourning excitement] at the end of the new nation's civil war. The place to look for an explanation of their prestige, then, is not in their personal traits or achievements but in the immediate situation wherein these were perceived and judged.

When the Civil War ended, Northerners knew they had passed through a momentous crisis and felt that America would never be the same again. Reverend George Boardman believed that God Himself had wrought the transformation: "He will not allow us to return to a state exactly the same as that which we held before" (1865, 10–11). A *New York World* editor wrote that "our gigantic civil war," having at last resolved the question of whether the United States could exist in permanent union, "marks a new era in our national life," a historical turning point comparable to the French Revolution (May 2, 1865, 4). In William Kip's opinion, the country had begun a "new career," because it was energized by a sense of "nationality such as never before existed" (1865, 8). The war, in John Egar's words, marked "the beginning of the modern history of the republic" (1865, 11). James McPherson (1991) has described this change as the "Second Revolution" of America's political, economic, and social life. But there was an internal, moral revolution, too. Benson Lossing's *Common School History of the United States* explained to young readers that the national government's moral power was greater than ever; the terrible war had "purified" the republic (1865, 303).

The Civil War had destroyed the last remnants of aristocratic privilege and had begun to transform America from a rural republic into a new, industrialized democracy. Feeling the change but having difficulty conceiving it, Northerners communicated their sense of what was happening in the only way they knew—by comparing it in historical significance to the American Revolution. In relating Washington, the great symbol of that revolution, to the most prominent representative of their own age, the people articulated the importance of what they had passed through. They conceived their state as replicating the pattern set by their ancestors, but at the same time they asserted their independence from the past. To find a heroic age, the people no longer needed to look back. Comparisons of Washington and Lincoln were statements not about the equivalence of the two men but about the equivalence of two heroic generations.

The Presidency: Focal Point of National Communion

The millions who paid their respects to Lincoln at his funeral disagreed among themselves as to what kind of president he had been. But "what often underlies people's political allegiances," as David Kertzer observes, "is their social identification with a group rather than their sharing of beliefs with other members" (1988, 67). Lincoln, however, was more than just a handy vehicle for the ritual expression of a common social identity. His image was transformed by that expression, was never the same after it. The funeral attached Lincoln to the people's enlarged sense of themselves, transcending particulars on which few could agree and converting him into a symbol on whose significance all could agree.

Comparisons with other presidents who died in office deepen this understanding of Lincoln's symbolic role. The death of any incumbent president, even natural death, has always brought strong reactions. William Henry Harrison served only one month, but his death was an "astounding blow. . . . Never, since the times of Washington, has any event produced so general and so profound a sensation of surprise and sorrow." Cities and towns throughout the country solemnly observed his day of mourning. Washington, the capital city, hosted enormous crowds from nearby states. "Almost every private dwelling had crepe upon the knocker and bell-handle of the door. . . . The stores and places of business, even such as are too frequently seen open on the Sabbath, were all closed" (*Charleston Courier,* April

8, 1841, 2; April 12, 1841, 2). Similarly, when Zachary Taylor died after sixteen months in office, the whole population was "shocked, stupefied, almost paralyzed" (*New Orleans Picayune,* July 11, 1850, 1). In Philadelphia, as elsewhere, "business was suspended and work of almost every kind ceased. Citizens were met with the badge of mourning on their left arm, and the countenances of old and young wore a look of deep and sincere sadness." New York City, in addition, marked the day of mourning with a great procession, while the pageant in Washington "exceeded everything of the kind, in order and magnificence, that ever took place in the metropolis" (*New York Tribune,* July 14, 1850, 1). The ritual reaction to Lincoln's death reflected the same respect for the presidency that had prompted impressive reactions to the deaths of Harrison and Taylor. The superior dignity of the presidential office, even when its power relative to that of Congress is feeble—as it was when Harrison and Taylor occupied it—creates a floor below which the mourning for its incumbent cannot fall.

When a president dies by assassination rather than of natural causes, the public mourning is infused with anger. Context, however, modulates that feeling. The murders of James Garfield in 1881 and William McKinley in 1901 produced widespread sadness and were marked by profuse displays of funerary symbols, great crowds attending public ceremonies, the display of presidential remains in various cities, and immense press coverage. But the two most conspicuous elements of Lincoln's funeral were absent in theirs. First, no suggestion of greatness was made for Garfield or McKinley. As neither president managed the state during a time of national peril, neither was compared to the revered men of the past. Speaking about James Garfield, who had been a peacetime president for six months when he was shot, former Navy Secretary Richard Thompson may have been right when he said, "Assassination in a time of peace . . . [when] harmony prevails everywhere . . . is worse than assassination in a time of war" (*New York Times,* July 3, 1881, 2). But peacetime assassination evokes a milder public reaction. William McKinley served as president much longer than Garfield and made controversial foreign policy decisions, including war with Spain, but none of these endangered the nation. "If there had been any political crisis at this time, such as would distort men's judgements," one correspondent observed, "this act might be less amazing, but there is none." In fact, no more was said about McKinley's policies or accomplishments, or what his death would do to the nation, than was said about

Garfield's. McKinley, like Garfield, was "beloved," "trusted," "cheerful," and the reaction to his assassination was strong but tempered (*New York Times,* September 7, 1901, 3). The political sentiment animating the mourning of Lincoln—hatred of a powerful enemy—was absent in the cases of Garfield and McKinley. Most people regarded Charles Guiteau and Leon Czolgosz, Garfield's and McKinley's assassins, as lone madmen and quickly forgot their names. The funeral rites for these two presidents were less elaborate than Lincoln's because of the serene political context in which they died.[12]

The second factor determining the reaction to a president's assassination is the time trajectory of his death. Deaths that occur suddenly, such as Abraham Lincoln's, are shocks that arouse and concentrate strong emotions. One of the immediate sources of shock is the sudden appearance of funerary symbols and rites. Routine news about routine presidential activities is replaced abruptly by business closings, solemn processions, and memorial services. In contrast, deaths occurring gradually, such as Garfield's (after ten weeks) and McKinley's (after one week), produce muted reactions. When the initial news concerns injury rather than death, no symbols and rites exist for people to organize around. At the first news of Garfield's wounding, people in Washington were astonished, yet those gathering outside the White House were orderly. On hearing the news that McKinley had been shot, the people showed "suppressed excitement. . . . feeling more than they had the power to express." And when their deaths finally came, it took no one by surprise. After ten weeks of vacillating news, everyone was ready when Garfield died; and after McKinley's injury, the *New York Times* reported that the precariousness of his condition "has in some degree prepared us for the final outcome" (September 7, 1901, 1). In both cases, the emotional arousal was spread over time and diluted.

Abraham Lincoln's assassination occurred while he presided over the greatest crisis the nation had known since its creation, and the assassin's bullet caused him to die within hours. Since two conditions that promote the strongest public reactions—national crisis and sudden death—were both present in Lincoln's case, we find the most intense and prolonged expression of ritual mourning. These two conditions were unequal in their effects. If Lincoln had died a week or even months after his injury, his funeral observances would have been less emotional but just as elaborate—perhaps even more so, given the additional time to prepare for them. But if Lincoln had not been president during the years of the Civil War, his death would have been less traumatic.

This point can be sustained better by taking into account the case of John F. Kennedy. Kennedy was elected to office by a smaller margin of popular votes than Lincoln received, and just before Kennedy's death his public approval rating, which had been dropping for months, reached its lowest point. Major newsmagazines reported that he was in trouble, particularly on domestic issues, and expressed doubts about his reelection.[13] Nevertheless, when Kennedy was shot to death in November 1963, the people mourned him as intensely as they had mourned Lincoln a hundred years earlier.[14]

Kennedy's case is puzzling. The one element most likely to produce a reaction similar to the one to Lincoln's assassination—prolonged national crisis—is precisely the element that most clearly distinguishes their administrations. Lincoln spent his entire presidency supervising the nation's costliest war. In contrast, Kennedy's closest ideological friends complained that his administration was too serene, too peaceful. It moved from one skirmish to another. "What is missing, many feel, is the smell of battle, the drama of great forces contending for great stakes" (*New Republic,* June 1, 1963, 3; May 18, 1963, 2).

To assert that Kennedy accomplished nothing significant during his administration would be wrong. Not only his civil rights accomplishments (however reluctantly motivated) but also his management of the Cold War, including the Cuban missile crisis, was dramatic and important. Yet these were no more than *significant* events. Washington, Lincoln, and Franklin D. Roosevelt responded to crisis by placing the country on a different course. Kennedy had no opportunity to do this, but the people reacted to his death as if he had.

Kennedy's case suggests that it is not crisis itself that explains extraordinary reactions to a president's sudden death; it is the effect of the crisis on the salience and visibility of the presidency. To use Michael Schudson's (1989a) terms, crisis can make the presidency conspicuous, publicly "retrievable"; it can give presidential policies greater "rhetorical force" and make them more consequential. Any factor that produces such effects will enlarge the "cultural power" of the presidency, bring it closer to the life of the people, and add to its prominence as a symbol of society's consensus and divisions.

The factor enlarging the cultural power of Lincoln's presidency was war, and all his eulogists spoke at length about the way he conducted it. The factor enlarging the cultural power of Kennedy's presidency was Kennedy himself—or, more precisely, as Alan Wool-folk suggests, the stylistic traits that Kennedy's aristocratic (as opposed to patrician) appearance and demeanor embodied.[15] Kennedy's eulogists never failed to recount his idealism and achievements; however, the one tendency distinguishing their tributes from memorials to other national leaders is their emphasis on physical attractiveness, "brilliance," "class," "decorum," "charm," "style," "grace," and "wit."[16] These traits, so closely connected in the public mind with youth and vitality, were exaggerated by Kennedy's premature death. Kennedy may have been an exemplar of his class, but in him the public found "personal charisma," magnetic traits perfectly suited to and dependent for their effect on the relatively new medium of television.[17] Recognized by Kennedy's critics and supporters alike (*National Review*, August 13, 1963, 65; December 10, 1963, 1), these personal traits became politically salient as they fused with the presidency and enlarged it as a cultural object.

However, the connections among the presidency, the personal qualities of its incumbent, and public opinion are as complex in Kennedy's case as in Lincoln's. Many Americans polled at the time of Kennedy's death, including two-thirds of white Southerners who had voted against him, expressed personal grief—in particular, "I feel I have lost someone close and dear to me" (Sheatsley and Feldman 1965, 167). How one man can be regarded as close and dear to so many who never met him is a question that resolves itself in the context of two interrelated facts: (1) those who mourned this man had just spent hours watching his three-day state funeral; and (2) the function of this funeral, as of ritual in general, was precisely to produce a sense of closeness between ordinary people and the sacred powers of their society (Durkheim [1915] 1965, 257–58). That the sacred power in this instance was the presidency and not the president himself is suggested by the fact that public mourning during the days following Kennedy's death was not accompanied by public movement toward Kennedy's positions on the fundamental issues of the day, including civil rights. In 1963, as in 1865, the year Lincoln died, people had various opinions about the president's politics, but everyone revered the presidency. In the words of a *Time* magazine reader: "I did not vote for John F. Kennedy. But that murderer [Lee Harvey Oswald] killed MY President" (December 6, 1963, 17). Kennedy's magnetism enhanced the significance of his death because it had already enhanced the cultural power of his office. Thus conceived, the survey findings conform to Sidney Verba's claim (1965) that attachment to the presidency stems from a diffuse commitment that transcends ideological preferences—a commitment whose real object is the nation itself.

The Power of Ritual

Generalizing the contextual details of Lincoln's death and discerning the contingencies that mediate different reactions to presidential assassination, we can speak with more certainty about our immediate concern: the interaction of crisis, belief, and commemorative ritual. To articulate properly how this interaction was manifested in the Lincoln assassination, we had to reject the assumption that the most impressive rites are dedicated to the people whom society uniformly reveres. Lack of such consensus around Lincoln reveals a loose connection between belief and ritual and sustains David Kertzer's reinterpretation (1988) of Durkheim. Although Kertzer believes, with Durkheim, that ritual can produce solidarity by creating and maintaining a common belief system, he does not see this as its only use. "Far from always creating solidarity by reinforcing shared values," Kertzer observes, "one of the crucial functions of ritual is to produce solidarity in the absence of any commonality of beliefs" (66).

The public reaction to Lincoln's death supports Kertzer's claim. Although people disagreed intensely on Lincoln's worth as president, their common participation in his funeral expressed their common identification with the nation. In contrast, strong agreement on a leader's merit will actually weaken solidarity if it leads people to engage in separate commemorative celebrations. Kertzer shows this in his example of Joan of Arc. For the political left, Joan had always represented secular republicanism and the power of the people; for the political right, she represented French gentility and the link between patriotism and religious commitment. Everyone had something good to say about Joan of Arc, but what they said was different and reflected different values. Indeed, when French leaders arranged a national festival in her honor during the 1890s, they created more antagonism than they resolved, for the "two Frances" celebrated the festival as rivals, using it as an opportunity to condemn rather than embrace one another. The contrasting cases of Abraham Lincoln and Joan of Arc support Kertzer's claim that ritual builds cohesion through uniformity of action rather than similarity of belief (71–72, 76).

At a deeper level, however, the affinity between this case study and Kertzer's theory breaks down. Kertzer's weak point is his conception of belief itself. He declares that "one should be wary about attributing too much significance to a person's set of political beliefs, since these are neither consistent nor are they all equally developed and strongly held" (68). Moreover, political beliefs are not always salient parts of the lives of the people holding them. Such a conception does not conform to beliefs about Lincoln. Emerging out of the torment of war, these beliefs were coherent and informed by personal experience. Popular beliefs about Lincoln were diverse and ambivalent, but, on an individual level, surely not ambiguous or casual.

If Americans held differing beliefs about Lincoln, they did agree on the merits of their new political order. For this reason, Kertzer's conclusion that "solidarity is produced by people acting together, not by people thinking together" (76) also needs qualification. Controversial figures, such as Lincoln, promote solidarity only on condition that they represent noncontroversial realities whose sacredness all recognize, ultimate realities on which a fundamental consensus rests. Lacking such consensus, the commemoration of a universally revered Joan of Arc only widened the divisions of late-nineteenth-century France, while commemoration of a widely disliked Lincoln promoted unity in mid-nineteenth-century America. Durkheim was wrong, then, to overlook the many ways in which rituals produce solidarity without consensus, just as Kertzer observed; but so far as the ritual support of ultimate realities is concerned—in this case, the integrity and power of the state—Durkheim was right.

Durkheim believed that people are usually unaware of what causes their excitement during times of national crisis. They cannot explain their feelings to themselves "except by connecting them to some concrete object of whose reality they are vividly aware" ([1915] 1965, 251). If an impressive ritual is dedicated to a particular man, then people will believe that man to be the ritual's object. But they will be wrong. The majesty of society itself, according to Durkheim, is what the ritual truly affirms. The tangible man takes the place of an intangible social reality. It is now he that is loved and respected.

Although Lincoln aroused love and respect among many, he was also an object of hatred and disdain. Spectacular funeral rites suppressed the latter sentiments only temporarily, but the rites themselves were memorable and laid the groundwork for a literal cult of veneration that would form in the next generation. Abraham Lincoln's assassination and funeral would be remembered independently of the assassin's motives and independently of what Lincoln himself had done or failed to do as president. When the new century dawned, the American people visited the place where Lincoln was shot and the house where he died; they saw movies and read newspaper stories, reprints, and poems about the funeral and the weeks of mourning. The reaction to Lincoln's death became a central defining feature of his life, enhanced the power of its commemoration, and induced a generation removed from the experiences of civil war to see him in a permanently positive light. Memory of the man and memory of the rite became intertwined. As years passed, the events and interests of new generations from the end of the Civil War to the end of the Progressive era would be expressed in new commemorative intertwinings. In Jeffrey Olick's words:

Differences between commemorations are not only a function of the politics of the present or of immediate historical precedents, but of the forms and media available in different moments. Comparing commemorations in terms of the history of memory thus both helps to explain their differences and leads to epochal insights about the status of commemoration as a social practice within particular societies. (1999, 383)

The study of Abraham Lincoln answers questions about memory practices that Olick has raised: how have change and persistence in historical memory been affected by the availability of changing commemorative media technologies and preferences, changing generational experiences, and changing societal conditions? Once these questions have been answered, we will know how the American people's love and respect for Abraham Lincoln could rise after his death and then diminish as the decades passed, only to rise again in a new century.

Promoting Lincoln
in the Late Nineteenth Century:
Successes and Failures

The reputational entrepreneur's job is to make an ordinary person great, or, more commonly, to bring the person's greatness to public attention. The task is twofold: "to propose early on a resonant reputation, linked to the cultural logic of critical 'facts' and then to make that image stick" (Fine 1996, 1177). Many entrepreneurs, moved by ideals, interests, and opportunity, worked to promote Abraham Lincoln's reputation.

As soon as Lincoln's Springfield, Illinois, friends—Richard Oglesby, John Todd Stuart, Jesse Dubois, and James Conkling—learned of his death, they began to plan for his tomb. Soliciting contributions under the name of the Lincoln National Monument Association, they envisioned a shrine of supreme dignity. Oglesby, an intimate friend and Whig/Republican colleague, had served as Lincoln's campaign manager and had devised the plan to make him the rail-splitter candidate. After Oglesby finished a period of war service, Lincoln promoted him to brigadier general; Illinois voters later elected him governor. John Todd Stuart, Lincoln's first law partner and his political mentor, disagreed with his emancipation policy but was his wife's cousin and always enjoyed good relations with him. Jesse Dubois, an antislavery man, was one of Lincoln's most enthusiastic admirers and campaign managers. He was reelected to the position of state auditor when Lincoln won the presidency, and he continued to work for him during the 1864 election. James Conkling was also one of Lincoln's Whig/Republican political partners, and his antislavery commitments were no less deep than Lincoln's. These four men approved and commissioned the first great monument to Abraham Lincoln.

Larkin Mead, designer of the majestic Lincoln tomb, must have known what the association wanted, for he outdid himself. The tomb was grander and more complex than that of any other president. George Washington's Mount Vernon tomb consisted then, as now, of a small gated compartment within which his and his wife's remains rest. Thomas Jefferson's memorial marker is a stone shaft in the Monticello cemetery. Andrew Jackson's tomb, covered by a modest columned dome, is more elaborate than Jefferson's but is also located in the family burial ground. For other presidents, including William Henry Harrison and James Polk, provisions were made for special tombs outside public or family cemeteries, but their size and design bear no comparison to Lincoln's.

Although built in memory of "the people's president," the Abraham Lincoln Monument (as it was then known) in Springfield conveys a sense of domination and distinction (fig. 2.1). An obelisk, reminiscent of the Washington Monument, rises from the terraced roof of a memorial hall to a height of 117 feet; at its base is a fourteen-foot-high pedestal supporting Lincoln's statue. On twenty-five-foot-high circular pedestals at each of the four corners of the hall sit sculptures representing the cavalry, infantry, artillery, and navy. The top portion of the burial vault lies within the memorial hall at ground level; below ground level is the compartment with Lincoln's remains.[1]

On October 14, 1874, President Ulysses S. Grant dedicated the Lincoln Monument before a crowd of forty thousand people. General William T. Sherman and other old soldiers listened as one speaker after another eulogized Lincoln. When the ceremony ended, several marching bands paraded from the Monument into the brightly decorated city (New York Times, October 15, 1874, 1; October 16, 1874, 1–3). The day's activities rekindled memories of Lincoln's funeral nine years earlier. It was as if Americans had copied the ancient custom of two burials (Hertz [1910] 1960): the first, in 1865, to remove Lincoln from the world of the living; the second, in 1874, to induct him into the world of illustrious ancestors.

The Victorian era's preference for the physically imposing

Figure 2.1. Larkin G. Mead, *Abraham Lincoln Monument,* 1874, Oak Ridge Cemetery, Springfield, Illinois. Photograph courtesy of the Illinois State Historical Library.

as symbolic of the socially significant was the first reason that Lincoln's friends erected an ostentatious tomb for him. Massive monuments would commemorate not only Lincoln but also the Civil War's second Northern hero, Ulysses S. Grant, and the next assassinated presidents, James Garfield and William McKinley. Second, and most important, the Lincoln Monument was dedicated to a non-monumental man. For centuries, the commemorative power of tombs has enhanced the stature of national leaders. In Lincoln's case the epic tomb plays a special role, because Lincoln at that time seemed so unfit for epic portrayal. Since George Washington was universally adored when artists and sculptors portrayed him, the making of monuments to him seemed to understate his flawlessness. Lincoln, on the other hand, died a controversial man, and the task for artists of his own and later times was to make him godlike. This was always difficult, for they had to work in the face of popular ambivalence. Their depictions of Lincoln were often unnatural and forced—almost as if they doubted the appropriateness of their own work.

Monuments commonly make up for the shortcomings of their subjects through "elaborated" design. Karen Cerulo (1995) has shown that elaborated designs, applied to flags and anthems, are preferred by societies on the periphery of the world system in order to compensate for their economic and political weakness. Cerulo's interpretation is relevant to the strategy of Lincoln's reputational entrepreneurs. Lincoln had many supporters—people who had staked their own convictions on his wartime policies—yet their success in promoting him was limited.

Epic Scripture

"Chained by stern duty to the rock of state" (Mitchell [1911] 1970), Abraham Lincoln was more than a chief executive; he embodied the nation, and when he perished the cosmos shook:

> And so the Nation rested, worn and weak
> From long exertion—
> God! What a shriek
> Was that which pierced to farthest earth and sky,
> As though all Nature uttered a death cry!
> Awake! Arouse! ye sleeping warders, ho!
> Be sure this augurs some colossal woe;
> Some dire calamity hath passed o'erhead—
> A world is shattered or a god is dead! (Goodman [1911] 1970, 60)

Between 1865 and 1900, hundreds of prose and poetical works cast Lincoln as a demigod. His overcoming poverty to become president was mystical, part of God's plan for America; his freeing the slaves and guiding the nation through tragic war shaped history. "After one makes the obvious concessions required by mid-century morality and by the exigencies of a republican form of government," David Donald observed, "this Lincoln conforms very closely to the type of ideal hero in classical mythology" ([1947] 1989, 149). This classical hero, however, was mainly a product of Republican and antislavery imaginations.

Josiah G. Holland's *Life of Abraham Lincoln* (1866) was the first classical narrative, one that depicted Lincoln as an Old Testament prophet. "I know there is a God and that he hates injustice and slavery," Lincoln declared while discussing slavery adherents' quoting of Scripture. I see the storm coming, and I know that His hand is in it. If He has a place and work for me—and I think He has—I believe I am ready." As if to anticipate his own martyrdom, Lincoln exclaims, "I am nothing but truth is everything. I know I am right because I know that liberty is right, for Christ teaches it and Christ is God" (237). A New England moralist who had distinguished himself by uplifting poetry, essays, and novels, Holland never intended to write an analytic biography. His concern was to draw moral lessons from Lincoln's life and publish them for the public good. His biography, however, never saw a second edition.

Holland's was not the only failed effort to mythologize Lincoln. Former Lincoln assistant secretary William O. Stoddard's *Abraham Lincoln: True Story of a Great Life* (1885) lacked the religiosity of Holland's work, but its purpose was the same: to show how Lincoln's life and services "offer one of the noblest lessons to be found in the world's history." Stoddard meant his book, as Holland did his, not as a life to be analyzed but as a model to be followed. Few bought it. Francis Bicknell Carpenter's *Six Months at the White House* (1867) and Isaac N. Arnold's *The History of Abraham Lincoln and the Overthrow of Slavery* (1866) were equally hagiographic—praising Lincoln's moral character and describing his Emancipation Proclamation as the opening of a new historical era. Their close ties to Lincoln (Carpenter as artist-in-residence for half a year at the White House and Arnold as a political colleague) inspired their remembrances but induced few people to buy their books.

Lincoln's personal secretaries, John Nicolay and John Hay, composed their own epic chronicle: the ten-volume *Abraham Lincoln, A History* (1890), an insider's account of a powerful giant shaping history. They submitted the entire work to Lincoln's son, Robert, for approval and revised it upon his request. So partisan was their work that *Century*'s otherwise sympathetic editor, Richard W. Gilder, asked them for more restraint in their serialized articles; but even the unrestrained versions did not sell well.

Since Lincoln's historical achievement has never been as evident to ordinary Americans as his personal character and demeanor (Adams 1890, 590), the epic Lincoln required dense and imposing symbolism. Lincoln's frontier background, however, failed to harmonize with the image his admirers were trying to convey—hence the defensive tone in much of their work. John Nicolay went out of his way to stress Lincoln's gentility of dress and manners and his social ease among gentlemen like himself. David Locke, realizing that levity and joke-telling undermined epic heroism, emphasized that Lincoln was a master of satire, which was "at times as blunt as a meat axe and at others keen as a razor" (1890, 52). Locke transformed Lincoln's humor, generally regarded as an instrument of distraction, into an instrument of power. Poets, too, tried to resolve Lincoln's inconsistencies. "The Master," as Edwin Arlington Robinson conceived Lincoln soon after the Civil War, was a complex leader—laconic yet Olympian, mirthful yet titanic, a product of both civilization and wilderness. "Was ever a master yet so mild / As he, and so untamable?" However artful the qualifications, though, the readers' response remained subdued.

Between 1865 and 1900, hundreds of Lincoln biographies appeared. No writer, however, attained the popularity of George Washington's biographer, Mason Locke Weems, who published more than twenty editions of his initial (1800) *History of the Life . . . of General George Washington* between 1800 and his death in 1825—an average of about one edition per year. The best-selling Lincoln biography at the turn of the century was John Nicolay's one-volume abridgement of his and Hay's earlier ten-volume work. However, Josiah Holland's book, published thirty-five years earlier, had sold three times as many copies (Thomas 1947, 130). Lincoln's biographers were at least as talented as Weems, but none had Weems's audience. In the late nineteenth century, the epic Lincoln (in painting [see Schwartz 1993] as well as in literature) lacked appeal.

If Lincoln's reputation had remained as strong as it was during his funeral, then his commemoration would have been unproblematic. Lincoln's supporters, however, could not sustain his prestige once the funeral excitement dissipated. The history of his commemoration in the late nineteenth century thus documents a tension infrequently addressed in collective memory studies. So accustomed are we to seeing posthumous reputations created and sustained by reputational entrepreneurs that their activities alone seem sufficient to perpetuate fame.

Many case studies document historical reputations being "produced" and "sold," but we have good reasons to hesitate before committing ourselves entirely to a "production of culture" model

(Peterson 1976). First, the model implies that loss of a reputation results from lack of efforts to cultivate and defend it; second, it emphasizes entrepreneurial efforts—the constructive aspect of reputation-making—at the expense of their reception, which reflects those elements in the social environment that enhance public readiness to respond positively to entrepreneurs' claims. Lincoln's case highlights the failure of competent reputational entrepreneurs to sustain reverence after the disappearance of conditions under which it had emerged. Lincoln's reputation, in short, eroded even as his supporters, wielding the nation's most prominent pens, chisels, and brushes, continued to commemorate him.

Erosion is not synonymous with disappearance. Lincoln's reputation, although diminished after his funeral, remained stronger than it ever had been during his life. One factor preventing his reputation from falling further than it otherwise might have was that the growing state needed legitimating symbols. The Civil War, according to historian Frank Tariello (1981), superimposed upon Jacksonian anti-statist culture a democratic mentality that saw the state as having needs and interests distinct from the needs and interests of the individual. The formation of the American state, giving governing elites an "identity and interest apart from any class or partisan interest" (Bensel 1990, ix, 3), began with the Civil War. America's "statist sensibility" inhered not only in the development of powerful political and regulatory units but also in a commemorative self-consciousness manifested in battlefield parks, reenactments of battles, state funerals and national cemeteries, and the growing presence and salience of national symbols, including the flag, adoption of the Pledge of Allegiance, color symbolism (red, white, and blue), the eagle, Uncle Sam, and Washington, D.C., as a symbolic as well as executive and legislative center (Zelinsky 1988). Of this national symbol system Abraham Lincoln's commemoration was a conspicuous part, although it was more limited during the late nineteenth century than it would be afterward.

The overriding concern of post–Civil War governments was the establishment of national cohesion, and for this purpose Lincoln was hardly the best symbol. His posthumous reputation was restricted by the bitter rift between North and South, conflict between Republican and Democratic visions of the good society, resentment over war policies and war losses, and racial problems caused by emancipation. These strains, each produced or exacerbated by Abraham Lincoln's presidential decisions, are expressed in the words of a lullaby many *Northern* mothers used to sing their babies to sleep: "Old Abe Lincoln is dead and gone / Hurrah! Hurrah!" (Fess 1914, 3396).

Revisions

Abraham Lincoln's assassination did increase his stature and underscore the significance of his presidency. Once the emotional climate attending his death dissipated, however, divisions of opinion about him reverted toward (without actually reaching) their original state.[2] Conflicts of interest and opinion were not as severe as they had been during the war, but they could not be easily healed. Because Lincoln's war had brought unmitigated sorrow to a generation, his posthumous reputation could not peak until that generation passed on. Reservations about his historical role, while differing from one sector of the population to another, endured. Establishing this claim is essential to proving that Lincoln's late-nineteenth-century *celebrity* exceeded his *reputation* and that it was not until the early twentieth century that he became a national idol.

The First Lincoln Day

Many Northern Democrats disliked Abraham Lincoln because they did not believe in his war; many Northern Republicans disliked him because they opposed the way he had conducted that war. The concerns of both were summarized on February 12, 1866, when the U.S. Congress met in joint session to hear George Bancroft's extraordinary eulogy of Lincoln. Sixty-six years earlier, the highest compliment Congress could bestow on an American citizen was to invite him to deliver the George Washington funeral address. Henry (Light-Horse Harry) Lee—Robert E. Lee's father—received that invitation, and although personal troubles ruined his life soon after, he never forgot the day he stood before Congress and declared George Washington "first in war, first in peace, and first in the hearts of his countrymen" (1800, 14–15). George Bancroft had no such feeling for Abraham Lincoln.

Earlier, in April 1865, as Lincoln's body was carried from New York City after three days of public mourning, Bancroft rose to deliver the city's official funeral address. "Too few days have passed away," he told the crowd, "to permit any attempt at an analysis of [Lincoln's] character or an exposition of his career" (*New York*

Times, April 26, 1865, 4). Uttered by a man introduced as the nation's most prominent historian, that odd statement, made after three of the most momentous days in the city's history, must have sobered the crowd considerably. If it was too soon really to know anything about Lincoln, then what was all the commotion about? Bancroft did not answer this question. Instead, he raised other questions that implied that when the verdict on Lincoln was in, it might be less than positive.

Bancroft recognized Lincoln's benevolent conduct toward the enemy, but he formulated his observation in a peculiar way: "The slaughter of myriads of the best on the battlefields and the more terrible destruction of our men in captivity by the slow torture of exposure and starvation had never been able to provoke [Lincoln] into harboring one vengeful feeling or one purpose of cruelty" (*New York Times,* April 26, 1865, 3). Bancroft, a Democrat, may have meant this as praise, but in light of Republican impatience with Lincoln's coddling of the South, listeners could not have taken it as such. What is a commander in chief's duty when confronted with atrocities? Schoolchildren knew that when the British army threatened to abuse American prisoners, George Washington promised retaliation against his British prisoners and the threats stopped. What, then, was to be made of a commander who witnesses the enemy's tormenting of his own soldiers and does nothing about it?

What was the achievement of the war itself? Slavery "is dashed down, we hope, forever," Bancroft declared. What did he mean by "we hope"? Did Bancroft consider the Thirteenth Amendment, forbidding slavery and recently signed by Lincoln, unenforceable? He would only say that the old justifications for the slave system were still strong. "The cry is delusive that slavery is dead" (*New York Times,* April 26, 1865, 4). And so, as the body of Lincoln was carried out of New York, the people learned that the war he was honored for winning was actually unfinished.

The committee that invited Bancroft to address Congress must have known about his New York speech, and if they hoped his address to Congress might follow the same line, they were not disappointed. He delivered the most unflattering funeral oration Congress had ever heard or would ever hear again, but one that reflected the opinions of a large segment of the American public.

Bancroft's congressional address (1866) enlarged on what he had said in New York, with the high points of Lincoln's life toned down, the low points amplified. His first thirty-five pages provided an overview of American history to the close of the Civil War with an uncomplimentary assessment of Lincoln's contribution to the war's outcome. "The President was led along by the greatness of [the people's] self-sacrificing example; and as a child, in a dark night, on a rugged way catches hold of the hand of the father for guidance and support, he clung fast to the hand of the people, and moved calmly through the gloom" (35). There is no trace of Father Abraham here. Lincoln is the child; the people, the father on whom Lincoln depends for guidance. Lincoln appears as a "man of the people" not in the sense of emerging from among them to lead and inspire, but as one dragged toward decisions demanded by public opinion.

Lincoln, according to Bancroft, performed poorly on his own; his administration was "unsteady and incomplete" and, by departing from the standard ways of running his office, often "confused rather than advanced the public business" (46). He was also a terrible judge of talent and took years to appoint the right generals to the right positions. Before he succeeded, tens of thousands had died (45–46).

Bancroft also questioned Lincoln's reputation for sympathy and tenderness. Most Americans (along with their religious spokesmen) believed that Lincoln's soft heart often caused him to be slow to act on urgent matters. Bancroft's assessment was less generous. The president's slowness, he revealed, resulted from simple indecisiveness, "not from humility or tenderness of feeling." Indeed, his sensibilities were dull; "he had no vividness of imagination to picture to his mind the horrors of the battlefield or the sufferings in hospitals." What was tender about Lincoln, in Bancroft's view, was his *conscience* rather than his *feelings*—a distinction he did not bother to clarify (44–45).

Bancroft summarized his judgment of Lincoln by comparing him to Lord Palmerston, Great Britain's recently deceased prime minister. Palmerston was a skillful guide for an established aristocracy; "Lincoln, a leader, or rather companion, of the people" (48). Bancroft's decision to use the word "leader" but then immediately replace it with "companion" underscores his claim that Lincoln led inadequately. He knew only "how to poise himself on the ever-moving opinions of the masses" (48).

Few Republicans in Congress, let alone Democrats, found anything objectionable in Bancroft's unflattering address. Democrats opposing the war were glad to learn they were not the only ones who believed Lincoln had been insensitive to its costs. Republicans supporting the war—the vast majority in Congress—were reinforced in their belief that Lincoln had lacked the will to pursue it vigorously. As to Lincoln's reliance on popular opinion, no one knew this better or was more pleased to hear it criticized than the staunch abolitionist Republicans. Thus, while most congressmen shared Bancroft's view that Lincoln was a decent and honest man, they also shared his opinion about Lincoln's historic role. Not only was Bancroft convincing to his congressional audience; he and his fellow Brahmins, according to historian Richard Current, "contributed to forming the popular image of Lincoln that was to prevail for many years. In this picture the wartime president had little to do, as an agent in his own right, with the events of the Civil War" (1983a, 185). A better appreciation of Lincoln's role, Current adds, lay in the distant future.

Different Faces of Lincoln

Richard Current has probably underestimated Lincoln's late-nineteenth-century reputation. We have no way to gauge it conclusively, but it is reasonable to assume the assassination elevated Lincoln permanently, even though the emotional peak of his funeral could not be sustained. Most Southerners had learned to disdain Lincoln during the course of the war, while Northern attitudes toward him were split: most antiwar Democrats, radical Republicans, and families hurt by the war harbored negative attitudes toward him; staunch Unionists and moderate abolitionists admired or revered him. Ironically, Lincoln was probably the most hated of nineteenth-century presidents but also the most loved.

Where was admiration for Lincoln located, and how did he stand in relation to previous presidents? The first question is more difficult to answer than the second. Lincoln's presidential policies and war management were controversial, but his friends, more committed to preserving his memory than were his enemies to destroying it, were concentrated in two areas: the Midwest and especially New England, center of pro-war sentiment and home to the nation's most influential writers, poets, and artists, almost all of whom portrayed Lincoln positively after his death. The intensity of feeling among Lincoln's admirers and their determination to venerate his memory can hardly be overemphasized, for it was out of this core that affection for him diffused to the rest of the country—affection that would, in time, elevate him to first place in the American pantheon.

Another factor enhancing the influence of Lincoln admirers was

Northerners' reluctance to express hostile feelings about Lincoln publicly. Given his status as the first murdered president, the self-restraint
shown by opposition Democratic newspapers at the time of his death
endured through the postwar decades. Nothing was to be gained by
stirring up animosities with an attack on Lincoln. The silence of Lincoln's critics is one of the reasons that his reputation, although it fell
after his funeral, remained higher than that of any other nineteenth-
century president.

By the end of the nineteenth century, the strength of Lincoln's
reputation is evident in the 1890–99 *Readers' Guide to Periodical
Literature* citation counts showing that the annual average number
of articles on Lincoln exceeded the number of articles on Grant and
Jefferson by a ratio of 2.4 and 2.8 respectively; on Jackson, Madison,
and John Adams, by a ratio of more than 9 to 1 (see table 3.1). Between 1870 and 1900, the number of *New York Times* articles on
Lincoln exceeded the number on Adams, Jefferson, and Jackson by
a ratio of 8.8, 3.2, and 7.8 to 1 respectively.[3] Earlier presidents did
not become less heroic; Lincoln, with the help of his supporters, was
made to seem more so. For them the magnitude of the crisis he had
superintended overwhelmed the events of earlier days. During this
period, only George Washington was written and read about more
often than Lincoln. In the *Readers' Guide* (1890–99), *Congressional
Record* (1875–99), and *New York Times* (1875–99), Washington
entries exceed Lincoln entries by ratios of 1.1, 2.3, and 2.6 respectively (see tables 3.1 and 3.2).

That powerful men are disliked by many is a necessary fact of
strong leadership; however, Lincoln is a special case not only because
so many disliked him so intensely but also because their hostility resulted from personal suffering occasioned by the war he had initiated.
Lincoln's assassination, not his military victory, did the most to reduce this hostility. The realization by Lincoln's friends that his continued fame depended on their bringing his death to mind in such a
way as to preserve its emotional effects affirmed Emile Durkheim's
insight into the precariousness of ritually induced sentiments:

Though very strong as long as men are together and influence each other
reciprocally, [sentiments] exist only in the form of recollections after the
assembly has ended, and when left to themselves, these become feebler and
feebler; for since the group is now no longer present and active, individual
temperaments easily regain the upper hand. The violent passions which may
have been released in the heart of a crowd fall away and are extinguished

when this is dissolved, and men ask themselves with astonishment how they could ever have been so carried away from their normal character. But if the movements by which these sentiments are expressed are connected with something that endures, the sentiments themselves become more durable. These other things are constantly bringing them to mind and arousing them; it is as though the cause which excited them in the first place continued to act. Thus these systems of emblems, which are necessary if society is to become conscious of itself, are no less indispensable for assuring the continuation of this consciousness. ([1915] 1965, 263)

The "systems of emblems" to which Durkheim refers are commemorative symbols—hagiographies, shrines, statues, place-names, memorial celebrations institutionalized in the holiday schedule; or "sites of memory," as Pierre Nora (1996) recently called them, designed to offset the otherwise unpleasant truths of history. These sites of memory, however, did not succeed entirely in preserving Lincoln's newly elevated reputation, let alone universalizing it. In 1865 there were twenty-six million white people in the United States, of which five million—about 20 percent of the total—resided in the South. White Southerners' feelings about Lincoln warrant attention.

In Southern Memory

Northern journalists traveling through the South reported genuine sorrow at Lincoln's death. Across the northern tier of the Confederacy, newspapers commented on extensive insanity in John Wilkes Booth's family and dissociated the South from his crime.[4] J. G. Hamilton, a University of North Carolina historian, observed in 1909 that even before the war ended, many Southerners reciprocated Lincoln's affection toward them. One-third of the many residents turning out to welcome Lincoln during his tour of Richmond in early April 1865 were poor whites, and their numbers would have been even greater if there had been no curfew. After Lincoln's death, their affection for him grew (*New York World*, April 19, 1865, 8; *Boston Journal* article reprinted in *Littrell's Living Age*, April 22, 1865, 137–38; Hamilton 1909).

In the Deep South, too, Lincoln was mourned. Memorial services on Savannah's main square were so well attended that one witness could not recall "so large an assemblage of human beings collected together in our city." A historian of the city observes, "Savannah was at peace with the United States of America" (Lawrence 1961, 217, 218–19). Elsewhere, Confederate government officials, including

Jefferson Davis and Robert E. Lee, expressed regret over Lincoln's murder, and the wide publication of their statements heightened sympathy for him. Lee is reported to have said that he surrendered his forces with "Lincoln's benignity" in mind as much as "Grant's artillery" (*New York World,* April 19, 1865, 8). Atlanta's mayor may or may not have shared this feeling about Lincoln, but in June 1865, he declared publicly that he had always opposed secession and wished to return Georgia to the Union. The city's other officials agreed (Miller 1949, 23).

Southern sympathy for Lincoln must be recognized but not exaggerated. Every Southern city marked his death with formal orations and mourning rites, but these public representations did not accurately reflect the full reality of private feelings. Since the cities were under occupation, civic bodies needing the military's cooperation to rebuild could not fail to express their regrets. Everywhere, in fact, disrespect for Lincoln resulted in punishment. Churches refusing to hold appropriate mourning services were compelled by military authorities to appoint new boards of directors, just as hostile newspapers were shut down and reopened under friendly editorship (Capers 1965, 176–83; Fraser 1989, 273). Nineteen-year-old Sarah Morgan of Baton Rouge, Louisiana, described the situation in her diary:

To see a whole city draped in mourning is certainly an imposing spectacle. . . . So it is, in one sense. For the more violently "secesh" the [residents], the more thankful they are for Lincoln's death, the more profusely the houses are decked with emblems of woe. . . . Men who have hated Lincoln with all their souls, under terms of confiscation and imprisonment which they *understand* is the alternative, tie black crepe from every practicable knob and point, to save their homes. (1991, 608)

Thus, though Southerners mourned Lincoln publicly, his death, after the devastation caused by his war against the South, seemed to many "like a gleam of sunshine on a Winter's Day" (Davis 1971, 99). The tyrant at last was gone. Abraham Lincoln had waged war against innocent people, burned their homes, sacked their farms, starved their children. A Texas editor could not forget:

In one of his messages [Lincoln] said, with grim and terrible satisfaction, "that *under all circumstances our Land would remain.*" Where the fierce Attila, calling himself "the curse of God," swept with his barbaric hordes, records as the marks of his terrible wrath, that "he left only the sky and the earth remaining . . . ," *Sic Semper Tyrannis.* Not in a fair fight merely, not on the field of honorable battle, not by the law's formal sentence, but every where and by all means, *Sic Semper Tyrannis*. Whoever would impose the fate of servitude and slavery on these Confederate States, whatever fatal Providence of God shall lay him low, we say, and say it gladly, God's will be done. (*Houston Tri-Weekly Telegraph*, April 25, 1865)

Not only were Southern mourning rites often meaningless; the commemorations sustaining pro-Lincoln sentiment in the North through the late 1860s and 1870s never affected the South. So greatly had Reconstruction (1865–76) alienated Southern sentiment that even Fourth of July was "not much in vogue" (*Atlanta Constitution*, July 2, 1876, 2). Ending Reconstruction added nothing to Southerners' interest in Lincoln. The making of Lincoln prints and paintings, the carving and dedication of Lincoln statues, the establishment of immense Lincolniana collections, the founding of Lincoln clubs and memorial associations, the observance of his birth, the writing of poetry and of articles, essays, and books about his life—these were exclusively Northern enterprises.

As Southern intellectuals contemplated Reconstruction and the imprisonment of their president and symbol, Jefferson Davis, they were disinclined to pay respects of any kind to their former enemy. Paul Hamilton Hayne, a South Carolina man of letters, remembered Lincoln in 1871 as a "commonplace Vulgarian" who "mistook blasphemy for wit," a "gaudy, coarse, not overly clean" man whose "idealization by Yankee fancy . . . would be ludicrous were it not disgusting" (Moore 1982, 93). "Putting all partisan feeling aside," William Hand Browne wrote in *Southern Magazine*, "we look back at the men who once were chosen by their countrymen to fill the places that this man has occupied—a Washington, a Jefferson, a Madison, an Adams . . . men of culture and refinement, of honor, of exalted patriotism, of broad views and wise statesmanship—and measure the distance from them to Abraham Lincoln, [and] we sicken with shame and disgust" (1872, 374).

Albert Bledsoe, Lincoln's friend and legal colleague in Illinois, was repelled by his conduct of the war against the South and turned against him. In 1873, he reported knowing Lincoln to have been more than an atheist: Abraham Lincoln believed that Christ was born a bastard. As president of the United States, he was also an unkind and ungrateful man, a man of "brute force, blind passion, fanatical hate, lust of power, and the greed of gain." Ward Lamon, whose biography Bledsoe was reviewing, believed these traits proved Lincoln's humanity and made him all the more venerable; for Bledsoe, they proved him to be no more than "the lowbred infidel of Tyson Creek, in whose eyes the Savior of the world was 'an illegitimate child,' and the Holy Mother as base as his own" (1873, 364).

Although Northern occupation forces limited the influence of Lincoln's critics by forbidding reproach in public media and public places, Southern hostility toward Lincoln did not depend on the press and pulpit to sustain itself. Indeed, as the Confederate "Lost Cause" tradition grew stronger throughout the 1880s and early 1890s, anti-Lincoln sentiments increased.

In African American Memory

That Abraham Lincoln would fail to achieve widespread respect among Southern whites during the postwar years is understandable, but ambivalence was also common among the tens of thousands of free blacks and four million emancipated slaves. On the surface, they worshipped Lincoln. In Washington, D.C., free blacks gathered at the White House ahead of everyone to convince themselves that he was really gone. During the funeral rites, "[t]here were no truer mourners when all were sad, than the poor colored people who crowded the streets, joined the procession, and exhibited their woe, bewailing the loss of him who they regarded as a benefactor and father" (Welles 1909, 590). The scene in Washington was generalizable to every American city and town. As a black commentator in San Francisco put it, Lincoln's memory would "be held in adoration, but one degree inferior to that which we bestow on the Savior of all mankind" (*Elevator,* April 21, 1865).

Blacks' affection for Lincoln endured decades of hardship. In 1937, the Works Progress Administration initiated a slave narrative project based on interviews with former slaves from the Southern states. Some narratives reflect their authors' childhood experiences on the plantation; others reflect the experiences of parents, family members, and friends. All reveal something of the structure of the myth grown about Lincoln.

An analysis shows that in 11 percent of the stories, Lincoln travels through the South in disguise. The archetypal, dreamlike account of Mary Wallace Bowe, enslaved in North Carolina when Lincoln supposedly paid his visit, is representative. She tells of Lincoln's tiring trip, his coarse, unpleasant appearance, and his hospitable reception:

In dem days dey wuz peddlers gwine 'roun' do country sellin' things. Dey toted big packs on dey backs filled wid everythin' from needles an' thimbles to bed spreads an' fryin' pans. One day a peddler stopped at Mis' Fanny's house. He was de uglies' man I ever seed. He was tall an' bony wid black whiskers an' black bushy hair an' curious eyes dat set way back in his head. Dey was dark an' look like a dog's eyes after you done hit him. He set down on de po'ch an' opened his pack, an' it was so hot an' he looked so tired, dat Mis' Fanny give him er cool drink of milk dat done been settin' in de spring house. All de time Mis' Fanny was lookin' at de things in de pack an' buyin', de man kept up a runnin' talk. He ask her how many niggers dey had; how many men dey had fightin' on de 'Federate side. . . .

Two or three weeks later Mis' Fanny got a letter. De letter was from dat peddlar. He tole her dat he was Abraham Lincoln heself; dat he wuz peddlin' over de country as a spy, an' he thanked her for de res' on her shady po'ch an' de cool glass of milk she give him. (Rawick 1977, 14:150–51)

Slave narratives of the traveling Lincoln are framed by the belief—then common in the rural South, as in most traditional western communities where hospitality to strangers was expected and common—that Christ assumed the human form of a traveler seeking assistance. None of the narratives suggest that Lincoln is divine, but their vein is positive: among the 112 slave narratives about Lincoln from six (mainly Deep Southern) states, 43 percent define him as a savior and liberator. "Lincoln died for we, Christ died for we, and me believe him de same mans" (Litwack 1979, 527)—this was a common kind of claim.

Yet blacks' admiration for Lincoln must have been qualified. Doubts about his reason for issuing the Emancipation Proclamation, if the slave narratives are to be taken as even weak indicators of what slaves believed, were extensive. Slaves had heard about the Emancipation Proclamation through the "grapevine telegraph," but not everyone accepted it as evidence of Lincoln's humanitarianism. One of their stories tells about his falling into a drunken stupor and issuing the Emancipation Proclamation by mistake (Wiggins 1987, 72). Another story, formulated after the war, relates his racial attitudes to the crack in the Liberty Bell: "Do you know how they got the crack in the Liberty Bell? Well, it happened this way. The whites were mad at Abraham Lincoln for all he'd done to free the Negro. They told him about it and Lincoln told them, 'I'd wade up to my neck in blood before I'd forget my race.' When the whites heard that good news they rang the Liberty Bell 'till it cracked" (Wiggins 1987, 72).

Many other emancipated slaves who recognized Lincoln as their liberator were realistic in assessing his friendship. Charlie Davenport recalled from Mississippi: "He went all through de country just a-rantin' an' a-preachin' about us being his black brothers. . . . It sure riled de niggers up and lots of 'em run away. I sure heard him, but I didn't pay him no mind" (Rawick 1977, 8:562). Louis Davis, another former Mississippi slave, could only think of Lincoln by comparing him to his mistress, remembered fondly as "Ole Miss." Recognizing Lincoln's fear of blacks immigrating to the North, he said:

I knows a lot about Abraham Lincoln. They say he is the man that set the niggers free. He might have done that for some of them, but he sure wasn't the one to set me free. Ole Miss was the one that set all of us free, and Mr. Lincoln didn't have nothing to do with it. All of us belonged to Ole Miss and if she hadn't said we was free we would have still belonged to her regardless of what Mr. Lincoln said. There was another great man in what they called the rebel army, his name was Robert E. Lee. Some like him and some don't. Some says it was him that tried to keep the niggers slaves. That wasn't what the war was about. That slavery didn't have nothing to do with it. You see it was this way. Jefferson Davis wanted to let the slaves go up to the North, and Abraham Lincoln wouldn't allow it, cause he didn't want no slaves up there, and that's what the whole thing was about. (Rawick 1977, 8:586–87)

Mr. Davenport was uncannily right. Lincoln "didn't want no slaves up there."

Emancipation's negative effect on the conditions of black life further mitigated reverence for Lincoln, to the surprise of many whites. Thomas Nast's print *Emancipation* (fig. 2.2), sold in 1865 to both black and white customers, pictures the white community's perception of emancipation as an unalloyed benefit. At the center of the print is Lincoln's portrait, above which a black family is shown seated happily around a stove. On the viewers left is a series of scenes depicting the cruelty of slavery; on the right, from top to bottom, a black man (with banjo) and wife relax outside their home, black adults watch their children run off to school and draw pay for their work. Life before and after emancipation is aligned with pain and happiness respectively.

In fact, the end of slavery brought uncertainty and want. Thomas Hall, formerly a slave in North Carolina, asked bitterly: "Lincoln got the praise for freeing us, but did he do it? He gave us freedom, [but]

Figure 2.2. Thomas Nast, *Emancipation,* 1863 print. Photograph
courtesy of the Historical Society of Pennsylvania (Bc 95 N269).

we still had to depend on the southern white man for work, food,
and clothing. . . . Lincoln done but little for the negro race and from
the living standpoint nothing" (Rawick 1977, 14:449).

Lincoln may have been the savior of the black people, but he was
remote, and his gift of freedom was too abstract to have significance
for all its recipients. The help of the kindly slaveholder, on the other
hand, was tangible and memorable. John Beckwith, another North
Carolinian, recalled: "We wuzn't happy at de surrender an' we cussed
ole Abraham Lincoln all ober de place. We wuz told de disadvantages
of not havin' no edercation, but shucks, we doan need no book lar-
nin' wid ol marster ter look atter us" (Rawick 1977, 14:90). Another
North Carolina man felt the same way: "Of course I hear about Abraham Lincoln and he was a great man, but I was told mostly by my
children when dey come home from school about him. I always think
of my Old Master as de one dat freed me, and anyways Abraham
Lincoln and none of his North people didn't look after me and buy
my crop right after I was free like Old Master did. Dat was de time
was de hardest and everything was dark and confusion" (Yetman
1970, 224). Emancipation indeed brought "dark and confusion." No
consideration more often qualified praise of Lincoln or more often

soured his memory. Henry Henderson summed it up as he remembered his Oklahoma days: "I guess Lincoln was a good man, but I was getting along alright anyway" (Rawick 1977, 12:180).

The frustrations of emancipation, mentioned in 1937 by more than 20 percent of the former slaves answering questions about Lincoln, were intensified by their understanding that "forty acres and a mule" were promised to them from confiscated slaveowner property. Hundreds of thousands of the newly emancipated suffered under this illusion. Turner Jacobs remembered how in Mississippi "we all thought [Lincoln] was a young Christ come to save us, cause he promise every nigger forty acres and a mule. We never did get dat mule or dose forty acres either, cepten by hard work but we all lakked him and thought he was a great man" (Rawick 1977, 10:1119). They would have liked him more and thought him a greater man if he had kept his promise. Lincoln, instead, was the Lord who would not provide.

Douglass's Lincoln

Former slaves' memories depended not only on their impressions of Lincoln while they were in bondage but also on impressions formed after emancipation. Many people who knew or worked with Lincoln told stories about him. Frederick Douglass was one of the few black men who had known Lincoln well, and his portrayals were influential.

From the time Lincoln was elected president, Douglass watched him closely and commented on his policies and conduct. In his *Douglass's Monthly,* he wondered why Lincoln was so solicitous about the constitutional rights of seceding slaveholders, naming him "the rebels' lawyer" ([1862] 1969, 4–5:694). And in Lincoln's manner of addressing blacks, Douglass saw common bigotry:

Mr. Lincoln assumes the language and arguments of an itinerant Colonization lecturer, showing all his inconsistencies, his pride of race and blood, his contempt for negroes and his canting hypocrisy. . . . [T]hough elected as an anti-slavery man by Republican and Abolition voters, Mr. Lincoln is quite a genuine representative of American prejudice and negro hatred. (4–5:707–8)

A week after Douglass wrote this, Lincoln announced the preliminary Emancipation Proclamation, but he had been so hesitant to confront slavery during the previous year that antislavery people feared he would rescind his statement or never sign it into law. Douglass disagreed. He regarded the proclamation as a product of events, not Lincoln's personal preference. Douglass's reasoning diminishes Lincoln's historical importance: "[E]ven if the temper and spirit of the President himself were other than what they are, events greater than the President, events which have slowly wrung this proclamation from him may be relied on to carry him forward in the same direction" ([1862] 1969, 4–5:721).

A year later, Lincoln approved the enlistment of black men into the Union army and met Douglass himself at the White House. Unable immediately to grant Douglass's petitions for equal treatment of black soldiers, Lincoln still impressed him with his sincerity and manner (Douglass 1962). Douglass eventually learned to respect Lincoln, but never without reserve or doubt. When Lincoln died, Douglass's eulogy at the New York City Cooper Union was deferential but realistic: the colored people, he said, "believed in Abraham Lincoln, had loved him even when he smote and wounded them," and their faith was rewarded by emancipation. Nevertheless, they "would have been pleased if he had confined his reasons to other motives than expediency or military necessity" (*National Anti-Slavery Standard,* June 10, 1865, 4).

Why were Lincoln's attitudes so important to begin with? Was not his accomplishment—emancipation—enough? As far as Lincoln's public identity is concerned, the answer is no. Public identity, as Harold Garfinkel observed, rests on intention, not achievement, referring "not to what a person may have done, . . . but to what the group holds to be the ultimate grounds or reasons for his performance" (1956, 420). The ultimate grounds or reasons for Lincoln's racial policies greatly impressed—and depressed—Frederick Douglass. Eleven years after the assassination, he revealed his thoughts at the unveiling of Thomas Ball's statue depicting Lincoln liberating a slave. It was the first statue of its kind, commissioned and procured exclusively by black Americans, but Douglass disliked it. His opinion of the statue was of a piece with his opinion of the man.

The monument (see fig. 2.3) marked the Emancipation Proclamation, but the obsequious position of the slave caused Douglass to think Lincoln was receiving more gratitude than he deserved. The slave is on one knee beside the shackles that have been struck from his wrists. Lincoln stands above him, his right hand, resting on a pillar of state bearing George Washington's profile, grasping the

Figure 2.3. Thomas Ball, *Emancipation Group,* 1876, Lincoln Park, Washington, D.C. Photograph courtesy of the Library of Congress.

proclamation; Lincoln's left hand, palm down, extends above the slave paternalistically, as if to bless him. Ball had attributed to Lincoln a nobility Douglass knew he lacked; but how was this sculptor to carry out his commission of ennobling Lincoln if not with the symbolic conventions of his day? Those conventions explain why most blacks admired the monument, why the African American organizations of Washington, D.C., attended its dedication, and why white admirers, including important public officials, also showed up in great numbers. The president of the United States, his cabinet, the justices of the Supreme Court, and many U.S. senators, representatives, and foreign dignitaries sat on the platform as Frederick Douglass rose to give the dedication address. Douglass honored Lincoln's "exalted character" and "great works," but only after jarring his audience by candidly portraying Lincoln's conception of black rights:

> It must be admitted—truth compels me to admit—even here in the presence of the monument we have erected to his memory, that Abraham Lincoln was not, in the fullest sense of the word, either our man or our model. In his interests, in his associations, in his habits of thought and in his prejudices, he was a white man.
>
> He was preeminently the white man's President, entirely devoted to the welfare of white men. He was ready and willing at any time during the first years of his administration to deny, postpone, and sacrifice the rights of humanity in the colored people in order to promote the welfare of the white people of this country. In all his education and feeling he was an American of the Americans. He came into the Presidential chair upon one principle alone, namely, opposition to the extension of slavery. His arguments in furtherance of this policy had their motive and mainspring in his patriotic devotion to the interests of his own race. To protect, defend and perpetuate slavery in the states where it existed Abraham Lincoln was not less ready than any other President to draw the sword of the nation. He was ready to execute all the supposed constitutional guarantees of the United States Constitution in favor of the slave system anywhere inside the slave states. He was willing to pursue, recapture, and send back the fugitive slave to his master, and to suppress a slave rising for liberty, though the guilty master were already in arms against the Government. The race to which we belong were not the special objects of his consideration. Knowing this, I concede to you, my white fellow citizens, a preeminence in this worship at once full and supreme. . . . You are the children of Abraham Lincoln. We are at best only his stepchildren, children by adoption, children by force of circumstances and necessity. (*New York Times,* April 22, 1876, 1)

Douglass explained that Lincoln's feeling toward African Americans was the very key to his success against slavery. If he had professed affection for blacks and made slavery his main issue, Lincoln would have failed. Slavery could only be abolished as a war measure designed to save the Union for whites. Lincoln's greatness inhered not in his love for the slave, said Douglass, but in his personal hatred of the slave system and in his decision to include its destruction among his war aims.

What Commemorative Symbols Mean

African Americans' affection for Lincoln was qualified but strong. Northern whites, on the other hand, were sharply split. Most were indifferent to emancipation; many opposed it. Whites favoring the war wished to save the Union; whites opposing it believed the Union could survive as well with slavery as without. But if Lincoln's presidential accomplishments seemed less adequate to whites than to blacks, pressures existed in the society to give Lincoln the benefit of many doubts.

No period in American history could have been more conducive to commemorating Lincoln than the late nineteenth century. This Gilded Age, according to Michael Kammen, was not only an age of industrial expansion and urbanization; it was also "the age of memory" (1991, 12). Industrialism brought deep cultural and political change to the society, and the unsettling experience of this change enhanced the appeal of a settled past. "The decades between 1870 and 1910 comprised the most notable period in all of American history for erecting monuments in honor of mighty warriors, groups of unsung heroes, and great deeds" (115). Conditions that stimulated commemorative impulses provided the means for realizing them. Rapid economic growth brought the wealth that supported commemorative organizations; the rapid growth of cities made these organizations numerically strong; the rapid growth of railroads and urban transit enabled people to assemble and mark the past in greater numbers than ever before.

Acting spontaneously and independently of one another, private and public bodies throughout the North worked to honor Lincoln's memory. Businessmen and professionals, including Daniel Fish, Frederick H. Meserve, and Osborn Oldroyd, amassed great collections of Lincolniana. Northern state and municipal governments, historical societies, museums, business groups, professional and trade associations, churches, political and social clubs, veterans' groups, and local Lincoln clubs—the organizational infrastructure of commemoration—kept records of Lincoln's life, collected artifacts, commissioned paintings and statues, named streets, held public exhibitions. Northern public schools performed the most important role of all: they put Lincoln on their calendar and in their curriculum, making an entire generation familiar with his life. As organizational sponsors multiplied, a commemorative topography formed. Lincoln's Springfield residence and tomb, Gettysburg, Ford's Theater, the Peterson house in which he died—these and scores of other sites kept his memory alive.

What do these sites mean? Who built, drew, painted, and sculpted them? What ideas did they convey? Did they resonate with the values of the society for which they were made? Observers at the end of the twentieth century can only answer these questions through inferences about the late-nineteenth-century mind, an uncertain mind still ruminating over the question of whether the Civil War's benefits had justified its costs. When Lincoln had mobilized men for war, everyone knew that the preservation of the Union was his only purpose. Since millions of Northern families could see no other reason for sending their sons off to die, they must have recoiled at the sight of statues portraying Lincoln as an emancipator—commemorating the very motive (to sacrifice white boys for the liberation of blacks) his adversaries had attributed to him.

That Abraham Lincoln became the primary symbol of national unity was not inevitable. Throughout the nineteenth century, George Washington symbolized the nation's union; Lincoln's significance inhered in his being associated with Washington's legacy. After Lincoln was assassinated, mourning portraits joined his image to Washington's. Here George Washington clasps Abraham Lincoln to his bosom and holds a laurel wreath above his head (fig. 2.4); elsewhere Washington, with open arms and in the company of angels, welcomes Lincoln to Glory (fig. 2.5). Associating contemporary leaders with images of George Washington was conventional and had wide appeal. Mourning portraits with a narrower appeal included Columbia, standing above the Confederate dragon she has slain, weeping as she leans on a granite monument bearing Lincoln's image (fig. 2.6). Behind the monument, covering his face in grief, stands a slave—half-naked but free. Depicting Lincoln as an emancipator, and in such graphic detail, could not have appealed to the many Northern families who believed their sons had died to save the Union rather than to free slaves. Such prints must have indeed outraged grieving families and could have done little to enhance Lincoln's stature.

The emancipation theme also appears in Lincoln paintings made during and immediately after the Civil War. David Gilmour Blythe's portrayal of Lincoln writing the Emancipation Proclamation, Edward Dalton Marchant's portrait of Lincoln next to broken chains, Francis Bicknell Carpenter's giant painting of Lincoln announcing the Emancipation Proclamation to his cabinet—these are among the very best known of the Civil War–era history paintings (Schwartz

Figure 2.4. *Washington and Lincoln Apotheosis*, 1865 print. Photograph courtesy of Lloyd Ostendorf.

1993). To viewers who were not committed to emancipation, however, they could not have been heroic. Many of the bronze and marble statues of Lincoln erected between 1865 and 1899 similarly distorted the war's purpose. Lincoln's supporters believed in a war for union, but eight of the eleven publicly dedicated statues portray him as emancipator. Henry Kirke Brown's depiction of Lincoln pointing to the Emancipation Proclamation (fig. 2.7) and Randolph Rogers's statue of Lincoln signing it (fig. 2.8) are good examples.

Adalbert Volck's rendition of Lincoln writing the proclamation (fig. 2.9) may have represented public sentiment better than artistic celebrations of emancipation. Volck, a Baltimore dentist, sympathized with slavery more than did most Democrats, but his crude drawings, whose publication was forbidden during the war and

Figure 2.5. *Abraham Lincoln: The Martyr/Victorious,* 1865 print. Reproduced by permission of the Huntington Library, San Marino, California.

which were distributed underground, also expressed Northern anti-war opinion during and after the fighting. Volck's *Writing the Emancipation Proclamation* (1864) portrays Lincoln on a chair bearing a carving of the Devil as he inscribes his proclamation with Devil's ink. His table is supported by cloven-hoofed legs beneath Satanic symbols; the window, opening to a scene of vultures, is draped with curtains tied back with a vulture's head. On the wall hang pictures canonizing John Brown and the murder of white women and babies by

Figure 2.6. To / Abraham Lincoln / the / Best Beloved / of the / Nation. / In Memorium. 1865 lithograph. Photograph courtesy of Harold Holzer.

Figure 2.7. Henry Kirke Brown, *Abraham Lincoln Declaring Emancipation,* 1869, Prospect Park, Brooklyn, New York. Photograph courtesy of the New York City Parks Photo Archive.

Santo Domingo slaves. In the corner stands the figure of Liberty, which Lincoln, the coward, uses as a hat rack for the tam-o'-shanter he wore shamefully as a disguise to avoid assassins on his way to assume the presidency. Against the wall stands the liquor that spurs his baseness, while his left foot profanes the sacred Constitution of the United States. Together with the statues commissioned by abolitionists and radical Republicans, Volck's representation, using popular religion to intensify anti-Lincoln sentiment, provides fuller access to the breadth of America's postwar memories.

Figure 2.8. Randolph Rogers, *Abraham Lincoln,* 1871, Fairmount Park, Philadelphia. Photograph courtesy of the Fairmount Park Art Association. Photographer, © Franko Khoury.

To infer Lincoln's reputation directly from the number of objects commemorating him is surely misleading; but as the remaining years of the nineteenth century unfolded, his place in history became more secure. Commentaries and poems about him appeared frequently, and artists worked hard to meet the public demand for his portraits. Still, something was missing, something making the difference between an intensely admired man and a great man, between a folk hero and an epic hero. That missing element was universality. The Southerners whom he had defeated in war were not inclined to revere him. They were busy building a cult around one of their own leaders, Robert E. Lee. Genteel people everywhere found Lincoln's earthiness offensive. Others were repelled by his policies. Pro-Confederate ("Copperhead") and antiwar Democrats on the one side and extremist abolitionists and Republicans on the other continued to look down on him.

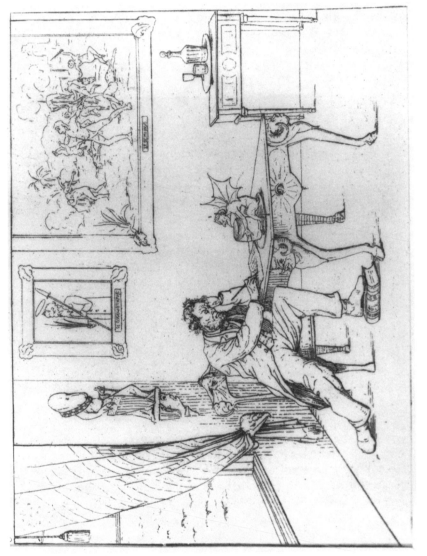

Figure 2.9. Adalbert Johann Volck, *Writing the Emancipation Proclamation*, 1864 ink drawing. Photograph courtesy of the Lincoln Museum, Fort Wayne, Indiana (3252).

Postwar writers and publicists did much to sustain admiration for Lincoln; however, the very best hagiographies, including Holland's, Arnold's, Carpenter's, Stoddard's, and Nicolay and Hay's, were not, as noted, overwhelmingly popular. Among the best-known efforts to portray the "folklore Lincoln" (Donald [1947] 1989, 144–66), two were scarcely read. William Herndon and Ward Lamon sincerely felt that the truest version of Lincoln's life would be the best tribute to him (Herndon and Weik 1889; Lamon 1872). It was not unusual, they thought, for a man to be a national treasure and at the same time a teller of vulgar stories and insulter of Christianity. The reading public was not ready for this kind of biography, and when the publishers realized how offensive it was, they stopped the presses and canceled arrangements for subsequent volumes.

Writings about Lincoln accumulated nonetheless, and although they failed to transform him into a national idol, they did keep him in the collective imagination and reflected the people's affection for him. Meanwhile, other lineaments of his cult were developing. Postage stamps bore his image. His sculpted countenance appeared conspicuously in the U.S. Capitol building. Counties, towns, streets, and businesses were named for him. By the end of the century, many states were considering making the anniversary of his birth an official holiday. On the other hand, Lincoln's was not the only claim on the American memory. The last quarter of the nineteenth century, in particular, was filled with reminders of the Revolutionary era. From 1876 to 1889 and beyond, great centennial celebrations marked the nation's founding. These enlarged George Washington's already paramount role in the nation's representation of itself, overshadowing Lincoln and leaving him in second place.

Washington and Lincoln

Collective memory is more than a means of transmitting the past or gaining advantage in the present; it is sense-making through time. Thus far, we have assessed Lincoln's reputation largely through inferences based on what we know about the immediate context of opinion within which Lincoln was recalled. Now we can use these inferences to claim that (1) Lincoln's nineteenth-century prestige was inferior relative to the standard of the day, George Washington; and (2) it was vastly inferior to what it would become in the twentieth century. Considerable evidence, much of it bearing on Washington's and Lincoln's relative stature, supports these claims.

The power of George Washington's image was not as great among members of the post–Civil War generation as it had been for their forebears, yet that image had been so exalted that it remained great even when diminished. Lincoln had stood in George Washington's shadow when he died, and as the decades passed the shadow remained. Many of the same organizations working to preserve Lincoln's memory worked even harder to preserve Washington's, for Washington united the nation as Lincoln never could. James Russell Lowell expressed the sentiments of many when he wrote "Under the Old Elm" for the July 1875 centennial of Washington's assuming command of the army in Cambridge. It was there that he

> Unsheathed the sword whose fatal flash
> Shot union through the incoherent clash
> Of our loose atoms, crystallizing them
> Around a single will's unpliant stem
> And making purpose of emotion rash. (1978, 368)

After Lowell read this poem in Baltimore, he reported: "I actually drew tears from the eyes of bitter secessionists" (364). Indeed, no one can grasp the status of Lincoln's reputation in the late nineteenth century without understanding Washington's.

Washington had died in December 1799 as "the man who unites all hearts" (Schwartz 1987, 85), and communities in every part of a still localistic nation vied with one another to show him reverence. When civil war broke out in 1861, Washington was embraced by both sides as the personification of their cause: union in the North, liberty in the South. No such consensus had emerged around Lincoln.

George Washington not only transcended regional divisions, he was also the focal point of late-nineteenth-century centennial celebrations. His stature, however, hardly depended on these observances; during the seventy-six years between his death and the national centennial, he had become the American Revolution's most prominent hero. Washington had stood the test of time even as America had changed from a rural to an industrial society.

Abraham Lincoln, in contrast, received less attention at the time of these celebrations than at any time since his death. For example, the city of Philadelphia had agreed to furnish one of the four military statues planned for Lincoln's tomb in Springfield, but as 1876 approached, "the people of [the city] have been so engrossed by the Centennial scheme that little or nothing has been accomplished by them" (*New York Times,* November 26, 1875). Congress could do nothing to make up for Philadelphia's reneging, for it had just appropriated funds to complete the Washington Monument. As 1875 ended, the prospect of the 1876 Centennial grew brighter. Binghamton, New York, marked New Year's Day 1876 with a mass meeting at the courthouse, the tolling of church bells, a thirteen-gun salute, grand decorations, and a torchlight procession at midnight. In Harrisburg, Pennsylvania, streets were jammed on New Year's Day with people watching parades with bands and drum corps. Cities everywhere invoked the memory of Washington at the beginning of the Centennial Year (*Philadelphia Inquirer,* January 2, 1876, 1). In Philadelphia five weeks later, Washington's Birthday closed all banks, exchanges, courts, schools, and large businesses, and people enjoyed banquets, parties, balls, militia parades, patriotic speeches, sports, and games. It was "the most heartily observed event that has ever been accorded public recognition of the kind in this, or, perhaps in any other city in the United States" (*Philadelphia Inquirer,* February 23, 1876, 2). Springfield, Illinois, like other Midwestern cities, marked the day with joyous receptions and a grand parade (*Chicago Daily Tribune,* February 23, 1876, 5).

Washington's presence was dramatic because the Centennial came just eleven years after a shattering civil war, before the nation's regional fractures could heal. Lyn Spillman (1997) has emphasized how Centennial organizers marked the occasion with the most unifying symbols they could find. Because America's founding moment was central to the Centennial's symbolic repertoire, Spillman shows, images of George Washington abounded. Centennial guidebooks, almanacs, poems, and speeches praised him. His uniforms, weapons, utensils, and other possessions went on display. As a symbol of the nation, George Washington was the perfect vehicle for anti-Lincoln sentiment. Many Northern Democrats would have agreed with the Virginia critic of the official Centennial medal:

> The U.S. design
> Of medal and sign
> Of Washington, 'tween Lincoln and Grant in relief,
> Find parallel fact
> To counsel the act,
> Of Christ crucified by each side a thief. (Spillman 1997, 72)

The limerick worked because national consensus was limited to Washington.

In many places, the 1889 centennial of Washington's first inauguration was marked as enthusiastically as the 1876 centennial. No Lincoln Day celebration approached these in scope or enthusiasm. President Benjamin Harrison reenacted Washington's ferry trip to New York City to take the oath of office as more than two million people filled the streets. To the west, Chicago had never been so profusely decorated. "The city was alive with processions, whose bands were playing, drums beating, and banners flying. . . . There were military processions, civic processions, Grand Army processions, and processions organized and unorganized." Conceived independently and held in local neighborhoods, these events, according to one observer, expressed profound grassroots esteem for the first president (*Chicago Daily Tribune,* May 1, 1889).

Throughout the 1890s, Washington remained prominent. Visitors to the 1893 World's Columbian Exposition in Chicago could take home a wide variety of Washington images and mementos but few souvenirs of Lincoln (*New York Times,* July 10, 1893). In May 1897, hundreds of thousands of Philadelphians watched President McKinley dedicate Rudolph Siemering's massive equestrian statue of Washington, then broke up for a day of parades and banquets (*Philadelphia Inquirer,* May 31, 1897). Two years later, on December 14, civic groups, patriotic societies, and city and state governments observed the centennial of George Washington's death (*New York Times,* December 10–15, 1899).

Whenever hard decisions on memorial resources had to be made, they favored Washington over Lincoln. One year after the U.S. Centennial, New York's governor approved an appropriation for a bust of George Washington while vetoing a request to frame a Lincoln portrait already in the state's possession (*New York Times,* May 25, 1877). Opposition in most states to attempts to make Lincoln's birthday an official holiday was based partly on the conviction of Washington's uniqueness. Lincoln's home state, Illinois, was an exception, but even there community leaders declared: "[W]e are not eager, not ready to disparage what we owe to George Washington" (Hirsch 1927, 197). There may have been plenty of prestige to go around, but people elsewhere felt differently. Above and beyond the practical problem of establishing two official holidays ten days apart (Lincoln's on February 12, Washington's on February 22), "it may be doubted," as one observer pointed out, "whether the distinctive honor conferred on the memory of WASHINGTON should be divided even in the case of ABRAHAM LINCOLN" (*New York Times,* February 10, 1890).

Washington's overshadowing of Lincoln is also evidenced by citation counts in the popular literature. Between 1875 and 1899, the
Congressional Record accumulated 184 entries for Washington (relating mainly to speeches and legislation on monuments) compared
to 80 entries for Lincoln. The *New York Times* shows an even greater
discrepancy: 678 articles related to Washington, 256 to Lincoln.
Poole's Index for 1882–92 contains 181 Washington entries and 54
Lincoln entries.

Late-nineteenth-century prints of American presidents provide
further evidence of Washington's symbolic dominance. Historian
Noble Cunningham (1991) has suggested that printmakers' depiction
of new presidents in the company of their predecessors celebrates the
institutional stability of the presidency. George Washington came
first, but as the years passed, Cunningham shows, the prints became
more crowded, evolving from group portraits of Washington, Adams, Jefferson, and Madison to collections of individual portraits of
all presidents. Arrayed in order of incumbency, the presidents sustain
one another's prestige and affirm the integrity of their office. To depict prestige differences, however, printmakers must violate order of
incumbency. When a substantial number of printmakers, independently of one another and over an extended period of time, violate
order of incumbency in the same way and successfully market their
products, their work may be used as a rough gauge of general opinion
about presidential reputation.

Printmakers commonly used centrality, size, foreground, and vertical prominence to represent George Washington's place in the nation's memory. *Our Three Great Presidents* (1872), designed at the
end of Grant's first term in office, shows George Washington at the
center, with Lincoln and Grant at his right and left respectively. Four
years later, *Our Presidents,* one of many Centennial prints, makes
Washington the central figure and places Lincoln at his remote left.
Our Presidents (1882) shows Lincoln in the center of the picture, but
Washington occupies the foreground. *Our Twenty Two Presidents,*
produced in 1884, highlights Washington and Lincoln, aligning them
vertically (Washington above) with images of Columbia and the Capitol. In the 1897 print *Washington and His Successors,* a large image
of Washington dominates the composition; a small image of Lincoln
appears at his lower right (fig. 2.10). Political campaign prints conformed to the pattern of Washington's dominance.

By century's end Abraham Lincoln's reputation, according to all
indicators, exceeded that of every president except George Washing-

Figure 2.10. *Washington and His Successors,* 1897 print. Photograph courtesy of the Lincoln Museum, Fort Wayne, Indiana (4281).

ton. Yet the relation between the two figures was complex. On the one hand, the inertia of Washington's fame was difficult for Lincoln to overcome. On the other hand, Washington's memory was a resource from which Lincoln's memory gained strength. The more often Lincoln was paired with Washington, the more his reputation grew and the more widespread his commemoration became. Here we return to this chapter's question: how effective is reputational enterprise as a determinant of historical reputation? Lincoln's entrepreneurs could not convince their own generation of Lincoln's unique greatness, but their efforts left behind a vital residue of commemorative symbols that could be and were exploited by later generations whose members were far enough away from the consequences of Lincoln's war to begin revering Lincoln himself.

PART TWO

Twentieth Century:
Symbolizing Industrial Democracy

3

Lincoln and the Culture of Progressivism: Democratizing America

Many young men participated in the Civil War resentfully, many enthusiastically, all painfully. Their elders—mourners of the war's dead and caretakers of its wounded—differed in their feelings about Lincoln. Supporters of the war embraced Lincoln as they tried to justify their loss and ease their sorrow; opponents of the war carried their sorrow, and their disdain for Lincoln, to their graves. During the first decade of the new century, however, Lincoln's prestige rose as a new generation able to think about him and his war in new ways replaced the old.

The new generation, inhabiting an industrial society of factories and cities, was more diversified than the old. Socialists, conservatives, suffragists, African Americans, immigrants, and Southerners of the day saw Lincoln through different lenses, but there were similarities in what they saw. Belonging to the same generation endows its members with "a common location in the social and historical process" and predisposes them "for a certain characteristic mode of thought and experience" (Mannheim [1928] 1952, 291). Thus, social and historical changes enveloped Abraham Lincoln's image in a new "period-wide" (Schuman and Corning, Forthcoming) consensus.

Lincoln's reputation changed rapidly during the first decade of the twentieth century. Only 20 percent of Americans born before the

Civil War were still living in 1900, and most of them regarded George Washington as the nation's treasure; few could imagine Abraham Lincoln in the same light. Their children, however, had not lived through Lincoln's war and, for reasons to be explored presently, conceived him as "a half-mythical figure, which in the haze of historic distance, grows to more and more heroic proportions" (Schurz 1891, 750).

"Revalued Year by Year"

After the twentieth century began, Abraham Lincoln became at once a standard for and a reflection of America's political aspirations. The problems American society then faced might not have been more urgent than the problems of earlier generations, but they were new in content and configuration. How to adjust the relation between capital and labor, bring half the population—women—into the political process, assimilate millions of immigrants arriving from Europe, reconcile the former Confederate states with the rest of the country—these problems were evident at the beginning of the industrial revolution but did not provoke widespread and effective reaction until the early twentieth century. Lincoln's transformation into a national idol articulated this reaction.

Without national opinion surveys, Lincoln's reputation is difficult to establish, but many independently formulated testimonies show a consistent pattern. Signs of Lincoln's transformation were evident as early as 1891, when A. E. Chittenden, Lincoln's former secretary, reported that the public's interest in the martyred president's memory "has been gradually rising" (1891, 385). Three years later John Coleman Adams also noticed "the increase of his fame in the years since he died" (1894, 590).[1] When the new century began, signs of Lincoln's transformation became more frequent and insistent. In March 1906 a *Review of Reviews* commentator observed that "during each succeeding decade, since the tragic end of that remarkable life, the American people have through the perspective of time, found their appreciation of his great character and achievements constantly growing" (294). Seven years later, a writer in *Nation* observed: "His rank as an embodiment of popular ideals and as an object of national homage is today vastly higher than it was when a quarter-century, instead of a half-century, separated us from the time of his labors and his martyrdom" (February 26, 1913, 196).

An important and decisive change in Americans' understanding of Lincoln had occurred. By 1917, when the United States entered World War I, Abraham Lincoln had become "America's most quoted man" (*Literary Digest,* January 6, 1917, 18). By the end of the war, his fame, "revalued year by year," was still growing (*New York Times,* August 15, 1920, 2). Contemplating this transformation, an *Outlook* contributor declared: "At no time in a long period has more attention been given to the character, influence, and steadfast qualities of Abraham Lincoln than seems to have filled the minds of men, both here and abroad, during the last two or three years, especially since the armistice" (September 29, 1920, 186).

Corresponding changes appeared in Lincoln's relationship to George Washington. The February 1913 issue of *Nation* noted that "while the birthday of Washington has been observed for more than a century, Lincoln's birthday has within the last two decades assumed something like a coordinate place in the national thought." The writer added: " 'We are doing just what Lincoln would do if he were living' has become a familiar catchword in these latter days. But nobody says 'we are doing just what Washington would do' " (196–97). Another observer came to the same conclusion. "No longer," he declared, "is Washington first in the hearts of his countrymen. Lincoln [is] secure in that place" (*Dial,* August 9, 1919, 93). Arthur H. Vandenberg sustained these points with his 1921 Grand Rapids, Michigan, poll of one hundred leading citizens' view of who was "the greatest American." Almost half the respondents—49 percent—named Lincoln, 32 percent named Washington (Adair 1974, 238).

Few changes in American culture were more vivid during the first two decades of the twentieth century than Abraham Lincoln's new place in the collective memory. Each year more observers noticed that Lincoln had become more exalted than ever. That Lincoln was admired more by some than by others is certain. He was admired more by Northerners than by Southerners, more by Midwesterners than by Easterners, more by New Englanders than by people in the Mid-Atlantic states. Among all categories of people and sections of the country, however, his reputation had grown. By 1922, the year of the Lincoln Memorial's dedication, he had become America's most prominent historical figure.

Dating the onset of Lincoln's new fame is critical to our understanding of his transformation. This point can be estimated by examining not only the subjective observations of people living at the time but also surveys and objective counts of biographical and artistic works. Surveys in public schools, showed Washington and Lincoln, in that order, rated the two greatest Americans. Lincoln's recognition was weakest among students in the early grades, probably because elementary school curriculum stressed the Revolution rather than the Civil War; high school students rated Lincoln as high as Washington (Barnes 1900; Chambers 1903, 110).

Because the school surveys just described were conducted only once, they do not permit us to compare Washington's and Lincoln's reputations across time. For this, citation counts are useful indicators. Merely enumerating entries from sources such as the *Readers' Guide to Periodical Literature* (see table 3.1) does not afford a precise measure of Lincoln's standing over time, but it does reflect something of the changing demands of a general adult reading audience and the way these demands were met. In addition, we can gauge Lincoln's standing relative to George Washington's.

Tracing the volume of articles from 1890 to 1904, we find a declining trend for both Washington and Lincoln, with about one Lincoln article published for every Washington article. At this time, Washington and Lincoln, as noted in the previous chapter, are still written about far more often than any of the other early presidents, including Madison, Jefferson, and John Adams, and more often than the most popular of the other later presidents, Jackson and Grant. After Lincoln passes his 1900–1904 low point, however, he pulls away from Washington. In 1905–9, two Lincoln articles appear for every Washington article. By 1921 the ratio in Lincoln's favor reaches 3 to 1.

The same pattern appears in the *Congressional Record*. Between 1875 and 1889, as table 3.2 shows, there are four entries on Washing-

Table 3.1 Average Annual Number of Entries in the *Readers' Guide to Periodical Literature*: Selected Presidents, 1890–1921

Readers' Guide Interval	Washington	Lincoln	Grant	Jackson	Madison	Jefferson	John Adams
1890–99	10.0	9.0	3.7	.9	.7	3.2	.6
1900–1904	7.2	7.6	1.2	1.0	.8	4.6	.8
1905–9	7.0	14.2	3.6	3.4	1.4	3.6	.4
1910–14	5.4	14.0	2.0	.4	.2	3.4	.4
1915–18	4.5	23.0	1.0	.2	.2	3.0	.2
1919–21	6.3	20.7	1.0	.3	—	.7	.7

Table 3.2 Entries on Abraham Lincoln and George Washington: *Congressional Record* and *New York Times*, 1875–1919

| Year | Congressional Record | | New York Times | |
	Lincoln	Washington	Lincoln	Washington
1875–99	4	22	55	58
1880–84	21	66	74	80
1885–89	8	51	45	309
1890–94	12	11	30	111
1895–99	35	34	52	120
1900–1904	15	19	18	30
1905–9	55	33	236	82
1910–14	76	46	125	81
1915–19	61	47	164	104

ton for every one on Lincoln, a ratio that reflects the centennial events associated with the nation's founding. From 1890 to 1904, fluctuation in the number of entries follows the same pattern revealed by *Readers' Guide* article counts: Washington and Lincoln are the subjects of almost the same number of entries. For the next fifteen years, 1905–19, Lincoln surpasses Washington by a ratio of about 1.5 to 1.

The trend of *New York Times* articles on George Washington is similar to the trend in the *Readers' Guide* and *Congressional Record*. It peaks in 1889, the year of Washington's inauguration centennial, and exceeds the number of Lincoln articles until the turn of the century. During the next five years, the volume drops sharply for both men, with Washington only slightly ahead of Lincoln. After 1905, the volume rises, and Lincoln's coverage outpaces Washington's by a ratio of almost 2 to 1.

The number of items added to the *Lincoln Bibliography* of the Illinois State Historical Library Collection also increases abruptly during the early years of the twentieth century (see table 3.3). In the five-year periods beginning in 1870 and ending in 1904, the number of acquisitions grows steadily, from 24 to 168. In the next five-year period, 1905 to 1909, it rises to 452. In the next two five-year periods, the number of acquisitions drops to 270 and 260 respectively but still exceeds by far all pre–1905 levels.

Poetry production provides another index of Lincoln's growing reputation. Roy Basler's bibliography (1935), among the most comprehensive available, shows that 5 of the 6 anthologies of Lincoln poetry to 1919 appeared after 1905 (table 3.3). It also lists 3 new nonanthologized poems about Lincoln in all but one of the six

Table 3.3 Additions to the Lincoln Bibliography and Poetry Counts, 1870–1919

| Year | Additions to the Lincoln Bibliography | Lincoln Poetry | |
		Anthologies	Nonanthologized Poems
1870–74	24	—	3
1875–79	25	—	—
1880–84	46	—	3
1885–89	50	—	3
1890–94	97	—	3
1895–99	118	1	3
1900–1904	168	—	6
1905–09	452	1	28
1910–14	270	2	15
1915–19	260	2	14

Sources: Illinois State Historical Library Collections; Basler 1935.

Table 3.4 Unveiling of Outdoor Statues in Bronze of Abraham Lincoln, 1865–1919

Year	Number of Statues
1865–69	2
1870–79	5
1880–89	1
1890–99	3
1900–1909	5
1910–19	17

Sources: Bulletin of the Lincoln National Life Foundation, February 1962; Bullard 1952, replicas excluded.

five-year intervals between 1870 and 1899. The number of such poems rises to 6 between 1900 and 1904, then to 28 in 1905–9; it drops afterward to 15 between 1910 and 1914, then to 14 between 1915 and 1919—several times higher than the average before 1905.

Lincoln's memory was also enlivened by the production of outdoor bronze and marble statues. Table 3.4 shows that from Lincoln's death to the turn of the century, a period of thirty-five years, 11 Lincoln statues were unveiled—one every 3.2 years. In the first decade of the twentieth century, another 5 statues appeared—about 1 every two years. The second decade, 1910–19, witnessed the unveiling of 17 statues—about 1 every seven months. "Scripture" and "icon," written and pictorial images of Lincoln, thus display an identical pattern: abrupt growth of interest in Lincoln during the first two decades of the twentieth century.

The Great Centennial

In America, as elsewhere, communities commemorate the past by setting aside time and means for their members to contemplate in common the memories they cherish and wish to preserve. The mood resulting from these observances is expansive, fostering communion with objects that transcend individual lives and infuse them with meaning. This ritual process established Lincoln's reputation after his assassination and revitalized it forty-four years later.

A year-by-year analysis of the *New York Times Index* suggests that 1909, the centennial of Lincoln's birth, was also the turning point of his historical reputation. Between 1875 and 1907, a thirty-three-year period, no trend in the production of *Times* articles on Lincoln is evident; a mean of about 10 articles appeared annually. In 1908, the number of articles rises to 36, a level higher than ever before, then leaps to 162 in 1909 before settling at a new equilibrium. Between 1910 and 1919, the number of articles varies substantially, but the average is about three times higher (29 articles annually) than before. Likewise, an average of 3 entries per year on Lincoln appeared in the *Congressional Record* between 1875 and 1908; in 1909, the number of entries rises to 41 and averages 14 annually during the next ten years.

Analysis of the *Lincoln Bibliography* catalog of the Illinois State Historical Library Collections reveals the same pattern. The number of volumes added to the collection gradually rises from a yearly average of 5 in the 1870s to 10 in the 1880s, 22 in the 1890s, and 35 in the years 1900 to 1907. The number of acquisitions increases to 82 in 1908 and 258 in 1909, then averages 53 per year during the subsequent ten-year period.

The number of *New York Times, Congressional Record,* and Illinois State Historical Library entries rose so high on the one hundredth anniversary of Lincoln's birth because more local officials than ever perceived the anniversary as an opportunity to celebrate his life and achievements and because more people than ever were eager to participate in the celebration. Lincoln's centennial intensified his memory by encasing it in ritual activities of unprecedented scale. Concentrated as they were in one to several days, centennial events reflected the truth of Emile Durkheim's ([1915] 1965) theory of periodic assemblies:

> There can be no society which does not feel the need of upholding and reaffirming at regular intervals the collective sentiments and the collective ideas which make its unity and its personality. Now this moral remaking cannot be achieved except by the means of reunions, assemblies and meetings . . . which do not differ from regular religious ceremonies, either in their object, the results which they produce, or the processes employed to attain these results. What essential difference is there between an assembly of Christians celebrating the principal dates of the life of Christ, or of Jews remembering the exodus from Egypt or the promulgation of the decalogue, and a reunion of citizens commemorating the promulgation of a new moral or legal system or some great event in the national life. ([1915] 1965, 474–75)

In content, commemoration and reunion rites differ from rites of mourning, but they are identical in their ability to unite people, to concentrate their attention, to increase the volume and intensity of communication. In remembrance as in mourning, the ritual excites and stimulates. In remembrance as in mourning, heightened feelings are rationalized by idealizing the person for whom the ritual is undertaken. So it was for Lincoln in 1909. The day off from work, the impressive displays of patriotic symbolism, the enormous numbers of people attending events throughout the community not only reflected the Lincoln panegyric but also enlarged it.[2]

Cities conducted the most elaborate centennial celebrations, but participation was effusive everywhere. In almost every Northern classroom, new portraits of Abraham Lincoln appeared, and extensive lessons about him were taught during the days leading up to the centennial. On February 12, businesses closed while churches, veterans' groups, and business, professional, and trade organizations mobilized their members for ceremonies, banquets, and parades. "Never before in the history of the world," wrote one *Review of Reviews* commentator, "has the one hundredth anniversary of the birthday of any man been celebrated with such depth of feeling and such widespread concurrence of opinion" (February 1909, 131).

Lincoln's centennial, like his funeral, was a refreshing and energizing release from ordinary activities; his commemoration was an "active, positive good" and aroused people from their "workaday lethargy" in a way that only catastrophes and recent presidential elections (McKinley's and Roosevelt's) had done (*Chicago Daily Tri-*

bune, February 13, 1909, 3). The spirit of the occasion thus proved that an order of wondrous existence transcends the routine of everyday life, and making contact with this transcendent order was exciting. Remarked one commentator, "The nation hasn't felt this deeply since Lincoln's death" (*Chicago Daily Tribune,* February 7, 1909, sec. 2, p. 4).

In an exploration of the reasons for this great outpouring of sentiment, the city of Chicago merits special attention because (1) the sheer volume of its ritual activities allows us to clarify the details of the commemorative process; and (2) since this city was populated by a large number of immigrants who knew little or nothing of Lincoln, it provides an opportunity to witness commemorative rites affecting people independently of their preconceptions.

An Effervescent City

On Lincoln Day 1909, collective effervescence and collective memory drew force from one another. At the Chicago Women's Press League, General Frederick Denton Grant—son of the famous general and president—made a courtesy call during a luncheon lecture. Expecting no outside visitors, the toastmistress became excited and mistakenly introduced him by his father's name. The effect on the women was "electrical," for "the air was already heavy with reminiscence." In response, one of the league members declared: "Why, she might almost as well have introduced Lincoln!" (*Chicago Daily Tribune,* February 12, 1909, 2). The inference seemed a non sequitur, but collective excitement fuses images that normal circumstances distinguish. In an emotion-charged environment where symbolic connections were occurring rapidly, the women could not help responding to a man indirectly connected to Lincoln (through his father) as if he were Lincoln himself.

The scope of the centennial is evident in its use of public places. As Lincoln Day 1909 approached, classes were suspended and forty-nine school buildings throughout the city were designated as commemorative program sites. Every school filled to capacity as prominent speakers explained the reasons for Lincoln's greatness and the importance of recognizing his birth centennial. Ceremonies were also held in local religious and ethnic clubs, political party headquarters, municipal and state offices, settlement houses, professional, business, and trade organizations, veterans' halls, and a host of other social clubs and associations. At fifteen city parks, patriotic programs fea-

turing oratory and music drew large crowds, including parents eager
to hear the one- to six-hundred-voice choirs in which their children
sang. (See, for example, *Chicago Daily Tribune*, February 12, 1909,
2; February 13, 1909, 3.)

Chicago newspapers captured and magnified the excitement of
the day. Emile Durkheim has shown how "the demon of oratorical
inspiration" ([1915] 1965, 241), expressed in a speaker's exaggerated gestures and tone, gives voice to the mood of his audience. So
too the demon of authorial inspiration, expressed in the journalist's
exaggerated phrases and bold print, reflects the newspapers' reaction to Lincoln's commemoration. Prior to radio and visual media
such as television, print was the only way to describe and communicate collective mood. With the *Chicago Daily Tribune*'s reaction
conforming to the mood of the city, its headlines seemed nothing
less than collective effervescence in print. "Spell of Lincoln over
Whole City," announced the February 10 issue. A February 12 headline read "Crowds Flock to Halls," where speakers gave details of
Lincoln's life and achievements. Another article emphasized that
the city recognized not merely the former president's name: "Deeds
of Lincoln Sway All Chicago" (February 12, 1909, 1). According
to the headlines, the oratory was always "stirring," the crowds
were "throngs," and what they learned of were Lincoln's "eternal
triumphs." For a generation attracted to melodrama (Thrall, Hibbard, and Holman 1960, 280–81), such rhetorical excess was normal. The centennial headlines exaggerated the surface reality of the
commemoration, yet they captured its deeper mood and reflected
a collective influence that transcended everyday curiosity. Stories
about vicious crimes, scandals, and tragedies that typically captured
the public's attention appeared under smaller headings. Overheated
headline prose reflected an overheated social climate.[3]

Frothy rhetoric appeared not only in newspaper headlines but
also in churches, banquet halls, and other public places. Intellectuals,
too, were carried away. "This centennial in honor of Abraham Lincoln's birth," explained sociologist Albion Small, "is a national sacra-
ment of purification." If Americans failed to follow Lincoln's example, Small added, then the holy day would become "humiliating," a
reminder of the nation's vice rather than a celebration of virtue (*Chicago Daily Tribune*, February 12, 1909, 8).[4]

Lincoln's centennial, like his funeral rites, was an occasion not
only for expressing feelings about his personal accomplishments but
also for performing ritual acts of national affirmation and national

communion. The centennial rites concentrated their participants, stimulated their emotions, and made them conscious of themselves as a single people. In 1909, as in 1865, corteges and ritual excitement established collective identity; ritual participation was a source as well as an expression of nationalism—a meaning-machine making concrete sense out of political abstractions (for detail, see Spillman 1997). The centennial rites, like the earlier funeral rites, were commitment practices dramatizing the bond between individual and society.

The Progressive Era

Enthusiasm over Abraham Lincoln's centennial presents a puzzle. The anniversary of his birthday had been observed every year in every part of the country outside the South, and the day came and went without much apparent change in Lincoln's reputation. Why was the 1909 observance so different?

The Lincoln centennial rites took place during a critical phase in the country's social development, lasting from approximately 1900 to 1920. The massive pageants and civic celebrations characteristic of this time were deliberately staged with a view to revitalizing American society by fostering new morals through heroic models from the past. In this Progressive era, David Glassberg observed, pageant masters and commemoration managers were strongly committed to social reform and regarded public spectacles as didactic instruments, modern equivalents to the ancient morality plays. Progressive rituals also performed integrative functions: they "grew with civic officials' efforts to create a coherent 'public' out of a hodgepodge of classes, interests, and immigrant groups" (1986–87, 965). To discern which of Lincoln's personal characteristics and achievements had the most significance for the twentieth-century American and why their commemoration was so widespread, we must study the Progressive era's defining aspects.

From Rural Republic to Industrial Democracy

The *Chicago Daily Tribune* chose for the cover of its special Abraham Lincoln centennial issue (February 7, 1909) a drawing of Lincoln seated against a background of skyscrapers and smokestacks. Lincoln was rarely associated with symbols of industrialization during the nineteenth century, but this was a new day. Prior to the 1890s, the voice announcing America's identity came from the past; America's cultural elite aimed to preserve the inspired design of the founding era and to realize that design through institution building and moral development. As the twentieth century approached, however, the orientation changed from past to future, from preservation to growth. In Henry Steele Commager's words:

The decade of the nineties is the watershed of American history. . . . On the one side lies an America predominantly agricultural; concerned with domestic problems; conforming, intellectually at least, to the political, economic, and moral principles inherited from the seventeenth and eighteenth centuries. . . . On the other side lies the modern America, predominantly urban and industrial; inextricably involved in a world economy and politics; troubled with the problems that had long been thought peculiar to the Old World; experiencing profound changes in population, social institutions, and technology; and trying to accommodate its traditions and habits of thought to conditions new and in part alien. (1950, 41)[5]

In modern America's first discernible phase, the Progressive era, a new order of cities and factories superimposed itself on a traditional rural order. The progressive impulse combined tendencies traceable to the beginning of the industrial revolution and reaching into the New Deal, but its social and cultural forms made it distinct.[6]

Two lines of development, the expansion of global power and maturation of industrialism, distinguished early-twentieth-century America from the world its oldest residents remembered. The nation's first line of development, growing international influence, was accompanied by a great surge of nationalism. The Spanish-American War, more than any other single event, altered America's global position. Fought and won in ten weeks during 1898, at low cost and with few casualties, this "splendid little war," as Secretary of State John Hay called it, yielded high returns in unity and self-conception. America's war against Spain satisfied the country's need to reaffirm its own unity—a need that had been building since the Civil War—as it signaled America's change from a hemispheric to a global power, not yet a dominant power, to be sure, but a key actor on the world stage. By the victory over Spain, Hay explained, "[w]e are all prouder to be Americans, and have a broader and truer understanding of the greatness of our country and of the grander destiny which lies before the American people." John Henry Barrows, president of Oberlin College, called the event of 1898 a "miracle." All previous conceptions of national pride, including the insular nationalism of the pre–

Civil War years, were, he felt, obsolete: "God has made us a world power" (Nagel 1971, 258–59). With this divine grant came a crop of new heroes, including Admiral George Dewey and Theodore Roosevelt, to furnish further inspiration. For perceptive men such as Charles Horton Cooley, "[I]t was easy to see during the Spanish-American War that . . . enthusiastic admiration of every trait of heroism was renewing and consolidating the collective life of the nation" ([1902] 1964, 326–27).

Aggressive participation in international affairs strengthened the presidency as it shaped the heroic vision. For Woodrow Wilson, the "greatly increased power and opportunity for constructive leadership given the President" was the most striking consequence of the Spanish-American War. Not since Lincoln, Wilson observed, had the presidency been so much "the front of affairs" (1966, 11:570). The stronger the demands and opportunities of the presidency, the more imperative the need for legitimating symbols—symbols to frame the new powers of the office so as to clarify for its incumbent as well as his patriotic constituents the traditions within which those powers must be exercised. Such was the context in which Abraham Lincoln's image became entangled.

The Spanish-American War consolidated and intensified what historian Stuart McConnell calls "the patriotic boom of the 1890s" (1996, 103). Not only the cult of the American flag, with its new oath of allegiance, laws against flag desecration, and new flag etiquette and ritual, but also the first signs of significant North–South reconciliation, deteriorating regionalism, new battlefield parks and monuments, the building of libraries and museums, and the rapidly increasing symbolic importance of the national capital of Washington, D.C.—all these developments, well established by the end of the century, crystallized by 1910 (McConnell 1992, 230; Goldstein 1995; Zelinsky 1988).

American nationalism had formed during the eighteenth century but ebbed and flowed throughout the nineteenth century in concert with the state's size and influence. The new industrial order, free of the semifeudal interests attending slavery, carried a new problem: "It consists in defining, or trying to define, a collective subject to whom the actions of the state can be internally connected, in creating, or trying to create, an experiential 'we' from whose will the activities of government seem spontaneously to flow" (Geertz 1973a, 240). Nationalism's devices, from flags to statues to monuments, render this experiential "we" explicit, casting it into tangible, usable, and describable form. Nationalism, the culture of industrialism, is the only ideology that can connect anonymous, mobile, and atomized individuals to an object transcending their private experience.

Victory in the Spanish-American War, in this connection, was less a military victory than an aspect of the United States' power in industry and trade. Like England, America acquired its empire, such as it was, "in a state of absence of mind" (Gellner 1983, 42). Between the time of the 1898 war to make Cuba and the Philippines safe for democracy and the time of the 1914–18 war to make the world safe for democracy, however, Americans concerned themselves more critically than ever before with the industrial order's internal effects. The industrial system that produced a culture of nationalism was now under scrutiny, and nationalism itself would be, ironically, a critical tool.

The Meaning of Progressivism

The Progressive movement involved a number of interacting forces: pressures to reconcile expansion of private wealth with expansion of public power; the coalescing of interest groups, bureaucracies, and political leaders around self-serving programs; and the mobilization of dispossessed sub-populations in their own behalf (Lichtman 1998). All progressive reformers confronted the adverse consequences of industrial growth, but since different reformers had different ideas of what improvement meant, no unified movement emerged. Labor reformers were not necessarily women's rights champions; child welfare advocates were not necessarily concerned about corporate greed and monopoly.[7] The movement's coherence was in the character of progressivism itself. Never before had so many different people engaged in so many organized activities to improve their society. "Progressivism," Arthur Link and Richard McCormick explain, "was the only reform movement ever experienced by the whole American nation. Its national appeal and mass base vastly exceeded that of Jacksonian reform. And progressivism's dependence on the people for its objectives and timing has no comparison in the executive-dominated New Deal" (1983, 9).

The progressives, as Eldon Eisenach (1994) has recently observed, advocated civic obligation, legal activism, nationalism, and the Social Gospel against the inertia of Jacksonian individualism, regionalism, and denominational conservatism. Progressivism involved ordinary people (farmers, small business owners, workers) asserting

and defending their rights (Dewitt [1915] 1968); well-educated, urban, Anglo-Saxon Protestant professionals and affluent businessmen concerned to protect their interests and status (Mowry 1958;
Hofstadter 1955); and forward-looking engineers, scientists, social
workers, intellectuals, businessmen, and physicians who rarely identified with the masses but wished to improve the lives of the masses
by rational means (Wiebe 1967; Hays 1995; Fink 1997). How federal
regulation affected these groups is the source of much controversy.
Some historians assert that regulation was undertaken in order to
preserve the general welfare (McCraw 1975, 163). Others, including
Gabriel Kolko (1963), believe that progressives were manipulative
elites, allied with business interests and concerned to control rather
than liberate the working class (see also Domhoff 1996). In this same
vein, Fred Block (1996) has argued that the Progressive era never
eliminated the selection mechanism that automatically chose policies
consistent with capitalism.

Understanding the development of the progressive state, however, requires that we attend not only to the interests of state managers and entrepreneurs but also to social forces from "below" that
provoked, demanded, or directed a state response (Sanders 1990).
Eileen McDonagh (1989, 1992), to take one example, discovered that
House votes for women's suffrage resulted from an increase in the
number of representatives from states permitting women to vote in
statewide and local elections. Other manifestations of federal intervention in the economy and local community, including Prohibition,
resulted from the extension of state and municipal practices. The
practice of social work, whereby national bodies of experts replaced
local philanthropy based on noblesse oblige, is also an instance of
change originating independently of corporate and business interests
and diffusing from the municipal realm to the state (Carson 1990).
Thus, competing interests at the grass roots, including business, professions, labor, consumers, and government, shaped the details of
progressive reform at all levels of government.

Bernard Weisberger (1994) has recently condemned critics of the
Progressive era, including Richard Hofstadter and Gabriel Kolko, for
arbitrarily discrediting the motives of the progressives, trivializing the
problems they addressed, underestimating the power of their adversaries, and ignoring the passion with which they struggled. Rectifying
this bias, however, requires not only reassessment of elite motives
but also understanding of public reaction to progressive programs.

Whatever the interests of the reformers themselves, the public responded enthusiastically to their efforts. Infused with indignation, the public mood—exemplified in the popularity of Upton Sinclair's 1906 novel *The Jungle* (which describes the working conditions and tainted products of Chicago meatpackers) and in the funeral procession of eighty thousand people along New York's Fifth Avenue in a driving rain to protest the Triangle Shirtwaist building fire, which trapped and killed more than 150 workers in 1911—was a key element of progressive culture. The Progressive era, to be sure, was not and could not have been programmed by the masses, but as Link and McCormick point out, "The dynamics of progressivism were crucially generated by ordinary people—by the sometimes frenzied mass supporters of progressive leaders, by rank-and-file voters willing to trust a reform candidate." Since the chronology of progressivism was a chronology of events arousing moral passion, the "popularity of individual leaders, the widespread anger at the corruption which they exposed, and the exhilaration of reformers when they defeated a hated boss or businessman" (1983, 8) were typical.

Progressivism was characterized not only by moral outrage against corporate wrongdoing and greed but also by the belief that government must regulate the free-market economy. Widespread poverty was the trunk out of which these and other branches of the movement grew. During the relatively prosperous Progressive era, approximately 10 percent of the population lived in poverty—not the kind of poverty that could be mitigated by publicly guaranteed housing, clothing, and food, but an abject poverty of misery, sickness, and death. The poverty of the late industrial revolution meant children and women laboring long hours, uncompensated work injuries and fatalities, tuberculosis, the ignoring of the aged and infirm, unsanitary tenements. Addressing these conditions, progressivism challenged the traditional idea that democracy meant no more than an equal starting place in the race of life. The new democracy, as conceptualized by the social sciences, with their confidence in rational solutions to social problems, and by the Social Gospel, which aligned the church with the downtrodden and the poor, was part of a more general, political movement to make the essential needs and dignity of the citizen a major state and federal concern.

The Progressive movement grew out of the conditions of urban life and was centered in the expanding cities. From 1860 to 1910, America's population more than tripled, from 30 million to 92 million; the urban population increased from 20 to 46 percent of the total. Some cities grew phenomenally. New York City had half a million inhabitants in 1867, 3 million in 1900—a sixfold increase in less than thirty-five years. Chicago's population grew from 30,000 in 1861 to over 2 million in 1910.

The growth of cities fundamentally altered the American class system. In 1860, social prestige still adhered to traditional distinctions based on taste and refinement. By 1900, money mattered most. Its possessors employed most of the population (including most of the twenty-three million immigrants who entered the United States between 1860 and 1910) and brought the country to an unprecedented level of productivity. Yet the condition of the average city dweller worsened.

Against the problems of the industrial revolution—the widening gap between rich and poor, unregulated immigration and urban growth, massive slums, a decline in moral values—the Progressive movement, animated by both scientific and evangelical beliefs, initiated public health (including eugenic) and welfare measures, regulation of business, and restriction of immigration. In this interventionist context, the century-old temperance movement achieved unprecedented influence. With new scientific evidence on alcohol's physical effects (cirrhoses, heart disease, and delirium), social effects (unemployment and deterioration of the family), and economic effects (absenteeism and lowered productivity), the Anti-Saloon League formed in 1895 and grew rapidly.[8] By 1920 the Eighteenth Amendment, making illegal the production and sale of alcoholic beverages, had passed.

The accomplishments of progressivism, although controversial, were considerable. Antitrust legislation, a pure food and drug law, child and sweatshop labor laws, federal workmen's compensation, the progressive income tax—these and other measures helped to transform the competitive jungle of the nineteenth century into the humane capitalism of the twentieth. Equally extensive were the effects of political reform, including women's suffrage, the direct election of U.S. senators, voter initiative, referendum, primary elections, and corrupt-practices acts. "Each one of these movements," William Allen White observed, "is a leveling process, a tendency to make money, capital, property, wealth, or financial distinction count for nothing save as an indirect influence in the ballot box" (1910, 48).

Progressive reforms were less visible in the agricultural South, but they were pressed vigorously nonetheless. Southern reformers, inspired by remnants of populist egalitarianism, strengthened oil and public utility commissions; forced down utility rates; fiercely prosecuted railroad, insurance, and other trusts; and passed unfair-practices laws, safety and inspection laws for mines and factories, pure food and drug laws, penitentiary reforms, and much humanitarian legislation. Southern states also adopted the election reforms established elsewhere (Woodward 1971, 369–95). In the South, as in the North, feminism rose in tandem with the gains of progressivism (Wheeler 1993).

In hindsight, the Progressive era was an aspect of America's transformation into a modern "mass society." As Edward Shils (1975b) conceived it, mass society possesses, and must possess, a "center" managed by political, economic, and cultural elites, but the people stand in closer relation to their center than before and interact with it more frequently. As the Progressive movement helped transform American society from a nineteenth-century rural democracy based on "liberty and order" into an urban democracy based on "liberty and justice" (Kammen 1986), it carried America in the direction of mass society. Linking issues of personal well-being to national democracy, the progressives placed issues of citizen rights and citizen obligations within a single political framework (Eisenach 1994, 221).

Progressive reforms made the United States a more democratic society, but they were not revolutionary. They were meant to protect, not undermine, free enterprise and property. The progressive state of the prewar years, no less than the conservative state of the 1920s, ruthlessly suppressed radicals' efforts to ameliorate the condition of labor (Cohen 1990). But few workers wished to challenge the capitalist order; on the contrary, workers were staunchly committed to private property, confident that in the long run they would receive their fair share. This long-run attitude was important, for the short run brought little material gain to the poor: the gap between rich and poor was greater at the end of the reform era than at its beginning. Racial justice was not even a marginal part of the progressive agenda. Still, progressivism had succeeded in inculcating a stronger regard for egalitarian *ideals* than had ever existed before.

Although progressivism's chief economic goal was to restore fair competition, many looked to the movement as a way to humanize capitalism by transcending competition. Christian reformers—notably adherents of the Social Gospel—looked forward to replacing a competitive system of production and distribution with a cooperative system (Danbom 1987, 38). Given their establishment of day care centers, soup kitchens, and settlement houses, their criticism of laissez-faire economics, and their support for moderate labor unions, the Social Gospel advocates represented an important communitarian wing of progressivism.

Social scientists such as Charles Horton Cooley and George Herbert Mead, educators such as John Dewey, settlement house pioneers such as Jane Addams, and religious leaders such as Jenkin Lloyd Jones were also powerful advocates of communitarian values; their critiques of competitive individualism had widespread and lasting influence (Noble 1958, 103–24; 1970, 53–80; Shalin 1988; Rice 1993, 166–72). Woodrow Wilson summarized their sentiments in one of his essays on the New Freedom: "There has been something crude, heartless, and unfeeling in our haste to succeed and be great. We said, 'Let every man look out for himself, let every generation look out for itself,' while we built giant machinery which made it impossible for anyone except those who stood at the controls to have a chance to look out for themselves" (1917, 17:7868–70). Populists had articulated this critique in the last decade of the nineteenth century, but the progressives extended it to urban industrialism and institutionalized it.

For supporters, the Progressive movement's merit resided in its climate of aspiration as well as its economic and political achievements. The Progressive era was an ideological era witnessing the arousal of a new political spirit, a revitalization of democracy and unprecedented concern for the rights and well-being of ordinary people. For William Allen White, progressivism was a "spiritual growth in the hearts of the American people . . . a moral movement in democracy" (1910, 50). Richard Hofstadter was less optimistic but conceded that progressivism, whatever its shortcomings, "must be understood as a major episode in the history of American consciousness" (1963, 15). True, the progressive emphasis on expertise and reliance on science to improve the lot of the people resulted, in the short run, in bureaucratic and consumer values rather than perfect social justice, but the imperfections of the era detract nothing from its successes. Oriented by "civic alertness" and a "combative mood," the extraordinary texture of the Progressive movement is perhaps best attested to by the phrase "return to normalcy," which was the slogan of those who wanted to see the movement end. (See also Commager 1950; Mann 1962; Noble 1970; Roosevelt 1961; and Wilson, Pilgrim, and Murray 1979.)

Lincoln: Symbol for an Era

Lincoln's status as a symbol of the Progressive era cannot be established until his image is considered apart from trends coincident with progressivism, especially a growing and increasingly resonant nationalism. Echoes of the patriotic boom of the 1890s backgrounded but could not explain Lincoln's emergence as a national idol, for it was not until the end of the century's first decade that Lincoln's prominence abruptly rose. American patriotism enlarged Lincoln's prestige only when ignited by Progressive-era ideals.

The first progressive "champion of the people's cause" against plutocracy was Theodore Roosevelt (Blum 1980). A patrician lacking strong attachment to the new entrepreneurial class, Roosevelt determined to harness America's unregulated economy. Critics accused him of making a show of federal regulatory authority in order to hasten public acceptance of big business, but most progressives saw him as an ally in their struggle against business's power. Roosevelt personalized the modern presidency, but he also shaped it politically (Gould 1991). The public, convinced of his ability to deal with recalcitrant corporate bosses, elected him by a landslide in 1904. After reading the thousands of letters written to Roosevelt (an unprecedented volume of correspondence), Kathleen Dalton (1979) concluded that people disagreed on the nature of the plutocratic threat but embraced equality and wanted strong leadership to protect it— precisely what progressivism and the Lincoln legacy were about.

The First Progressive

Roosevelt's fondness for Abraham Lincoln contributed to Lincoln's as well as his own prestige. During his presidency (1901–9), Roosevelt's program became increasingly focused, eventually including the establishment of a tariff commission, expansion of the Interstate Commerce Commission and Federal Bureau of Corporations to regulate private corporations, new laws providing for graduated inheritance and income taxes, conservation of national resources, workmen's compensation and laws on children's and women's labor, and direct primary elections. He invoked Lincoln to explain and defend his progressive program. As Roosevelt conceived it, this program had to be moderate in order to succeed, and he repeatedly held up Lincoln as a paragon of moderation: Lincoln "endeavored to get the best results he could out of the warring forces with which he had to deal" (Roosevelt 1904, 1:331–32). President Roosevelt likened his opponents, led by Wisconsin reform governor Robert La Follette, to Wendell Phillips, William Lloyd Garrison, and Lincoln's other radical abolitionist adversaries.

When Roosevelt ran for the presidency again in 1912 as the Progressive Party candidate, he identified with Lincoln more closely than ever. Lincoln, he said, led the formation of a new Republican Party when the old Whig Party ceased to "help the people"; Roosevelt followed in his footsteps. Lincoln hated slavery and fought it all his life; Roosevelt hated and fought the idea that "it is one man's duty to toil and work and earn bread and the right of another man to eat it." Alarmed by his support of the public's right to recall elections and of voter initiative and referendum, business leaders accused Roosevelt of favoring "pure" over representative democracy and condemned him for abridging business owners' right to conduct their affairs as they saw fit. Roosevelt responded by reasserting the ultimate grounds of his position: "[T]he Progressive platform of to-day is but an amplification . . . of Lincoln's," while "Lincoln and Lincoln's supporters were emphatically the Progressives of their day" (Roosevelt 1913, 1–6).

During Roosevelt's terms in office, the presidency expanded its historic role, representing the nation over the party to a greater extent than before (Schudson 1982, 104). Roosevelt, like other effective reputational entrepreneurs, knew how to exploit the memory of Lincoln for his own good. That Roosevelt's reputation was secure before he wrapped himself in Lincoln's mantle, however, was reason to believe that his affection for Lincoln was real. No president admired Lincoln more than Roosevelt did. His father had been a staunch Lincoln supporter. As a child in New York City, young Theodore had watched Lincoln's funeral procession pass his home, and he never forgot what he had seen. The Civil War preoccupied his early interests and remained his constant reference point for current affairs. "Constant reference point" is not too strong a concept: as a New York state representative, he believed that efforts to deal with the new danger of his time—monopoly—were direct extensions of the antislavery crusade. His thinking about strong central government was shaped by Lincoln's example. Long before he assumed the presidency, his feelings about Lincoln were reinforced by John Hay, who had been one of Lincoln's private secretaries, McKinley's secretary of state, and his father's friend. Roosevelt visited Hay often, and the two became close. Knowing that Roosevelt thoroughly understood and appreciated Lincoln, Hay gave him a ring containing a lock of Abraham Lincoln's hair as a gift for his 1904 inauguration. No other president, Roosevelt wrote in his acknowledgment letter, had ever received such a treasure. Nine years later, Roosevelt recalled in his biography how this relic sanctified his own convictions: "The ring was on my finger when the Chief Justice administered to me the oath of allegiance to the United States; I often thereafter told John Hay that when I wore such a ring on such an occasion I bound myself more than ever to treat the Constitution, after the manner of Abraham Lincoln, as a document which put human rights above property rights when the two conflicted" (1913, 385). In the White House, he saw Lincoln walking from one room to the next and up and down the corridors. "For some reason or other he is to me infinitely the most real of the dead Presidents" (quoted in Hanna 1992, 8).

The frequency with which Roosevelt mentions Lincoln in private correspondence, never intended for public display, lessens any doubt in the sincerity of his feelings. Most of Roosevelt's admirers knew what Lincoln meant to him. An editorial cartoon in the *New York Mail and Express* titled "Led by Lincoln's Principles" (August 3, 1904) showed Lincoln holding Roosevelt's hand and pointing him in the direction of the common good (fig. 3.1). A month later, the *Mail and Express* depicted Roosevelt under the guiding hands of Lincoln and Uncle Sam. Thus, when Roosevelt publicly claimed Lincoln was his guiding light, he was merely reminding his supporters of what they already knew.

Theodore Roosevelt never doubted that Lincoln's Republican Party had replaced the Whig Party in 1856 for the same reason his Progressive Party had had to replace the Republican Party itself in 1912. Both organizations had become moribund from having lost touch with the people. Roosevelt could not help thinking of William Howard Taft, the Republican filling the presidential chair that he had vacated, as a modern counterpart to Lincoln's do-nothing predecessor, James Buchanan. Roosevelt's opponents, on the other hand, scoffed at his efforts to identify himself with Lincoln, and some brought out extensive evidence to show how far short of Lincoln's ideals he actually fell (see, for example, Stewart 1912). Roosevelt's opponent in the 1912 presidential race, Woodrow Wilson, also admired Lincoln, but he drew on Lincoln's frontier self-reliance and individualism (rather than his coercive presidential efforts to regulate the political and economic order) as a blueprint for his progressive efforts to perfect economic competition and free trade. Both efforts, however—Roosevelt's and his opponents'—affirmed the esteem in which Americans held Lincoln's memory and showed them relying on it as a moral and political model.

Progressives promoted Lincoln as a model for their era of reform

LED BY LINCOLN'S PRINCIPLES.

Figure 3.1. "Led by Lincoln's Principles," cartoon, *New York Mail and Express,* August 3, 1904. Photograph courtesy of the Abraham Lincoln Museum, Harrogate, Tennessee.

because of who he was and what he did. They promoted him because his character inspired and guided them. They believed his emancipation policy expressed his convictions about the relationship between labor and capital, and the different sides of Lincoln's personality— kindness and identification with ordinary people on the one hand, aggressiveness in the practice of law and the waging of war on the other—became apparent to many progressive leaders.

Symbolic Diffusion

Widespread support for progressive reform strengthened the offices and symbols of state. Congress's approval of the 1909 minting of a new penny bearing Lincoln's profile testified that the public's affection for Lincoln was embedded in new political attitudes. Ever since the 1794 Mint Act had rejected the plan to set President George Washington's image on federal coins and notes, Americans have regarded portraits of public figures on their coins as a mark of state arrogance. Lincoln's appearing on the 1909 penny reflected the people's growing trust in their government and approval of its democratic direction. "A penny," explained Carl Sandburg, then a young socialist working for the *Milwaukee Daily News,* "is strictly the coin of the common people. . . . you find it stops at many cottages and few mansions" (Callahan 1970, 41).

By the early 1900s, Lincoln's name had become a familiar part of anti-corporate as well as populist rhetoric. Frederic Hinckley asked his Philadelphia Unitarian Society audience ironically to "[i]magine Washington or Lincoln connected in some legislative or executive capacity with the government of a large city, wherein the rights of the people are largely surrendered to the interests of great corporations; to political cliques and bosses" (1897, 2). Twelve years later, Rabbi Harrison explained to a Lincoln centennial audience how Lincoln would have opposed the prevailing "snobocracy." He would have fought "the class spirit and the growth of the so-called 'four-hundred.' " He would have put down lawless wealth and insolence. After a side comment on the "political filth" of his hometown, St. Louis, and why the city would benefit if its mayor were more like Theodore Roosevelt, Rabbi Harrison brought Lincoln back into the picture. If Lincoln were alive, "he would defend the humble against the powerful; the small trader against the monopolist that seeks to crush and ruin him by immoral tricks. . . . To regulate and control great corporations . . . would surely be the first task that he would make his own, so that the plain man may not be robbed of his unalienable rights." Harrison's audience, which included a thousand Civil War veterans, gave him a standing ovation (*Chicago Daily Tribune,* February 13, 1909, 3).

The issue of corporate power and privilege connected Lincoln more centrally to the progressive program than any other issue. When Theodore Roosevelt laid the cornerstone for Lincoln's birthplace shrine in Hodgenville, Kentucky, he remarked on the "social and industrial problems of the day" and how Lincoln's own "reform" (emancipation) would apply to them (*Atlanta Constitution,* February 13, 1909, 2). At about the same time, Jane Addams devoted a chapter of *Twenty Years at Hull-House* (1910) to her family's profound affection for Lincoln and to his influence on her own belief in democracy and civic cooperation (1910, 23–42). Many politically moderate leaders worked away at this theme. Lincoln would oppose child labor and the exploitation of adult labor. He would recognize that "socialism is the new slavery" but would say the same about "corporations that break the laws with insolence and impunity" (*Outlook,* February 27, 1909).

The anti-corporation Lincoln found his way into labor songbooks. The fourth voice in "Lincoln, Oh! Lincoln, We Honor You Today" (Douglas and Hoschna 1906) sings in *allegro marziale:*

> Oh, for an hour of Lincoln now,
> To make the power of money bow.
> To curb and crush monopoly,
> And set the common people free
> From graft and greed and exploitation
> And bring content to this our nation.

Lincoln was a natural "labor leader" who recognized not only the legitimacy of property but also the rights of the working man. A commentator in *Arena* therefore defined the centennial of Lincoln's birth as a major event giving "a new inspiration and hope to thousands who were all but despairing of the success of popular rule. . . . It has flooded the imagination of the rising generation with the light of democracy, so hated and feared by the reactionary interests of privileged wealth" (July 1909, 480). What better way to condemn antidemocratic interests than by placing them in Lincoln's light? Thus, an artist who wished to depict President Taft's break with the progressive wing of his party showed him openly disparaging the masses as Lincoln, the Man of the People, looks down in sorrow (fig. 3.2). The more credible the progressives' claims, the greater the enhancement of Lincoln's stature. As the *Chicago Tribune*'s centennial editorial explained, "demand for popularization of the senate, for the democratization of party organization . . . , for the initiative and referendum, and even the recall" had all converged into a "tide of democracy." And "in this ripe hour the American people turn to their noblest memory. . . . For Lincoln's life and Lincoln's character illustrate more perfectly than that of any other of America's great men the essential rightness and practicability [of these political reforms]" (*Chicago Daily Tribune*, February 13, 1909, 2; see also February 7, 1909, 4; and February 19, 1909, 1).

Figure 3.2. "William Howard Taft and the Spirit of Abraham Lincoln," cartoon, 1910. Photograph courtesy of the Library of Congress.

As Lincoln's presidency became the first phase of the Progressive movement, the Gettysburg Address became its manifesto. By 1913 *Nation* was complaining: "Nobody knows, and there is nothing in Lincoln's acts or words to tell, whether or not he would have been for the initiative and referendum, for endowment of motherhood, or for single tax; yet enthusiastic advocates of almost any 'advanced' proposal of our day find little difficulty in persuading themselves that it is a corollary of the Gettysburg address" (July 10, 1913, 27). The address's cultural resonance, in turn, had grown. It seemed natural that James T. McCleary (1908), realizing that Lincoln's eulogy "will be recited by school boys a thousand years from now," should propose to acknowledge the 1909 Lincoln centennial with a memorial highway connecting Washington, D.C., and Gettysburg, Pennsylvania.

No single group, according to Kathryn Kish Sklar (1988), profited politically from the Progressive era more than women, and no group found the Civil War a more powerful analogy of their situation. Women reformers pursued many goals, but the most basic was voting rights. To this end, suffragists wrote militant lyrics and set them to the tune of "Battle Hymn of the Republic" and "When Johnny Comes Marching Home." They referred to themselves as "Lincoln Soldiers," fighting the modern equivalent to slavery. Lincoln, the "Pioneer Suffragist," was a model for the time, and those opposing the extension of democracy to women had to answer to him. "I go for all sharing the privileges of the government who assist in bearing its burdens, by no means excluding women": billboards, along with several years' February issues of the *Woman's Journal,* carried this quotation by Lincoln under his picture. Demonstrating in front of Woodrow Wilson's White House in 1917, protesters exclaimed on placard and banner: "Lincoln stood for woman suffrage sixty years ago. Mr. President, you block the national suffrage amendment today. Why are you behind [i.e., lagging] Lincoln?" (*New York Tribune,* February 13, 1917, 8). By 1920, Wilson's last year in office, women had gained the right to vote—which they saw as the realization of Lincoln's will.

Abraham Lincoln had never written or spoken at length about women's rights, but he became their champion nonetheless. Not only his early support of women's suffrage but also the prominent maternal strain of his nature made him an attractive vehicle of gender politics. As his own mother "left on Lincoln's memory an overwhelming impression, so Lincoln himself physically and mentally 'mothered' his neighbors, his State, his country" (*Literary Digest,* January 6, 1919, 19). In his many acts of personal kindness, including his famous letter of consolation to Mrs. Lydia Bixby for the loss in battle of her sons, "he displays an understanding of motherhood unsurpassed in English literature" (*Outlook,* October 17, 1917, 241). Indeed, he "embodied the universal motherhood as no man has since Christ" (*Outlook,* December 27, 1916, 891; see also Lemmon 1909).

Julia Ward Howe, author of the "Battle Hymn of the Republic," reinforced the Civil War's legacy when she wrote a poem in Lincoln's praise and read it before a national meeting of suffragists. In New Jersey, a local suffragist society printed postcards with Lincoln's picture placed beside his statements on equality and liberty. The keynote speaker at a Chicago meeting during Lincoln's centennial expressed hope that "a hundred years from today America will be celebrating the birth of some woman wise enough and noble enough to be the liberator of women from a slavery far worse than that from which Lincoln freed the negro" (*Woman's Journal,* February 27, 1909, 34). Identification of Lincoln with the cause of underdogs is a constant that runs through every interpretation of his historical significance. The future hero of women's equality, in particular, would be a second Lincoln.

The same ideals that went into the making of the Nineteenth Amendment, providing for women's suffrage, went into the Eighteenth Amendment, which abolished the manufacture and sale of alcohol. Progressivists knew they could count strong temperance advocates, including Lincoln admirers Ida Tarbell and Samuel S. McClure, among their number. Lincoln himself, described by opponents as an alcoholic, was in fact a nondrinker and championed abstinence earnestly. Not until the early twentieth century, however, did his views on drinking become publicly significant. Temperance advocates often invoked his 1842 Washington's Birthday address to the Springfield Temperance Society. "Whether or not the world would be vastly benefited by a total and final banishment from it of all intoxicating drinks," he said, was no longer debatable. "Three-fourths of mankind confess the affirmative with their tongues, and I believe the rest acknowledge it in their hearts." This statement, along with affirmations of abstinence in Lincoln's own handwriting and testimonials of his disdain for alcohol by his contemporaries, appears in Samuel Wilson's booklet (1910) on Lincoln as an "apostle of temperance and prohibition." Nine years later, temperance advocates celebrated the ratification of the Eighteenth Amendment by reprinting Lincoln's

1842 address in its entirety and, to prove that Lincoln never changed his views, reproduced his 1863 letter to the Sons of Temperance, asserting that "intemperance is one of the greatest, if not the very greatest, of all evils among mankind" (*Lincoln on the Liquor Question* 1920, 16).

The vast majority of writings and orations during and after the centennial concerned themselves with Lincoln's private life, tastes, and preferences, for in the end it was less important to know what contemporary measures Lincoln would have supported or opposed than to know what traits of character were revealed in that hypothetical support or opposition. Hence the inexhaustible reminiscences about Lincoln's ascetic tastes, his simplicity and unpretentiousness, his merciful attitude toward condemned soldiers, his accessibility and responsiveness to people without influence and power, his profound sympathy for the casualties of war and their families. Saturating the yearly February issues of popular magazines and the Lincoln Day editions of local newspapers, these reminiscences blur hierarchical distinction by depicting the common people in interaction and close moral affinity with the state. Lincoln's character and life on the one hand and twentieth-century political and economic reforms on the other were thus infused with the same egalitarian principle, and the invocation of one invariably brought to mind the other. In Lincoln, the people had found the most compelling emblem of the Progressive era's democratic aspirations.

Progressive Media

America's burgeoning magazine industry and literacy rate (Kaestle et al. 1991) strengthened Lincoln's affinity with progressivism. In a very real sense, progressivism, the printed materials of the day, readers' attitudes, and their preferred images of the past were produced in the same shop. Between 1890 and 1921, the *Readers' Guide to Periodical Literature* listed 575 articles on Lincoln published by 58 different magazines. Half the articles (50 percent), however, were published by just 8 magazines, of which 6 had both strong commitments to progressive programs and a history of admiration for Lincoln.[9] Their editors and contributors were reputational entrepreneurs in the strong sense—deliberately invoking the memory of Abraham Lincoln in the pursuit of goals they thought, rightly or not, to be in the interest of society at large.

Century magazine, the largest producer of Lincoln articles, began publishing in 1881 and replaced *Scribner's,* whose only editor, Josiah Holland, had written the first popular life of Lincoln. Richard W. Gilder, *Century*'s editor during its first twenty-eight years, was intensely interested in municipal reform, served on city boards, and wrote about New York's "rotting tenements." Gilder had fought briefly with a Pennsylvania artillery unit in the Civil War and believed that the conflict was the most significant event in American history. As public memories of the war receded, he published many articles related to it, including the serialized version of Nicolay and Hay's Lincoln biography. Later he published his own biography, *Lincoln the Leader* (1909a). *Century* also produced *St. Nicholas,* a children's magazine in which Lincoln articles were common fare (*Dictionary of American Biography* 1931, 7:273–77; Mott 1957, 3:470).

Outlook magazine was in some ways the most aggressive exponent of the progressive program. Published from 1870 to 1893 as *The Christian Union* and edited for its first eleven years by abolitionist Henry Ward Beecher, *Outlook* emerged in 1893 with a vital sense of purpose. It believed "in the immortality of the spirit and in change of forms, in the old religion and in a new theology, in the old patriotism and in new politics, in the old philanthropy and in new institutions, in the old brotherhood and in a new social order." For this purpose—the unification of tradition and progress—Lincoln was an ideal symbol. Under the forty-two-year editorship of Lincoln admirer Lyman Abbott, *Outlook* became both a large repository of Lincoln commentary and a vehicle of progressivism. In 1912 it supported the candidacy of Theodore Roosevelt (one of its regular contributors) and the platform of the Progressive Party (*Dictionary of American Biography* 1:24–25; Mott 1957, 3:429).

Collier's magazine, another rich source of Lincoln articles, was established in 1888 by Peter F. Collier—the man who had purchased Lincoln's birthplace and made it into a national shrine. Between 1902 and 1912, under Norman Hapgood (author of *Abraham Lincoln: The Man of the People* [1899]), the emphasis of *Collier's* changed from short stories to public affairs. Hapgood's editorials led the magazine's crusade on the issues of income tax, women's suffrage, direct election of senators, child labor laws, railroad rate regulation, and patent medicine. He, like many other progressives, regarded these reforms as extensions of Lincoln's principles (Mott 1957, 4:462, 467).

From 1913 to 1916 Hapgood took *Harper's Weekly* in the same direction he had taken *Collier's*. His predecessor George William Curtis, editor from 1863 to 1892, had established a tradition that made *Harper's* compatible with the goals of the influential Hapgood. During the Civil War, Curtis had been a supporter of Lincoln's policies, and in 1903 he wrote a book about him (*The True Abraham Lincoln*). As the industrial revolution unfolded, he recognized labor's rights as well as its obligations to capital and was among the first to advocate women's suffrage and civil service reform.

Review of Reviews, another outlet for progressive ideas, was first published in London in 1890 by William Thomas Stead, a "daring social reformer" (Mott 1957, 4:657). Albert Shaw edited the American edition and included in it a large number of Lincoln articles. A schoolmate and lifelong friend of Woodrow Wilson and a close friend of Theodore Roosevelt, Shaw studied and wrote about social movements and municipal government. He also wrote a two-volume biography of Lincoln and, with Collier, organized the Lincoln's Birthplace Shrine Committee.

Nation magazine, edited from 1881 to 1906 by Wendell Phillips Garrison, son of abolitionist William Lloyd Garrison, concerned itself with civil service reform, voting reform, and the well-being of African Americans. Progressive on many political issues, *Nation* consistently sided with capital in its disputes with labor. It supported William Howard Taft and Woodrow Wilson, but strongly opposed William Jennings Bryan and Theodore Roosevelt. *Independent* magazine's link to the Progressive movement was more inconsistent than *Nation's*, but since it had been established by abolitionists in 1848 as a medium for antislavery views, its early editors wrote about Lincoln often (Mott 1957, 2).

Many magazines publishing large numbers of articles about Lincoln were unconcerned with progressive issues. *Literary Digest* had no definite policy on domestic concerns, but it was one of the most prolific publishers of Lincoln articles during and after World War I. Some magazines publishing an average or below-average number of Lincoln articles (for example, *Munsey's* and *Cosmopolitan*) were staunchly progressive (Schneirov 1994). Some progressive publishers deliberately chose to print a limited number of very well researched, groundbreaking articles on the former president. *McClure's* published only eight Lincoln articles between 1890 and 1921, but the affections of its owner and manager, Samuel S. McClure, ran deep. McClure had graduated from Knox College (Galesburg, Illinois), a traditional center of Christian reform, site of the fifth Lincoln-

Douglas debate (1858), and bestower of Lincoln's honorary law degree (1860). When McClure established his publishing business, he
reinforced his own interest in Lincoln by surrounding himself with
staff members who were also graduates of Knox College. Although
he never found time to write his own Lincoln biography, he published
a useful collection of anecdotes about Lincoln, financed Ida Tarbell's
search for new information on Lincoln's youth, and published the
books resulting from her work. (Tarbell herself was a staunch progressive who embraced temperance and believed in the parallel between trusts and slaveholding, the latter evident in her book assailing
Standard Oil Company. For both her antitrust and her anti-alcohol
activities, Lincoln was her exemplar.)

Thus, articles on Lincoln appeared frequently in the popular magazines of the early twentieth century but had a special affinity for the
most progressive of these. The result was a tighter coupling of Lincoln's image with the reforms of the day.

Beyond Progressivism: Washington, Lincoln, and
the New Morality

American newspapers and magazines frequently compared Abraham
Lincoln to George Washington, and the contrast revealed a growing
nation assuming an increasingly democratic conception of itself. For
immigrant as well as native-born Americans, the title "Father of His
Country" meant that Washington had played selfless military and
political roles in the war for independence. During eight years of
fighting, he had renounced the wealth and comfort that populist critics condemned him for possessing. After winning the war, he turned
down every opportunity to convert his prestige into political power,
and when coaxed into accepting the presidency, he served with a
studied disregard for partisan interests. To call him "Honest George"
would not go far enough in capturing the people's confidence in his
political virtue. Renunciation of self-interest and satisfaction with
"fame" rather than power or wealth as the reward for public service
are patrician traits Lincoln never possessed. A shrewd and partisan
politician, Lincoln could not have been as morally upright in his society as Washington was in his. Lincoln's policies, personality, background, and demeanor were more compatible with an industrial democracy than a rural republic ruled by an unpaid class of gentlemen.

Lincoln's displays of expressive folksiness intensified his affinity for industrial society, with its loosening of institutional restraints, its enhanced appreciation of the emotions and the senses, its growing emphasis on rights over obligations. In industrial America, Lincoln was loved; Washington, merely revered. Norman Hapgood (1919) explained:

[M]en live little in their judgements, much in their sentiments. Lincoln was a great man; Washington was even greater; but Lincoln lived and expressed the sorrows, the longings, the humor of us all, and the abilities and character of Washington are not easy of approach. . . . The man around whose gigantic figure the American nation was formed is not romantic and he is not to a high degree articulate, there is in the actual Washington little to reach the sentimental soul.

For Hapgood, as for other commentators, Washington's distinguishing trait was devotion to duty. His "was a nature fit for bearing the greatest load ever carried by an American" (Hapgood 1919, 93). but it was precisely that nature that made him unattractive. He spent his life, from adolescence to old age, in positions of responsibility. Sacrificing youth, he grew into a stately and aloof adult, a man of virtue and dignity but little warmth. Lincoln's youth, on the other hand, was coarse and mischievous—just like any other boy's—which is precisely why it helped make him the perfect American symbol.

Washington and Lincoln, as Lyman Powell described them, are two trees, two giants of the American forest. The Washington tree draws the eye upward toward leafy crown and sky; the Lincoln tree draws the eye downward to massive roots and to the earth in which they are set. To this contrast between leafage and roots, sky and earth, corresponds another contrast—that of Old World and New. The leaves crowning the Washington tree reflect "the autumnal tints of Europe," while the roots of the Lincoln tree go deep into the New World soil (1901, 192). Washington, the high-born man of stately demeanor, devoid of tender sentiment yet utterly just and incorruptible, differs thus from Lincoln, the low-born man of ungainly demeanor, yet sentimental, plain, humorous, and friendly. Washington is to Lincoln as restraint is to release, gravity to lightness, or, in the words of a poet, silence to sound: "The one impregnable, austere; / The other vibrant like a horn" (*Independent*, January–June 1911, 387).

As the twentieth century's second decade drew to a close, the difference between Lincoln's sounds and Washington's silences seemed clearer than ever. Washington, compared to Lincoln the common man, seemed all the more an English country gentleman, symbol of a culture of deference. Contrasting achievements highlighted the contrasting images. Lincoln's opposition to the slave power "gives countenance to emotional agitation in the name of a vague humanitarianism," whereas Washington's opposition to British power gave him a reputation for nonsentimental firmness and resolve (*Nation*, February 27, 1913, 197), for being "more a general and statesman," as Charles Sumner put it, "than a philanthropist" ([1900] 1969, 12: 242). Washington and Lincoln thus symbolized contrasting ideals of social order. The first ideal, embedded in the community of a semifeudal gentry, was based on the ancient, class-bound concept of honor; the second ideal, embedded in the industrial state, was based on the modern, class-free concept of dignity (for detail on the social correlates of honor and dignity, see Berger, Berger, and Kellner 1973, 83–96).

A Malleable Symbol

The rise of Abraham Lincoln's historical reputation was not something waiting to happen, a kind of cultural Sleeping Beauty to be awakened when conditions were right. The roots of Lincoln's new prestige were deep, growing within a broader field of events: the rapid disappearance of a generation that had experienced the hardship of the Civil War and known Lincoln as a cause of personal suffering; and the maturation of a new generation adapted to industrial order, political and economic reform, and vigorous nationalism. If these transformations had matured while the population was still embittered over Lincoln's policies, his reputation would not have grown as much as it did. Alternatively, if the new generation, innocent of the tribulations of war, had not come of age during a period of intense social and moral change, the need for Lincoln to symbolize the age would have been less acute. The sudden rise of Lincoln's prestige resulted from the coincidence of generational transition and political-economic change.

The Progressive era was the beginning of American capitalism's "late stage," wherein government intervened to correct the free market's failures. Since active governments, according to Jurgen Habermas (1975), require heavy doses of legitimacy, Abraham Lincoln's sudden elevation during the early twentieth century might be interpreted as the progressive state's effort to legitimate itself. Progressive administrations recognized the value of Lincoln's reputation and consciously drew on it to elicit support for their programs; yet Lincoln's image was much more than a tool for manipulating public opinion. It was hardly needed for this purpose. Progressives did not require more legitimacy because they were interventionist; rather, they intervened so effectively in the workings of the economy and polity because they already possessed legitimacy. To sustain this legitimacy, moreover, they did not need to appropriate Lincoln, for their Republican Party had already traditionally identified with him. The memory of Lincoln was not so much an instrument of progressive interests as a language through which they communicated to one another about these interests.

Abraham Lincoln, however, "stood for" the Progressive era in two senses. He was a model *for* progressivism, shaping and illuminating its values and framing its members' experiences; he was a model *of* progressivism, mirroring progressive ideals that were not altogether his. In truth, the substance of progressive issues concerned but never absorbed Lincoln. He subordinated economic matters to his passion against slavery and, eventually, his preoccupation with war. During a thirty-year political career he made many remarks about capital, labor, and the economy, but these statements, although frequently quoted, were disconnected and sometimes contradictory. Lincoln was not indifferent to economic issues; he endorsed the Whig economic program centered on protective tariffs and internal (infrastructural) improvements—"the American System," as it was known. Nothing in this program, however, provided for the state to sympathize or to side with the interests of labor against capital. When twentieth-century economic progressives invoked Lincoln, they were mirroring their own generation's perspectives.

Faced with the unprecedented problems of an industrial society, progressive reformers invoked Lincoln's moral and political character, asking what he would do in this situation or that. Reformers referred to Lincoln because they knew their audience would be receptive to him. For an entire generation of Republicans, socialists, suffragists, African Americans, temperance advocates, and conservatives of all stripes, he modeled progressivism's deepest tendencies.

The need for new ways to represent American society made Lincoln appealing, but the industrial society also drew on preindustrial agrarian symbols to represent itself. Since the American common people—counterparts of the French *paysans,* Russian *narod,* and

German *Volk*—arose out of agrarian life, Americans represented their industrial society, expanding sense of nationhood, and "labor patriotism" with symbols of family, village, and valley.[10] The image of the common man, based on the peasant ideal, is a universal of industrial nationalism, and the next chapter shows how Lincoln personified it.

Lincoln, a Man of the People:
Dignifying America

Several days before William Jennings Bryan spoke at the Springfield, Illinois, Lincoln centennial celebration, he had an automobile accident. "Motor Car Strikes Bridge Crushing Commoner Severely," a newspaper headline announced (*Chicago Daily Tribune,* February 7, 1909, 1) Everyone knew that "Commoner" was short for "the Great Commoner," Bryan's political epithet.[1] The words *common* and *commoner* possessed great resonance in the early twentieth century. The centennial edition of the *Chicago Daily Tribune,* for example, said that Lincoln "was the common man serving with the common wisdom and the common powers the common good in its noblest aspects." One story after another explained how Lincoln's "homely power" and "noble commonness" affirm the "sanctity of everyday life." "Mysterious flames" of genius burn in great men's minds, but "common thought" has its own "clear, steady and life-giving flame." European aristocrats, a *Tribune* writer added, scorn the common as they scorn the people, but Americans cherish commonness as they cherish democracy. Since "the meek shall inherit the earth," Lincoln fulfills the prophecy of "the greatest of democrats, that carpenter's son of Nazareth" (February 7, 1909, sec. 2, pp. 2–7).

Americans have long deemed equality the source of all their virtues—the "fundamental fact from which all others seem to be derived," in Alexis de Tocqueville's words. Equality, he said, "is their idol . . . they would rather perish than lose it." Its importance to the texture of the nation's life cannot be overemphasized: in America "the passion for equality is ardent, insatiable, eternal, and invincible" ([1840] 1945, 102).

The American concept of equality, rooted in a past devoid of feudal distinctions, consists in the belief that all people, no matter how poor in wealth or talent, deserve dignity and fair treatment. Even before Tocqueville, J. Hector St. John Crèvecoeur, in *Letters from an American Farmer,* emphasized that the American "dictionary" was "short on words of dignity, and names of honor"—short, that is, on words describing a lower stratum subordinating itself morally to a higher one ([1782] 1963, 46–47).

Americans imagined that Abraham Lincoln embodied their belief in equality in God's sight, but the real Lincoln was not an altogether satisfactory model of egalitarian ideals. The real Lincoln believed in social distinctions; he had been transformed into an egalitarian symbol by the stories told about him. Lincoln stories—as vehicles of information and moral discourse—affected the way Americans interpreted their world and helped them reiterate their history and traditions, and shape and preserve their mores and identity. People everywhere define themselves by asking and answering the question, "Of what stories do I find myself a part?" (MacIntyre 1981, 201; see also Hauerwas and Jones 1988, 19–20), but the function of these stories is not totally dependent on their authenticity.

The Authentic Lincoln

John Vance Cheney's poem "Lincoln," written for the centennial, tells of how "Earth held to him." Truly are "his roots deep in the earth." Earth meant only one thing: democracy. To be of the earth is to be of the people:

> Ay, Earth's he is; not hers alone
> Blood of our blood, bone of my bone,
> Love folded him to rest
> Upon a people's breast. (1909, 278)

Common men representing and never leaving the masses are folk heroes. Symbolizing society's elemental tendencies, folk heroes are imperfect, touchable, human. Folk imagery from frontier lore humanized Lincoln, made him a man with whom ordinary people could identify, and enhanced his reputation. Lincoln the folk hero reflected traditional American thinking about the relation between leaders and masses. Alexis de Tocqueville explained that in America, leaders "take care not to stand aloof from the people; on the contrary, they constantly keep on easy terms with the lower classes; they listen to them, they speak to them every day. They know that . . . in democratic ages you attach a poor man to you more by your manner than by benefits conferred . . . and even want of polish is not always displeasing" ([1840] 1945, 111). Tocqueville's account, based on observations made at the midpoint of Andrew Jackson's presidency, reflects the Democratic-Jacksonian view of democracy, one that stresses the common man's dignity and capacity for self-rule.

But Tocqueville overlooks the strain of American democracy legitimated by America's "hierarchical" values (Ellis and Wildavsky 1988). Vestiges of hierarchical society lived and influenced thinking when Tocqueville visited America in 1832. The genteel class no longer ruled, but its cultural fragments, including honor, good manners and breeding, and responsibility and duty, had been appropriated by ambitious men and women seeking respectability. Tocqueville recognized the remnants of this aristocratic culture but never understood or discussed its tension with democratic culture. Abraham Lincoln, in particular, symbolized egalitarian ideals but personally embraced hierarchical ones.

Gentleman and Whig

Abe Lincoln? Wull, I reckon! Not a mile f'om where we be,
Right here in Springfiel', Illinoise, Abe used to room with me.
He represented Sangamon, I tried for Calhoun,
And me and Abe was cronies then; I'll not forgit it soon.

Robertus Love ([1911] 1970, 21) wrote these words in 1895 and attributed them to Jason Pettigrew of Calhoun City, Illinois, a former judge with whom Abraham Lincoln rode circuit. Lincoln's speech, the poet implies, was as vulgar as his colleague's. Can this be the man whom so many regard as America's most eloquent president?

Don Fehrenbacher, a prominent Lincoln scholar, presents the most widely accepted account of why Jason Pettigrew's "crony" occupies such a central place in America's historical imagination. Fehrenbacher believes that nineteenth-century America needed a "heroic *common* man—a representative not only of American national-

ity but of American democracy. Lincoln fitted the role perfectly—
fitted it in his background, in his outlook, in his appearance, in his
style, and in the very structure of his life" (1987, 176). Although
Fehrenbacher was right about Lincoln's meeting the common people's need for a hero out of their own ranks, the real Lincoln did not
fit this role as well as Fehrenbacher suggests. As Lincoln grew from
a boy into a young man, the "structure of his life" became less, not
more, suggestive of the common people. Mostly an exaggeration of
authentically distinguishing traits, Lincoln the Commoner was part
fabrication and part false inference based on Lincoln's own claims.
To appreciate the effect of these distortions, we must grasp certain
realities of Lincoln's life.

As Abraham Lincoln became more of a public figure, his identification with ordinary people weakened. William Herndon, Lincoln's
law partner, described Lincoln as "always calculating, and always
planning ahead. His ambition was a little engine that knew no rest"
(Herndon and Weik 1889, 2:375). In saying this, Herndon was not
referring to the classic conception of ambition as lust for power and
control over others; he was talking about Lincoln's passion for self-
improvement—moving beyond, and above, his early environment
and social circles.

During the early nineteenth century, unsettled western lands attracted many families seeking to better their lives. Jefferson Davis
was born seven months before Lincoln in a log cabin in Christian
County, Kentucky.[2] In log cabins and other wilderness dwellings were
born Andrew Jackson, James Polk, Millard Fillmore, and thousands
of other powerful men in federal, state, and local government. To be
born on the frontier in those years was not necessarily to be born
poor. Belief in an inevitable connection between frontier life and poverty results from the log cabin myth, whose purpose, according to
Edward Pessen (1984), is to legitimate the privileges of the "self-made
man."

The log cabin myth exaggerates the deprivations of Lincoln's
background as it reflects popular understandings of the frontier.
"One of the most stubborn myths of American history," according
to David Hackett Fischer, "is the idea that the frontier promoted
equality of material condition" (1989, 749). In fact, landed wealth
was more concentrated on the frontier than in any other rural re-
gion of the United States. Most adult males living in America's "backcountry" during Lincoln's lifetime were in truth landless tenants and
squatters. In eleven Kentucky counties from 1792 to 1819 (Lincoln

was born in 1809), for example, Gini ratios (a measure of wealth inequality) ranged from .66 to .92—far greater than in comparable rural areas of New England and Delaware (752). In the average Kentucky county, approximately 60 percent of adult males were landless; 20 percent were large landholders owning 85 percent of the land; and the remaining 20 percent were small landowners. This latter group—a "middle class of yeoman farmers" (753)—is the class into which Abraham Lincoln was born and reared. Being born of industrious but illiterate parents made Lincoln's cultural background typical. That this family had acquired so much land and property, however, made his economic background atypical.

Lincoln's family legacy was unusual in yet another way: his southeastern England roots, traced through the 1629–40 wave of Puritan migration, differed from the English highlander roots of most of his American backcountry neighbors. The first Lincoln to settle in the New World, Samuel, became a prosperous businessman in Hingham, Massachusetts; subsequent generations of Lincolns migrated to Virginia and to Pennsylvania and became Quakers. Lincoln's mother, Nancy Hanks, who died when Lincoln was ten years old, was also descended from Pennsylvania Quakers. Lincoln's stepmother, Sarah Bush Johnston—who, by his own account, influenced him considerably—was a New Englander. On the other hand, his paternal grandfather, Abraham Lincoln, was a slaveholder owning two hundred acres in Virginia. In 1782, this farmer moved his family to the western frontier of Virginia (now Kentucky) and soon acquired more than fifty-five hundred acres of prime land. Under Virginia's primogeniture law, Lincoln's eldest son, Mordecai, inherited his father's estate; Thomas, like all later-born sons of the day, had to make his own way—and it was a hard way. But if Thomas inherited none of his father's money, he learned from his father's resourcefulness and energy. Thomas's son, named Abraham after his grandfather, thus belonged to "the seventh American generation of a family with competent means, a reputation for integrity, and a modest record of public service" (Donald 1995, 21).

The log cabin in which Lincoln was born was central to the myth of his poverty; however, it did not become a *distinguishing* symbol of Lincoln's life until the twentieth century. Most children born in the early-nineteenth-century West were reared in rough-hewn wooden homes. When Lincoln was born, nine years after George Washington's death, western society was a temporary society—temporary because it was growing and prospering. Brick homes, or sturdier homes of any kind, were impractical for families on the move socially and geographically. Even in towns such as Springfield, Illinois, as late as 1837—when Lincoln arrived there—most dwellings were made of logs. Some temporary wooden houses, however, were better-built, larger, and better-appointed than others. The log home in which Lincoln was born has been considered simple and rude, but in all probability it was much larger and more comfortable than the average western home.

Abraham Lincoln's father, Thomas, built his son's childhood homes in Kentucky and Indiana. Born in 1776, Thomas Lincoln was a skilled carpenter, surveyor, and farmer. He was a conservative, antislavery Whig and, like his son, had a reputation for industriousness and a talent for storytelling. There is strong evidence that Abraham and his father disagreed on most matters, but none that shows Thomas to have been a cruel or neglectful father.[3] At the time of Abraham's birth, Thomas owned a farm of three hundred acres with livestock and horses, and several town lots—more than an average accumulation of wealth. Five years later, he belonged to the richest 15 percent of taxpaying property owners in his community (Donald 1995, 22). During most of his time in Kentucky, Thomas owned three farms. His failure to properly determine liens cost him two tracts of land, but this loss was not a mark of carelessness in a state known for its anarchic array of surveys and landholding laws.

In 1816, the year Indiana entered the Union, Thomas Lincoln moved there along with a wave of other settlers. He chose Indiana because titles to the land, which had been surveyed by the federal government, were secure. According to legend, Thomas, his wife Nancy, and their children Sarah and Abraham, then eight and seven years of age respectively, lived in a lean-to—a rude shelter open to the elements—during their first winter in Indiana. How a family could survive the cold, windy, and wet Midwestern winter in such conditions is difficult to imagine; yet this image of Abraham Lincoln's early Indiana days remains with us today. In fact, as soon as Thomas reached Indiana, he built a large house, began working as a wage laborer, and soon started acquiring land and property. Two years after they settled, Nancy died, and within another year Thomas had paid the debts of the respectable Sarah Bush Johnston and married her. Active as a church deacon, Thomas was also well respected and trusted by his community, and he gave his son Abraham a better start than most frontier boys enjoyed.

The chores and odd jobs young Lincoln performed on his father's

Indiana farm were no different from the kind of work performed by most boys. Abraham, however, had no taste for rural life, and at the age of twenty-two he moved to the small trading center of New Salem, Illinois, where he worked as a clerk and postmaster and undertook his first business venture (which failed). At twenty-five, Lincoln was elected to the state legislature. Soon he took up the study of law, moved to Springfield, and, at the age of twenty-eight, was taken in by Mary Todd Lincoln's cousin, John Todd Stuart, whose political reputation and established practice assured him an abundance of clients. Later, he set up a partnership with another lawyer, Stephen T. Logan. Although Lincoln chose law as his profession, no one possessed direct knowledge of the kind of legal work he handled, or how he approached it, until the Lincoln Legal Papers project was established in 1986. The project, directed by Cullom Davis, recovered from Illinois county courthouses and elsewhere more than 70,000 documents related to the 6,000 cases Lincoln managed.[4] We now know that Lincoln was a principled but not idealistic attorney. He opposed slavery, yet represented both escaped slaves and owners seeking their capture. Lincoln's main practice, however, consisted of contract and real estate disputes, including divorce work. He represented his clients conscientiously, but when they failed to make timely payment, he sued them. From 1836 to 1861, Lincoln won about half his cases and was one of the state's most energetic lawyers, handling more than five thousand clients.[5] At the age of thirty-three, this "country lawyer" was earning twice as much as circuit judges.

Lincoln was industrious, but effort explained only part of his success. Almost anyone willing to work hard in fast-growing central Illinois could build a professional career. Sociologists distinguish between the exchange mobility of stagnant economies, where individuals succeed only at the cost of others' failure, and the structural mobility of expanding economies, where individuals move up the social ladder together. To recognize that Lincoln came of age in an expanding economy is not to deny his ambition or talent but rather to understand the kind of world in which he lived. Many people in this world were less fortunate than Lincoln and were born poor, yet they were carried by this same rising economic tide to wealth, power, and fame. Lincoln's presidential predecessor Andrew Jackson and his successor, Andrew Johnson, are the most notable examples.

Just as Jackson and Johnson had "married up" to women of higher status, Lincoln's marriage into Mary Todd's wealthy family enhanced his professional standing and gained him a solid position among Springfield's elite. When Lincoln was thirty-six, he and his new law partner, William Herndon, were employed by five different railroad companies. By the time Lincoln reached his early forties, he was representing banks, insurance companies, gas companies, and large manufacturers. Between 1845 and 1855, he and his partners managed more than 300 Illinois Supreme Court cases and over 350 federal court cases—the largest practice in the southern (and largest) part of the state. He had become one of the wealthiest lawyers in Illinois, and his political career progressed apace. After four successive terms in the state legislature, mostly as Whig floor leader, Lincoln won election to the U.S. House of Representatives.

Lincoln's Springfield neighbors regarded him as a distinguished man, as he regarded himself. In public and professional affairs, he was congenial but formal. Few people called him "Abe"; he referred to himself as "Old Abe" (as early as his late thirties), but in the sense of distinction and propriety, not backwoods informality. In his domestic life, too, distance prevailed. Lincoln, like all middle-class men, addressed his wife by her first name, but she addressed him as "Mr. Lincoln." This sophisticated man was at home in the city; he remembered nothing pleasant about his youthful farm years and rarely talked about them.

Eastman Johnson captures Lincoln's "self-education" in *Boyhood of Lincoln* (fig. 4.1), an 1868 painting that strongly and permanently affected the popular image of Lincoln's youth. Johnson portrays the future president as an early adolescent leaning toward the fireplace to catch enough light to read his book. On the dark side of the painting appear a table, bowls, and other common objects of farm life, including a rifle affixed to the wall and tobacco hanging from the ceiling. To this scene viewers could bring their own experience and understandings, for few early-nineteenth-century children, especially Southern children, received formal schooling. Even prominent men—such as Lincoln's model, Henry Clay, reared in an upper-middle-class Kentucky family—had spent their childhood literally reading before the fireplace.

Lincoln's few recorded comments about his father ridicule Thomas's illiteracy: he "never did more in the way of writing than to bunglingly sign his own name" (Neely 1982, 188). And though Abraham had somehow succeeded in educating himself, he believed Exeter Academy and Harvard would do a better job for his son, Robert. Abraham Lincoln, however, did not wish to put on airs. Running for office as a member of the Whig Party, regarded as the home of the

Figure 4.1. Eastman Johnson, *The Boyhood of Lincoln*, 1868.
Photograph courtesy of the University of Michigan Museum of Art, Ann
Arbor, Michigan (bequest of Henry C. Lewis, 1895.90).

rich and conservative, he complained about being "put down here
as the candidate of pride, wealth, and aristocratic family distinction";
but even before he left his father's house for New Salem, he had renounced the rustic mentality of his neighbors and embraced the bourgeois outlook of the rising class (Hofstadter [1948] 1974, 128; Howe
1997, 138).

In his early-nineteenth-century world, where the concept of "gentleman" still carried connotations of merit and superiority, Lincoln
may have been ashamed of his family background. On his parents
Lincoln was silent, and his distance from relatives was evident. To
witness his marriage to Mary Todd, a French-speaking Kentucky
aristocrat, Lincoln did not invite a single member of his family. In
personal affairs he was no less distant. On his deathbed, Thomas
Lincoln bade his son come to him that he might see him one last time.

Abraham for some reason declined.[6] This pattern—the renouncing of family obligations and disregard for local expectations—was common among self-made men of Lincoln's generation, men who celebrated the cosmopolitan and national over the provincial and local; rationality and self-control over irrational spontaneity and self-expression. In this culture, self-improvement—character development through self-mastery—was a moral duty. Against these ideals, made tangible in upward mobility, Lincoln measured himself (Howe 1997, 122–28).

At a time when leadership was passing from the gentry to self-made men like himself, Lincoln joined the Whig Party; yet he was inwardly committed to the genteel values of the preceding generation. In 1842, for example, he was challenged to a duel by a man whose personal character he had, without provocation, insulted. Dueling was illegal in Illinois and Lincoln personally opposed it, but as Douglas Wilson observes, "In the self-consciously aristocratic class with which Lincoln was increasingly associated as he ascended the social ladder, fighting was more formal. . . . It was bound by a code of honor, with clear rules and procedures, and, as Lincoln advanced in society he had more to do with people who considered themselves bound by this code" (1998a, 69). Lincoln, as the challenged party, chose for his weapon a broadsword (in whose use he was practiced); but his second negotiated a settlement, and the contest was canceled.

As Abraham Lincoln advanced socially and professionally, he retained his western accent, along with knowledge of country people's figures of speech and informal demeanor. His gift for metaphor, for finding simple phrases to express complex ideas, made him a superb communicator. An effective trial lawyer, he informed and persuaded unsophisticated juries without patronizing them. The step from Lincoln's forensic skill to his reputation as a storyteller is logical and short; yet he never enjoyed sitting around a wood stove telling stories for fun. In his own words: "I often avoid a long and useless discussion by others or a laborious explanation on my own part by a short story that illustrates my point of view. . . . Story-telling as an emollient saves me much friction and distress" (Gilder 1909, 489).

Lincoln's every political act was self-conscious, including his performance as "man of the people." Waldo Braden observes that from the time he entered politics to his election as president, Lincoln "actively projected the persona of a poor man's son." "I was born and have ever remained in the most humble walks of life," he announced in his first political handbill (1832). Debating Stephen Douglas, the

Democratic candidate for the Senate in 1858, he continually compared "the giant" to himself, "a common mortal" and "small man" (1988, 4). Ironically, Douglas represented the party of "small men"; Lincoln, the party of "big men."

The Whig Party was Lincoln's natural political home. As a young politician, he distrusted the masses and thought their Democratic leader, Andrew Jackson, a demagogue who pandered to the mob. Jackson's successor, Martin Van Buren, sought for office "agents who would execute the [people's] will," as Van Buren put it, while the Whigs "cast around for great men" (Ellis 1993, 68). Lincoln, campaigning in behalf of William Henry Harrison, took Van Buren's insult as a compliment. Along with his fellow Whigs, Lincoln believed that leaders must define rather than represent the interests of the people; they must be men in whom the people "can confide better than in themselves" (Howe 1977, 215). Lincoln's ideal government, run by intellectually and morally superior men, would be the "parent of the people" and would seek to maintain "a prevalent spirit of subjection to established law and constituted authority" (quoted in Ellis and Wildavsky 1988, 178).[7]

Believing that a publicly responsible government had to be active, Lincoln considered economic growth and internal improvements its vital responsibility. He also believed that a publicly responsible government must be just, and he shared the Whigs' aversion to the injustice of slavery while rejecting Democratic assumptions about human differences. Egalitarian Democrats could justify their disdain for blacks only by denying their humanity; Lincoln, the Whig, could affirm the humanity of all underdogs, including blacks, and even assert their right to a measure of equality under the law because he could never conceive them as his equals (Howe 1979, 38).

Lincoln never extolled manual labor; he deemed it a temporary condition leading to proprietorship. As a gentleman in a capitalist rather than late-feudal world, he was fascinated with mechanical things as instruments of personal profit and economic growth, not as ends in themselves. In 1849, Lincoln had patented a device designed to buoy vessels over shoals and had written a series of lectures on the history of discovery and invention. He believed that the principal shortcoming of American labor was inefficiency, and he developed the concept of "thorough work" as a means to remedy it (Lincoln 1953–55, 2:437–42; 3:356–63, 474–77). In all matters, he valued order, self-control, reason, industriousness, money, and property.

That same driving ambition that lifted Lincoln above his origins also showed up in the resolve with which he fought the Civil War and the pain he was willing to cause to win it. Against military advice, he ordered the construction of the ironclad *Monitor*—"one of my inspirations," he called it (Cousins 1900, 10)—and he purchased supplies of the latest and most devastating weapons: repeating rifles, mortars, machine guns, and incendiary shells. Exploding bullets, which shattered bone, muscle, and tissue through which ordinary bullets might pass, repulsed the most hardened Union generals; however, Lincoln placed a big order for them. And if Lincoln never said anything harsh against Southerners during the war, he never said anything good about them. His only public statement on this matter expressed his policy: the Union army must kill as many Southern soldiers as quickly as possible (Current 1958, 176–81).

Although Lincoln had a generous nature, this alone fails to explain his acts of kindness and clemency. He never doubted the justice or value of capital punishment. Most condemned soldiers were in fact shot after he signed their death warrants, while all his pardons resulted from interventions on behalf of condemned soldiers by a political representative. Indeed, one of his own supporters, Donn Piatt, declared most of his pardons to be political favors. And the reason Lincoln ordered the release of Confederate war prisoners in return for a mere oath of nonbelligerence was to entice more Confederate soldiers into surrendering (for detail, see Current 1958, 164–86).

Lincoln's reputation for clemency bolstered his image as the "people's president," but the "people's presidency"—and here we come to the final, ironic feature of Lincoln's image—was more a collective representation in which Lincoln clothed himself. He had acquired this image in 1860 by campaigning "down to the people" according to the "log cabin and hard cider" model created for William Henry Harrison twenty years earlier. Harrison, a wealthy gentleman farmer and member of one of the nation's most distinguished families, successfully exploited the politics of personality and symbolism in tandem with the ideological content of *The Log Cabin,* the Whig Party's campaign weekly, by transforming himself into an ordinary frontiersman. Lincoln's managers did the same for him. Their job was relatively easy because Lincoln had always presented himself as an unaffected, small-town lawyer with whom ordinary people could identify; the managers reaffirmed this identity by enlarging and decorating it. The intensity of the presidential campaign amplified this representation and fixed it for good. Within months, one of Illinois's most powerful and dignified politicians had become "Honest Abe," the rail-splitting, down-to-earth, common man.

Lincoln's campaign posters (see Holzer 1993) show that he appealed to an antislavery constituency composed of both sophisticated and ordinary people, but it was his appeal to the latter that distinguished his campaign. As rural symbols enveloped Lincoln's presidential candidacy, Republican clubs named themselves "Rail Splitters," and one of them even devised a parade march formation to imitate the shape of a split-rail fence. Lincoln's managers associated his candidacy with the western frontier and symbolized both with the ax. "Honest Abe of the West"; "The Great Rail Splitter of the West Must and Shall Be Our Next President"—these were the kinds of slogans that transformed Lincoln's public identity and helped him get elected president (Fischer 1988).

After the election, Lincoln found that ax-and-log-cabin imagery undermined his presidential dignity, and he tried to dissociate himself from it. When Philadelphia supporters of the Emancipation Proclamation commissioned Edward Dalton Marchant to paint his portrait, Lincoln arranged for the artist to live at the White House and recalled Marchant's son from military duty to assist him. As soon as Marchant left, Lincoln turned his quarters over to another artist, Francis Bicknell Carpenter, who painted a gigantic portrait of the president reading his proclamation to his cabinet; Bicknell later wrote a flattering book (1867) describing his six-month White House stay. Sporting his first beard, which he grew just before he assumed office, Lincoln spent a considerable amount of time posing for photographers as well as painters. Lincoln did not sit for these artists solely for the purpose of enhancing his presidential authority. He felt entitled to individual recognition. His personal secretary observed, "It is absurd to call him a modest man. . . . It was his intellectual arrogance and unconscious assumption of superiority that [political colleagues] never could forgive" (John Hay, writing in 1866, quoted in Herndon and Weik, 1889. 3:516–17). Lincoln, thus, felt presidential, but no matter how hard he tried, he could not make the public forget he had once been a backwoods rail-splitter.

Supporters conjured Lincoln's plebeian background because it proved his identity with the common people, but critics emphasized it because it justified their claim that he was a boorish country lawyer, unfit for any public office. The presidency above all was too important to be occupied by a man of unrefined accent and ungainly demeanor. Thus Richard Dana complained:

He does not act, or talk or feel like the ruler of a great empire in a great crisis. . . . He likes rather to talk and tell stories with all sorts of persons . . . than to give his mind to the noble and manly duties of his great post. It is not difficult to detect that this is the feeling of his cabinet. He has a kind of shrewdness and common sense, mother wit, and slip-shod, low leveled honesty, that made him a good western jury lawyer. But he is an unutterable calamity to us where he is. (Adams 1890, 2:264–65)

Given the credibility of the backwoods image Lincoln had cultivated for himself, it is no wonder his critics could so convincingly turn it against him.

The Making of a Heroic Common Man

After Lincoln's death, symbols that had helped him gain election reappeared, with a positive twist, in his funeral eulogies. His "ungainly and unpolished" figure, in Edward F. Cutter's view, embodied the virtues making him "a man of the people . . . whose exponent and executive he was proud to be" (1865, 10, 12). Repeatedly, the eulogists politicized common traits by defining them as foils to aristocracy. Homely in speech, uncouth in manners, Lincoln "was yet not so barbarous" as his aristocratic betters (Briggs 1865, 30). Labor being dishonorable in the aristocratic South, it was no coincidence that the emancipator of the slave was a plebeian. Lincoln's life denied the necessity of impermeable classes, proved that the republic could thrive without aristocracy. James Russell Lowell explained why Lincoln symbolized this new democratic order in his 1865 "Commemoration Ode":

> For him her Old-World moulds aside she threw,
> And, choosing sweet clay from the breast of the unexhausted West,
> With stuff untainted, shaped a hero new.
> . . . .
> New birth of our new soil, the first American. (1978, 344)

Lowell articulated a vision of human greatness embodied in the low and humble rather than the high and proud (1978, 342–47). The practical result was a new and more intimate relation between the presidency and the people. Horace Greeley, although critical of Lincoln's policies, affirmed this relationship when he expressed doubt whether anyone "reached forth a hand to Abraham Lincoln, and detected in his countenance or manner any repugnance or shrinking from the proffered contact, any assumption of superiority or betrayal of disdain" ([1868] 1891, 381).

As the years passed, Lincoln's friends and acquaintances supplied local newspapers with letters recalling his love for plain things and plain people. They remembered him as a marksman, matchmaker, diligent student, friendly advisor, ambivalent suitor, kindly father, humorous chief executive. Dwelling on his youthful experiences and on the private scenes of his presidency and domestic life, a growing body of revelations established the affinity between Lincoln and the common people.

Herndon's Lincoln

Lincoln biographies were published and read during a period in which literary realism was dominant. Realism, a post–Civil War development, depicted life in a new industrial society candidly, stressing "the common, the average, the everyday" aspects of life rather than idealizing it (Thrall, Hibbard, and Holman 1960, 397–99). Realism, in addition, blurred the boundary between the common and the vulgar.

Lincoln's former law partner, William Herndon, recognized that the public wanted to know about "the real Lincoln," but Herndon could not, or would not, depict him in a realist light. He devised a "naturalist" conception of Lincoln. Naturalism goes beyond realism by emphasizing reality's underside—the crude and the indecent rather than the plain and the normal.[8] Herndon had known Lincoln for many years (perhaps better than anyone alive outside his family), had been fond of him, and felt that a true version of his life would be the best tribute. It was possible, he believed, for a man to be a national treasure and at the same time tell dirty jokes and make do without a handkerchief. Herndon's Lincoln, born into a world of louts and ruffians to which he adapted readily, never acquired genteel habits. His mother, a product of this environment, was born out of wedlock, grew into a promiscuous girl, and conceived her son, Abraham, in the arms of a neighbor, Abraham Enloe. As a child, Lincoln was mischievous and often cruel. He would place a hot coal on a turtle's shell and take pleasure in watching it squirm. As a young man he used his wit not only to entertain friends but also to destroy slower, less gifted men who disagreed with him. He grew into a sometimes selfish and ungrateful adult who never outgrew his lascivious interests and fondness for smut.

Lincoln's married life, Herndon continues, was disastrous. So uncertain was he of his decision to marry Mary Todd that he left town a few hours before their wedding. The ambivalent suitor eventually decided marriage to an aristocrat would be too profitable to pass up, but he paid for his decision to marry with years of unhappiness.

Herndon's readers had heard these stories before and dismissed most of them, but nothing enraged them as much as his "revelations" about Lincoln's religious beliefs. Herndon wrote a full chapter "proving" that Lincoln was an atheist and hater of Christianity. As a young man, Herndon claimed, Lincoln had read all the freethinking literature, including Thomas Paine's *Age of Reason*. He had also written a book-length anti-Christian essay, which a good friend, fearing for Lincoln's reputation, destroyed.

Before Herndon published his three-volume *Life of Abraham Lincoln* in 1889 with the assistance of Jesse W. Weik (the work was retitled *Herndon's Lincoln* in 1922), he copied his documentation (mainly reminiscences by Lincoln's old acquaintances) and sold it to Ward Hill Lamon, a former Lincoln political supporter and bodyguard, who assembled it into his own *Life of Abraham Lincoln*, published in 1872. Although some readers applauded both books as great breakthroughs in the understanding of the "real" Abraham Lincoln, most were outraged. The public did not rush to buy either book. Lamon's biography sold fewer than three thousand copies. Herndon's sales were meager even before his publisher went bankrupt. A new publisher released the book after deleting the most objectionable material, and its sales, although steady over the years, remained unspectacular. William Herndon's claims were not widely known in the nineteenth century, but they do show where distortions of the heroic common man lead, how the buffoon and vulgar man appear when the folk hero is viewed close up. It remained for Ida Tarbell to set the record straight.

Tarbell's Lincoln

Contemporary authorities regard William Herndon, for all his faults, as the best informed of the nineteenth-century Lincoln biographers; but Ida Tarbell's depiction of Lincoln was the most popular. Tarbell did not create the heroic common man Americans have come to know so well. This image was deeply embedded in America's collective consciousness long before she wrote about it. But Tarbell articulated that image, enlarged the existing conception of it, and brought out its textures and tones more successfully than anyone had before. Most Americans embraced Tarbell's conception of Lincoln, not Herndon's.

The conservative business world resented Tarbell; she had never ceased criticizing business, had written an exposé about Standard Oil's shady practices implicating John D. Rockefeller. "[B]ut again and again," she found, "this asperity was softened by a man's love for Lincoln." Her editor and publisher, Samuel S. McClure, had known Lincoln personally, believed that no magazine could be great if it "overlooked the life and character of Lincoln" (Tarbell 1939, 282, 161), and backed up his convictions with money. Knowing that a decent life of Lincoln had yet to be written, he sent Tarbell to find out as much about the great man as she could. Unlike her predecessors, Tarbell had never worked for Lincoln or known him personally; yet he was very much a part of her life—a bridge between her private world and the broader society.[9] The years she spent working on Lincoln, as she recalled them, "did more than provide me with a continuing interest. They aroused my flagging sense that I had a country" (179).

An aggressive journalist, Tarbell was the first writer since Herndon to carry out extensive research on Lincoln's youth and adulthood. She challenged Herndon's conclusions about Nancy Hanks's promiscuity and Abraham Lincoln's illegitimacy. She discredited Herndon's story about Lincoln's failing to show up the first time for his wedding. But Tarbell's most important contribution was her solution to the puzzle earlier biographers had left unsolved: what conditions and qualities connected Lincoln the frontier youth to Lincoln the president of the United States? Lacking such a connection, Lincoln seemed like two men, one moving beside yet independently of the other.

Misunderstanding of Lincoln's early environment was the crux of the problem. The frontier had seemed to be the very last place a respectable family would want its children to grow up. Lamon called it a "dung hill" doubly cursed by poverty and "the utter absence of all romantic and heroic elements" (1872, 18); Herndon, a "stagnant putrid pool" (Herndon and Weik 1889, 1:ix). Tarbell, in contrast, believed the wilderness was challenging and intellectually invigorating—the perfect preparation for the life Lincoln would lead as an adult. The western frontier, more effectively than any settled environment, filled Lincoln's youth with excitement and adventure, caused him to be self-reliant and to understand the value of labor, induced him to probe and learn the ideas filling the minds of common men, enabled him to understand their passions and to communicate with them in their own language. For Tarbell, Lincoln personified Frederick Jackson Turner's claims about the significance of the frontier in American history, and this theme endured through all her writings, beginning with *The Life of Abraham Lincoln* (1895) to *In the Footsteps of Lincoln* (1924)—a codification of the new evidence on Lincoln's life and a revisiting of her own Lincoln biographies. In this work, her most reflective and penetrating, Tarbell reemphasizes the richness of Lincoln's youthful environment. "The horse, the dog, the ox, the chin fly, the plow, the hog, these companions of his youth became interpreters of his meaning, solvers of his problems in his great necessity of making men understand and follow him." Above all, he had learned labor's role in advancing civilization. "The trees must be cut and the fields cleared before food and shelter were possible. Roads must be opened and wagons built before barter of extra produce could begin." Young Abraham Lincoln saw in labor the common man's contribution to the building of a nation. (Tarbel 1924, 137).

By tracing Lincoln's individualism and egalitarianism to his youthful years in the wild, Tarbell ennobled his early life and stripped it of all vulgarity. She appreciated the earthiness of his mature personality without denying the depth and permanence of his refinement. Tarbell first published her Lincoln portrait in *McClure's* during 1895 and 1896, and within three months the magazine gained one hundred thousand new readers (Thomas 1947, 184).

Progressive Man of the People

In the late nineteenth century, Lincoln's egalitarian image not only retained its salience but was promoted in new ways. Rural and small-town society could appreciate Tarbell's Lincoln, and many urbanites who affirmed her image of him in their own memories had been young Union supporters when Lincoln assumed his presidential duties. As the celebration of the 1909 Lincoln centennial drew closer, more and more reminiscences by Lincoln's young contemporaries appeared in print. "Recollections of Lincoln," "An Audience with Lincoln," "Intimate Personal Recollections," "Impressions of Lincoln," "Lincoln as I Knew Him," "A Boy at Lincoln's Feet"—these and similar titles filled popular magazines in unprecedented numbers during the first decade of the twentieth century. This centennial, then, was in one respect unlike the rituals described by Durkheim—rituals symbolizing a distant past whose events transpired long before the birth of those who were now celebrating. The Lincoln centennial included an orgy of autobiographical remembrance.

Heard by the native-born, immigrants, socialists, conservatives, blacks and whites, Northerners and Southerners, stories told about Lincoln in the early twentieth century were produced by a narrower set of people—almost all white, native-born Northern men, middle-of-the-road to conservative in their politics, and having been alive during the Civil War. If these stories originated from a narrow segment of society, however, their influence was wide. They enable us to understand how Lincoln's image was transmitted and what it represented.

Abraham Lincoln stories are not to be understood as parables of the new Progressive era, but they gave their readers some sense of their own relationship to it. Ironically, the distinguishing features of progressivism—didacticism and reforming zeal, concern for order and self-control, rational administrative planning and control, modernization, confidence in technology and industrial capitalism, the application of science to social problems—were shared by Lincoln the man but were rarely associated with Lincoln in the public imagination. Lincoln stories were commemorative narratives (Zerubavel 1995, 6) embodying progressivism's moral and political, not technological, virtues.

Defining the cultural contexts within which present predicaments were understood was the social burden of the Lincoln stories. Like a magnifying glass, the stories enlarged Lincoln's every contour, revealing precisely what admirers meant by designating Lincoln the "man of the people" and precisely what Lincoln did to warrant this designation. Most of the stories fall into three categories. The first type of story, concerning Lincoln's simplicity and his similarity to ordinary people, explained why every person, no matter how humble, could identify with him. The second type depicted Lincoln's accessibility to the masses, even in the midst of war. Finally, there are the stories about his kindness and compassion, which embraced even those who hated and opposed him.

These three themes paralleled the concerns of progressive culture, and they were embodied in the rhetoric of the progressive presidents. Woodrow Wilson expressed the first theme, the dignity of the ordinary people, more clearly than any other president. Wilson's New Freedom *ideals* were more compatible with Jacksonian democracy than with the centralized power of Theodore Roosevelt's New Nationalism, yet Wilson's *rhetoric* expressed convincingly the needs of progressive democracy. His commitment, or at least sensitivity, to the culture of progressivism is evident in his constant assertion that America was a land of common people—one in which class differences were losing significance. "Where did all of us come from except from the ranks of average men?" he asked in 1912 (1966, 25:505). The function of the political leader was therefore representational. "You are justified," Wilson told Chicago Democrats that same year, "in judging your public men by their ability to think your thoughts and judge of your interests" (24:261). Lincoln was great, in Wilson's view, because he rose above common people without abandoning their sentiments and thoughts. And these sentiments and thoughts were essential because a nation, like a tree, gets nourishment from its unnoticed roots, not its conspicuous branches and fruit. Among "the speechless masses of the American people is slowly coming up the great sap of moral purpose and love of justice and reverence for humanity which constitutes the only virtue and distinction of the American people" (37:335). Wilson's goal was to "fill up the intervals between classes," to establish "connections" between the haves and the have-nots. "What we have got to do is to see to it that each class realizes that it is part of the other class, that there is not any line of division, that the blood of the body politic will not flow if there is any interruption in the connection, in the intimate connection between class and class" (38:535).

The second aspect of progressive culture was the state's accessibility to the masses. Wilson always believed that the ultimate purpose of the state was "to aid the individual to the fullest and best possible realization of his individuality, instead of merely to the full realization of his sociality" (1889, 647; see also 659). In other words, the common man was to be treated with respect and not dismissed as merely a source of faceless labor and military manpower. While governor of New Jersey, Wilson also condemned universities for promoting elitism by encouraging students to "forget their common origins, forget their universal sympathies." [10] Since the nation was "fed from the mass of obscure men, not from the handful of conspicuous men, . . . the American college must become saturated in the same sympathies of the common people" (1966, 20:375, 366, 365). [11]

A third feature of progressivism, the selection of leaders from the stratum of men and women most sympathetic to the interests of the common people, is manifested in Wilson's First Inaugural Address

(1913), which includes remarks on the cost of industrial achievement—"lives snuffed out, energies overtaxed and broken, a fearful
physical and spiritual cost to men, women, and children upon whom
the burden has fallen. The groans and agony of it all has not yet
reached our ears. The great government we loved has too often been
used for private and selfish purposes. And those who used it had forgotten the people" (1917, 17:7868). From the beginning of his academic career, Wilson believed that the industrial order had distorted
competition and induced the powerful to combine against the poor
and the weak. But there could be no "equality of opportunity, the
first essential of justice, if men and women are not shielded from
the consequences of great industrial and social processes which they
cannot alter, control, or cope with by themselves" (1889, 659). Wilson found Abraham Lincoln's greatness in his realization of these
truths, and he invoked Lincoln when he uttered them.

Common Man

Like Wilson's speeches, stories about Lincoln provided listeners with
a pattern for their own lives and articulated, in ways everyone could
understand, the nature of a new political and economic order. The
stories communicated to the average American what it meant morally
to live in an expanding industrial democracy. Most of the Lincoln
stories had a basis in fact but were stretched in one direction or another in order to fit the situation of their teller.

"Homely," "homespun," "cracker box," "uncouth," "plain,"
"rugged," "ungainly," "simple"—these are some of the adjectives
that were routinely applied to Lincoln. The more closely the use
of these terms is examined, however, the more evident it becomes
that their referent transcends Lincoln. Twentieth-century writers who
knew Lincoln personally, or had had occasion to meet him, often
described his appearance. He was not a vulgar man, they explained,
but the figure he presented was less imposing than that of aristocrat
George Washington, whose "gift of making a fine public appearance
Lincoln had none" (Nadel [1917] 1965, 132). Lincoln's imperfection,
however, was one of democracy's signs. If the seated Lincoln looks
awkward in photographs, Gutzon Borglum (1910) explained, it is
because American chairs are mass-produced for the average citizen;
only aristocrats sit on chairs custom-made to fit their bodies.

Tension between commonness and gentility was further expressed through Lincoln's actions. In 1909, the *Chicago Daily Tri-*

bune considered sculptor Leonard Volk's commentary on his visit to Springfield important enough to print in full. After Lincoln's election to the presidency, Volk had come to take measurements and casts for a statue. But the sculptor was shocked by "the man's democratic bearing and absolute lack of pretension." A small incident was most telling. When the time came for a cast to be made of the forearm, Volk asked Lincoln to choose and grasp some object. The president-elect went out to the yard, sawed off an old broom handle, and returned with it. "Would it not have been more fitting for a servant to do that kind of work?" the sculptor asked. Lincoln could only laugh and say, "We're not much used to servants about this place; besides, you know, I have always been my own wood-sawyer" (*Chicago Daily Tribune,* February 12, 1908, 7). The Lincolns did keep servants in Springfield, and these men did whatever sawing the household required, but the vignette is worth repeating because it contributes to a broader pattern of stories in which Lincoln serves as a foil for gentility.

In his choice of friends, too, Lincoln's sense of where he belonged, and to whom, was dramatized in Ida Tarbell's popular children's stories about Lincoln's fictitious neighbor, Billy Brown. In one story, Billy visits President Lincoln in Washington but is about to see the door slammed in his face. "Tell him Billy Brown's here, and see what he says," the visitor requests. In about two minutes the beaming president is at the door.

He saw me first thing, and he laid hold of me, and just shook my hands fit to kill. "Billy," he says, "now I am glad to see you. Come right in. You're going to stay to supper with Mary and me." . . .

Well, we had supper and then talked some more, and about ten o'clock I started down town. He wanted me to stay all night, but I said, "Nope, Mr. Lincoln, can't; going back to Springfield tomorrow."

Well, sir, I never was so astonished in my life. He just grabbed my hand and shook it nearly off, and the tears just poured down his face, and he says: "Billy, you'll never know what good you've done me. I'm homesick, Billy, just plumb homesick, and it seems as if the war will never be over." (*Chicago Daily Tribune,* February 1, 1909, 11)

As we move from Lincoln's being awkwardly seated in a mass-produced chair to his doing his own tasks without resorting to servants and being relieved of homesickness by an old friend, the same opposition appears—the tension between the culture of gentility and the culture of commonness. In each case, Lincoln resolves this tension by ignoring the boundaries separating the genteel and common people.

The Billy Brown story recounted above, described in the *Chicago Tribune* (February 1, 1909, 11) as a real event, advertised scores of other Lincoln stories that would appear in the newspaper's special centennial issue of February 7, 1909. Everyone "will be a better man, woman or child for having read it," the advertisement declared, for knowing about Lincoln conveyed to everyone, regardless of social station, a sense of personal dignity. The *Tribune* was not pandering but reflecting changing beliefs about the political role of the masses. Princeton University president Woodrow Wilson expressed these same beliefs after a losing battle with trustees over the exclusiveness of Princeton's student organizations:

I have been struck sometimes with the thought: would Lincoln have been a better instrument for the country's good if he had been put through the processes of one of our modern colleges? I believe in my heart he'd have been less instrumental for good. . . . The great voice of America does not come from seats of learning. It comes in a murmur from the hills and woods and the farms and factories and the mills, rolling on and gaining volume until it comes to us from the homes of common men. (1966, 20:365, 375)[12]

Lincoln, representing the "great voice of America," became even more meaningful in this respect when compared to other presidents, especially George Washington. When retired general James G. Wilson was a child, he mentioned to President Lincoln that Washington was the strongest man of his generation, a famous wrestler who had never been thrown. Lincoln replied: "It is a curious thing, my young friend, but that is precisely my record: I could out-lift any man in Illinois when I was a youth, and I never was thrown. If George was around now, I should be pleased to have tussle with him, and I rather believe that one of the plain people of Illinois would be able to keep up his end against the aristocrat of Old Virginia" (Wilson 1904, 458).

The words attributed to Abraham Lincoln in this memoir (and it is certain that Lincoln's reverence for Washington would have prevented him from uttering them as reported) refer to the Father of His Country with an air of mock hostility. Washington's aristocratic background is mentioned in a context of conflict. "George" is not an object of respect but an opponent in a wrestling match—a competitor whom the plain Lincoln claims he could "keep up" with, or even beat. Conveying Lincoln's remark, the author recapitulates America's evolution from a republic to a democracy and avows the ascending virtues of the people. General Wilson does not portray Washington in 1904 the way Brahmin James Russell Lowell portrayed him in 1876—as

> this imperial man
> Cast in the massive mold
> Of those high-statured ages old
> Which into grander forms our mortal metal ran. (1978, 369)

Instead, we have an "aristocrat of Old Virginia"—"old" meaning obsolete rather than venerable.

Lincoln's moral superiority was also celebrated in stories about his writing and oratorical skills. Critical historians Charles and Mary Beard described Lincoln as "a man of the soil, the son of poor frontier parents," whose influence as an adult resided in his "simple and homely" language (1921, 342). Richard W. Gilder, on the other hand, reminded the reader that simple Abe, whose use of English outshone that of contemporaneous British prime minister William Gladstone, had produced prose masterpieces that were miracles of democracy (1909, 487). Although Gladstone, being one of the most ponderous writers of the nineteenth century, was not the best choice for a comparison, Gilder's statement seems reasonable. But how did Lincoln's prose become so powerful?

Lincoln acquired his literary eloquence on the frontier, where a man had to teach himself. The process, *Outlook* magazine told its readers (February 13, 1909), was tedious. Coming across an unknown word, Lincoln was at a disadvantage because he had no dictionary. He proceeded by pondering the word until he discovered its meaning on his own, then drew up a list of synonyms for it. "It became a habit with him to put plain words in place of complex ones, Saxon words in place of Latin derivatives, the vernacular in place of the special dialects of cultivated people" (328). Mastering the vernacular, and so democratizing the English language, Lincoln saved himself from his own genius.

Lincoln's story, thus, culminated in the rags-to-riches myth that had become a staple of America's industrialization. Rags-to-riches tales have been told in many ways, but they have a common denominator. The hero, usually coming from a foreign or rural background, begins life in poverty but through hard work and strong character achieves success. This plot may have borne some resemblance to reality in the early years of the industrial revolution, but during the twentieth century, business and political leaders came from economically privileged families, were college-educated, and assumed pivotal positions in established corporate bureaucracies. The theme of rising from poverty to success nevertheless continued almost unchanged. Eyal Naveh (1991) suggests that the rags-to-riches story was resilient during the Progressive era because it legitimated social privilege. But no American embodied this story more dramatically than Abraham Lincoln, and critics of privilege used that story more often to criticize the dominant class than defenders did to legitimate it. The Lincoln version of the rags-to-riches myth celebrates the moral virtues of the common people, not the elite.

Lincoln is, clearly, represented selectively in these stories. None were told by people who disliked him or held grudges against him. Many people living in the early twentieth century still considered Lincoln responsible for the tragedy that civil war had brought their family, but their views were rarely represented in the popular media. Lincoln's admirers told most of the stories, and even they remembered selectively things that seemed important in the twentieth, not the mid-nineteenth, century. This selectivity does not mean that every story about Lincoln distorted the realities of his life; it means that only certain portions of that life were relevant as models for dealing with the new century. Abraham Lincoln's accessibility to ordinary people, a second distinguishing feature of his presidency, lent the contemporary stories even more power.

Accessible Man

During the opening decades of the twentieth century, one observes not only an increasing amount of discussion about Lincoln but also a different way of talking about him. As we follow the thread of the Lincoln narratives, it becomes clearer that their new meaning turned on new understandings of the role of the presidency and the state. That the state should be at once a center of authority and a steward for the people—a representative of the people's emerging sense of entitlement to a minimal level of physical and economic well-being—had been alien to the late-nineteenth-century mentality. Lincoln, as a symbol of the people as a whole, reinforced this new conception: the meaning of "people's president" changed from "president *of* the people" to "president *for* the people."

Abraham Lincoln's presidency was "not solitary, like Fuji; it was neighborly, like the peaks of the Rockies, which rise from a wide tableland" (*Outlook*, April 14, 1915, 859). Mount Fuji was remote and inaccessible; the Rockies, familiar and accessible. Lincoln's was the presidency of a familiar friend who knew the needs of the common heart.

Shortly after he became president, Lincoln set aside weekly hours to receive citizens needing help. As the burdens of war accumulated, he sharply curtailed this practice, but even the limited amount of time he devoted to it was symbolically important and became a key element in his presidential image. Lincoln, assisted by a secretary, occupied a desk and spoke to the petitioner in the presence of other petitioners scheduled for that day (see, for example, Bancroft 1909).

In 1907, John Hay described one of the scenes he had witnessed as Lincoln's secretary. A woman widowed when her husband was killed in combat petitioned President Lincoln to allow one of her three sons, all soldiers, to return home. The president instantly wrote out an order for discharge, but when the poor woman showed up at her son's regiment, she learned that he, too, had been killed. Would the president give this afflicted woman one of the two remaining men in her family? She approached him again. At first he was annoyed by her return. "What is the matter now?" he asked. His tone frightened her, but she managed to explain. Struck by her further misfortune, "Mr. Lincoln responded with sententious curtness, as if talking to himself, 'I have two, and you have none'; sharp and rather stern, the compression of his lips marking the struggle between official duty and human sympathy." Lincoln defined the situation in egalitarian terms, comparing the number of sons under his authority to the number belonging to the petitioner. The second death, however, made the discharge of another son even more costly to the national cause. Reminding himself of his duty, Lincoln hesitated; but he soon gave in. The nation and the widow would now each have the services of one able-bodied man. When he sat down at last to write a second discharge order,

the woman as if moved by a filial impulse she could not restrain, moved after him and stood by him at the table as he wrote, and with the fond familiarity of a mother placed her hand upon the President's head and smoothed his wandering and tangled hair. Human grief and human sympathy had overleaped all the barriers of formality, and the ruler of a great nation was truly the servant, friend, and protector of this humble woman, clothed for the moment with a paramount claim of loyal sacrifice. (Nicolay 1912, 703)

This blurring of hierarchical distinction took on great significance in an industrial society whose masses stood in closer affinity with their elites and interacted with them more frequently than ever before. Lincoln stories treating this topic served as allegories of an ongoing democratic revolution, and their meaning must have been enriched by comparison with older tales about George Washington. When Washington's personal diplomatic representative, Gouverneur Morris, audaciously placed his hand on the president's shoulder, as the probably apocryphal story goes, the great man stepped back and condemned him with a devastating look of displeasure. In the greater liberties a lesser petitioner took with his person, President Lincoln saw no offense. Memories of Lincoln constituted a field in which real democracy could be appreciated.

As Lincoln's admirers recollected his accessibility, they recalled his dependence on the very people seeking his help. The result was role reversals, where the elevated were brought low and the lowly elevated—an epitome of democratic ritual. *Outlook* magazine (February 13, 1909, 39) provided an example in its story of a Quaker nurse visiting Lincoln on her way home from an army hospital. The story had been passed down third-hand, reported by an interlocutor of one Dr. Cookman, to whom the nurse herself had told it. The woman wanted to see Lincoln in order to convey greetings and support from the wounded and dying men for whom she was caring. The president had emerged from an all-night meeting with his cabinet. Exhausted, he agreed nevertheless to see the woman and receive her messages. But she demanded more than his attention:

'Abraham Lincoln, I have somewhat more to say to thee—I cannot go till I have prayed with thee.' In her own words to Dr. Cookman, which I made note of at the time of our interview, 'I kneeled and Abraham Lincoln kneeled and the Spirit did give me utterance, and I did pour out my soul for Abraham Lincoln; and when we arose, with tears rolling down his cheeks he took both my hands in his and said, God bless you forever. . . .'

No brush nor pencil could fill out the details of this picture as it grew upon me, while Dr. Cookman, deeply moved, described it.

The early morning light filling the room as with a baptism from above: the majestic, crownless king kneeling humbly, as a little child before the Supreme Majesty of the King of Kings, and the low-voiced woman radiant with a halo of purity and peace, entering with awe, and yet with confidence, the audience-chamber of the Most High, to bring down strength and comfort and blessing on the head and heart and work of her Nation's chief!

This "Touching Episode in the Public Life of Abraham Lincoln" (as the article title put it), however exactly or inexactly recalled, highlighted a new dimension of political openness, depicting the president as a beneficiary who embraces rather than suffers his petitioners and in the process dissolves the boundary separating them from his office.

Countless other stories acquainted the twentieth-century reader with Lincoln's openness to the people. Some of these stories are fictitious and quaint, such as the one describing the president's showing to his Springfield neighbor, Billy Brown, a hospitality worthy of the highest political official. Other stories are authentic and solemn, including the one about Lincoln's old friend Colonel Elmer Ellsworth from Springfield. After Ellsworth was killed in Alexandria, Lincoln brought his body into the White House and placed it in state. In both cases, the president embraces common men—not reluctantly or under a burden of moral obligation, but voluntarily and earnestly as is emphasized in many other stories by his shedding tears. Lincoln himself breaks down the wall separating the dignity of his office from the dignity of the people.

"A Man Who Would Leave His Position" Although petitioner stories affirmed presidential accessibility, they also affirmed presidential authority, because they depicted the people going to the president rather than the president going to them. Political power is governed by what anthropologist Raymond Firth called the "principle of energy conservation": the higher the rank of an office, the less energy its incumbent expends in fulfilling his duties (1973, 311). Not only do the benefits Lincoln confers prove how powerful he is; his beneficiaries are compelled to visit and to wait upon him.

Before a man assumes political power, however, he must first be a candidate who goes to and waits on the people. The author of "A Boy at Lincoln's Feet" (Newkirk 1921), for example, recollected in 1909 how Lincoln arrived to make a political speech during his 1858 senatorial campaign against Stephen Douglas. Did he enter the scene as would an actor, from a separate entrance? Did he address the people with remote eloquence? No. The candidate for the U.S. Senate arrived in a wagon pulled by two steers. He was carried directly to the spectators and would try to stand to acknowledge their cheers, but the wagon would hit a bump and he would be jolted back into a sitting position. "The entire combination was so ludicrous that the crowd went wild. Mr. Lincoln laughed with them, and decided to keep his seat, raising his hat and bowing while he made the circuit of the half-mile track." He then gave his talk. As the correspondent—then still a child—looked up to the man speaking just above him, "I was conscious now and then of falling mist upon my brow. . . . I had to keep my red bandanna in hand for use whenever he leaned directly toward me; and yet I had no thought of changing my position till the last word was said" (217). To be thus showered with saliva was equivalent to being touched. A common thread of contact united the people to their representative.[13]

Lincoln's tearing away of the harness of distinction was realized even more dramatically among children. The drama was not so much in the stories as in the resonance between the stories and the times. Organizations calling for the protection and welfare of children had moved into the era with a cluster of activities numerous and coherent enough to be dubbed the child welfare movement—itself part of a larger "child-saving" crusade that included the establishment of juvenile courts, germ-free milk, improvement of recreational facilities and orphanages, Girl Scouts, Boy Scouts, pensions for mothers, and settlement house programs (Link and McCormick 1983, 79). In 1912 the Children's Bureau was established in the Department of Labor with the mandate to address "all matters pertaining to the welfare of children and child life" (see Lindenmeyer 1995).

Given its intense concern for children's welfare, the public was especially moved by the story of Abraham Lincoln's reception in Ohio on his way to assume the presidency. The president-elect cheerfully greeted everyone, including a young child whom he stooped to kiss. "You can say, when you grow up, that Abraham Lincoln bent half-way to meet you," he remarked, interpreting his own gesture (Busbey 1911, 282). Another correspondent remembered Lincoln's visiting and playing baseball at his grandfather's Maryland farm. "I remember vividly how he ran with the children; how long were his strides, and how far his coattails stuck out behind, and how we tried to hit him with the ball as he ran the bases. He entered into the spirit of the play as completely as any of us" (*Chicago Daily Tribune,* February 7, 1909, sec. A, p. 4).

The president of the United States entering into the spirit of the play as completely as any child mocks hierarchical order. As stories such as this worked their way through the Progressive era, they became entangled with the issue of inequality and social class. The *Chicago Daily Tribune*'s special centennial section (February 7, 1909, sec. C) described a presidential reception at which

many persons noticed three little girls, poorly dressed, the children of some mechanic or laboring man, who had followed the visitors into the White House to gratify their curiosity. They passed around from room to room and were hastening through the reception room with some trepidation when the President called to them. "Little girls, are you going to pass me without shaking hands?" Then he bent his tall, awkward form down and shook each little girl warmly by the hand. Everybody in the apartment was spellbound by the incident, so simple in itself.

Remembrances of Lincoln's hospital visits further enlarged his reputation for informal kindness. Lincoln could not have possibly seen many of the more than one million wounded Northern men, but his scattered hospital visits endeared him to the soldiers (Davis 1999) and became a key part of his early-twentieth-century persona. George Washington led a fighting army for eight years but was not remembered as a man who spent time visiting the wounded. Lincoln was, in contrast, his army's comforter. The following reminiscence of his conversation with a badly wounded soldier, one Captain Houghton, is representative; it was recorded by another wounded man who occupied the cot next to the captain's:

About 9 o'clock . . . the door which I lay facing opened and from the surgeon in charge of the corps hospital, Dr. McDonald, came the command. "Attention! The President of the United States."

Raising my eyes to the doorway I had my first sight of the president, and it was not an impressive one. His clothes were travel stained, ill-fitting, and dusty; his hat was an immensely exaggerated type of the 'stove-pipe' variety; his neckwear was awry, and his face showed pressing need of the services of a barber. In short, his whole appearance seemed to justify the caricaturists of those days in their worst cartoons.

Unescorted, except by the surgeon, the president, bowing his tall form to enter the low doorway, stepped in, turned a step or two to the right, and, tenderly placing his hand on Houghton's forehead, stood for an instant looking into his face; then, bending down to the low cot, as a mother would to her child, he kissed Houghton's white cheek.

In a voice so tender and so low that only my near proximity enabled me to hear, [the president] began to talk to him. . . . Poor Houghton could only reply with faint smiles and whispers that were too low to reach my ears, but Mr. Lincoln heard and a smile came to his grave face. Turning to his surgeon, the president asked to be shown the major's wounds, especially the amputated limb. Dr. Mcdonald tried to dissuade him by saying the sight . . . would be too shocking, but the president insisted, turned down the light coverings, and took a hasty look. . . . "Poor boy! Poor boy! You must live! You must." This time the major's whispered answer, "I intend to, sir," was just audible. [And here let me say, in parenthesis, he did live, many long and useful years.] With a tender parting hand stroke and a "God bless you, my boy" the president moved to the next cot in line and to the next. (*Chicago Daily Tribune,* February 7, 1909, sec. D, p. 7).

The old soldier who told this story recognized that Lincoln was much more than a kindly man. He did not enter the hospital ward unceremoniously, as would a doctor or nurse. His entry, announced by the highest official on the scene, affirmed the authority of his office. The formalities, however, were overwhelmed by the president's touching the wounded man's forehead, kissing his cheek. The president came not only to console him in his pain but to see his wound and feel the suffering his command had caused, to identify himself with the fate of the soldier as well as the consequences of the battle. The deeper structure of this story shows formality opposed by informality, distance by intimacy, legal authority by personal warmth.

From stories of the president's leaving his executive mansion to sympathize with ordinary people, one learns about the workings of the American mind. One recognizes, with David Donald, that Americans have attributed to the central hero of their mythology "all the decent qualities of civilized man" ([1947] 1989, 166).

Although today's readers might fail to contemplate, let alone understand, the stories, the audience for whom they were written took them seriously, delighted in reading them, never thought them saccharine or corny. The stories were part of life, and early-twentieth-century life was everywhere hard and cruel—especially in the burgeoning cities, where traditional relations of obligation and dependence were eroding fastest. The growth of the city was the context in which Lincoln stories were heard and contemplated. As industrialism matured, cities expanded opportunity but provided little for misfortune or illness, no safety net, nothing to mitigate the calamitous effects of even minor or temporary failings. In these circumstances tales of Abraham Lincoln were told and understood. Workmen's compensation laws and regulation of women's and children's labor expressed the state's compassion for the casualties of the market-place, just as Lincoln's hospital visits symbolized the state's compassion for the casualties of war. Graduated income and inheritance taxes helped make the industrial society more like Lincoln's frontier society was thought to be—a level playing field where the poor could rise above the circumstances in which they were born. In a very real sense, the Lincoln stories were strategies for reforming a world of privilege and inequality. As a model for the Progressive era, his life, comprised a repertoire of ideals (Swidler 1986, 277) from which people could select to interpret their situations, construct lines of action, and interpret the actions of others. Lincoln was a credible model for the era because his life, as it was imagined, was rooted in his life as it was actually lived.

Compassionate Man

Abraham Lincoln's concern for human problems and suffering dramatized progressivism's alternative to the traditional indifference of the state, while Lincoln stories formulated for their readers an interpretation of progressive ideals. In the progressive mind, these stories distinguished Lincoln from all his predecessors.

Andrew Jackson, like Lincoln, was born on the frontier and worked his way to positions of national prominence. Jackson's attitude toward the masses was warmer and more trusting than Lincoln's; his attitude toward the privileged, harsher. Lincoln the Whig wished to limit direct democracy; Jackson the Democrat wished to extend it. Andrew Jackson's appearance may have been more dignified, his manner more polished, than Lincoln's, but he never admired gentility as much as Lincoln did, and he resisted its political claims with greater determination. Nomination of presidential candidates in open conventions, election of the president by direct popular vote, assignment of important governmental responsibilities to those previously excluded on the pretext of inferior background and education, veto of public projects designed to serve private interests, abolition of the national bank in favor of state banks sensitive to the needs of the majority of Americans—these were the kinds of programs that Jackson the Democrat carried through. Lincoln the Whig would have opposed most of them.

However, a president's attention to the interests of the people does not in itself induce the people to idolize him—at least not permanently. Jackson's memory was certainly warm in the minds of many Americans during and immediately after the Civil War, but by the early twentieth century it had become vague. The memory of Lincoln totally eclipsed it, and magnanimity was the trait that made the difference. Referring in the narrow sense to kindness toward an opponent, magnanimity is ennobling because it demonstrates mastery of the natural inclination toward grudge and vengeance. In the broader sense, magnanimity refers to warmth of heart and tenderness of feeling— the capacity to perceive and be moved by human weaknesses that smaller souls exploit. Whether narrowly or broadly defined, magnanimity is the one virtue with which Andrew Jackson's memory has never been identified. His own generation, as John Ward (1955) points out, saw gentleness beneath his iron exterior, but as the years passed, that perception diminished. His expeditious if not illegal hanging of British soldiers in Florida, his outbursts of temper in the Senate, his indifference to the suffering of Indians whose expulsion he approved—these and similar actions convinced Whig rivals of his cruelty and "excessive passion." By the twentieth century, these had become Jackson's defining traits.

Sternness alone, on the other hand, does not injure one's reputation. In 1779, after a military court convicted British major John André of espionage and sentenced him to death, an influential group of American officers endeavored to commute his sentence. General Washington would go no further to accommodate their wishes than to utter a sigh as he signed André's death warrant. George Washington never let his emotions get in the way of justice. His posterity, at least, believed this. Jackson, on the other hand, acquired a reputation, rightly or wrongly, for malice and narrow-mindedness, and this made him an ineffective symbol for an ethnically diverse industrial democracy.

During and after the Civil War, many Americans felt the country would be better off with a leader like Jackson, who always did what had to be done, than with Lincoln, who had allowed sympathy to prevail over duty. Many believed that God had arranged for Lincoln's assassination in order to save the Union from his excessive leniency toward the Confederacy. America needed its own Joshua, they said. By the turn of the century, however, Exodus images had become less vivid; New Testament models replaced the Old Testament as sources of biblical inspiration. The tenderheartedness that had dismayed Lincoln's nineteenth-century contemporaries became the principal source of his twentieth-century greatness. In this new age, compassion seemed godlike. It seemed proper, therefore, to J. Stanley Webster, a legal scholar addressing Seattle's Young Men's Republican Club, to "pause and note the great similarity between the lives of the Great Emancipator and the Man of Galilee" (1916, 1):

Each lived a life of pathetic sorrow and sadness, and was frequently the object of ridicule and scoffing. As the mission of Christ, as Christians believe, was to strike the moral shackles from a sin-cursed world, and to establish mankind in its true relationship to God, the mission of Abraham Lincoln was to strike the physical shackles from millions of God's people, and to place them in their true relationship to their neighbors. While Christ fought and condemned sin, He loved and ever dealt gently with the sinner; and while Lincoln hated and condemned the institution of slavery, he ever dealt gently and considerately with the slaveholder. (2)

Plainly, Abraham Lincoln was to Andrew Jackson what Jesus was to Jehovah. Beneficence and forgiveness, not power and vengeance, were at the core of his virtue.

It seems no accident that Herbert Croly (1909) chose Lincoln and Jackson to articulate the impact of industrialism on American life. In Croly's view, Jackson was an enlarged version of the typical American; Lincoln was "more than American" because his fierce will to preserve the union was accompanied by a radical loving-kindness and forgiveness. Because the "promise of American life," based on inclusive nationalism rather than divisive regionalism, needed a God of love rather than a God of battle, it ignored Jackson and deified Lincoln (91–99).

Fledgling Birds and Sleeping Sentinels Moral character is an essential and distinguishable aspect of a person that is present throughout life. Tenderheartedness was part of Lincoln's character, and it appeared redundantly in stories about his youth. He was tenderhearted all along, from the very beginning. If redundancy clarifies messages, myth must be stated in a variety of ways, and its essence, in Claude Lévi-Strauss's words (1955), always consists "of all its versions"

(435). Each version of the myth includes what others omit or fail to emphasize.

Redundancy is apparent in stories about young Abe Lincoln's relationship to animals. Nineteenth-century stories depicted Lincoln tormenting animals; twentieth-century stories depicted him protecting them. One story published during Lincoln's centennial recalls him as a boy searching for hours, despite his friends' protest, to recover the nest of two fledgling birds he has found trembling on the ground. "I couldn't sleep tonight if I didn't put these little birds back into their nest," he says (*Los Angeles Times,* February 7, 1909, pt. 7, p. 7). In a second story, the young man Lincoln is riding in a stagecoach when he spots several baby pigs trapped in a stream. He receives the other passengers' permission to stop the coach, then steps out and runs to the animals' assistance. He liberates the little pigs, "while the sow, that had been fairly shrieking in terror over their danger of drowning, ran to them as fondly as ever [a] human mother did to her rescued offspring." Returning to the coach, he explains to his fellow passengers, "I couldn't have had any peace of mind if I'd gone on and left that old sow to worry about her pigs" (*Los Angeles Daily Tribune,* February 12, 1909, sec. 2, p. 1). In a third story, Lincoln's family, bound for Indiana, has just completed a difficult crossing of an ice-covered river when they discover that their dog is stranded on the opposite bank. The others wish to move on without it, but Abe cannot bear the thought of the dog by itself in the bitter cold. He convinces everyone to wait, recrosses the river, fetches the dog, and carries it back.

A common structure unites these three stories: Lincoln finds young animals in trouble and is moved by an irresistible impulse to come to their aid. By deciding to help the animals, he inconveniences his companions, but by saving the animals and returning them to their parent or human guardian, he attains peace of mind.

Remembrances of President Lincoln's pardoning of condemned soldiers expressed this same narrative structure. Lincoln was always faced with cases of young soldiers in trouble. They were not professional soldiers, often neglected their duty, and sometimes found themselves in front of a firing squad before they knew what had happened. Because Lincoln usually commuted death sentences on political request, generals complained about his abuse of his power to pardon. If he kept interfering with military courts' verdicts, they said, all discipline would be gone. One day, Indiana representative Schuyler Colfax came to the White House seeking a pardon for a constituent's son, and Lincoln used the occasion, as Colfax recalled, to explain himself: "Some of my generals complain that I impair discipline by my frequent pardons and reprieves; but it rests me, after a day's hard work, that I can find some excuse for saving some poor fellow's life, and I shall go to bed happy tonight as I think how joyous the signing of this name will make himself, his family and friends." Lincoln dipped his pen into the inkwell and signed the pardon (Current 1958, 164). Formal controls were again overcome by spontaneous sympathies.

The best-known clemency story of all, Lincoln's pardoning of the "Sleeping Sentinel," concerns a Vermont farm boy named William Scott, who, after a night of guard duty and a long day's march, volunteers to stand guard for a sick friend. Overcome by exhaustion, he falls asleep and is discovered, convicted, and sentenced to be shot. Lincoln learns about the incident from the soldier's friends and personally goes to the place where he is being held for execution. Lincoln questions him about his home, neighbors, farm, schoolmates, and mother. He urges the condemned youngster to try to make his mother proud of him and never cause her sorrow, then orders his release (Chittenden [1891] 1909).

The "Sleeping Sentinel," as the story goes, later died in battle, vindicating the president's kindness. Lincoln's concern for the soldier's mother, however, is the story's characteristic and moving feature. In almost every clemency tale, the family rather than the soldier himself is the ultimate beneficiary. Since popular magazines and newspapers printed so many anecdotes of this kind, the believing public must have welcomed J. L. G. Ferris's *Lincoln's Last Official Act* (fig. 4.2). In this painting, Lincoln is petitioned by a condemned man's wife. With head in handkerchiefed hand, the woman inclines in gratitude toward the president, who holds an order that will prevent her husband's execution. He does his good deed at an inconvenient time. The desk is covered with papers, the floor strewn with office debris. Behind the guard at his office door wait others with pressing business. Still, the president finds time to convert a young wife's grief to joy.

The politically resonant aspect of the painting is its subjects' physical proximity. A powerless petitioner sits on the president's own chair (presumably by his invitation) and rests her arms on his desk. Her mobile left hand pivots on the elbow, seeking the president, wanting to touch him. Lincoln leans compliantly toward the grateful

Figure 4.2. Jean Leon Gerome Ferris, *Lincoln's Last Official Act*, 1912.
Photograph courtesy of Elizabeth Ryder, Brewster, New York.

woman, placing his hand upon her head, more aware of her anguish than of her husband's offense. This is, in truth, not only a ruler but also a friend.

In Lincoln clemency stories, the characters differ but the plot is the same: Lincoln sees a fellow creature in danger and indulges himself by rescuing it and restoring it to its family over the objections of less sympathetic associates. Such stories could fill a volume; and, with their deep cultural significance, they were broadcast through short story, essay, poetry, and painting.[14] And they fed the new movie industry. In *The Reprieve* (1908), President Lincoln stops the execution of a young soldier condemned for falling asleep at his post. *The Sleeping Sentinel* itself was filmed in 1914. *The Heart of Lincoln* (1915) draws on the same material: a distraught daughter appeals to the president to release her father, held in a federal prison, and gets her wish. *The Highest Law* (1921) is about a Civil War veteran telling two veterans of World War I how he was spared execution through Lincoln's mercy.

Clemency narratives are about compassion and sympathy overriding the demands of justice. They say nothing directly about the society, but their themes typify the political context in which they are told. Stories about Lincoln's pardoning of soldiers assimilate the changing relationship between the state and the individual; they tell of the state's discounting the wishes of the privileged and using its powers to protect the least of its citizens. The progressive ideal of the beneficent state is the context that made clemency stories so meaningful.

Man of Sorrows Of the many tales of Lincoln's softheartedness, one resonated with the people's taste better than any other: Lincoln's first love. This story did more than provide romantic relief from the tragic narrative of Lincoln's life; it was part of that tragedy and strongly affected the way his life was interpreted. The myth's function need not be exaggerated for its importance to be appreciated. People would have thought much the same about Abraham Lincoln without Ann Rutledge, but by the turn of the century she had become an inseparable part of his life story. Ann was the opposite of Lincoln's wife, Mary, in background and personality; her presence in Lincoln's narrative clarifies his relationship to the culture of democracy. The story, relayed by William Herndon in a public lecture shortly after Lincoln's death, then detailed in the chapter-length discussion in

Herndon's and Weik's biography (1889, 1:128–42), goes something like the following.

When Abraham Lincoln was a twenty-six-year-old postmaster in New Salem, Illinois, he became attracted to his landlord's pretty daughter, Ann. She was already betrothed to John McNamar, an Easterner who had come to Illinois to make a new life for himself. McNamar, having established a successful business, returned to the East to reunite with his family, bring them to Illinois, and marry Ann. Many months passed, however, and because Ann received no letter from McNamar, she and her family assumed he would never return. At this point, young Lincoln expressed his tender feelings for her and proposed marriage. She consented, but somehow could not dismiss from her mind her original promise to McNamar. An intense conflict between her duty to her fiancé and her love for Lincoln weakened her physically. The tortured young girl contracted a fatal "brain disease," struggled for a while, then died. For many days after Ann's death, Abe wandered about in the woods, muttering incomprehensible sounds. He stopped eating and sleeping. He began to embrace the "shadows and illusion" of his own "heated brain." Friends watched as "his mind wandered from its throne." The damage was permanent. Abraham Lincoln recovered his mind, but he never loved again.

Granting Lincoln's grief (Wilson 1998b, 114–26), no evidence proves that Ann Rutledge's death affected him permanently. Yet the business of all myth, according to Joseph Campbell (1973), is to guide the individual through the psychological traumas of living: "The happy ending is justly scorned as a misrepresentation; for the world, as we know it, as we have seen it, yields but one ending: death, disintegration, dismemberment, and the crucifixion of our heart with the passing of the forms that we have loved" (1973, 25–26). Ann Rutledge was central to the Abraham Lincoln myth because she embodied this tragic element. She made Lincoln's life a more effective model for living.

The story of Ann Rutledge became increasingly popular during the early twentieth century because it resonated powerfully with democratic ideals. Over many years, symbolic anthropologists influenced by Emile Durkheim, including A. R. Radcliffe-Brown and Claude Lévi-Strauss, have shown how the relationship between objects in the natural world, such as totemic animals and plants, "encodes" the relationship between individuals and groups in the social world. Ann and Abe perform this "totemic" function: their relationship to one another idealizes the relationship between the masses and the state. Ann's love for Abe dramatically formulates the people's growing attachment to the state (manifested in the hypernationalism preceding and following World War I); Abe's love for Ann articulates the state's progressive concern for the welfare of the people.

Abraham Lincoln grieving over his sweetheart's death—was this not the perfect Man of Sorrows? Democratic societies require a Man of Sorrows to define themselves. In him they see their own suffering and struggle and recognize both as central to their collective experience. So critical was the Man of Sorrows symbolism to the Progressive generation that *Harper's Weekly* marked the Lincoln centennial with a cover illustration of a bereaved Lincoln, awkwardly bent over a chair, his right arm resting helplessly on its back, his left holding a crumpled list of casualties (fig. 4.3). Great wars had been fought before Lincoln assumed office, and greater wars—world wars— would be fought after; but no American president has ever been thought to possess so great a measure of compassion.

Whether grieving over the death of soldiers or a sweetheart, visiting the wounded, showing kindness to animals or leniency toward wrongdoers, Lincoln stood for compassion at a time when growing numbers of citizens expected a more humane state. Of Lincoln's compassion much has been written, many pictures drawn, but the Man of Sorrows in marble and bronze (a unique theme in American sculpture) is most striking. Gutzon Borglum's statue, erected in 1911 in Newark, New Jersey (fig. 4.4), represents Lincoln during his presidency, with beard and formal dress; but he does not look presidential. He is slightly stooped and careworn. His face exudes weariness, sorrow, and failure. His body is tilted slightly forward. His left hand, resting on his right knee, hangs limply. The right hand, extended in front of his hat, lies flat upon the bench. As his hand bears no weight, Lincoln's torso appears twisted when viewed from the front. The strange posture is exaggerated by the lowness of the seat, which raises and elongates Lincoln's knees and causes them to jut forward awkwardly. There is no pedestal. Lincoln sits at eye level at the end of a simple, backless bench, where viewers and passersby can sit down beside him. Borglum explained publicly that his statue portrayed Lincoln sitting alone at night and grieving over battle casualties outside the White House telegraph office. The statue did not represent a specific moment in the war but rather the hundreds of dreaded moments when Lincoln had to contemplate its costs.

Figure 4.3. *Bearing the Nation's Burden,* cover, *Harper's Weekly,*
February 13, 1909. Photograph courtesy of the Hargrett Rare Book and
Manuscript Library/University of Georgia Libraries, Athens, Georgia.

Figure 4.4. Gutzon Borglum, *Seated Lincoln,* 1911, Newark, New Jersey. Photograph courtesy of the New Jersey Historical Society.

Daniel Chester French's and George Ganiere's statues, erected in 1912 and 1913 respectively, portray Lincoln with the same lowered head, bereaved expression, and prayerful posture. Lincoln's sorrow became more defining as the years of reform drew to a close and the prospect of war and death loomed greater. Andrew O'Connor's statue erected at the Illinois state capitol in 1918 shows Lincoln bidding a sad farewell to his Springfield neighbors before leaving for Washington to assume the presidency (fig. 4.5). A second O'Connor statue, unveiled four years later at Fort Lincoln Cemetery, Maryland, depicts a seated Lincoln grieving over war casualties. Alonzo Lewis, faithfully depicting "the long, lank, shambling Lincoln . . . with the huge flat feet that had followed the furrows, the gnarly hands bred to the ax," fits his Lincoln nicely to the new genre (fig. 4.6). His statue, installed in Tacoma, Washington, in 1918, has the right kind of awkwardness, the appropriate stooped-over look, the correct "unpicturesque fidelity" (Bullard 1952, 246). Lewis's Lincoln is surveying the Gettysburg battlefield. His face is tired, worn, and aggrieved. He appears as he did at the White House telegraph office and the Springfield train station. Lewis has created another Man of Sorrows.

Figure 4.5. Andrew O'Connor, *Lincoln of the Farewell Address*, 1918, Springfield, Illinois. Photograph courtesy of the Illinois State Historical Library.

Figure 4.6. Alonzo Lewis, *Lincoln Surveying the Gettysburg Cemetery,*
1918, Tacoma, Washington. Photograph courtesy of the Illinois State
Historical Library.

To regret leaving others or to mourn them is to esteem them. This
esteem is why the Man of Sorrows is such a powerful democratic
symbol: it makes the people an object of grief rather than authority.
The democratic icon achieves here its ultimate conception.[15]

Appearance and Reality

Throughout this chapter, we have seen stories defining the character
and virtues of Lincoln that bear close affinity with Progressive-era
ideals. To say that Lincoln "reflected" or "expressed" progressive
aspirations in some strict sense, however, would be imprecise, for

reality constrains the kind of man we imagine him to be. Since memories of Lincoln were externalized by storytellers and other witnesses, hardened into an objective reality transcending their own lives, then internalized by the next generation, it might seem that we are observing people venerating a past they have themselves created. The problem with this account is that it takes for granted what must be demonstrated: why Lincoln memories assumed their particular form. So far as images of Lincoln model reality, they reflect the interests of the storytellers and artists who create them and the critical powers of the audience that reads or views them. In a democratic society where more and less credible versions of the past compete for acceptance, the stories and pictures of Lincoln that are "externalized" must be consistent with Lincoln's actual accomplishments, failures, and personality. The real Lincoln could not determine, but did limit, the range and quality of his representations.

Between the true Lincoln—middle class, proper, ambitious, respectful of refinement—and the imagined Lincoln—working class, informal, content with his lot, respectful of the average man and woman—a gap appears that must not be exaggerated. Lincoln was never close to poverty, but he was reared on the frontier, grew up among people on the move and on the make. His was a society containing many coarse, uneducated men drinking themselves to distraction, trading obscene stories, threatening and fighting one another, scheming for place and privilege, yet essentially fair and decent. Lincoln knew them well. He knew and liked plain people (however superior he may have felt toward them), got along with them, and sympathized with them. In this respect, he never changed. Lincoln also knew men determined to refine themselves in any way they could, men who sought stability, money, power, status, and justice. Lincoln respected these men and eventually became one of them, but his affinity with the masses remained.

PART THREE

Twentieth Century: Symbolizing Unity

Lincoln and the Culture of Inclusion: Integrating America

If an American had returned to the United States in 1922 after a fifty-year absence, he would have been impressed by the capital city's new Lincoln Memorial and surprised to find so many other monuments to Lincoln: forty heroic-size statues throughout the country, a gigantic tomb in Springfield, Illinois, a birthplace shrine in Kentucky. He would have seen many other new memorial sites: the completed Washington Monument along with a score of new George Washington statues, beautifully wrought and centrally placed; hundreds of recently unveiled monuments to past wars, from the Revolution to World War I. Surrounded by this forest of remembrance, the returning American would have realized at once that Lincoln's prominence had increased during a period of nationalism and symbol-making. The spectacles would have astonished him, for many people who gathered at these monuments on Lincoln Day, Washington's Birthday, Memorial Day, and July 4 were not American-born. The familiar, patriotic songs were being sung and the old oaths sworn by foreigners—yet with great dedication. Never before had the country seen so much foreign dress and heard so many foreign accents; never before such spectacular displays of patriotism.

To his own generation the range of admiration for Lincoln would have been incomprehensible. How could socialists and conservatives alike celebrate his memory? And if African Americans still recognized Lincoln as their deliverer, how could Southerners bring themselves to embrace him? How could such consensus form around a man who had so divided his own generation? This question evokes one of collective memory theory's important issues. Every generation has a culture of memory that aligns emerging social structures with traditional culture. In the introduction to this work we saw that Emile Durkheim, Edward Shils, and Robert Bellah provide partial answers to the question of how collective memories remain intact while society changes. Their solutions centered, in different ways, on tradition. Tradition sustains memory, even as society changes and as new cultural groups arrive. Unprecedented labor unrest, immigrating European families with their own traditions and memories, and migrating white and black Southerners to Northern industrial cities pressed the integrative power of American communities to its limit.

At the turn of the century, according to dominant ideology theory, official programmers exploited tradition through patriotic symbols contrived to subjugate immigrants, women, blacks, and working-class people while promoting their sense of well-being and loyalty to the state (Bodnar 1992, 13). Patriotism itself, as Stuart McConnell explains, was devised within "ethnic and class hierarchies, with certain groups [notably the petit bourgeois] privileged to dictate the terms of entry to others" (1996, 117).

Late-twentieth-century adherents of "multiculturalism" and "cultural diversity" conceive the early twentieth century a dark age of chauvinism and bigotry, but this is to see the era in only one of its aspects. The state, not the petit bourgeois, dictated the terms of incorporation to every citizen (not only the foreign-born). States that fail to thus affirm themselves, fail to resist disruption, whether from the arrival of immigrants or from claims of political or regional minorities, lack stability and continuity; they become lifeless receptacles taking the shape of whatever enters or develops within them. In Emile Durkheim's words:

Every strong state of conscience is a source of life; it is an essential factor of our general vitality. Consequently, everything that tends to enfeeble it wastes and corrupts us. There results a troubled sense of illness analogous to that which we feel when an important function is suspended or lapses. It is then inevitable that we should react energetically against the cause that threatens us with such diminution, that we strain to do away with it in order to maintain the integrity of our conscience. ([1889] 1964, 96)

With no collective conscience, no pattern of belief and value to defend, cultural diversity fragments and weakens society, and a centerless society enters a state of constant flux as successive new cohorts divide it in new ways.

Massive immigration from nondemocratic European countries threatened the common conscience of American society, a young society whose government was scarcely one hundred years old. Long-standing concerns culminating in the immigration restrictions of 1921 and 1924, although motivated in part by racism, nativism, and anti-Semitism (which a majority of progressives probably shared), entered into the progressives' effort to substitute rational planning for a free-market approach to managing international labor streams. Social workers and labor organizations were immigration's opponents; large corporations, which progressives opposed, vigorously sought to liberalize immigration policy.

Unfriendliness toward immigrants and other minorities was not the salvation of American society. Rather, the same nationalism that produced chauvinism and bigotry sustained ideals that resisted them and facilitated the assimilation of new peoples. Native-born Americans, a minority in many American cities, had a strong interest in the rapid assimilation of immigrants. The native-born were sensitive to minority-group indifference toward American values. If self-styled patriots oppressed many immigrants, they also provided a framework that strengthened society by shaping immigrants' political preferences and loyalties.

Minorities, it is true, competed against dominant (Northern-born white male) Americans for economic and political advantage, but if that had been the only threat they posed, then only the economically vulnerable would have worried about them. Many Americans, however, were reacting not so much *against* marginal people as *for* something to which they were attached, something above and beyond themselves that the stranger somehow threatened. The threat may have been an illusion, but reactions to that illusion did more than torment minorities; they also generated sentiments reinforcing the values of their new society. Although not always evident in the conduct of their defenders, these values were the ones Lincoln represented—the ideals, not the reality, of American democracy.

If the early-twentieth-century patriotic boom was a defense mechanism against equality and justice, as dominant ideology scholarship claims (Bodnar 1992; 1996, 3–10), then Lincoln, as a prominent symbol of the day, must have been one of that mechanism's key parts.

The minorities—not only immigrants, socialists, and African Americans but also antiprogressive conservatives and Southerners—against whom the ruling class imposed its image of Lincoln, interpreted him differently on some levels, similarly on other levels. Of what did the latter, consensual interpretations consist, and what sustained them? Did they refer to superficial matters of lifestyle and taste or deep transformations that brought the state into more continuous and effective contact with the people? If this consensus and these transformations were not objects of progressive reform, were they part of the culture of progressivism? Mini–case studies, the first of which concerns America's immigrant communities, enable us to address these questions.

Lincoln and the Newcomer

Amos H. Van Horn, like many native-born Newark leaders, feared foreigners; he wanted to see them assimilated and their cultures forgotten. To this end he bequeathed $50,000 for statues of Abraham Lincoln and George Washington and another $150,000 for a great monument commemorating America's wars. Van Horn's will contained only one specification for the Lincoln statue: it had to be placed in front of the Essex County courthouse. Van Horn believed that "in front of the Courthouse the statue would be seen by the many foreign-born who seek citizenship in the county building" and "would tend to awaken patriotism in them" (*Newark Sunday Call,* February 12, 1909, 1).

New Jersey State Chancellor Mahlon Pitney worried about immigrants as much as did Van Horn. His dedication address at the Lincoln statue's unveiling had the tone of a colonial missionary seeking to convert the heathen to the true faith. Pitney noted that the county courthouse was the place "whither aliens of many a race and from many a clime come to abjure old allegiances and to claim adoption into American Citizenship." To them "this monument of Lincoln . . . shall stand as a perpetual reminder of his life and its lessons." The next year the Newark Free Public Library published a small book to mark the first anniversary of the statue's dedication. Its text mentions the "physical and industrial expansion of the city, with its correlative accretion of foreign-born population." In this dangerous environment Lincoln's image was a taming talisman: "The nations move and mingle in this melting pot of ours . . . but of one spirit we are sure they all will be while ideals like this of Lincoln are held before their uplifted eyes" (*Newarker,* February 16, 1916, 83; October 1912, 192).

Authorities knew how much Lincoln attracted the newcomers, how much he induced them to identify with the nation—even as that nation's citizens rejected them (as they rejected, to a considerable degree, one another). Parents and grandparents of native-born Americans remembered Lincoln as the source of their greatest sorrow as well as pride, but immigrants brought to their history lessons no negative preconceptions. Moored in Old World neighborhoods and communities, they could not renounce entirely their ethnic identities, but they had no trouble embracing Lincoln. As they embraced him without qualification, they contributed to his stature and enhanced the strident nationalism that helped to make him so relevant in the first place. Not every immigrant shared the "melting pot" image of America, but most could understand Lincoln as their new nation's symbol.

"Far more than any other American," a schoolteacher observed in 1917, "Lincoln makes the immigrants feel this is their country as well as the country of the native-born" (Humphrey 1917, 237). The capacity of great men to promote social cohesion was a central focus of Max Weber's (1968, 1:266–71, 2:1113–115) account of charisma, Sigmund Freud's ([1921] 1960) analysis of group psychology and collective behavior, and Thomas Carlyle's (1966) depictions of heroes and hero worship. Lincoln's case enlarges their discoveries. They believed that ethnically homogeneous nations sustain their integration by relating the memory of great men to the shared concerns of citizens. Lincoln's commemoration, on the other hand, engaged ethnically diverse communities by appealing to their members' *distinct* concerns. All immigrant schoolchildren were "drawn close to the ragged boy whose childhood was filled with struggle and hardships"; but Polish children "appreciate more Lincoln's economic struggle, the limitations of his country life, for they come of a long line of tillers of the soil; Jewish children, on the other hand, are more interested in him as the epic rescuer of the oppressed, the man who freed the slaves" (Humphrey 1917, 238).

Beneath the immigrants' diverse experiences of Lincoln was the common belief that he would have understood and respected them in their singularity. To them he seemed the patron saint of all marginal and despised peoples. In this sense, Lincoln was the perfect symbol of the inclusive dispositions of mass society (Shils 1975c, 91–

110), mediating the primordial solidarity of the ethnic community and the transcendent solidarity of the nation. Since Jews epitomized the marginal and despised, their representations of Lincoln illustrated newcomers' feelings best of all.

"Why, this man was just one of us," a Jewish schoolboy remarked. He was "one of us"—a spiritual Jew—because he was for the little man. Victor Brenner, Jewish immigrant and designer of the Lincoln-head penny, took Lincoln's identification with the underdog for granted: Lincoln and the penny belong together: "the smaller the value [of his coin], the more people would handle it" and come to know him. Washington and Jefferson are inspiring, Brenner believed, but only Lincoln's profile "can touch a burdened heart." (Humphrey 1917, 237, 238).

Sentiments about Jewish schoolboys and burdened hearts eventually appeared in popular song (Johnson, Bibo, and Klein 1925):

> You say you're ridiculed by all the boys in school . . .
> But when they call you Abie don't you mind.
> There was a man named Abraham not many years ago,
> A better man you'll never find.
> We didn't have the power to make you look the same,
> The best we could do was to give you his name.

Traditionally, Jews name their children after deceased relatives, not public figures. Since the American nickname for Abraham, however, is "Abe," not "Abie," and since "Abie" is a Jewish nickname prompting derision, the song ("Don't Be Ashamed of the Name of Abraham") must have been written for Jewish consumption. Few Jewish families actually named their children after Lincoln, but even a fictional account of their doing so shows how far they had identified with him. Fiction appeals to fantasy and voices possibilities too deep to see.

Jews routinely invoked Lincoln to express their new loyalties. A. E. Chittenden's *The Sleeping Sentinel* ([1891] 1909), for example, provided the model for E. A. Steiner's *Uncle Joe's Lincoln* (1918). Chittenden told about a soldier who dies in battle after being saved by Lincoln from the firing squad. Steiner tells about Uncle Joe, sentenced to be shot for desertion, pardoned by Lincoln, and redeemed by valor.

Immigrant Jews associated the Great Emancipator with their own liberation. In the 1919 Milwaukee pageant of Jewish history, adults and children, in modern and traditional garb (including two boys with greasepaint sidelocks), are introduced to Liberty by Abraham Lincoln (fig. 5.1). At her feet appears the motto "The Wanderer Finds Liberty in America." All adore her elevated figure yet find her remote and untouchable. She does not acknowledge their presence but stares into eternity.[1] Lincoln, in contrast, stands at the people's level, looks at them directly, his arms seemingly extended in welcome. The Statue of Liberty stands for the Jew's Promised Land; Abraham Lincoln, their deliverer. It seemed right. Was not Lincoln like the "first great emancipator of mankind?" Rabbi Abba Silver asked. "Both Lincoln and Moses were born poor. Both were handicapped—one by a defect in speech, and the other by his physical unattractiveness" (1927, 648).

Rabbi Silver's analogy, although slightly far-fetched, shows that Jewish, like Christian, immigrants learned much of what they knew

Figure 5.1. *The Wanderer Finds Liberty in America,* 1919, Milwaukee Americanization Pageant. Photograph courtesy of the State Historical Society of Wisconsin, Madison (WHi [X3]22831).

about Lincoln from the pulpit as well as from songwriters and novelists. Ten years after "Don't Be Ashamed of the Name of Abraham" appeared, Emanuel Hertz, foremost Jewish interpreter of Lincoln, assembled his *Abraham Lincoln: The Tribute of the Synagogue* (1927)—a selection from more than fifty years of rabbinical commentary on Abraham Lincoln's virtues. From these sermons it is evident that immigrant Jews did not learn to admire Lincoln, as John Bodnar (1991) believes, through the clever tactics of WASP "programmers" seeking cultural hegemony, or by what their children learned in schools dedicated to the destruction of their culture. Their own spiritual leaders taught them to admire Lincoln. It was the rabbi, not the Protestant board member worried about property values, who defined Lincoln as the "Saint of Democracy" (Silver 1927, 646). True, American society was no utopia, no paradise of justice, but Lincoln, compared in almost all rabbinical testimony with the ancient prophets, was the vehicle through which Jews thought about their country's faults. As Rabbi Leonard Levy worried about commercialism, he also found the antidote: the "type of aristocracy that is growing up in America, whose coat of arms is a money bag . . . is the type Lincoln hated, and in his name every American is invited to hate it" (1927, 331). America's messiah will surely resemble Lincoln. "The voice of despair, the cry of injustice, is aloud in the land," declared Rabbi Joseph Krauskopf. "That cry will be heard. The emancipator will come, perhaps again from the lowly, out of the hiding place whence Moses came, or out of a log-cabin whence Lincoln arose" (1927, 278–79). In the end, one could not distinguish the sense in which the Jews had assimilated Lincoln from the sense in which Lincoln had assimilated them. But how did the Jewish and other immigrant communities come to revere Lincoln in the first place? The facts of his life framed their experience, but the appeal of these facts is problematic.

Since philo-Semitism and xenophilia were never dominating aspects of Lincoln's historical reputation, something about the way Lincoln's character was represented, or the context in which it was represented, must account for his popularity among Jewish immigrants. Character and context are interdependent. Progressives were by no means friendly to outsiders, but they were far more friendly to immigrants, according to Eric Goldman (1956), than were their populist forebears. Although never eager to see more foreigners in their country, progressives were prepared to accept the ones who had already settled. Progressives spearheaded the settlement house movement to promote Americanization, and they were delighted with their successes. It was also the progressive audience who best understood *The Melting Pot* (1914), a play written by Israel Zangwill, a British Jew, concerning religious intermarriage and celebrating "the glory of America, where all races and nations come to labour and look forward!" Zangwill's play "provided for thousands of progressives an exciting expression of their desire for an attitude toward the immigrant that was more generous and hopeful than Populist snarling" (Goldman 1956, 60–61, 62).

Centennial and Assimilation

Not only the progressive school system and citizenship lessons induced immigrant communities to admire Abraham Lincoln. All "public addresses in churches or schools, plays and exhibitions—in a word, whatever draws men [and women] into an intellectual and moral communion" (1974, 92), Emile Durkheim would have said, also upholds their appreciation of Lincoln. Durkheim would have been essentially right, but the process was complex.

Between 1880 and 1920, historian Eric Hobsbawm asserted, the main political problem of the United States was to assimilate a heterogeneous and almost unmanageable mass of working-class immigrants (Hobsbawm1983). "The invented traditions of the U.S.A. in this period," he added, "were primarily designed to achieve this objective":

On the one hand, the immigrants were encouraged to accept rituals commemorating the history of the nation—the Revolution and its founding fathers (the 4th of July) and the Protestant Anglo-Saxon tradition (Thanksgiving Day)—as indeed they did, since these now became holidays and occasions for public and private festivity. . . . On the other hand, the educational system was transformed into a machine for political socialization by such devices as the worship of the American flag, which, as a daily ritual in the country's schools, spread from the 1880s onwards. (279–80)

To this list Hobsbawm could have added Lincoln's Birthday, celebrated with unprecedented enthusiasm during the first two decades of the twentieth century.

Hobsbawm's belief that immigration was America's principal problem would have made perfect sense to native-born Americans. Immigrant waves fueling the industrial revolution had, by the first decade of the twentieth century, changed the face of the largest cities.

In 1910, New York's population was 36 percent foreign-born; Boston's, 32 percent; Cleveland's, 30 percent; Detroit's and San Francisco's, 29 percent; Philadelphia's, 22 percent. Of fifty-six non-Southern cities with 100,000 or more inhabitants, thirty-five had foreign-born populations of 20 percent or more. Furthermore, many native-born Americans were the children of foreign-born parents. In Chicago, for example, 35 percent of the white population were foreign-born; 42 percent, native-born having one or two (mostly two) foreign-born parents. Only 23 percent of the city's white population—a distinct minority—were the American-born children of two American-born parents. Chicago was not unique. Fifteen of America's fifty-six largest cities of 100,000 or more inhabitants had a native-born nuclear family population of 29 percent or less; in only sixteen of these cities were such families a majority (U.S. Department of Commerce 1920, table 15).

In 1909, integrative commemorative rituals were a matter of practical concern. To assimilate immigrant populations, however, was not the principal purpose of commemorating Lincoln. If there had been no immigrants at all, the Lincoln centennial would have been celebrated widely and enthusiastically. To understand the centennial's inclusiveness, nothing is more essential than an accurate account of the relationship between its planners and participants. Given recent interpretations of Progressive era commemoration, particularly assertions about upper-middle-class planners using public holidays to manipulate the masses into uncritical loyalty (see, for example, Bodnar 1992), this relationship can be difficult to grasp. Organized around instructional devices and public oratory, centennial activities were openly didactic in their aim, but few who observed or participated in them attributed sinister motives to their organizers or felt themselves being manipulated.

In Chicago, arrangements for the Lincoln centennial were supervised by an elite committee of native-born male citizens. Such was the case in most cities, but in Chicago the planning process was widely publicized and transparent. The Chicago Centennial Planning Committee organized events indirectly through eager community leaders who wanted to make the celebration a success. Local representatives had no trouble persuading constituents to participate. Arranged from bottom up rather than top down, the celebrations took place in ethnic neighborhoods having little contact with one another.

Chicago's Lincoln Week celebrations were centered around neighborhood churches. Hundreds of centennial sponsors were listed in the *Chicago Daily Tribune* (February 5–11, 1909), but the churches appeared most often, contributing 28 percent of the total number of public announcements. The frequent listing of churches reveals their importance as a catalyst of assimilation. For most immigrants, the church provided the link between the New World and the Old, the present and the past, at once undermining and upholding the cultural distinctiveness of their community.

Many native-born Lincoln admirers wanted foreigners to live their lives in their own communities, but municipal institutions, including newspapers, represented their city as being free of internal strife, prejudice, and injustice. The *Tribune,* for example, idealized the unity underlying Chicago's ethnic divisions in its February 13 front-page cartoon (fig. 5.2). A symbolic representation of the Lincoln Day parades, the image depicts people marching down an imaginary Chicago business street, each of whose stores is owned by a member of a different ethnic community. On the reader's left is Schmidt's, O'Donovan's, and MacGregor's, then Svensen's, Brunelli's, and Rosenthal's. On the right, from front to back, are Kostakos', Pulaski's, LaRoche's, Klewicz's, and Smith's. The latter is the only English name among the eleven, and it is farthest from the viewer. Although the names are different, the Lincoln portraits placed between store signs are the same, and they give the impression of a chain linking names and places together. A sense of unity is also embodied in flags carried by paraders and waved by spectators, attached to rooftop poles and windowsills, and installed with patriotic bunting behind every one of the ethnic name-bearing signs. To witness the commemoration of Lincoln, as this picture suggests, is to witness nationhood transcending ethnicity.

The *Tribune*'s cartoon appeared one day after the centennial's "Grand Memorial Climax," which began with a February 12 morning assemblage at the city's auditorium. There, Princeton University's president, Woodrow Wilson, addressed five thousand people. Three afternoon events took place at armories located in Chicago's north, west, and south sides. "Every one of [these places] was crowded with men and women, who entered into the spirit of the occasion with every fibre of their beings." The culminating event was held at night at the Dexter Pavilion, near the stockyards, where twenty thousand people gathered. Planners underestimated the turnout. People stood shoulder-to-shoulder, and as the evening progressed they became "joyfully riotous." Reverend Jenken Lloyd Jones, reformer, defender of minority interests, and fanatic Lincoln admirer,[2] tried to give a

Figure 5.2. "Lincoln Centennial Parade," cartoon, *Chicago Daily Tribune*, February 13, 1909. Photograph courtesy of the *Chicago Tribune*.

lecture on Lincoln's life, accompanied by a stereopticon presentation, but few could hear him. When he projected the log cabin on the screen, however, the audience recognized it and erupted with mighty applause and cheers "that must have been heard for many blocks." As one picture followed the next, the cheers grew ever louder. The program ended as five hundred red-, white-, and blue-clad boys and girls formed a human flag to the tune of the "Star-Spangled Banner" and held their positions for ten minutes. A great murmuring arose from the crowd as it watched the extraordinary display, and when the children were dismissed, a final convulsive roar of approval resounded (*Chicago Daily Tribune*, February 13, 1909, 1, 7).

The Dexter Pavilion program was designed to draw people out of their local neighborhoods into a multiethnic assemblage—a kind of temporary settlement house to promote Americanization. People at the pavilion and elsewhere, however, thought of Lincoln in different ways. Some considered him to be the preserver of national union, some an emancipator, some a kindly leader, some an epitome of the common people's virtues. At his centennial, as at his funeral, people expressed their solidarity not by thinking about him in the same way but by assembling in his name—by ritually honoring the same person despite their disagreements about what he stood for. True, people were embracing their nation and its past, not one another, but harsh realities made the ideal of solidarity—expressed in conceptions of a harmonious Chicago—all the more salient. All who attended the centennial observances knew the city's ethnic and class antagonisms firsthand, but the centennial enabled them to feel beneath their differences a common identity as they shared contact with the nation and its past. The next day they despised one another as much as ever— but with a renewed and authentic sense of having something essential in common.

What, then, did the centennial mean? It could be argued that Lincoln's popularity was essential to employers' and managers' efforts to dominate the immigrant working class. They accomplished this, according to Eric Hobsbawm, by entertaining and brainwashing. The problem with this conclusion is that it is based not on evidence but on assumptions about what officials had in mind while organizing the celebrations, and why working-class immigrants chose to participate in them. It portrays the state in the role of deceiver; the masses in the role of deceived.

Early-twentieth-century pageantry was, it is true, a control mechanism designed to express and propagate progressive ideals (Glassberg 1990). "Coercive progressives"—native-born Americans concerned to impose their own ways of living on racial, religious, and ethnic minorities—were minor participants. The vast majority of progressives, were "social progressives" interested mainly in poverty-related issues, and "reforming professionals" who applied their scientific and technical skills to social problems, including physical and mental illness, city planning, and illiteracy. Dominant ideology scholars and new cultural historians, by reducing progressive reform to coercion, fail to capture fully the reformers' impact. Immigrants chafed not so much at bigotry and political oppression as at Sunday blue laws, women's rights, and prohibition of strong drink (Link and McCormick 1983, 99).

Organized around instructional devices and public oratory, Lincoln centennial activities sought openly to inculcate values; but few people felt themselves being brainwashed. Members of the Chicago Centennial Planning Committee certainly had a stake in the institutional structure of the city, and most probably disliked foreigners, but few believed that immigrant masses threatened society or that the centennial should be used for "fostering order" and collective discipline or for "organizing the diverse population of the [city] into manageable categories," as Mary Ryan believes (1989, 136, 152). Committee members possessed power and privilege, but their values were not utterly different from those whom they were trying to enlighten. The committee realized its plans because of immigrants' readiness to adopt them, or to their having already internalized them. Even the dominant ideology theory's moderate version—that "cultural programmers" (as Bodnar designates them) used their wealth and privilege to make Lincoln in their own image—is untenable. The mass media, as has already been shown, placed Lincoln in a progressive, not pro-corporate, or even pro-business, light. Moreover, immigrant and working-class people knew very well that the affluent were paying for the propagation of this image, but they saw beneath this beneficence a sense of obligation, not manipulation. "The centenary observance will be popular wherever the name of Lincoln is venerated," said one Grand Army of the Republic official, "but those who go to the front this time will have to be those who have the money" (*Chicago Daily Tribune,* February 12, 1908, 2). This official also knew that the elite's wealth did not enable it to depict Lincoln or manage the centennial any way it pleased. Lyn Spillman, in this regard, has shown how cultural centers preserve and cultivate society's symbolic repertoire by inviting members of cultural peripheries to participate in their programs (1997, 34–37). But even in Spillman's moderate version of dominant ideology theory, emphasizing invitation rather than manipulation, the readiness of peripheries to accept the center's proposals, although crucial, remains unexplained.

As Chicago's communities could follow only leaders whose direction was familiar and meaningful, the locally arranged celebration had to reflect local values. Middle-aged and younger members of these communities, morally attracted by progressive democracy, participated in the centennial and realized their own interests too directly and in too many different ways—as parent, church member, veteran, businessman—to be characterized as victims of false consciousness or nativist hegemony. Every immigrant community would take some part "in the magnificent democratic ritual of hero worship" (*Chicago Daily Tribune,* February 7, 1909, 1), a ritual which promoted a level of cohesion that could not be reduced to the interests of an elite.[3]

Socialists and Lincoln: A Peculiar Affinity

Lincoln, symbol of ethnic inclusiveness, also articulated the yearning for economic equality. Since there was little in Lincoln's presidency to warrant his becoming a symbol of economic reform, the era's mentality must have included a will to believe that transcended the factual record. In the socialist community, this will to believe was as compelling as it was anywhere. Socialists' political and economic views were marginal, but their way of drawing inferences about Lincoln were typical. The socialist case is good for learning about dynamics that induce everyone, including nonsocialists, to ignore inconvenient facts.

Socialists defined their program as an alternative to progressivism; their aim was to abolish capitalism, not fine-tune it. Yet socialists could not have failed to see their affinity with progressive causes, including the control of plutocracy and improvement of the living conditions of common people. Indeed, by the turn of the century there had developed a moderate socialist movement consisting almost entirely of native-born Americans (Goldman 1956, 58).[4] Concerned to remedy the industrial revolution's excesses (the keystone of the progressive agenda), socialists gained popularity. In 1912, according to Fink and McCormick's count, a thousand socialists held offices in thirty-three states and 160 cities, including the mayoralty of Milwaukee and 70 other towns (1983, 40).

Progressives and socialists found in Abraham Lincoln the personification of their cause, but among orthodox socialists the fit was logically problematic. Socialist intellectuals doubted Lincoln's commitment to equality. Herman Schluter concluded in *Lincoln, Labor, and Slavery* that Lincoln's real attitude toward the working class has been totally distorted by "mythical tradition." He has been extolled as a friend of the working man, almost as a socialist; yet he never claimed to be in favor of the working class, much less considered himself part of it. The few thoughts he expressed on the matter show that while he preferred "free labor" to "slave labor" (as did many Northerners of his time), he was totally committed to the middle-class ideal of people getting rich at one another's expense. His distance from socialism is evident in "his glorification of property and its owners, and by his warning to workingmen not to make war on property." Indeed, if Lincoln "was at all aware of Socialist views and had formed an opinion concerning them, it must have been a hostile one" ([1913] 1965, 180).

Socialists understood and partly shared Schluter's views. They believed Lincoln had been too much the politician: ungrateful to friends but eager to appease political enemies; tolerant of slavery as long as it remained within an outmoded constitutional framework; proclaiming emancipation halfheartedly and conditionally, and at the insistence of more daring and heroic men. Yet socialist communities celebrated Lincoln Day as if these faults were someone else's. Throughout the country socialist clubs and organizations conducted lecture programs and dramas; socialist newspapers displayed Lincoln's picture, printed stories about his achievements, and extolled him as America's greatest president. Children's sections revealed him as "A Great Example for Young America" (*Call,* February 13, 1909, 7); cartoons showed him confronting industrial capitalism (represented by Theodore Roosevelt) by asserting the need for a proclamation to break the workers' chains (fig. 5.3). In federal and state legislatures, socialists quoted the International Workingmen's Association statement applauding his reelection, his struggle against slavery, and his revolutionary efforts to reconstruct the world for the benefit of the working class (see, for example, U.S. House of Representatives 1918, p. 1993). The socialist press quoted endlessly Lincoln's own statements on the relationship between capital and labor:

Capital is only the fruit of labor and could never have existed if labor had not first existed. Labor is the superior of capital, and deserves much the higher consideration.

[It] has so happened in all ages of the world that some have labored, and others have, without labor, enjoyed a large proportion of the fruits. This is wrong and should not continue. To secure each laborer the whole product of his labor, or as nearly as possible, is a worthy object of any good government.

I am glad to see that a system of labor prevails in New England under which laborers can strike if they want to.

The strongest bond of human sympathy outside the family relation should be one uniting all working people of all nations, tongues and kindreds.[5]

The rank and file embraced these principles, but ideologues knew that Lincoln was not and could not have been one of their own. He did not regard the Civil War as a working-class revolution, and since he believed in private property, competition, and inequality, he could not stand for anything connected with socialism. The contradiction was formidable, but not invulnerable. "In his economics," one observer noted, Lincoln "was an individualist; in his ethics he was a Socialist" (*New York Evening Call,* February 13, 1909,6).

What, then, is to be said for Andrew Neather's distinction between nineteenth-century "labor republicanism" (militant and dedi-

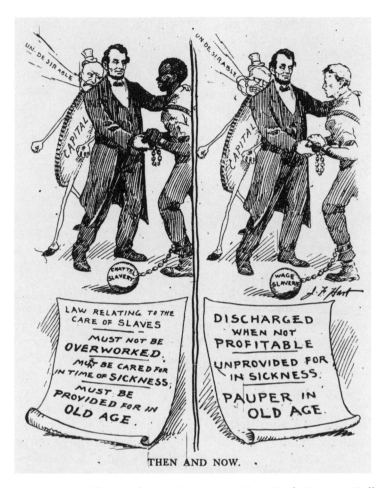

Figure 5.3. "Then and Now," cartoon, *New York Evening Call,*
February 12, 1909.

cated to promoting workers' interests) and Progressive era "labor
patriotism" (a counterfeit movement whose celebrations, framed in
flags and patriotic images of Lincoln, disguised its recognition of capitalist hegemony)? "In its American context at least, even for socialists, patriotism was and is a peculiarly coercive ideology. . . . Business
Americanism forced organized labor to direct more energy into a patriotism that emphasized loyalty at the expense of the radical anti-
capitalist currents of republicanism, a shift toward the '100 percent
Americanism' of the 1920s" (1996, 101). Whether employers self-
defensively mobilized patriotic symbols in the defense of capitalism is

contestable. Socialists invoked Lincoln regularly, but not to disguise a longing to surrender to their employers. Throughout the country socialists agreed that "[t]he figure of Lincoln remains a grand and a beautiful one—a figure to love as well as to admire" (*Call*, February 12, 1909, 6; February 13, 1909, 6). More specifically, and militantly, "[o]nly the tradition of Lincoln" can overcome "evil capitalism" and redeem the nation (*New Republic*, December 31, 1919, 148; also see *Century*, February 1920, 448–50.) Where Marx and Lenin were, there shall Lincoln be. Abraham Lincoln was no mere trinket of "Business Americanism."

Conservative Lincoln

Lincoln would have been surprised to be placed among the critics of capitalism, but the construction is not entirely groundless. If Lincoln's public statements on the relationship between labor and capital, his identification with the common people, and his hatred of slavery did not make him an "ethical socialist," nothing would. Yet the conservative interpretation of Lincoln is no less convincing; its factual foundation, no less solid. Just as progressivism's radical opponents accepted Lincoln, its conservative opponents embraced him because he personified their political and economic ideals.

As the number of immigrants to the United States swelled and the industrial revolution's labor shortage ended, native-born Americans worried about the integrity of their country. In Lincoln they found a remedy. He was not only the greatest American but also "the ideal by whose standard true American is measured" (Bland 1920, 4479). Immigrant minorities "knew" of the attempt "to introduce into American life a spurious Americanization process with the nominal intent of helping America, but with the real purpose of restraining the liberty of 'aliens'" (Teller 1927, 679). But who was restraining whose liberty? The real Americans were the ones being cheated. So it seemed to Reverend John Wesley Hill, respected president of Lincoln Memorial University and sentinel of Lincoln's reputation: "We have substituted the melting pot for the log cabin." Instead of educating white Appalachia's six million "undiluted Americans," the government was spending millions on "the Sicilian, the Turk, the Greek, the Portuguese, the Pole, the Russian."[6] Accustomed to despotism, Southern and Eastern (never Western or Central) Europeans had brought socialism to the United States. How to control socialism was the question of the hour. "This is the decisive moment," declared Hill. "National stability is at stake. We are in the midst of the wrecking forces of ignorant, vicious, un-Americanized alienism. The red flag has been lifted; its glow has fallen upon our National Capitol." Never before, Hill believed, were the ideals of Lincoln more relevant and commitment to them more imperative (U.S. House of Representatives 1925, 4448).

As the prewar goal of "unhyphenated Americanism" was replaced by the postwar goal of "100 percent Americanism," the United States moved into the twentieth century's most important nation-building phase, one that provided a basis of solidarity on which the fighters of its next battles would draw. In the midst of the latest battle, World War I, the concerns of the 100 percenters seemed understandable. How to shape an ethnically diverse society into a unified force? Their measures, based chiefly on exhortation, seem innocent enough, at least when compared to the excesses of European nationalism. Even the tribalisms of the 1920s—racism, anti-Semitism, Ku Klux Klan ascendancy—were symptomatic of nobler attitudes. For Americanism was much more than a crude assertion of Anglo-Saxon superiority, more than a disguise for racial and religious bigotry. Americanism reflected something bigger. Even if there had been no immigrants, no minorities to fear and despise, the United States' new world role would have made its citizens more aware of their distinctiveness as a people. A heightened sense of dignity and power made Americanism one of the decade's defining cultural traits. Class-linked chauvinistic bigotry was an effect, not a cause, of surging nationalism.

Harvard president Charles W. Eliot, like many other Americans, believed that an aristocracy of talent is the keystone of democracy. Staunchly opposed to the leveling of class differences, he was proud that "democratic freedom permits the creation and perpetuation of greater differences as regards possessions than the world has ever known before." Lincoln, he assured his young readers, was as great a protector of these differences as George Washington (Eliot 1906, 55). The *Los Angeles Daily Times* also explained how people would value the American system of opportunity and inequality if they would just think about Lincoln rather than the muckrakers and reformers, "each with a way of making all the successful fail and making all the failures succeed" (February 23, 1909, sec. 2, p. 4). The

National Industrial Conference Board (1920), for its part, drew from Lincoln's speeches the words that most vividly described "the American system," then set them before the public:

The man who labored for another last year, this year labors for himself, and next year will hire another to labor for him.

If any continue through life in the condition of the hired laborer, it is not the fault of the system, but because of either a dependent nature which prefers it, or improvidence, folly, or singular misfortune.

That men who were industrious, and sober, and honest in the pursuit of their own interests should after a while accumulate capital, and after that should be allowed to enjoy it in peace . . . is right.

Property is the fruit of labor; property is desirable; it is a positive good in the world. That some should be rich shows that others may become rich and hence is just encouragement to industry and enterprise. Let not him who is houseless pull down the house of another, but let him work diligently and build one for himself, thus by example assuring that his own shall be safe from violence when built.

Few people alive during the early twentieth century doubted Lincoln's belief in these precepts. Lincoln, as evident in the widely used and understood expression "from log cabin to the White House," symbolized the chance of everyone to advance through hard work. That men shared not only legal rights but also equality in the marketplace regardless of family name, ethnicity, or religious beliefs was a new idea at the time Lincoln grew into adulthood. When U.S. Representative Benjamin Focht told a Republican Club meeting in Lewistown, Pennsylvania, that "around the whole of Lincoln's life was spun the great central idea of human equality . . . expanded and glorified into a fair chance in the race of life" (1920, 8850), he was using the very same words Lincoln had used in his wartime speech to an Ohio regiment: "[T]hat you may all have equal privileges in the race of life, with all its desirable human aspirations—it is for this the struggle should be maintained." For Lincoln, competitive capitalism was more than a system of production and distribution; it was a system of morality, an "inestimable jewel" worth fighting for (1953, 7: 512).

Conservatives had good reason to embrace Lincoln as a representative of their beliefs and values. Lincoln, as Wisconsin Representative Neil Brown explained, "did not need to fawn upon the people and assure them of his democracy." Indeed, if current democratic reforms—the primary election, referendum, and recall—had been in place during Lincoln's own presidency he would have been expelled from office by popular demand after any one of a number of Confederate victories (1912, 2, 6). A staunch Whig, Lincoln believed in both a strong central government and the rights and dignity of labor; but this hardly made him a socialist. "Unlike Lenine [sic], Lincoln did not believe in a free lunch; he believed in the right to accumulate goods and property by hard work" (Williams 1922).

Lincoln, in truth, never believed in a free lunch. But he never believed that the mass of men would always be wage laborers, perpetually dependent for their livelihood on the wealthy few; he believed in mobility—precisely what corporate monopoly inhibits. Such was the progressive understanding of Lincoln's economic philosophy (see, for example, Abbott [1909]). Conservatives, on the other hand, were no defenders of plutocracy. "Grasping and unrelenting monopoly," in their view, strengthened the socialist case and stimulated the strong government controls that would wipe out free enterprise (Goldman 1956, 57). Conservative-progressive tension was, in this sense, centered on contrasting conceptions of economic liberalism superimposed on common problems. Lincoln became a conductor through which these conflicts were expressed rather than a fuse that muted them. Conflict, in turn, enlarged Lincoln by causing everyone to focus and project their preferences on him. Conservatives' efforts to make him in their own likeness were limited, however, by the fact that progressives were trying to do the same and enjoying the greater success. But if Lincoln's presumed friendliness to workers resonated with a progressive ideological climate, America's deeply rooted individualism limited the length to which the progressive image of Lincoln could be developed.

Lincoln's Stepchildren

Immigrants, socialists, conservatives—all were connected through their belief that Lincoln symbolized the justice they desired. The relation between Lincoln and the black community, however, was more complex. From the very start of Lincoln's presidency, informed blacks were aware of his ambivalence toward them, yet they admired him more than any other group in the nation—more than Northern whites, more than immigrants, more than socialists. In the anticipation and aftermath of Abraham Lincoln's 1909 centennial, his reputation among African Americans grew.

Black and white Americans admired Lincoln separately. Excluded from the formal Springfield, Illinois, centennial festivities, the black Springfield Law and Order League condemned the all-white Lincoln Centennial Association, then organized their own celebration. "We don't care that much about mixing with the other race," one spokesman declared (*Broadax* (Chicago), February 18, 1909, 1).

African American experience has moved back and forth between assertiveness and accommodation. When white society has been in a reform mood, August Meier observed (1963), black spokesmen have demanded full rights and total integration. When white society has been in a racist mood, African American spokesmen have urged black solidarity and self-help. During the Progressive era, few reform-minded whites were in a mood to do anything about race relations. As the Jim Crow system, instituted in the last decade of the nineteenth century, became established in the South, segregation crystallized in the North. Even settlement houses, so solicitous of the interests of European immigrants, rejected needy blacks.

African American society became profoundly accommodative and insular during the Progressive years. As blacks were excluded from every aspect of national life, their leaders believed they should replicate the system they could not join by establishing their own businesses and training schools and employing and serving members of their own race. No single leader articulated this enclave ideology more clearly or persuasively than Booker T. Washington. Throughout his public life, Washington conciliated whites, secured their support in the building of schools and businesses, conceived civil rights as an ultimate rather than immediate aim, and believed that blacks must advance economically without whites. To whites he promised: "In all things that are purely social we can be separate"; from blacks he asked for self-improvement through "severe and constant struggle," for no race "that has anything to contribute to the markets of the world is long in any degree ostracized" (Meier 1963, 101. See also Woodward 1971).

Washington knew he could not depend on progressive reforms to facilitate his program. In his Lincoln centennial address he announced, "We as a race, should, like Lincoln, have moral courage to be what we are, and not pretend to be what we are not." He then urged blacks to be hardworking and useful (*World's Work*, April 1909, 11420). That Washington's philosophy summarized the profound dilemma of American culture is evident in its consistency with the premises of the Supreme Court's (1892) Plessy-Ferguson decision. Although never justly implemented, the "separate but equal" doctrine reflected a real tension between America's egalitarian and racist ideals.

A certain kind of Lincoln was needed to represent the realities that Booker T. Washington acknowledged. Lincoln would not be credible if he were a race relations reformer. On the front page of the February 12, 1914, *New York Age,* to take one example, Lincoln displays a scroll that connects the Emancipation Proclamation to the ideal of self-reliance: "TO BE REAL CITIZENS," the proclamation declares, "YOU MUST BE SELF SUPPORTING. THAT IS WHAT YOUR FREEDOM MEANS" (fig. 5.4).[7] African Americans paired this cartoon with Booker T. Washington's agenda,[8] for Washington invoked Lincoln as he urged black men throughout the nation to obey the law and work diligently to learn skilled trades (*New York Age,* February 12, 1914, 1). Proclaiming emancipation through training and investment, Washington became the black Abraham Lincoln; proclaiming self-reliance to be the purpose of emancipation, Lincoln became the white Booker T. Washington.

W. E. B. DuBois's vision of Abraham Lincoln—a man "big enough to be inconsistent—cruel, merciful; peace-loving, a fighter; despising Negroes and letting them fight and vote; protecting slavery and freeing the slaves" (1922, 103)—was more true to life than Booker T. Washington's. But Washington's understandings were the more relevant. As African American political prospects shrunk to nothing, Washington's model of politically docile blacks purchasing farms, going into business, and acquiring industrial skills was practicable and noble. One need not underestimate the assertive side of the era's black politics to appreciate Washington's appeal. His vision of the past, like his diagnosis of the present, was spiritually fulfilling, and the black masses saw in him the revered and beloved leader they saw in Lincoln.

The *Emancipation Proclamation,* a print produced in 1919, articulated the African American predicament (fig. 5.5). In this print the egalitarian ideals of the Progressive era appear vividly, but they are unaccompanied by any reference to justice. The picture, produced for display within the home, represents Lincoln holding an excerpt from the Declaration of Independence: "All men are created equal . . . ." When drafted by Thomas Jefferson in 1776, this assertion of *legal* equality for white citizens took for granted their *social* inequality;

Figure 5.4. "What Lincoln Would Say If Alive To-day," cartoon, *New York Age,* February 12, 1914.

Figure 5.5. *Emancipation Proclamation,* 1919 print. Photograph courtesy of the Lincoln Museum, Fort Wayne, Indiana (3842).

but it is identified in the print as the Emancipation Proclamation, dated September 22, 1862, when presented to the Cabinet, and signed "A. Lincoln." Segregation is thus reconciled with freedom. Blacks who had grown up believing that self-help would make them equal saw themselves in the *Emancipation* print. Located next to Lincoln, Booker T. Washington holds a diploma in his right hand; beneath his outstretched left arm is a rural scene and a table full of books and work instruments. "We have cleared the forests," he says, and are "building cities, railroads, and great institutions." Beneath, a prosperous husband and wife, whose children "are being educated and will become . . . a power in all affairs of life" personify Washington's claim. At the top of the print, cameos of Frederick Douglass and poet Paul Dunbar, and, at the center, high-ranking army officers, exemplify the powers of self-help. On the viewer's lower left, black soldiers, "the bravest of the brave," attack their country's foes. Above the battle, America embraces a black child and a white child. The slogan "Look forward! There is room . . . for achievements of both," implies that, looking backward, even amid idealizations of black progress, the achievements of only one race, the white, have been significant. Abraham Lincoln thus remains the friend of a backward and separate people.

African Americans purchased prints bearing Abraham Lincoln's likeness because—and here we touch on the ultimate purpose of commemoration—something about the prints rendered their experience in a hostile world meaningful. The symbolic Lincoln asserted black obligations rather than black rights, but black writers and publicists represented him persuasively as a man with whom the black masses could identify. They succeeded by emphasizing Lincoln's poverty. His work on his father's farm "was of the very hardest kind. He was ragged and otherwise unkempt. His poorly constructed bed . . . consisted of dry leaves spread on the floor with skins for covering. . . . In winter time his food was even worse than it was in the other seasons of the year," often consisting of "simply raw potatoes" (*Broadax*, February 13, 1909, 1). Lincoln's situation, as described by the *Broadax*, reflects the life conditions of a substantial portion of the black masses during the early twentieth century and these conditions in turn affected the way they conceived Lincoln. To toil endlessly for scant reward, to be at once politically aware and politically impotent, to fight a war yet be despised more than the enemy—these experiences were framed by images of Abraham Lincoln, images that enabled African Americans of the Jim Crow era to find dignity in a world that denied it. Not to avoid suffering but to comprehend and cope with it—such was the aim of the politics of accommodation; such was the function of Abraham Lincoln's commemoration.

No community could fully realize America's political ideals. African Americans had to accept their equality separately from the white world. Immigrants had to be content with equality at the voting booth, for there was no room for them elsewhere. Socialists had to learn to accept the disdain of a nation whose economic and political order they despised. Conservatives would never see the competitive individualism they so fervently idealized. Yet ideals, which are by definition unfulfillable, are nonetheless compelling. The reconciliation of the South is another case in point.

Lincoln, the Blue, and the Gray

In 1909, the melding of diverse ethnic populations into a single national society was a pressing concern, but the most pressing concern of all was regional solidarity. Stitching together the fabric of national unity after the most ferocious war in American history, however, proved difficult. Postwar reconciliation, like race relations and immigrant assimilation, was a social problem, separate from the progressive political and economic agenda; yet it was conceived in this agenda's context. Southerners were utterly serious when they defined the Jim Crow system as a progressive reform: segregation of blacks was essential to unifying America's white population.

The contempt in which Southerners and Northerners held one another lessened as the Civil War generation passed. By the turn of the century, most of the Northern Democrats who had fought so hard against Lincoln and his policies had died; so had the radical Northern Republicans who wished to see the South humbled and transformed. In the South, the Lost Cause tradition had lost most of its appeal. Veterans died; Southern cities industrialized; the new generation, untouched by the Civil War, took pride in their forebears' gallantry but shared only little of their forebears' devotion to the Confederate state (Foster 1987).

Global events accelerated reconciliation. In 1898, as Northerners and Southerners fought a common enemy for the first time in more than sixty years, it seemed as if the nation were stronger for having once been divided. "Old Glory, the Blue, and the Gray," sung in march time, captured the effervescent mood:

> Who dares to say our noble sons won't do and die for right,
> Who dares to say we are divided still,
> 'Tis ninety-eight, not sixty-one, and we went forth to fight,
> United, one flag, one cause, one will. (Murphy 1898)

Notation accompanying the musical score instructs the chorus to conclude "with emotion": "We can defy creation with our fighting combination: Old Glory, the Blue, and the Gray." The basis of reconciliation is clear: Old Glory comes first, then the blue, and, lastly, the gray. Regional identity is acknowledged, but subordinated (the South's more than the North's) to national loyalty. While the nation savored its first foreign conquest, the South's sense of separateness diminished but never disappeared completely. Reconciliation remained an urgent matter.

The Lincoln centennial did not eliminate regional antagonism, let alone hatred of Lincoln himself, but it helped dissipate contentious feelings by providing occasions for Northerners and Southerners to think about the ideas they shared. Northern and Southern leaders, representatives, and veterans traveled to one another's cities and participated together in the Lincoln Day ceremonies. As North and South "stand side by side with clasped hands," the *Chicago Daily Tribune*'s editor exclaimed, the immortals "can see that the Union which Lincoln loved has been saved" (February 13, 1909, 7). In Atlanta, a Union veteran presided over the Trinity Methodist Episcopal Church's first tribute to Abraham Lincoln (*Atlanta Constitution,* February 24, 1909, 6). In Lexington, Kentucky, where Lincoln's wife, Mary Todd, was born, five thousand children paraded. In New Orleans, President-elect William Howard Taft joined with city leaders in a lavish Lincoln Day banquet. In Savannah, the holiday was celebrated in a wide array of public and private meetings. In Lincoln's Hodgenville, Kentucky, birthplace, President Theodore Roosevelt laid the cornerstone for a monument. The speakers included Union and Confederate veterans, the governor of Kentucky, and Secretary of War John Wright, a Confederate veteran. Southern newspapers covered the proceedings in detail and claimed Lincoln as one of their own. Reciprocally, President Roosevelt ordered Jefferson Davis's name restored to Washington's Cabin John Bridge: it had been inscribed when the bridge was built in 1857, but removed during the war.

Southerners were inclined to identify with Lincoln when he was characterized as a Southern man born in circumstances similar to their own, a man in fact closer to them socially than the aristocrat-warriors they had been taught to adore. But it was Lincoln's attitude toward them as Southerners that appealed most. They believed that Lincoln never uttered an unkind word against the South because he understood the forces with which it struggled. On this topic Lincoln's words made his radical contemporaries wince, but they were music to the Southern ear. In 1909, Henry Watterson, then in Richmond, quoted him at length:

The people of the South are not more responsible for the original introduction of [slavery] than are the people of the North, and, when it is remembered how unhesitatingly we all use cotton and sugar and share the profits of dealing in them, it may not be quite safe to say that the South has been more responsible than the North for its continuance. . . . If slavery did not now exist among them they would not introduce it. If it did now exist among us we would not instantly give it up. (375)

Many Southern writers commented on Lincoln's belief in Northern guilt; some attributed it to his moral character. "Too long," as one writer would later put it, "the opinion has prevailed that the North was the only party who had anything to forgive. Lincoln knew better. He planned to forgive and hoped to be forgiven" (Rutledge 1928).

Centennial spokesmen made these points time and again. In Hodgenville, President Roosevelt asserted that Lincoln's most important trait was that he "could fight valiantly against what he deemed wrong and yet preserve undiminished his love and respect for the [people] from whom he differed" (*Charleston News,* February 13, 1909, 2). Secretary of War Wright added that the Civil War was produced by "the stern logic of events," not Lincoln's will. Lincoln would have worked hard to forget and make the new union succeed. Since slavery, the issue that led to war, was supported in one way or another by "all our people [North and South], it was a burden which should be borne by all alike" (*New Orleans Times,* February 13, 1909, 4). Throughout the South, Lincoln symbolized Northern readiness to reconcile on equal terms. Confederate veterans contradicted themselves when, on the one hand, they told *Chicago Daily Tribune* reporters that Reconstruction and slavery were equally vile sins that Lincoln would have condemned, but on the other hand, that Lincoln sought union, not emancipation (February 13, 1909, sec. F6). No one noticed, or cared, about the contradiction.

Great rhetorical skill was brought to bear on the problem of separating Lincoln's presidency from Southern suffering. In Atlanta, Reverend James Lee presented his public audience with a neo-Hegelian interpretation. Abraham Lincoln and Jefferson Davis were identical in character but differed in their relation to "the divine idea at the bottom of American Union." With that idea, Reverend Lee concluded, all Americans, including Southerners, were now in perfect harmony (1909, 13). New Orleans city attorney John Gilmore made the same point: Abraham Lincoln expressed the "inarticulate thought of a whole nation" when he abolished slavery. He wished to soften the blow of emancipation, however, with monetary compensation to slaveholders, which Congress rejected to his great sorrow. So tender were his feelings toward the South that when John Wilkes Booth appears before God on Judgment Day, it was said, Lincoln the lawyer will plead his case (*New Orleans Times,* February 13, 1909, 5).

In Savannah, the rhetoric was equally imaginative. One resident noted that the three marriage candidates in Lincoln's life—Ann Rutledge, Mary Owens, and Mary Todd—were all Southerners (*Savannah Morning Post,* February 11, 1909, 9). The nativity of Lincoln's succession of sweethearts, in an uncanny way, recapitulated history. Ann Rutledge, the first girl, wished to marry Lincoln just as the slaveholding South wished union with the North, but both the girl and friendly slaveholders died. The second girl, Mary Owens, spurned Lincoln just as the South did after his election. The third girl, Mary Todd, married Lincoln and bore him children, just as the North and New South would productively unite. The union of Abraham and Mary prefigured regional bonds.

The nation's preoccupation with regional reconciliation contributed to the great popularity of D. W. Griffith's film, *Birth of a Nation.* Thomas Dixon, author of *The Clansman* (1905), on which the film was based, loved Lincoln and considered him one of the greatest men who ever lived. A former Baptist minister, Dixon left the church to write novels and plays about race relations in the South. His *Clansman,* which sold more than a million copies, portrayed Lincoln in the context of the Reconstruction and origin of the Ku Klux Klan. Opposing radical Republicans' desire to invest blacks with political power, Dixon's Lincoln argues: "We can never attain the ideal Union . . . with millions of an alien, inferior race among us, whose assimilation is neither possible nor desirable" (46). Dixon developed his portrait further in *The Southerner* (1913) and *A Man of the People* (1920); however, it was the film version of *The Clansman* that brought his vision of Lincoln to the largest audience.

At *Birth of a Nation*'s 1915 opening night in New York, Thomas Dixon told the theater audience that he would have allowed no one but David Wark Griffith, son of a Confederate soldier, to direct the screenplay of his book. Only to the most liberal Americans did Griffith's film seem "inflammatory" and "prejudice-feeding" (*New York Times,* March 4, 1915, 9; May 2, 1921, 12); to most Americans it was a monument to North-South reconciliation.

Birth of a Nation's plot involves a network of love interests among the sons and daughters of Northern and Southern families. Before Griffith brings Lincoln into the lives of these families, he shows the Northern president wiping tears from his eyes after signing the call for seventy-five thousand volunteers to meet the Southern threat.

His wish is not to impose Northern will, harm the Southern people, or destroy their institutions, but "to enforce the rule of the upcoming nation over the states." No theme could have been more congruent with the aims of progressive collectivism and centralization. Nationhood cannot be realized, however, until the powers that separate North and South (disorderly blacks and their white sponsors) are conquered. This was the progressive solution, as Northerners and Southerners alike conceived it: to prevent the racial issue from ever dividing the nation again.

The film depicts Reconstruction's "black brute" pillaging, rioting, and raping. Lincoln, however, is above the race war—not so much the black man's enemy as the white man's friend. In the defining scene he is petitioned by the mother of the Southern protagonist, who has been unjustly convicted of spying and condemned to death. At first, the "Great Heart" resists her plea, but she persists and he relents. As he writes out his pardon, the grateful mother bends down to kiss the kindly president but stops and backs away respectfully. "Mr. Lincoln has given back your life to me," she later tells her boy.

That Lincoln would have protected the entire South from its Northern enemies and prevented Reconstruction is affirmed in the scene following his assassination. The story's villain, representing Thaddeus Stevens, is told by his ambitious mixed-race admirer (symbolizing Stevens's enduring love for a black woman) that Lincoln is dead, that now he, Stevens, is the most powerful man in the country—free to wreak vengeance upon the South.

Before Griffith's film appeared, Lincoln's prestige throughout the South had already been enhanced by his centennial. Lincoln Day observances were described in county and small-town newspapers. In Georgia, extended accounts of Lincoln's character, leadership, and reputation—apparently drawn from unnamed external sources—appeared in the *Griffin Daily News, Thomaston Times, News-Herald* (Lawrenceville), *Waycross Daily Journal, Oglethorpe Echo, Blackshear Times, Turner County Banner, Lavonia Times,* among other newspapers. Lincoln's image thus seeped into the Southern countryside, where it had been known only vaguely before.[9] Southerners in 1909 were far from uniform in their respect for Lincoln, but the centennial had made a difference, affirming that Northerners and Southerners were of one land.

The Lincoln Memorial, conceived in its present form during the centennial and erected in 1922, symbolized the reunification explicitly. On the memorial's northern wall is engraved the portion of Lincoln's Second Inaugural extending a hand of friendship to the South; on the southern wall, his Gettysburg Address, which Southerners took to refer to Southern as well as Northern soldiers; atop these walls are Jules Guerin's panels depicting emancipation (which no one confused with racial integration) and regional unity, marked by the Angel of Truth joining the hands of female allegories of the North and the South.

The Language of Dissensus

Variant perspectives on Lincoln—immigrant, socialist, conservative, African American, and Southern—show how the content of collective memory is influenced by the experiences and mentalities of the communities invoking it. Different memories result, however, from a common method of making them meaningful: selecting the elements of Lincoln's life to be included in its representation and translating these into a form that will maintain their relevance. Thus, immigrants emphasized Lincoln's belief in the dignity of all people; socialists commemorated his views on labor and interpreted them in conformity with their priorities; conservatives saw the guiding force of Lincoln's life to be his respect for the right to accumulate property; blacks celebrated their emancipation and regretted that conservative whites did not put into practice Lincoln's belief in a fair starting place in the race of life; Southerners recalled his understanding of the Confederate cause, affection for the South and its people, and longing for regional reconciliation.

That different groups, positioned differently and moved by different interests and following different interpretive conventions, arrived at different images of Lincoln does not mean that the real Lincoln is unknowable and that all images of him are contrived. Through the deliberately selective conceptions of artists, writers, editors, clergymen, newspaper reporters and commentators, booksellers, and teachers, separate communities become aware of alternate conceptions of Lincoln and, indeed, agree with many if not most of them. Thus, blacks reading about Lincoln in city newspapers and whites reading about Lincoln in black newspapers would notice variations on the image to which they had become accustomed, but they would find these accounts of Lincoln familiar and often acceptable.

The concepts of Ferdinand de Saussure (1966), the linguist, can be usefully applied to this situation. Saussure considered language in terms of two fundamental dimensions: *langue* and *parole*. His notion of *langue* is equivalent to the abstract system of vocabulary and grammatical rules which in English we call "language." His notion of *parole*, which we call "speech," refers to the infinite number of concrete utterances made by the speakers of a language. Extending Saussure's distinction, diverse images of Lincoln appears as different "utterances" of the same language. They refer to different aspects of the real Lincoln, matters of liking or disliking him in different degrees, of emphasizing different parts of his life. Thus, not everyone remembers the man in the same way, but everyone recognizes the same man. As different sentences enact the unseen reality of a single language, so different depictions of Lincoln enact one of the many sides of the same man. This does not mean that some groups were more justified in identifying with Lincoln than others; it means that Lincoln himself was ambiguous, complex, and many-sided, and that different communities, according to their experiences and interests, saw one side more clearly than others.

Collective memory proceeds from historical realities admitting of both divergent and unifying conceptions. Rarely has the unifying conception of Lincoln been more compelling than during World War I. During this great war, we learn readily that collective memory articulates widely shared ideals—in this case progressive ideals—about how a virtuous world must be structured.

Abraham Lincoln in World War I: Strengthening America

From Abraham Lincoln's death in 1865 to the 1922 dedication of his memorial in Washington, D.C., different communities, ranging from immigrant and native-born men and women to blacks and Southerners, found different meanings in his life and presidency. Partisans did the most to promote Lincoln's memory. Political officials organized his funeral rites, Republican organizations covered most of their expense, while Lincoln's personal friends and political supporters—influential businessmen, attorneys, and politicians—contributed most to the construction of his statues and monuments, and the organization of annual Lincoln Day festivities. A broader range of communities arranged his centennial celebration and the planning of his national memorial.

Lincoln's nineteenth-century admirers failed to persuade the nation to adore him; their efforts, however, laid the basis for his expanded twentieth-century reputation. During the Progressive era Lincoln's image framed a wider range of experience than ever before. He appeared as the first progressive, embodying the ideals of universal suffrage, temperance, just distribution of income, fair treatment of labor, and help for the poor. His life and labors justified election reform, anticorporation legislation, and regional reconciliation; his moral values justified self-sacrifice and war.

War weakens routine and causes fear and death. World war, in addition, threatens national existence and requires universal sacrifice. In wartime, more than ever, people seek orientation by linking present troubles to the challenges of the past. Linked to their national heritage, new forms of authority, cooperation, and sacrifice become meaningful. During America's first Great War, World War I, the invocation of Abraham Lincoln's memory aligned America's new geopolitical situation to its political traditions.

The Past in the Present

World War I provided new lessons on how we learn about and distort the past. Film, magazine, and newspaper accounts of the war and its aftermath, raised questions about commemoration and history, social networks as repositories of memory, partial or complete forgetting of events, official memories and counter memories, successful and failed interpretations of the past. World War I was also a *site* of memory, and by analyzing it as such we move from memory *of* crisis to memory *in the time of* crisis. Since crisis gives nations their strongest incentive for invoking the past (Bellah 1975, 141), Abraham Lincoln's function in World War I warrants close examination. Previous chapters have shown Lincoln's memory framing an era of reform; this chapter shows Lincoln's memory framing an era of war. At no time between 1865 and 1922 did the Lincoln image better lend itself to this purpose. World War I was the pivot of twentieth-century American history because it transformed the United States from a regional into a global power, and Americans explained to themselves this new sense of political responsibility by looking backward.

Memory as a Social Frame

Looking backward enables people to frame their experience of the world. My model of the framing process, although tentative, rests on a strong premise: "Every conscious perception is . . . an act of recognition, a pairing in which an object (or an event, an act, an emotion) is identified by placing it against the background of an appropriate symbol" (Geertz 1973b, 215).

Two concepts explicate memory as a "recognizing" and "pairing" accomplishment. First, shared memories become appropriate symbols—backgrounds for the perception and comprehension of current events—when organized into what Goffman called a "primary framework": *primary* because "application of such a framework or perspective is seen by those who apply it as not depending on or harking back to some prior or 'original' interpretation; indeed a primary framework is one that is seen as rendering what would otherwise be a meaningless aspect of the scene into something that is meaningful" (1974, 21). I have changed this model slightly. Instead of comparing primary events to secondary copies, I consider how participants in one primary event, the First World War, interpret their experience by aligning it to another primary event, the Civil War.

Keying transforms the meaning of activities understood in terms of one event by comparing them with activities understood in terms of another. Reactions to Woodrow Wilson's death in 1924, for example, assume new meaning when keyed to reactions to Lincoln's death in 1865. "Keying" is more than a new word for analogical thinking, more than a way individuals mentally organize their social experience (Goffman 1974, 40–82, especially 43–44); keying transforms memory into a cultural system because it matches publicly accessible (i.e., symbolic) models of the past (written narratives, pictorial images, statues, motion pictures, music, and songs) to the experiences of the present (Geertz 1973b, 214). Keying arranges cultural symbols into a publicly visible discourse that flows through the organizations and institutions of the social world. Keying is communicative movement—talk, writing, image- and music-making—that connects otherwise separate realms of history.

Abraham Lincoln was good for thinking about World War I, just as he had been good for thinking about the Progressive era.[1] Critical historians define World War I, no less than the era's progressive reforms, as an event consolidating capitalist exploitation and domestic injustice for the next several decades. The triumph of state liberalism, in John Bodnar's words, led directly to the glorification of state power, masculine aggressiveness, the "idealization of male warrior heroism and aggressive nationalism" (1992, 13). True, American nationalism became more aggressive during the war, but the war itself was more than the celebration of aggressive manliness.

The moral bent of Americans' martial attitudes made Lincoln the perfect symbol for perceiving and comprehending their first global war. Protestant-inspired moralism, Seymour M. Lipset has argued, determines the way Americans have always gone to war. "To endorse a war and call on people to kill others and die for their country,

Americans must define their role in a conflict as being on God's side against Satan—for morality against evil" (1996, 20). This morality is why American publicists summoned Abraham Lincoln so often during the Great War. All belligerent nations convened their past heroes to mobilize wartime motivation, but not as often as Americans convened Lincoln. Lincoln's face appeared on domestic propaganda literature because it infused the war effort with an egalitarian-individualist legacy no other American hero so well embodied.

Lincoln was not the only symbol of the egalitarian-individualist legacy, but his image was most relevant because the generation that fought the Great War lived in an environment filled with his memories. For years this generation had heard stories idealizing Lincoln and making him relevant to domestic political and economic problems; now it found him relevant to global and military ones. Thus, the patriotic song "Abraham Lincoln, What Would You Do?" (Hirsh 1918) defined the war's purpose in terms of the people's debt to Lincoln: "Abraham Lincoln, we owe it to you, to protect this great country today. . . ." That Lincoln represents a guide as well as a creditor is evident on the sheet music cover, which shows America, in her unprecedented predicament, looking up to Lincoln's statue (recently dedicated at his birthplace in Hodgenville, Kentucky),[2] her arms open and receptive to his example (fig. 6.1). Songwriters Alfred Bryan and Harry Tierney, too, explained that "It's Time for Every Boy to Be a Soldier" (1917) so that "the nation of the people, by the people, for the people shall not perish from the earth." No man represented the cause better than Lincoln, and one song after another invoked him to communicate the war's meaning. Song lyrics interpreted the war by embedding it in the story of the nation. "Don't say that all the statesmen died with Lincoln. . . . You'll find we've still the power to produce men of the hour" (Moore and Williams 1917). America's legacy is secure because its men and women are greater than the crises they confront.

Throughout World War I, the American Revolution was also conjured; its hero, George Washington, also recalled. But the Civil War (the "Second American Revolution," as McPherson [1991] calls it) established the democracy for which the World War I generation fought. Morality is the "cultural code" to which a historical event must fit rhetorically if it is to become a model for current events (Smith 1991, 191). Civil War memories include the clearest examples of moral virtue, like endurance in the face of great loss; moral goals, like emancipation and the preservation of the Union; moral values,

Figure 6.1. "Abraham Lincoln, What Would You Do?" 1918 sheet music cover. Photograph, from the DeVincent Collection, courtesy of the Archives Center, National Museum of American History, Smithsonian Institution.

like equality and dignity of the common man, moral exemplars, like Abraham Lincoln. Thus, the Civil War furnished the themes of American civil religion: death, sacrifice, and rebirth (Bellah 1970, 177–78); and throughout the Great War Lincoln's image, alone and joined with George Washington's, legitimated, oriented, clarified, inspired, and consoled.

History as a Vehicle of Conception

World War I established the United States as a world power, but the American experience of the war resulted as much from its unprecedented violence as from its geopolitical consequence. Europeans made sense of the loss of thirteen million lives by viewing the war as a sacred event (Mosse 1990). Their allegorical images, including military versions of the *Pietà*—statues of dead soldiers borne in the arms of angels (keyed to the dead Christ borne in the arms of Mary)—idealized the war by fusing political and religious sentiments. America's fatalities, 117,000, were relatively light, but its mood, influenced by Europe's, was somber. Americans realized they were engaged in the greatest war in human history, a war for which no precedent existed—which is why they so often invoked the Civil War, the greatest war in American history. The narrative of the Civil War "suggests many points of likeness between the America of 1860–5 and that of today [1917]: there was the same prolonged hesitation as to the moral issues of the war, and the same inexorable determination of the country when the decision was reached" (Macdonell 1917, 562). Looking to the past for present bearing, everyone needed to know what Lincoln would do were he alive and president again.

Lincoln, emblem of progressivism, framed the Great War so suitably because the latter, in many important respects, incarnated the spirit of the Progressive era. Many progressives opposed the war from beginning to end, but most supported it and viewed war preparation through progressive lenses. Assertion of federal power in national affairs, subordination of self-interest to the collective good, equal imposition of duty, regardless of birth, wealth, or status, were as evident in military mobilization as in progressive political ideals. Since the draft was the essence of democracy, it contributed in the long run to social improvement. Military training epitomized citizenship training, and fighting Germany abroad was no different morally from fighting corruption, exploitation, and vice at home. Progressives therefore stood prominently among the war's supporters, and their magazines and journals (Decker 1986; also see Meigs 1994) projected the ideals of the Progressive era beyond the domestic scene to the entire world (Current 1987, 68). Just as Lincoln had earlier become a vehicle of progressive reform, he now articulated the meaning of America's military struggle. Images of Lincoln clarified the war by defining the goals of the president, spelling out the war's purpose, and interpreting its suffering.

Lincoln and Wilson

No reason exists to bring up the past, George Herbert Mead believed (1929, 1932), if some significant problem is not disrupting normal patterns of life or effective action. Woodrow Wilson's problem was his and the public's reluctance to go to war. Hesitation was natural, even after the May 1915 sinking of the *Lusitania,* because America's interest in the war was problematic; its experience at waging full-scale foreign war, nil. Some Americans, however, were eager for war, and they could find no better model than Lincoln for criticizing Wilson's caution. Denouncing Wilson's explanation of his policy of non-belligerence, the *New York Tribune*'s editor observed that Lincoln "never considered, before calling the country to arms, whether, after all, he might not 'serve humanity' better by being 'too proud to fight.'" The *Tribune* editor pursued the parallel in biting detail:

Lincoln did not demand a disavowal of Beauregard's attack on Sumter and reparation for injuries done to its defenders. He did not conduct precarious negotiations for nearly two years thereafter, submitting to various repetitions of the original attack and finally obtaining some qualified promises that such attacks would cease. He did not remain on amicable relations with the Confederacy until the latter decided to cancel its qualified pledges and to resume the bombardment of Federal forts. And, finally, he did not wait after receiving notice that the Confederacy no longer admitted that the United States had any rights which it was bound to respect, for some "overt act" which was to prove beyond peradventure that the South's leaders meant what they said. (February 12, 1917, 8)

At length, Wilson asked Congress to declare war, and on Good Friday 1918, fifty-three years after the very day Lincoln was shot, sent American troops to Europe. As American armies engaged the enemy, Wilson and Lincoln began to look increasingly alike.

Given Wilson's professed appreciation of the common man and disdain for elitism, it seemed right for admirers to compare him with Lincoln. Parallels appeared in congressional addresses, magazines, newspapers, and sermons: Lincoln suffered attacks motivated by meanness and partisan prejudice. So does Wilson. Lincoln was accused of waiting too long to go to war. So is Wilson. Lincoln's war policy was designed to reorder society permanently and prevent future wars. So is Wilson's. Lincoln was magnanimous to his enemies. So is Wilson. Lincoln enlarged the power of the presidency. So has Wilson. "Lincoln was the apostle of democracy and before he died he lived to see the whole of America come to him. Today we have a new apostle of democracy: we will live to see the whole world come to him" (*Milwaukee Journal,* February 12, 1918, 6).

Wilson's conduct became more comprehensible when defined as a version of Lincoln's. Recognizing that legal authority is rooted in tradition, "the sanctity of the order and the attendant powers of control as they have been handed down from the past and always existed" (Weber 1947, 341), Wilson men called on historical precedent. In the Senate, Thomas Hamilton Lewis declared: "Let the world know that as George Washington fought for democracy as a right to America and Thomas Jefferson proclaimed it as a necessity to mankind, while Lincoln made it his creed of emancipation for all color and all clime—so, too, Wilson fights for democracy as a right of the whole world" (U.S. House of Representatives 1918, pp. 1984–85).

Why should Lincoln's presidency be invoked to begin with? Wilson's supporters knew the difference between the Civil War and the fighting then raging in Europe, and they could have justified his actions simply by arguing they served the national interest. But they were not trying to perform a technical analysis; their aim was to connect Wilson's measures to the sacred narrative of the nation. Keying World War I measures to the Civil War was an ideological exercise, not to be assessed in terms of historical evidence but by its ability to grasp and communicate present realities that the language of history cannot express.

The alignment of Wilson and Lincoln was nowhere closer than in newspaper and poster iconography. In one editorial cartoon after another, Lincoln appears as a moral model. Here, Lincoln helps Wilson fend off special interests and draft a letter to Germany (fig. 6.2); there, Wilson grimly witnesses violent storm clouds gathered around the executive mansion while Lincoln, his left arm under Wilson's right, steadies and emboldens the president as he looks upon the perilous scene (fig. 6.3).

Parallels extended to public information posters defining World War I as an episode in the larger experience of the nation. The triangular appearance of Washington, Lincoln, and Wilson in prints and

Figure 6.2. "Lincoln Steadying Wilson's Hand," 1918 cartoon.
Photograph courtesy of the Abraham Lincoln Museum, Harrogate,
Tennessee.

cartoons, for example, was a regular element in the wartime iconography. In one of these, the three presidents appear utterly resolute above a picture of battleships crossing the sea to confront the enemy. In another poster (fig. 6.4), Washington and Lincoln, America's founder and savior, frame Wilson and the "Brave Boys of 1917," who extend their forebears' legacy to the world. These pictures are "frame images" (Schwartz 1998a)—artistic devices that define the meaning of present events by linking them to great and defining events of the past.

Toward this same end the theater made its mark. Seeking to explain the great success of John Drinkwater's *Abraham Lincoln* on both the New York and London stages, *Literary Digest's* reviewer observed: "We have a well defined suspicion that if one were to pull

Figure 6.3. "Lincoln and Wilson Facing the Storm," cartoon from *Philadelphia Press*, reprinted in *Cartoons Magazine*, February 1918.

Figure 6.4. *The Brave Boys of 1917,* 1918 poster. Reproduced by
permission of the Huntington Library, San Marino, California.

the beard from Drinkwater's *Abraham Lincoln* he would find Woodrow Wilson" (January 3, 1920, 32).

Framing War

Aligned with the Civil War and Abraham Lincoln, World War I became a moral movement. Vachel Lindsay gave this point clear poetic
expression. "It is portentous, and a thing of state" that Lincoln
should appear at midnight at Springfield's courthouse square during
the Great War. "He cannot rest until a spirit-dawn / Shall come;—
the shining hope of Europe's free. . . ." As Gods appear at critical
moments to be with their people, so Lincoln arises from his tomb

and broods over America's dangers. This god, however, is no different from his worshipers. He is lanky, and wears a stovepipe hat, black suit, and shawl to keep away the cold. Before attending to mankind's burden he pauses where his children once played (Lindsay 1945, 53–54). His concerns and interests, even his appearance, prefigure Wilson's desire to make the world safe for the democracy of ordinary people. Clarifying the parallel further, Lincoln, accompanied by George Washington and Uncle Sam, walk beside Woodrow Wilson and lead civilians to the Great War (fig. 6.5). Recruitment for World War I occurs within a narrative context composed of past wars.

Invoking Lincoln's memory helped legitimate war mobilization. Whereas *legitimation* discourse justifies mobilization, *clarification*

Figure 6.5. "Onward," 1917 cartoon, from *Philadelphia Press,* reprinted in *Cartoons Magazine,* May 1917.

discourse dramatizes the values making mobilization necessary. Bringing these values to bear on public understanding of the war, however, was problematic, and no other home-front task was assumed by as many different media. Shortly after the United States entered the war, the U.S. Office of Public Information and private corporations (fig. 6.6) distributed posters carrying the last line of the Gettysburg Address: "That government of the people, by the people, for the people shall not perish from the earth." To save democracy was what the war was about.

Figure 6.6. "Warriors All," 1918 Havoline Oil advertisement. Photograph courtesy of the Abraham Lincoln Museum, Harrogate, Tennessee.

Orators, printmakers, and cartoonists have always visualized democracy through slavery images. Slavery, the negative term giving freedom and equality their positive sense, is central to America's self-conception[3] and was aligned time and again to World War I. "A world divided against itself cannot stand," declared Reverend James Huget in a sermon titled "What Would Lincoln Say to This Generation?" He answered the question by paraphrasing the rest of Lincoln's "House Divided" speech in terms of the present struggle: "The world must become all autocratic or all democratic. In a new sense it must become all slave or all free. This is the far reaching significance and must be the far reaching outcome of the world war. Just as Lincoln declared that no man is good enough to own another man, so now he would say that no nation is good enough to control the destiny of another." Just as the proslavery faction of Lincoln's own time was "blowing out the moral lights around us," so do those who now "invade and oppress neutral nations, and endeavor to gain military advantage and ill-won victory by the devices of the savage" (1918, 13–14). Accordingly, on Lincoln Day 1918, a state leader aroused great enthusiasm when he asked a Springfield, Illinois, gathering: "Is there any difference in essentials between the enslavement of the Negro and such enslavement as Germany today practices under the gospel of world domination?" (*Chicago Tribune*, February 13, 1918, 7). At the same time, the *New York Herald Tribune* observed that if the murder of Illinois abolitionist editor Elijah Lovejoy, "standing as he did for the freedom of the press and the freedom of the slave, was to the wise and clear-sighted Lincoln the most important single event that had ever happened up to 1857 in the history of the New World, should we not be steadied and heartened for the mighty task in hand across the sea?" (February 12, 1918, 8).

The match was exquisitely detailed. Woodrow Wilson's response to German peace overtures, also reported in the 1918 Lincoln Day issue of the nation's newspapers, required German recognition "that peoples and provinces are not to be bartered about from sovereignty to sovereignty, as if they were mere chattels" (*New York Herald Tribune*, February 12, 1918, 1). In its front-page cartoon (fig. 6.7), the *Tribune* visualizes a new emancipation by depicting Wilson addressing a joint session of Congress under Abraham Lincoln's specter. Standing before a full auditorium, Lincoln's words frame Wilson's: "This nation cannot endure permanently half slave and half free." History repeats itself, with Wilson reiterating Lincoln's position on the subjugation of the weak by the powerful. The actors differ; the

Figure 6.7. "Woodrow Wilson and Abraham Lincoln," 1918 cartoon, *New York Herald Tribune,* February 12.

plot is the same. Lincoln legitimates the course of action that Wilson is summoned to explain.

British prime minister Lloyd George grew up in a family that held Lincoln in high regard, and he would have appreciated the artist's point. Seeking support for Great Britain's cause, he knew that sympathetic Americans had referred to his predecessor, Prime Minister Asquith, as "the Abraham Lincoln of Great Britain" (Elmore 1917; *Current Opinion,* November 1916, 316) and that he would impress Americans, as he had already impressed himself, by keying his country's European War to their Civil War. The battle in Europe, George said, "is at bottom the same battle which your countrymen fought under Lincoln's leadership more than fifty years ago." Lincoln realized that "unless the Union abolished slavery, slavery would break the Union." Just so, there had grown up in Europe "a new form of slavery, a militarist slavery which has not only been crushing the freedom of the people under its control, but which in recent years has also been moving toward crushing out freedom and fraternity in all Europe as well" (*Survey*, February 1917, 564–65). Like so many of his countrymen, George saw in America's Great Emancipator—Lincoln—a pattern for his own time (Cooper 1918, 16).

Lloyd George plausibly defined World War I as a replay of the Civil War, but Americans interpreted his words differently than did many of his countrymen. For Americans, democracy meant the kind of equality that minimized distance between the people and their leaders. War information offices worked out the theme—the sacredness of egalitarian democracy—by showing citizens how to identify with Lincoln. One of their war bond posters (fig. 6.8) shows Lincoln's

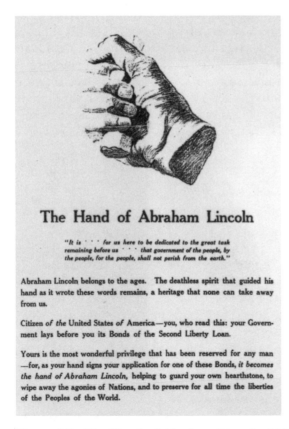

Figure 6.8. *The Hand of Abraham Lincoln*, 1918 poster. Reproduced by permission of the Huntington Library, San Marino, California.

fist grasping the broomstick he had cut off and held for sculptor Leonard Volk in 1861. By purchasing a war bond, the poster explains, one identifies with Lincoln, "for, as your hand signs your application for one of these Bonds, *it becomes the hand of Abraham Lincoln*" (italics in original). Likewise, parents decorated their homes with "A Tribute to Our American Soldier," a poster bearing the images of an eagle, American flags, and oval-shaped portraits of Abraham Lincoln, George Washington, and Woodrow Wilson. In the very middle of the poster was a cut-out square for purchasers to place a photograph of their son in uniform. As the soldier is literally framed by symbols of his nation's greatness, he becomes part of it himself.

The people identifying with Lincoln while Lincoln identifies with the people symbolizes the proximity of state and citizen. Lincoln believed that "a place equal to the most favored was rightfully to be given to the humblest toiler. So must we in this our day also ever recall that the men who perform the labor, bear the burdens . . . must be reckoned with by all who seek to rule" (Huget 1918, 12). Illinois governor Frank Lowden also saw this clearly. Contrary to the ideology of *Kultur,* based on the "Teutonic" doctrine that "the world belonged to the strong and the strong alone," Lincoln believed that the powerful must protect the weak (1919, 3). Progressivism's concept of the state as regulator of the plutocrat and champion of the common people paralleled this vision; to defend it, everyone knew, was the war's purpose.

Consolation

People who live through a war costing 170,000 lives and a half million injuries need more than inspiration. They need a theodicy. The discourses of theodicy and inspiration are comparable: both enable people to work together continuously and effectively despite loss. In spring 1917, when the first casualty lists were wired to America from Europe, the media linked them to casualty lists of the past. Civil War veterans were by then old men, but "[l]ads and striplings they were in the armies that fell in windrows on Antietam's cornfield, that were swallowed up uncounted in the Wilderness, that died yet held for all time the stone wall on Cemetery Ridge" (*New York Tribune,* May 30, 1917, 8).

Consolation discourse is formulated to make the ultimate loss, death, understandable and bearable. Two sacred documents of the Civil War performed these functions. Lincoln wrote the first document, the Gettysburg Address (part of the "New Testament" of "civil scripture" [Bellah 1970, 177–78]) for the dedication of a new military cemetery, but its substance was generalizable. As fatalities mounted, the Gettysburg Address grew more popular, and every recitation of it made the war more understandable. "The noblest of all Memorial Days," according to the *Chicago Daily Tribune* editor, "was not a 30th of May, but that 19th of November when President Lincoln journeyed to the Gettysburg battlefield to dedicate its hills still scarred with graves" (May 30, 1917, 8). Junius B. Remensnyder had been present at the Gettysburg dedication and recalled in 1918 how Lincoln eased the burden of the people by revealing "the generic truths of democracy" (1918, 243–44). For the last line of that revelation, concerning government of, for, and by the people, to appear on so many 1917–18 war bond announcements (see, for example, fig. 6.6) seemed natural. When World War I ended, Representative Wells Goodykoonts voiced the common realization that Lincoln's address was truly the perfect model *for* society: "the most perfect definition ever given of the word democracy" (U.S. House of Representatives 1920, 8785.

The second document of Lincoln's secular theodicy was his letter to Mrs. Lydia Bixby, a Massachusetts mother believed to have lost five sons during the Civil War. Realizing Mrs. Bixby's sacrifice to the Union cause, Americans found in Lincoln's letter the meaning of their own loss. The letter showed the president of a great nation identifying with the people by joining in their suffering. He does not address Mrs. Bixby as would a ruler his subject. No presumption clothes his words; indeed, he knows "how weak and fruitless" they will seem. And the consolation he offers is not his personal gratitude, but the thanks of the whole people. In the end, only God can relieve the woman's grief; a president can only pray that she can "cherish the memory of the loved and lost, and the solemn pride" to which so terrible a sacrifice entitles her. Lincoln signs his letter "Yours very sincerely and respectfully."[4]

Lincoln's words commemorated deeds greater than the words themselves, but which, in the absence of those words would have seemed less comprehensible. Kaiser Wilhelm's letter, reprinted beside Lincoln's on propaganda posters (fig. 6.9), had just the opposite effect. Addressed to a German mother who had lost not five but nine sons, the Kaiser's letter distinguishes itself by authoritarian presumption, evidenced in its third-person form and the accompanying photograph and autograph signature. Americans asking themselves what

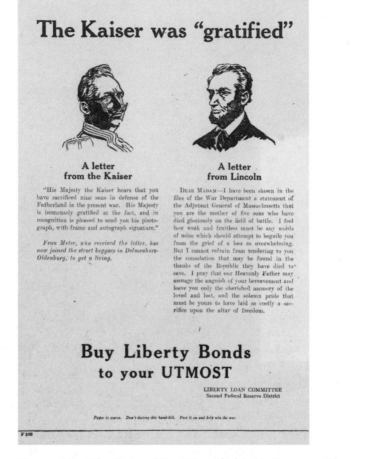

Figure 6.9. *The Kaiser Was "Gratified,"* 1918 poster. Photograph courtesy of the Lincoln Museum, Fort Wayne, Indiana (2531).

the war was about received an answer as their gaze shifted from the Kaiser's words to Lincoln's.

The Emancipator's War

That World War I was being waged to save democracy was not evident to the nation's black communities; but black loyalty remained nonetheless strong and became stronger when fixed on the image of Abraham Lincoln. In churches, schools, and association meetings, Lincoln appeared as a mediator—a bridge connecting the black community to the white nation, a translator expounding national concerns in local terms. In one World War I poster (fig. 6.10), Lincoln is etherealized and looks down on black soldiers fighting the German enemy. The picture leaves no doubt that the soldiers are fighting in a racially segregated army. Their sacrifice for the nation rejecting them, however, is justified by memory of the man who emancipated them. In another poster (fig. 6.11), a young black soldier is welcomed home by his patriotic family, on whose living-room wall hangs Lincoln's portrait. The actual war president, Woodrow Wilson, reared in Augusta, Georgia, believed in segregation and had no interest in improving black peoples' lives. His war was worth fighting, however, because it was also Lincoln's war. As Lincoln armed black men against

Figure 6.10. *True Sons of Freedom,* 1918 poster. Reproduced by permission of the Huntington Library, San Marino, California.

Figure 6.11. *Welcome Home,* 1918 poster. Photograph courtesy of
Lincoln Museum, Fort Wayne, Indiana (3843).

the slave power, America arms their descendants against slavery's
European successor. Ritual repeatedly affirmed the analogy. On
Lincoln Day 1918, for example, a host of twelve thousand African
Americans and white political and military officials gathered in the
Chicago Coliseum to hear black religious leaders declare: "Free the
World as Lincoln Freed Us!" And the sentiments expressed on that
occasion were sincere. "Never was [the song] *America* . . . given a
more emotional and impressive rendering," according to a white ob-
server. Shouts were heard from the five-hundred-voice chorus "and
the entire assemblage joined in with emphasis that rocked the build-

ing" (*Chicago Daily Tribune*, February 13, 1918, 7). Chicago's African Americans had situated World War I within the Civil War's realm of memory.

War and Union

Southern Americans, like African Americans, discovered the meaning of Woodrow Wilson's war by keying it to Lincoln's. Some Southerners, committed still to the Lost Cause, considered Kaiser Wilhelm, not Woodrow Wilson, the new Lincoln. Belgium, they believed, had been raped and pillaged by the Teutonic monster just as the South had by the Yankee monster. "If Belgium had its Louvain and Antwerp, so also had the South its Columbia, its Atlanta, its Savannah, its Charleston" (Blacknall 1915, 2). But the maker of this analogy realized he was in a minority. If the German government "sent to this country millions of dollars to buy up newspapers and newspaper men to abuse the allies, so Northern propagandists "have been successful in disseminating the idea that Lincoln was the great emancipator and that all his shuffling and equivocation was fine evidence of consummate leadership on his part" (Tylor 1921, 1, 17).

Initiated during the 1909 centennial, Southern reconciliation with Lincoln grew closer during the Great War. In February 1917, Kentucky made Lincoln's Birthday a legal holiday. One year later, as American troops fought in Europe, the Virginia legislature officially observed Lincoln's Birthday. The typical Southerner may have been ready to concede to Lincoln an important symbolic role; yet that role was not the same in the South as it had been in the North. For Southerners, Lincoln stood more plainly for union than for democracy. When, on the fiftieth anniversary of Lincoln's assassination, President Woodrow Wilson ordered the lowering of flags throughout the United States, Southern newspapers commented on the occasion and praised Lincoln for holding the country together. Senator Joseph Randall of Louisiana visited Boston to explain that a Confederate victory "would likely have made wars as possible in North America as they are in Europe . . . wars which doubtless would have involved Canada to the north and Mexico to the south of us—a repetition of the awful situation in Europe" (*New Orleans Times*, February 12, 1915, 2). The reestablishment of American unity seemed to be nearing completion: the Union had been broken in 1861, formally reestablished in 1865, then sanctified in 1917 as Northern and Southern men fought and died together in its name. "If it be true," said Representative Alben Barkley, "that the spirits of the departed take note of the movements and emotions of living men, may we not believe that the great souls of Lincoln and Davis rejoice together in Paradise because the children of those who followed them now stand arm in arm and shoulder to shoulder under the sacred banner of a single alliance, forgetting the misconceptions of past years . . ." (U.S. House of Representatives 1918, 1992). Barkley's words were visualized in the *Philadelphia Press*'s portrayal of flag-bearing civilian recruits being led by officers to training and war while great Northern and Southern heroes of the past—Lincoln, Washington, Grant, Sherman, and Lee—salute them (fig. 6.12): "And here's to the Blue and Gray as one; / As they'll meet on the fields of France; / May the spirit of God be with them all / As the sons of our flag advance" (U.S. House of Representatives 1920, 2792).

Figure 6.12. "They Will Fight as Their Fathers Fought," 1917 cartoon, from *Philadelphia Press,* reprinted in *Cartoons Magazine,* May 1917.

Into the small crevices of Southern life, lit by the glow of nationalism, Lincoln images slowly settled and accumulated. As the end of the war approached, Southern congressmen anticipated the erection of the greatest symbol to regional reconciliation ever devised—the Lincoln Memorial. Meanwhile, popular songs strengthened Lincoln's Southern ties: "My daddy fought with little Phil, the laddie said with pride. / But my dear daddy fought with Lee, the lassie proudly sighed." The scene is Gettysburg Cemetery, where romantic love and mourning connect Lincoln to the issues of regional unification, nationalism, and war. "My father wore a suit of blue and your dad a suit of gray, / That's why we both bring roses here, / On Decoration Day." Then the chorus—somewhat melodramatic, but meaningful in its day: "I love you just like Lincoln loved the old Red, White and Blue, / He gave his life for the dear old flag, / And I'd give my life for you" (Jerome, Young, and Schwartz 1914).[5] Remembering Lincoln's patriotism, the chorus enunciates the frame within which the romantic bond assumes meaning: old animosities are forgotten as new dangers and the prospect of new sacrifices arise.

An Image Crystallized

Victorious war and its symbols strengthen the state. "The fully successful functioning of a nation state," in turn, "demands and receives . . . an incandescent level of adoration" (Zelinsky 1988, 8). Abraham Lincoln's commemoration made the American state glow more brightly than ever. In 1922, the federal government dedicated the Lincoln Memorial as a monument to America's greatness and to what Lincoln had contributed to it. People were also tirelessly reading about Lincoln. Throughout the 1920s the number of popular magazine articles about Lincoln remained constantly high. The number of New York Times articles increased from 164 in 1915–19 to 176 in the years 1920–24, then rose sharply to 296 between 1925 and 1929. Between 1919 and 1921, 21 articles per year were listed in the Readers' Guide to Periodical Literature. Between 1922 and 1928, the number was 20. Congressional Record entries numbered 59 in 1915–19, 70 in 1920–24, and 73 in 1925–29.

While Lincoln's reputation grew, progressivism, which helped induce that growth, seemed itself to diminish. Vernon Parrington has argued that World War I destroyed the aspiration of progressive humanitarianism and prepared the ground for a conservative reaction beginning with Harding. Parrington was right as far as he went, but other conditions account for the progressive movement's institutional erosion: lack of a political organization capable of carrying progressives into national office, internal divisions, failure to agree upon a common program, lack of national leadership. The culture of progressivism, however, outlasted the progressive movement. Indeed, most of the federal legislation passed during the 1920s was progressive in character and attracted the support of farmers, organized labor, Democratic organizations, social workers, proponents of public power and centralization, and remaining social gospel adherents (Link and McCormick 1983, 105–18). That Lincoln's image grew as reform activity slowed was therefore no irony, for the political program of progressivism, resting on a new structural foundation, needed its original reformist impulse no longer. The newly centralized government, easily tooled for wide and intrusive controls and regulation and, above all, recognizing the principle of responsibility for the citizen's well-being, was in place, ready to be enlarged and utilized when the Great Depression struck.

Throughout the 1920s Lincoln symbolized political power and centralization; yet conservatives as well as reformers quoted and embraced him. His face adorned campaign posters and song sheets. As his images multiplied, they became more magisterial. In 1922, Nathaniel W. Stephenson published the first biography to emphasize the Civil War's effect on Lincoln's greatness. *Lincoln: An Account of His Personal Life, Especially of Its Springs of Action as Revealed and Deepened by the Ordeal of War* (1922) is by no means a psychoanalytic account of Lincoln's presidency, but it seeks understanding of Lincoln's personal assets and purposes. Stephenson's Lincoln is a man of mild sentiment but iron will, a man whose unwavering commitment to union changed history. Stephenson's article, "Lincoln and the Progress of Nationality in the North" (1919), first appearing in the *Annual Report of the American Historical Association* but deemed important enough to be reprinted in 1923 by the Government Printing Office, was, according to Mark Neely Jr. "the most nationalistic Lincoln portrait ever drawn" (1982, 291). It also emphasized the elitist (technocratic, expert-oriented) rather than populist elements of progressivism, asserting that Lincoln would have rejected the progressive plebiscite and referendum, for he never hesitated to suspend civil rights or to issue unpopular warrants for arrest. Abraham Lincoln "refused to be the mere spokesman of the people" (Neely 1982, 290).

Ida Tarbell had always portrayed Lincoln as the ultimate common man; however, during the postwar years she wanted everyone to know how uncommon he became. Her "Abraham Lincoln's Money Sense" (1923) proved that when Lincoln died he was worth $110,000—equivalent to a multimillionaire by present standards. Lincoln's admirers wanted the public to recognize his pedigree, too. Representative Frederick Dallinger of Massachusetts emphasized that he was from highly distinguished stock. George Washington's refined background, it is true, could be contrasted with Lincoln's, but "recent historical research has proved that the English progenitors of Lincoln were fully as high in the social scale as those of Washington" (1925, 4444).

The greater Lincoln became, the more expansive his role as a model *for* society. To say, as did New York's Governor Charles Whitman, that "The Republican party must conduct itself so that it tallies and squares itself with the life, example and manhood of Abraham Lincoln" (*New York Herald Tribune,* February 12, 1918, 9) is to say something simple and, on the surface, uninspiring, but it reflects the era's exalted conception of Lincoln. To "Lincolnize" America was then a well-understood phrase. Recognizing the growing power of the motion-picture industry, civic leaders urged movie-makers to strengthen their nation's morals by inducing viewers to "look at all questions of America through Lincoln's eyes" (*New York Times,* February 12, 1920, 10). When an Ohio judge answered the call to Lincolnize the country by recommending a year-long course on Lincoln as a high-school requirement, educators took him seriously. That Charles Evans Hughes urged college courses on Lincoln in order to reinforce the character of young students also made sense. As secretary of state, Hughes explained: "In making Lincoln the exemplar of the Nation, we are not merely recognizing heroic service but we are safeguarding our most vital resource. . . . So long as we cherish Lincoln's principles and so long as his virtues inspire our youth, our security and progress are assured" (Peterson 1994, 197).

In crisis, the idea that a nineteenth-century president should be a guide for twentieth-century living was self-evident. On Lincoln Day 1917, *Los Angeles Times* readers learned from the front-page headline, "Congress Turns to Teachings of Lincoln in Foreign Crisis," that their government was acting and measuring itself against Lincoln's example (*Los Angeles Times,* February 13, 1917, 1). For instance, just as the Civil War was needlessly prolonged by Lincoln's pacifist opponents, so anti-Wilson pacifists would make the European war more costly to America (Abbott 1916, 222; see also Lewis 1915). After the United States entered the war, the *Saint Louis Post-Dispatch* printed Lincoln's August 1863 letter to Illinois Republican leader James Conkling on the subject of pressures within his own party to compromise with the Confederacy. Published under the title "What Lincoln Said to Pacifists of His Day," the "letter is so astonishingly applicable to many phases in the present situation of the world war

Figure 6.13. "No American Home Is Complete without a Picture of Abraham Lincoln," c. 1916 cartoon. Photograph courtesy of the Abraham Lincoln Museum, Harrogate, Tennessee.

that . . . it may be read with profit and illumination today" (February 10, 1918, 1, 15).

Lincoln's enduring peacetime relevance was also manifest in his admirers' accounts. A Chicago businessman tells the story of his moving from a dingy loft into one of Michigan Avenue's finest new offices:

I bought and laid on the floor of my office the best rugs that I could find in town. I papered the walls with a plain, rich gray paper, put a big flat-topped mahogany desk in the center of the room, and on the opposite wall where my eyes would meet it every time I looked up from my work, I hung a portrait of Abraham Lincoln, for Abraham Lincoln has done more for me than any other man in the world—living or dead. ("A New Portrait" 1918, 18)

Portraying an admirer gazing at a portrait of his hero was a conventional form of representing deference at the turn of the century, and this form emerged in many media. In one of the era's cartoons, a boy appears with hat in hand studying a portrait bearing the slogan: "No American Home Is Complete without a Picture of Abraham Lincoln" (fig. 6.13). To gaze upon another person, psychoanalyst Otto Fenichel said, is to identify with him through "optical incorporation" and to make him part of one's own conscience (1953–54, 393). Accordingly, to be reared in a home without Lincoln's image was to be reared imperfectly.

Mirror, Lamp, and Frame

"People are not invariably seeking to legitimate their present interests [by invoking the past]. . . . They seek to know what is right, what is true. They seek some kind of direction when they are aimless. They seek in the past some kind of anchor when they are adrift. They seek a source of inspiration when they despair" (Schudson 1992, 213). Memory, in other words, is a cultural program that orients our intentions, sets our moods, and enables us to act. Studying memory during a national emergency gives us a grasp of how this program works.

Between April 6, 1917, and November 11, 1918, Abraham Lincoln framed a nation's war experience. His memory did not glorify the war or conceal its horror, as have other World War I commemorations (Mosse 1990); it formulated the war's meaning. His memory helped to legitimate the president's assumption of war powers, prepare the population to fight, clarify the ideals and values at stake in the war, and justify its injuries and deaths. The American people legitimated and oriented their actions, affirmed their values, and inspired and consoled one another in many ways. Lincoln's commemoration was but one part of the cultural template making war comprehensible, but it provides answers to one of the questions posed at the beginning of this book: what do we mean behaviorally when we refer to memory work as a model *for* society?

Our first step in answering this question has been to consider the social function of memory work. Memory work has at best a minimal instrumental function: it does not create and mobilize resources or make armies more effective. Its function is semiotic: to make tangible the values for which resources and armies are mobilized. Keying, the mechanism of memory work, realizes this function by a crossing of ideational wires—a forced juxtaposition of events in two separate wars, such that the events of one war are appropriated as a means to interpret the events of the other.

World War I era moralists, teachers, and propagandists appropriated Abraham Lincoln by applying a six-part keying method. If they had wished to make this method explicit, they might have given the following instructions:

1. *Selection.* Invoke the Civil War as a primary framework.

2. *Scanning.* Probe Civil War episodes with a view to locating actions relevant to World War I predicaments.

3. *Event Alignment.* Emphasize relevant similarities rather than contrasts in order to render World War I a "repetition" of the Civil War—"the same thing all over again."

4. *Identification.* Identify World War I participants with the Civil War generation, then construe the latter as "predecessors"; the former, "descendants."

5. *Values Alignment.* Depict World War I participants and their Civil War ancestors struggling for the same moral ends.

6. *Idealization.* Summarize complex Civil War realities in the familiar image of Abraham Lincoln, then enlarge that image in order to better articulate present purposes and apprehensions.[6]

Although Americans at war could invoke many events from their eighteenth- and nineteenth-century history, they chose the Civil War most often because it was the nation's defining moment—the moment that shaped and fixed the identity of generations. Makers of Civil War and Lincoln images could therefore count on their audiences' capacity to appreciate their work. The machinery of invocation (keying) presupposes rather than creates the affinity of the events it brings together, and this affinity warrants the invocation of a nineteenth-century president to reinforce twentieth-century values.

That the World War I generation so readily found itself in Lincoln is the condition defining the power of his image. If Lincoln's image had been hollow, a symbolic residue left over from the previous century, then the popularity of new Lincoln biographies, songs, dramas, and films, and the great volume of newspaper and magazine articles about him immediately before and during the war, would be unexplainable.

Although American people earnestly keyed problematic states of their present war to Lincoln's experience in the Civil War, the fit was imperfect—and this was necessarily so, for the past is at once an idealization and critique of the present world. Invoking Lincoln and the Civil War would have been pointless if they had resembled Wilson and the First World War too closely, for a past that merely reproduces the present suggests no answers to its dilemmas. Ideal models, not realistic ones, inspire. These inspiring models reveal themselves as well through cartoons as through any other medium. The *New York Tribune*'s front-page 1917 Lincoln Day cartoon captioned "'Lives of Great Men All Remind Us'—But They Don't Remind Us Often Enough" shows a midget politician, his arms full of documents titled "Pork Bill," "River and Harbor Graft," "$100,000 Post Office for Podunk," gazing up embarrassingly at a giant statue of Lincoln. The past appears here as a critique, not a reflection, of reality. On the other hand, abstractly simplistic ideals bear no credible relationship to a complex and imperfect present. Tension, not easy compatibility, defines the relation between memory and experience.

In the present case, tension is sustained in two ways. Since Lincoln's life is made up of more facets than can be applied in a given situation, its emulation requires selective remembrance. During Wilson's term as war president, for example, Lincoln's presidency was the main object of popular reflection; during Wilson's funeral, his death. This selection does not mean we ourselves create the object that instructs and inspires us. The question, "What *part* of Lincoln's life is a model *for* society?" is rather answered differently, evokes different sentiments, and appears with different relevance from one social context to another.

Tension between memory and experience is also sustained by the dynamics of distortion. If memory work does not create the past, it exaggerates it because invocation is rhetorically stylized. Invoking Lincoln in oratory and pictorial art makes him more decisive, relentless, clear-minded, democratic, and sympathetic than he could have been. This exaggeration, induced by twentieth-century problems, idealized Lincoln and made him credible as a model *for* a twentieth century society. But the exaggeration of Lincoln's virtues does not explain why he had become a model in the first place. Lincoln, in fact, was not a model because he was idealized; he was rather idealized because he was already a model. And he was already a model because of real, not imaginary, that is, constructed, accomplishments and traits.[7]

Models can be used in different ways. To understand the keying of any World War I situation to the Civil War, therefore, the role of "fabrication"—the intentional effort of one or more individuals to manipulate or even falsify the meaning of the past—must be discounted. (For detail, see Goffman 1974, 83–123.) What motives should we attribute to President Wilson and his administrators for resorting so often to Lincoln? What should we make of the work of cartoonists, editors, corporation heads, advertising departments, and the U.S. Committee on Public Information? Should we treat their appeals as keyings or fabrications? Was Lincoln's image invoked by the state and the media as Christ's image was invoked by the church? Or was his image used to manipulate the masses into supporting a cause toward which they might have otherwise been indifferent?

Influential people do not always consciously manipulate; they often believe their efforts to affect others' opinions are in the general interest. Fabrication is a useful concept, however, because it implies a distinction between reputational entrepreneurs who share their audience's values and those who induce their audience to adopt values that only entrepreneurs would otherwise approve. Conflict theories of memory are referring to this kind of fabrication when they assert that any image of the past is "a product of elite manipulation" (Bodnar 1992, 20). So far as the dominant class's images undermine the subordinate class's interests, these images "can be seen as a form of oppression" or, at best, baneful influence (Baigell 1993, 201, 204).

Whether elites are sincere or deceptive, assertions about their hegemony leave two essential and interrelated questions unanswered. First, of the infinite number of devices that could have been used for the purpose of inspiring and consoling the American masses, why was Lincoln's memory invoked more often than anyone else's? What is problematic is not only the *function* of memory—to console by making death meaningful—but also the *vehicle* of memory—to make death meaningful by invoking Lincoln. Secondly, dominant ideology theory assumes dissensus to be the natural state of society, dismissing the possibility of image-makers embracing the same values and goals as their audience and invoking shared symbols to articulate rather than manipulate its sentiment. This second point is the most fundamental. To focus exclusively on Lincoln's use by a dominant class or dominant institution is to offer a supply-side theory that attends to the production of images but ignores their reception. Reception, however, is always problematic. The state's success or failure in generating support for war by sustaining discourse on Lincoln is determined by the public's endorsement of the values Lincoln symbolized, its belief that those values are worth struggling to preserve, and its perception that the state is their custodian rather than their exploiter. Between the remembrance of Lincoln and the immediate imperatives of war exists a relation that neither the concepts of manipulation and propaganda, nor the related concepts of dominant ideology and false consciousness, can formulate.

Theories focusing solely on divergent memories rooted in competing interests cannot credibly depict American memory during the Great War. Throughout this war, political conservatives still regarded Lincoln as the antithesis of progressive reform and centralized power politics while progressives still saw him as the epitome of popular democracy. Those who considered diplomacy necessary to end the war no less than those wanting to fight to the finish found their own views in Lincoln's (Croly 1920, 350–51). The politics of memory, however, can be consensual as well as conflictual; by 1918 the former dominated the latter, and memories of Abraham Lincoln embodied a universal cultural presence. Common memories of Lincoln constituted common models for acting, common ideals for judging, common categories of understanding, common sources of inspiration, common interpretations of suffering and death. As a model *for* society, Abraham Lincoln was more than a unifying image of the moment. He was part of something deeper and more permanent—part of the soul of American society.

Two Lincolns:
Symbolizing America

Expanding international power and redistribution of domestic power limited the kind of man Americans could make of Abraham Lincoln during the early years of the twentieth century. Ordinary men cannot represent great and powerful nations; elitist strongmen cannot represent democracies. Lincoln's image was for these reasons pulled in contrary directions: not only toward plainness, familiarity, and sympathy, but also toward stateliness, authority, and dignity. Lincoln, in hindsight, had always embodied this dualism, but it did not figure so prominently in his commemoration until the twentieth century.

Since common people, as Herbert Croly observed, want common heroes, Americans still considered Lincoln a magnified version of themselves and continued "to disguise flattery of themselves under the form of reverence for him" (1920, 15). But Croly, an advisor and associate of Theodore Roosevelt, failed to appreciate how much the collective perception of Lincoln had changed. Throughout the Progressive era and World War I, people admired Lincoln's presidential simplicity, accessibility, and kindheartedness. They appreciated his humble background, seedy appearance, storytelling, and quaintness—which made him a kind of second cousin to America's frontier heroes—Davy Crockett and Kit Carson. At the same time, Lincoln's epic qualities became more apparent. The Union's savior, the prophet of democracy, the Great Emancipator, the giant who changed the course of history was a man, for sure, but too good and too big to be treated as one. By 1900 the coexistence of these contrasting conceptions had become discernible, and by the end of World War I they had crystallized. The burden of Lincoln's changing image was to help Americans express awareness of their new world role and the necessity of their performing it within the limits of values transmitted from the past.

Epic Heroism

Reflecting on World War I, William B. Guitteau explained in his textbook *Our United States: A History:* "It is time that our citizens realized that the welfare and the happiness of mankind are largely in the keeping of the great democracies of the world" (1919, v). To be responsible for mankind's well-being places great responsibilities and great prestige upon democratic leaders. In this climate, American intellectuals, developing a theme established by Ralph Waldo Emerson ([1850] 1900), began to contemplate systematically the great man's social role. Charles Horton Cooley ([1902] 1964; 1918) considered the American heroic vision an extension of Emerson's "representative men" (Schwartz 1985), but William McDougall, one of America's most influential psychologists, carried it farther than anyone by conceiving heroic leaders as the very wellsprings of their nation:

Any nation that has achieved a considerable development . . . has its national heroes whom it rightly glorifies or worships; for to them it owes in chief part its existence. To them also it owes in large measure the forms of its institutions, its religion, its dominant ideas and ideals, its morals, its art and literature, all that of which it is most proud, all its victories of peace as well as of war, the memory of which is the strongest of all national bonds. . . . Would Germany now be a nation, but for Frederick the Great and Bismarck? Would America, but for Washington, Hamilton, and Lincoln? (1920, 189)

As the prestige of the American presidency grew from the Spanish-American War to World War I, the presidential ideal changed. To images of a neighborly, rustic leader telling quaint stories were added less sentimental, more dignified elements. Signs of the revision were evident as early as 1890, when Stephen Douglas Jr.

ascended the Union League podium on Lincoln Day to talk about his father's old opponent:

I hope I may be pardoned for saying that in the generally accepted view of Mr. Lincoln's character there is a tendency to glorify his heart, to exalt what may be called the child qualities of his nature, while reducing to a minimum what may be called the man qualities. Many dwarf him of his manliness, because they make him a dreamy drifter, molded into shape by circumstances, instead of a clear-headed, kind-hearted, strong-handed man of iron will, who molded circumstances and compelled success. . . . In his soul he heard, no doubt, the music of wonderful melodies that none but angel harps could sound, but his hands sought only such work as human brain and brawn could do. (*New York Times*, February 13, 1890, 2)

Almost twenty years later, George L. Knapp criticized prevailing images of the sad-eyed emancipator and droll humorist who made do with intuition rather than brains. The public itself, Knapp asserted, has more heart than head and projects the same ratio onto its heroes, but the public is wrong about Lincoln. Yes, he was kindly and witty, but "with it all, and illuminating all, was a keen, incisive, forceful brain. I do not question Lincoln's moral greatness. I do not undervalue his broad humanity, his utter unselfishness, his elemental patience. But had these qualities not been guided by a great and oddly penetrating intellect . . . our national temple would be the poorer for the figure of one of its greatest heroes" (*Review of Reviews* 1909, 241).

By 1909, the plebeian side of Lincoln's makeup had already begun to lose part of its earlier appeal. The collections of "Lincoln jokes" published while he was still president continued to sell after his death. The popularity of the lighthearted Lincolniana grew, according to Roy Basler, "until about 1909, when the Lincoln centennial brought out every stock from the nook. Since then, interest has become more and more fixed in his dignified posture as America's greatest statesman and leader" (1935, 34). Contemplating Gutzon Borglum's bust of Lincoln, the latest to be added to the U.S. Capitol's iconography (1911), Rabbi Leonard Levy conveyed Basler's observation in different words: "It seems to me that the sculptor desired to indicate to us by this piece of statuary that Lincoln has grown greater and greater since his death. For you see this head is thrice, perhaps four times, the size of its natural prototype. Lincoln has grown in that proportion during the forty-five years since the assassin's bullet laid him low" (1927, 323).

Rabbis were unrepresentative of America's religious leaders, but their views on Lincoln were conventional. The *Chicago Tribune*, for example, believed that Lincoln's reputation had grown since 1865 by more than a factor of three or four. A cartoon in its February 12, 1912, issue depicts Lincoln in 1858, overwhelmed by his contemporaries. On his right stands Democrat Stephen Douglas, who defeated him in that year's senatorial election; on his left stand Republican leaders William Seward and Charles Sumner. The prestige and influence of these three men is symbolized by their deep black suits, which distinguish them from minor figures of the day, Edwin Stanton, Horatio Seymour, and Salmon Chase, who in turn appear larger than Lincoln. By 1865, however, everything changes. Lincoln is now distinguished in black, and he stands head and shoulders above the men who once dominated him. By 1912, the cartoon's bottom panel shows him towering over the U.S. Capitol and the Washington Monument, over nature's high mountains and the city's skyscrapers. Abraham Lincoln has become so big that he dominates an entire continent (fig. 7.1); he has been reincarnated into a higher version of himself.

The lighthearted, humorous Lincoln, the little man's president, was attacked: "Give us a captain bold and tried and true, / Not this gaunt, shambling homespun lout— / Railsplitter, backwoods jester, wrestling clown." So Richard Linthicum depicted criticisms of Lincoln during the early months of his presidency. That the poet himself shared disdain for peasant-presidents is evident in his regard for the kind of man he thought Lincoln actually to be: "As in a mountain range one giant peak / Lifts its tall head above its fellow crests, / A guide to all within the lofty land" ([1911] 1970, 155). An unnamed *Nation* poetry critic finds in such an impression the values of his readers:

The American folk has done nothing more imaginative, and nothing more revealing, than to build up this tender, merry myth [of Lincoln]. In the hands of our newest poets, however, the myth is changing. . . . Lincoln's laughter has lost something of its rusticity. . . . and with it have gone both the buffoonery of so much of the popular tradition and the sentimental humanitarianism. What survives is the elemental, ancient matter of heroic genius and wisdom. (May 7, 1919, 222)

As Americans reminded themselves of Lincoln's executive abilities, his personality commanded less attention; his achievements,

Figure 7.1. "Lincoln and His Contemporaries," 1912 cartoon, *Chicago Daily Tribune*. Photograph courtesy of the Library of Congress.

more. Count Bernstorff, German ambassador to the United States, searching for something appropriate to say on Lincoln's Birthday 1913, described Lincoln as a strong man who ignored his cabinet's reservations and recognized the necessity of war. During the great fight, the ambassador added, Lincoln's "native hue of resolution" was not "sickled o'er with the pale cast of thought" (1913, 10). Here was no figment of the Prussian imagination. Lincoln was fast becoming the American man of will and brawn. In the words of a *Nation* correspondent:

In America, our veneration of Lincoln is greater, because more intelligent, than it was in 1865. He is a far more commanding figure now than then, a more epic and less intimate hero. His personal character lent itself to a myth-making process. His homely humor led to ransacking of joke-books; his gentleness grew into legends of reprieve, pardons, and consolatory letters. This was a familiarity that bred contempt even with its affection; and it so defeated itself that historians have had a great work to do in restoring Lincoln as he really existed. We now care little for "Lincoln stories," yet we study his authentic life as that of no other national figure. (April 22, 1915, 434)

The most important element in the campaign to dignify Lincoln, this correspondent told his readers, was the discovery of his presidential aptitude:

A Lincoln myth that long had general vogue, but has now been thoroughly discredited with all who know the facts, is that he came to the Presidency a raw, untrained man. The common people like to think this was so, since it fit in so well with their belief, or hope, that mediocre intellectual attributes were sufficient. But we now fully understand that Abraham Lincoln became President with a disciplined and sinewy mind. (434)

Even H. L. Mencken, the greatest cynic of his age, had to admit that "Lincoln, in point of fact, was a practical politician of long experience and high talents" ([1918] 1920, 223–24).

Two narratives had come clearly into view. Egalitarian narratives, abhorring distinction, depicted Lincoln as being indifferent to social rank, ready to embrace the least of his admirers as men no different from himself. All could match his achievements with effort and luck. Competing portrayals, however, depicted a man of superior if not supernatural powers, and they changed Lincoln fundamentally by placing him beyond most citizens' reach. Because distinction is the basis of natural hierarchy, the new narratives showed Lincoln's personal assets to be unmatchable, and he became the remote demi-god with whom no ordinary mortal could compare.

Portraits of Greatness

Americans visualized Lincoln as they read about him. After the excitement of the Spanish-American War, Jean Leon Gerome Ferris, a master at rendering Lincoln as folk hero, recognized the national thirst for epic imagery in *Lincoln at Independence Hall* (1908). His painting (fig. 7.2) shows Lincoln delivering a Washington's Birthday

Figure 7.2. Jean Leon Gerome Ferris, *Lincoln at Independence Hall*, cover, *Ladies' Home Journal*, February 1919.

speech in Philadelphia, where he had stopped on his way from Spring-field to assume the presidency. In the address, Lincoln publicly defied a plot to kill him on his way to Washington. Rather than surrender the principle of equality for all citizens, he declared, "I would rather be assassinated on this spot." Ferris showed Lincoln having finished the speech. Lincoln steps to the flag and grasps its cord in his right hand; just before he raises it he points with his left hand dramatically toward the sky. The flag itself is a curtain that sets Lincoln in front of the platform's other occupants, and the minutely drawn audience exaggerates his prominence.

Lincoln's greatness was written all over his face. During the 1918 exhibit of a new Lincoln portrait (to which an infinite range of traits might be ascribed), one anonymous art critic pointed out: "There is no suggestion of the frivolous Lincoln—the story-loving rollicking one." Another critic noticed that "dignity is one of the marked char-acteristics of this interpretation. . . . Although it is not lacking in humanity, the emphasis is on the keen mind of the man who thought his way through the confusions and prejudices of his time."[1]

Sculptors portrayed Lincoln in the same manner. Neoclassical conventions, which resulted in heroic sculptures, remained dominant despite challenge. Of the twenty-two original Lincoln statues un-veiled between 1900 and 1919, ten were wrought neoclassically; seven "realistically" (i.e., they were "genrefied" statues, emphasizing his ordinary qualities); five were mixed. Neoclassical versions of Lin-coln not only outnumbered realistic ones; they had also broken from the nineteenth-century convention of depicting him as the Great Emancipator. Now he is simply, and greatly, head of state. Otto Schweizer's 1913 statue of Lincoln nobly delivering the Gettysburg Address (fig. 7.3) exemplifies the neoclassical mode. So does Adolph Weinman's first statue, unveiled in a small town square near Lincoln's birthplace (Hodgenville, Kentucky), depicting a dignified Lincoln sit-ting upon a chair of state (fig. 7.4); his second statue erected in Ken-tucky's state capitol building, shows Lincoln standing upright, his cloak draped over the chair of state. F. Wellington Ruckstuhl's model of Lincoln on his deathbed, with angels prepared to crown him with laurel (fig. 7.5), was never converted into bronze or stone but reveals further the impulse to commemorate Lincoln as a demigod. Sculptors produced comparable statues throughout the 1920s: Daniel Chester French's Lincoln Memorial statue, one of the largest marble statues ever made, is the prominent neoclassical example (fig. 7.6). The great chair is adorned in front with flat-faced pillars on which are carved the fascia of power and indivisibility. The expansive symbolism of the

Figure 7.3. J. Otto Schweizer, *Abraham Lincoln at Gettysburg*, 1913, Gettysburg Memorial Park, Gettysburg, Pennsylvania. Photograph courtesy of the Lincoln Museum, Fort Wayne, Indiana (803).

memorial building is also impressive, but Lincoln's image dominates everything. Here is no tribute to the common man. When the statue was dedicated in 1922, the name "Lincoln Triumphant" was suggested for it. Neoclassical statuary looked like the people felt: big, powerful, morally upright.[2]

A God in Human Form

By 1920, Lincoln had become a demigod. Parallels between his life and Christ's were drawn so often as to approach cliche. Reverend Sydney Strong denied that Lincoln was Christ's equal but insisted that "mankind's estimate of [Lincoln] more closely tallies with the estimate of Jesus, than does its estimate of any other man" (1920, 12). Poet James Oppenheim described "The Lincoln Child" ([1911] 1970, 196–202); Edwin Markham, "The Coming of Lincoln"

Figure 7.4. Adolph Weinman, *Abraham Lincoln*, 1909. Hodgenville, Kentucky. Photograph courtesy of the Lincoln Museum, Fort Wayne, Indiana (781).

([1911] 1970, 38–39). Samuel Kiser's appreciation was stronger and more direct:

> Lo, where the feet of Lincoln passed, the earth
>> Is sacred, where he knelt we set a shrine!
> Oh, to have pressed his hand! That had sufficed
> To make my children wonder at my worth—
>> Yet, let them glory, since their land and mine
> Hath reared the greatest martyr after Christ! ([1911] 1970, 11).

"The homespun mantle which Lincoln originally wore has entirely fallen away" (*Nation*, March 16, 1919, 777). The *Nation* was

Figure 7.5. F. Wellington Ruckstuhl, *Recumbent Lincoln,* clay model, in *Art World,* May 1917.

almost, but not entirely, correct. Just as Christ combined the attributes of god and man, so Lincoln's memory unified opposites. He was a mediator of the "world-spirit" and the "folk-soul," a mystical power bringing the higher realms of time and history to the lower plane of the people. Contrapuntal narratives sanctified Lincoln's memory at the end of the nineteenth century, but the theme became more pronounced during the first two decades of the twentieth. A sample of fifty poems about Lincoln, all written after 1900, most between 1900 and 1920 and published in two anthologies, show this dualism to be evident in the repetition of two sets of words broken down in table 7.1 into characteristic nouns and adjectives.

Words displayed on the left-hand side of table 7.1 depict Lincoln in the role of commander and ruler—a majestic, noble man of great but quiet strength. Words listed on the right-hand side of the table depict him in the role of frontiersman—a rough and humble man of the earth. A separate analysis shows the ratio of folk to epic words to be almost identical: the number of poems in which folk words outnumber epic words is the same as the number of poems in which epic words are most common. Table 7.1 as a whole shows Lincoln at once prophet, king, captain, and master; plowman, woodsman,

Figure 7.6. Daniel Chester French, *Lincoln Memorial*, 1922, Washington, D.C. Photograph courtesy of the Library of Congress.

and wrestler. He is a man of the sky and the mountain, but also of land, root, and ax; a great, stately, and divine man, yet also homely, unkempt, and rough. Thus, the poets, like their fellow artists—biographers, sculptors, and painters—looked for one man but found two.

Two Lincolns—the common man and the great man—matured in the early twentieth century. It was as if two tickets were issued for Lincoln, "one giving access to the almost superhuman savior of the Union and sad-eyed emancipator; the other to the droll humorist and the 'great heart' who subsumed reason to sentiment" (Peterson 1994, 176).[3] These two tickets, as is now clear, represent a cultural dualism—the kind one finds in a society that values both equality—the familiarity that makes people alike—and hierarchy—the powers that distinguish them.

Table 7.1 Types of Imagery Commonly Found in Fifty Lincoln Poems

Epic Terms			Folk Terms		
Nouns		Adjectives	Nouns		Adjectives
Social roles	*Other*		*Social roles*	*Other*	
Ruler	Strength	Great	Plowman	Land	Homely
Prophet	Power	High	Railsplitter	Clay	Shambling
Father	Heart	Mighty	Woodsman	Earth	Gaunt
King	Sky	Stately	Wrestler	Root	Unkempt
Prince	Mountain	Divine	Common	Ground	Uncouth
Crown	Depth	Majestic	Man	Cabin	Rough
Captain	Silence	Genius		Backwoods	Simple
Chief		Noble		Ax	Humble
Master				Tears	Quaint
				Toil	Kindly
				Laughter	

Sources: Osborn H. Oldroyd, ed., *The Poets' Lincoln* (Washington, D.C.: By Editor, 1915); Wright-Davis 1919; Basler 1935; William Wilson Betts, ed., *Lincoln and the Poets* (Pittsburgh: University of Pittsburgh Press, 1965); A. Dallas Williams, ed., *The Praise of Lincoln* (Freeport, N.Y.: Books for Libraries Press, [1911] 1970).

Contrapuntal Memory

Since cultural dualism had insinuated itself into the American mind as a schema, a mental framework for perception and memory, people spoke about Lincoln in two languages. One language evoked images of an epic Lincoln—a hero unconquerable and incorruptible, dignified and remote. The other language evoked images of a folk Lincoln, a hero acquainted with hardship and defeat, approachable and warm. Edwin Markham spoke both languages eloquently. Markham, a socialist entertaining a nonsocialistic belief in heroes, particularly heroes to lead America to a new brotherhood, saw in Lincoln "a man to hold against the world, / A man to match the mountains and the sea." Yet "The color of the ground was in him, the red earth; / The smack and tang of elemental things." The elemental, Markham added, prefigures the sublime:

> Up from log cabin to the Capitol,
> One fire was on his spirit, one resolve. . . .
> And evermore he burned to do his deed
> With the fine stroke and gesture of a king:
> He built the rail-pile as he built the State. ([1911] 1970, 13).

Between Lincoln as everyman and Lincoln as demigod is a complex relation many have tried to understand. Woodrow Wilson imagined a continuum, bounded at one end by Andrew Jackson, a frontier statesman alien to many parts of the country, and at the other by Henry Clay, familiar to East and West; friendly to both. Between Jackson and Clay stands Lincoln, in whom the nation's eastern and western cultures converge. "The whole country is summed up in him: the rude western strength, tempered with shrewdness and a broad and humane wit; the Eastern conservatism, regardful of law and devoted to fixed standards of duty." Andrew Jackson, it seemed to Wilson, could never be more than one man; Henry Clay could never be less than two. Lincoln was "all men by turns, as mood succeeded mood in his strange nature" (1966, September 15, 1893, 8:378; May 16, 1895, 9:270–71).

Lincoln's dual nature attracted many people. John Nicolay's Lincoln "combined in his character the people's virtues, while remaining untouched and untarnished by the people's vices" (1891, 935). Carl Schurz, on the other hand, deemed virtue and vice, the high and the low, as essential constituents of one another: "He had grown up among the poor, the lowly, the ignorant. . . . His mind was much larger than theirs, but it thoroughly comprehended theirs; and while he thought much farther than they, their thoughts were very present to him" (1891, 730).

The intellectual's self-conscious struggle to comprehend Lincoln's anomalous makeup reflected the people's unconscious recognition of his distinctiveness. Lincoln, thus, appeared a *coincidenta oppositorum,* an agency that integrates opposing qualities without modifying them. Memories of Lincoln varied from one part of the country to the next, from one person to the next. For most, the epic Lincoln dominated the folk hero; for others, it was the other way around. For all, Lincoln was a dual hero, not easily represented, let alone described, by one object or one script.

National Monuments for the Two Lincolns: Case Studies

Artistic representations of Abraham Lincoln capture but one of two opposing images. To portray properly the rail-splitter, the rude man from the prairie and the river bottoms, the storytelling folk hero of common touch and homely virtue, is to miss the savior of the Union, liberator of the slave, martyred hero of godly virtue. Likewise, to capture the demigod is to lose the man. In the collective consciousness, however, one side of Lincoln has never replaced the other. Two sides have always coexisted, and as the epic Lincoln became more salient their dualism became a topic of public discussion. Augustus Saint-Gaudens's and George Grey Barnard's statues of Lincoln, the establishment of the Hodgenville, Kentucky, Lincoln birthplace monument, and the design of the Lincoln Memorial made this discussion dramatic. Each case will be examined in turn, beginning with the great statue controversy.

Two Lincolns in Bronze

In 1913, the American Peace Centenary Committee, formed during the 1909 centennial of Lincoln's birth, chose to mark the anniversary of peace with Great Britain (scheduled for 1915) by sending to London replicas of Augustus Saint-Gaudens's statue of Lincoln (fig. 7.7)

Figure 7.7. Augustus Saint-Gaudens, *Abraham Lincoln,* 1879, Lincoln Park, Chicago, Illinois. Photograph courtesy of the Illinois State Historical Library.

and Antoine Houdon's statue of George Washington. The state of Virginia bore the cost of replicating the Houdon statue, but no benefactor appeared for Saint-Gaudens's. The onset of war in 1914 delayed the entire project, but as its resumption approached, the fund for a Saint-Gaudens replica remained empty. Realizing this, Charles Taft, half-brother of the former president, offered to supply the committee a replica of George Grey Barnard's Lincoln (fig. 7.8), and his gift was immediately accepted.

In 1910, Charles Taft had commissioned the original Barnard statue for the city of Cincinnati. Former president William Howard Taft officially dedicated the statue in that city on March 31, 1917—several few days before the United States entered World War I. In June, a periodical dedicated to cultivating traditional art forms, *Art World,* launched the first professional attack against Barnard's work,

Figure 7.8. George Grey Barnard, *Abraham Lincoln,* 1917, New York City (prior to permanent placement in Cincinnati, Ohio), in *Literary Digest,* January 6, 1917.

condemning it as a "mistake in bronze." Shortly afterward, when the American Peace Committee reported its decision to place this work on the British Parliament grounds, the merits of Saint-Gaudens's statue were rediscovered and the dispute over Barnard's statue intensified. The *New York Times* printed forty-nine articles on the disagreement, the majority during a three-month period—September, October, and November 1917. Popular magazines lagged newspapers by about a month. The *Readers Guide to Periodical Literature* lists twenty-four articles on the statue dispute, two-thirds published during October, November, and December 1917. Thus, media coverage peaked six months after the United States entered the war, four months after its first troop contingent arrived in Europe, but several months before these troops would be fighting and sustaining heavy casualties. The argument raged hottest at the height of martial enthusiasm.

The argument itself follows two lines, the first of which concerns refinement and simplicity as alternative prerequisites of political greatness. Barnard critics stated their position rhetorically: is Lincoln to be remembered as a man of dignified tastes and manner or as a backward man who never outgrew the rudeness of his early environment? An *Art World* commentary puts the question in political context:

> *First*—Was Lincoln a clean, dignified member of the bar, dressing in reasonably good taste and having a respect for common-sense social forms and beauty of environment, or was he a rough-necked slouch, dressing like a despiser of elegance in life and beauty of social environment?
>
> *Secondly*—Does democracy mean club-footed, inelegant, vulgar ugliness to the destruction of all social forms, or does it mean grace, dignity, self-respect, and ever-increasing beauty of social form and environment? (October 13, 1917, 30).

The issue could not be stated more clearly. Must democracy bring leveling and mediocrity, as many American intellectuals believed, or can it be reconciled with a culture of high achievement and good taste?

Revelation of Lincoln's true physical traits, *Art World* believed, entails an appreciation of his gentility, of the fact that he was never "a sufferer from the hookworm," that his "father and mother did not belong to the white trash but were really from Virginia stock passing through Kentucky." Clearly, Lincoln was "fully aware of the importance of elegant social forms." People in general think of the young Lincoln as a man "bent from hard labor," but this was not so. From the day he became a lawyer, "he never again did another day's work of rough manual labor." Also, he "hated ugliness, disorder and vulgarity," loathed beyond measure "the class of hobo-democrats and the mobocrats who, together, imagine that slouch-democracy is the salvation of the world, and the last expression of what democracy should mean" (June 1917, 191, 208, 213, 217, 218; August 1917, 416; December 1917, 190).

Such criticism might seem elitist today but was engaging when America's position as a world power was new and precarious, when many intellectuals, including sociologists—not to mention the people at large—took reactionary ideology about democracy's shortcomings seriously (Persons 1973; Cooley [1909] 1962). In this context, American democracy's vitality became an important issue, and around this issue formed the second dimension of the controversy: power versus weakness. Is Lincoln to be remembered as a man of capacity and initiative or as a weakling distinguishable mainly by his good nature? Since Barnard, according to his critics, never appreciated democracy's moral energy, it was no surprise that his Lincoln statue, according to the first in a series of *New York Times* editorials, portrays "a long-suffering peasant, crushed by adversity." It will not, and cannot, "symbolize to the coming generations the true spirit which animates the militant democracy of our times" (August 26, 1917, sec. 2, p. 2). On this same point, another commentator declares that a statue of Lincoln should represent "the triumph of the democratic principle" and depict "not the humble and despairing Lincoln, but the powerful, unshrinking, heroic, and triumphant Lincoln" (October 3, 1917, 12). Although treacherously assassinated, this man deserves our "stern admiration," not our tears; a loving man, his was yet "virile love"; magnanimous, he was never a "weeping willow." Throughout his public life, "Lincoln was a conqueror" (*Art World*, December 1917, 190, 192).

Two Values

George Grey Barnard's defense of his statue revealed a conception of Lincoln and of democracy that critics considered obsolete and unworthy of America's growing world-power status. He made an icon of equality when hierarchical values were, in their view, necessary. Yet the epic image of Lincoln never replaced but was superimposed upon the common Lincoln, and it was this original, realistic conception that Barnard sought to recapture.

Ignoring the real Lincoln, Barnard explained, insults the people and thwarts democracy's essence. And Barnard intended to represent democracy alone—American democracy. In demeanor and dress as well as physical appearance, Lincoln was American; he "carried his weight unconsciously, without pride in rank or culture." His clothing, "worn, baggy trousers, forgotten, unthought of, honored their history . . . of labor" (1917, 18–19). And so Barnard portrayed and made understandable the freedom that American democracy ensures. Expansive personal liberty shows up in looseness of personal appearance.[4]

Capturing Lincoln's rough appearance and manner, Barnard gave the American people a tangible portrayal of their democracy. Theodore Roosevelt, at least, saw in Barnard's accomplishment "the living Lincoln, the Great Democrat," as did sculptor Frederick Mac-Monnies, painters John S. Sargent and Abbot H. Thayer, illustrator Charles Dana Gibson, and art critic Richard Fletcher. As the debate wore on, other distinguished people, including President Woodrow Wilson and former president William Howard Taft, sided with Barnard.

Two Truths

"If that weird and deformed figure [by Barnard] really represents the results of democracy, we can hardly expect Europe to fight that democracy may be made safe" (New York Times, January 1, 1918, 17). This statement reflects not only the belief that Barnard's Lincoln portrays national weakness rather than strength but also the fear that it confirms America's cultural inferiority. A letter to the Times editor puts it squarely: "Don't give Britons proof of what they believe about the crudity of American democracy" (New York Times, January 1, 1918, 17). Likewise, Art World argues that "this slouchily dressed and presumably democratic despiser of elegant social forms will certainly give to every European reactionary and enemy of democracy a justification for saying: do you see the disgusting fruit of the vulgar social life of Democracy?"[5] Such talk alarmed Barnard's supporters: "Are we ashamed of Our Commoner, so that we want to hide his hands and feet and gaunt figure from British eyes?" (Roberts 1917, 62). The answer was a resounding yes.

Although many distinguished artists and politicians, and a few art journals, supported Barnard, the major art establishments and even certain political bodies opposed him. This institutional opposition reflected public opinion. In November 1917, *Independent* magazine, a general periodical, invited its readers to assess six Lincoln statues. Of more than twenty thousand replies, 49 percent preferred Saint-Gaudens's Lincoln. Statues by J. Patrick, Daniel Chester French, Thomas Ball (fig. 2.3, 88), and Gutzon Borglum (fig. 4.4, 183) received from 7 to 17 percent of the votes, and Barnard's only 6 percent, ranking last (*Independent,* December 29, 1917, 590–91). Although no model public opinion survey, the study's one-sided results warrant the tentative conclusion that Saint-Gaudens's image better reflected the public's conception of Lincoln than Barnard's.

Rejection of Barnard's statue did not result solely from its offending epic ideals. The major clue for understanding the uproar is that no opposition existed to locating the statue in Cincinnati; the storm broke only with the prospect of its placement in London. In a widely distributed public letter, Robert Todd Lincoln, the president's only surviving son, said that he understood "that the completed statue has gone to Cincinnati to be placed. As to that I have nothing more to say, but I am horrified to learn just now that arrangements are being made for a statue of President Lincoln by the same artist, and I assume of a similar character, to be presented for location . . . in London" (*Literary Digest,* October 4, 1919, 30). Since Lincoln knew that many Americans admired Barnard's work for reasons few Europeans would understand, he did everything he could to prevent the statue from leaving the United States. "I gave the best years of my life to accomplish this," he told an acquaintance. "I pulled every wire. I wrote, I spoke publicly and privately; I did everything I could to keep it out of London, and I consider that the last public service I shall ever render" (Thayer 1922). In Cincinnati, Lincoln reasoned, Barnard's portrayal of his father might elevate the dignity of the people; in London it would surely diminish the dignity of the nation. The *New York Times* opposed the London site for essentially the same reason: "We have often greatly admired [Barnard's] statuary, and to his Lincoln the only objection we have to make now is that it is not a fitting embodiment of the Emancipator to place publicly in London" (September 1918, 10).

Critics imply that Barnard may have accurately depicted at least one side of American democracy—its respect for the common man. At issue was the context in which this man, this typical American, should be celebrated. No absolute agreement on the matter was possible, but a working consensus emerged. To the local monument went the task of portraying the nation's commonness; the national monument, its greatness—this is what the critics seemed to be saying. Whatever Barnard's statue of Lincoln meant to the American viewer, it could only undermine America's image abroad.

In late December 1918, a year after the "American Committee" supporting Saint-Gaudens's statue was established, the British centennial committee declared both statues acceptable, each to be placed in a fitting location. In late summer 1920, Saint-Gaudens's statue was unveiled in London's Parliament Square before a group of distinguished citizens and high British and American officials. Barnard's statue had been affectionately received ten months earlier by Manchester, a city, as one observer put it "closer to America in thought than any part of the British Isles" (*Literary Digest,* October 4, 1919, 29). Thus, the two memorials, each representing a different facet of America's self-conception, found suitable foreign display in places that amplified one aspect of the democratic dualism they respectively embodied.

Two Temples

Unselfconsciously, Americans settled on a conception of Abraham Lincoln that reflected two irreconcilable parts of their political makeup: first, their love of democracy and preference for leaders they could reach, talk to, and touch; secondly, their pride in the swelling power of America and wish to embody it in impressively remote men. This dualism found expression not only in the genres of Lincoln's statuary but also in the architecture of his Hodgenville, Kentucky, and Washington, D.C., memorials.

Shrine of the Log Cabin

Abraham Lincoln's earliest memories went back to Knob Creek, a farm located ten miles east of his birthplace to which he and his family moved when he was two years old. Lincoln had forgotten his first home; his admirers did not. Because Lincoln's log cabin legitimated belief in America as a land where common people are respected and can improve themselves through work, great effort went into its "restoration."

About thirty minutes east of the interstate highway linking Louisville and Nashville sits Lincoln's birthplace—a relatively isolated spot which is, nevertheless, visited by more than three hundred thousand people annually. Rolling green land, lush trees, and abundant plants intersected by walkways and trails make this one of the most beautiful of all historical parks. The landscape is, in turn, made more pleasing by the park's relics and shrines. Sinking Spring, for example, merely supplied the Lincoln family with water, but it has become almost a holy place, as the Park Service's sign suggests: "The infant child Abraham had his earliest drinks of water from this source." The spring is physically unimpressive, but many visitors make their way down the steep and narrow walkway to see where "the infant child" drank.

Set on a hilltop and sheltered by a marble temple is the greatest relic of all, the log cabin. "The neo-classical structure in a farm setting may seem grandiose for a man who wrote: 'I was born and have ever remained in the humble walks of life.' But the rough cabin within the memorial dramatizes the basic values sustaining Lincoln as he led the Nation through its darkest period." Such is the United States Park Service's version of this greatest of monumental anomalies. What "basic values," precisely, does the memorial site dramatize? Why should an old symbol of democracy, the log cabin, be enveloped in an undemocratic temple?

These questions must be contextualized before they can be answered. The log cabin was symbolically important not only because it was Lincoln's birthplace. During the presidential campaigns of 1840 and 1860, the log cabin had been identified with democracy and the frontier spirit. At the turn of the century, as America grew into an urban industrial society, youth leaders—progressives in particular—invoked simplicity and renewed contact with nature as a source of democratic values.

Lincoln's birthplace shrine was dedicated in 1916, just one year before the United States entered World War I. Its developers adapted the "two Lincolns," the folk and epic Lincoln, in such a way as to communicate a particular way of knowing and feeling about the world. Their Lincoln monument expressed the same dual ethos animating the Saint-Gaudens/Barnard controversy. Specifically, the log cabin was to the marbled temple what Barnard's Lincoln was to Saint-Gaudens's. The story behind the development of this familiar symbolic structure, however, is strange.

After Lincoln's assassination in 1865, many people visited the Hodgenville farm but found there neither a log cabin nor any other structure. Thirty years later, in 1894, a Major S. P. Gross acquired an option to purchase the farm in order to build a historical site, but a log cabin never figured into his plans. Evidently the cabin in which Lincoln was born had long ago deteriorated. Gross went bankrupt before he could exercise his option, and the farm was purchased by Alfred W. Dennett, a New York–based entrepreneur who wanted to make it a national historical park, complete with a hotel, and to use the proceeds to fund missionary work. He had reason to believe that the original cabin was still standing on a nearby farm, for he instructed his agent, Reverend James W. Bigham, to purchase this cabin, move it to its "original location" and rebuild it with "identical logs that were in the original cabin" (Pitcaithley n.d., 4). Dennett's belief was possibly related to the local story that Dr. George Rodman had bought the cabin after Lincoln died, moved it to his farm, made alterations so that renters could live in it, and later sold the farm to the family from which Dennett made his purchase. Dennett's instruction to rebuild the "original cabin" with "identical logs" must have been based on his belief that Dr. Rodman enlarged the original cabin, for after Reverend Bigham bought the two-story cabin from the neighboring farm he converted it into a smaller, one-story dwelling. He called in a photographer and advertised it as "Lincoln's birthplace Cabin." Dennett displayed the cabin (along with Jefferson Davis's) at expositions in Nashville and Buffalo, but he went bankrupt and had to dismantle both cabins and store their logs together in Long Island, New York.

In 1899 and 1900, Dennett and Reverend Bigham tried to persuade the U.S. Congress and the Kentucky legislature to purchase the Lincoln farm. Both efforts failed. In 1905, after unsuccessful local efforts, the Hardin County court put up the farm for auction. Robert J. Collier, admirer of Lincoln and publisher of *Collier's* magazine, bought the property and, with his associates, including Albert Shaw, editor of *Review of Reviews,* formed the Lincoln Farm Association for the purpose of developing the birthplace into a national shrine. Besides Collier and Shaw, the association's twenty-eight-member board of trustees included Lincoln biographers Henry Watterson, Norman Hapgood, and Ida Tarbell, sculptor Augustus Saint-Gaudens, writer Mark Twain, labor leader Samuel Gompers, political leader William Jennings Bryan, and Secretary of War William Howard Taft. Joseph Folk, governor of Missouri, was presiding officer. The board represented such a wide range of political, economic, and regional interests because its task involved a nationwide money-raising effort.

"There is a natural human instinct," wrote Mark Twain in his widely published 1906 solicitation of contributions, "that is gratified by the sight of anything hallowed by association with a great man or great deeds." The benefits, in the Farm Association's view, extended beyond personal satisfaction. By 1906, the American people had become more wealthy and powerful than ever, but "our keen patriotic sensibilities have been dulled," explained association member Richard Jones (1906) and "greed, commercialism, and sectional strife" plague the land (18). As devotion is the nation's safeguard, this "altar of patriotism," according to New Hampshire Senator Jacob Gallinger, would be an object lesson "inculcating the principles of patriotism and love of the Union in the hearts of the coming generation." Representative John Williams of Mississippi agreed: patriotism and love of the Union meant "the coming together of Northern and Southern ideas, the essential unity of the American people" (quoted in Stephenson 1993, 55).

Raising money proved difficult, and work on the birthplace shrine did not begin until the 1909 centennial. To restore the log cabin to its original site and to build near it a historical museum containing Lincoln relics was the original idea. (Such a place, in President Theodore Roosevelt's words, would be a "temple of patriotic righteousness.") Insufficient funding caused the museum plan to be dropped in favor of a simpler one: the log cabin restored and protected by a marble temple.

Lincoln's birthplace logs were ready to be assembled, since Robert Collier had brought them to Kentucky at the time he purchased the Lincoln farm. Although mixed indiscriminately with the logs of Jefferson Davis's cabin, the "sacred pile" was placed on a flatcar, decorated with a portrait of Lincoln, covered with flags and bunting, guarded by Kentucky militiamen, and carried from New York southward to Philadelphia and Baltimore, then westward across Pennsylvania, Ohio, Indiana, and into Kentucky. As soon as the logs arrived in Louisville, Collier and the Farm Association retained a law firm to collect evidence and make a judgment on the original cabin's authenticity. The Farm Association's action indicates the cabin's symbolic importance, but affidavits collected by the firm were contradictory. Three supported the story of Dr. George Rodman, which asserted the cabin to be Lincoln's; one did not. The evidence, although indecisive, was persuasive enough to warrant confidence in the cabin's authenticity. Positive findings were transmitted to the Farm Association: "[T]he American people will not be so unreasonable or critical as to demand more conclusive evidence." (Peterson 1968, 28).

Not everyone was willing to suspend all doubt. Collier himself used guarded language when referring to the cabin as Lincoln's actual birthplace, but since there was no strong counterevidence, the Farm Association endorsed its authenticity. The Association's word was good enough for the U.S. Committee on the Library of the House and Senate. Given the Committee's approval, Congress voted to take over the site in 1916 "with all the buildings and appurtenances thereon, especially the log cabin in which Abraham Lincoln was born and the memorial hall enclosing the same" (Davis 1949b).

From a late-twentieth-century standpoint it may seem as if the Farm Association and Congress were victims of their own gullibility, but from an early-twentieth-century standpoint, when Lincoln's memory was more immediate and relevant than it is today, both acted prudently. Everyone knew why the Association's law firm deemed demands for "more conclusive evidence" to be unreasonable. When the object in question is a sacred object, being wrong about its authenticity would be the worst mistake possible. This decision rule must be recognized in order to understand the firm's recommendation. If facts fail to compel in so significant a matter, decisions must be based on faith. At best, then, the Farm Association had certified a sacred relic; at worst, a sacred symbol. If the cabin in question was not the authentic place of Lincoln's birth, then at least the country had a reminder of the kind of place in which he was born. This is what Lincoln scholar Louis Warren meant when he asserted, in 1950, that "unimpeachable evidence" of mistaken identity would be needed for rejecting an object that has "made a positive inspirational contribution to an ever-increasing number of pilgrims" (Peterson 1968, 96).

Another reason why the Farm Association took the prudent course in approving the cabin is that so little was needed to prove authenticity. Critics may have been right in denying the authenticity of the cabin *as a whole,* but that was not the issue. As Louis Warren later explained, they had failed "to prove that no logs in the present structure can be associated with the original birthplace" (Pitcaithley n.d., 13). Warren was referring to the fact that the cabin logs had been disassembled, moved, and reassembled so often and mixed in storage so indiscriminately with other logs (including Jefferson Davis's) that no one could be certain which were originally Lincoln's. However, one part of the original structure was enough to authenticate the whole. As Emile Durkheim observed, "when a sacred thing is subdivided, each of its parts remains equal to the thing itself" ([1915] 1965, 261). Warren recognized this intuitively. Likewise, when John Russell Pope discovered that the cabin was too big to allow ease of movement within the marble temple he had designed to house it, he immediately cut off several feet from the cabin's length and width. As the part stands for the whole, the remains were more than enough to represent the original. The direction of Pope's oversight, moreover, sustained the impression of Lincoln that the log cabin had always preserved. Pope, a talented architect, had not bothered first to take a measurement of the cabin because he could not believe it would be too big for the space he contemplated. Underestimating the size of Lincoln's birthplace reinforced the myth of Lincoln's humble origins. (For detailed discussion of the log cabin's enshrinement, see Davis 1949a. Also see Hosmer 1965; Stephenson 1993.)

In 1918, two years after the federal government assumed responsibility for the Lincoln Farm, John Lloyd Wright, son of famed architect Frank Lloyd Wright, patented "Lincoln Logs," a toy that has been marketed to this day. Wright came of age during the Progressive era, held the camping movement in high regard and had it in mind as he designed his logs. Lincoln's was the ideal name to attach to these logs, for the two—man and cabin—had become synonymous. Because each new box of toy logs contains instructions for building a replica of Lincoln's cabin, every child in the land could participate in keeping the truth of the log cabin myth alive.

Two Memorials in One

The log cabin represented a story Americans embraced. All memorial structures, however, must be worthy of what they represent. Just as an imposing grotto was built over the humble birthplace of Christ, so a temple was built over the humble birthplace of Lincoln. Lincoln's temple, like Christ's grotto, stands neither apart from nor against its relic, but rather constitutes it. The container and its content define one another.

John Russell Pope, architect of the Jefferson Memorial, National Gallery of Art, and National Archives, designed Lincoln's temple after the Pantheon, located it on a hilltop, and made it accessible by a long, wide flight of fifty-six steps, one for each year of Lincoln's life. The board of trustees, appointed to supervise the temple's construction, approved the following inscription above the five-columned entrance:

HERE

OVER THE LOG CABIN WHERE ABRAHAM

LINCOLN WAS BORN . . . A GRATEFUL

PEOPLE HAS DEDICATED THEIR MEMORIAL

The opening words of the inscription are designed to reinforce the
visitor's confidence in being in the presence of a sacred object—the
very place where Abraham Lincoln came into the world. The words
"Over the Log Cabin" convey an impression of certainty: the cabin
came first; the temple, afterward. The most visible and imposing part
of the Hodgenville shrine was thus reduced to a mere covering.

Popular media illustrations, on the other hand, featured the temple more often than the cabin. The February 1916 issue of *Collier's*
magazine marked the federal government's acquisition of the shrine
with a cover picture of hundreds of people outside the temple, ascending its steps, gazing at its stately columns. The temple's immen-

Figure 7.9. Abraham Lincoln's log cabin, 1916, Abraham Lincoln
Birthplace Memorial Park, Hodgenville, Kentucky. Photograph courtesy
of the National Park Service. Photographer, W. L. McCoy.

Figure 7.10. Abraham Lincoln Monument, 1916, Abraham Lincoln
Birthplace Memorial Park, Hodgenville, Kentucky. Photograph courtesy
of the National Park Service. Photographer, W. L. McCoy.

sity, these illustrations and their stories imply, define the cabin's significance. The cabin alone, like the commonplace it symbolizes, has
no power to attract; it must be enhanced by traditional symbols of
authority. The temple's distinction, on the other hand, is defined by
the humble building it contains. The two elements are connected, yet
separate: from outside, the log cabin is invisible; from inside, the temple's majesty is unapparent (figs. 7.9 and 7.10). Cabin and temple are
physically autonomous but symbolically interdependent. The cabin is
to the temple what humility is to pride, commonness to dignity, nature to culture, obscurity to fame, mediocrity to greatness, weakness
to power.

President Theodore Roosevelt laid the cornerstone of the shrine on February 12, 1909. Ten thousand people attended the dedication; most, conscious of its significance. A Lincoln shrine in Kentucky, after the establishment of the Lincoln Home and Tomb in Springfield, Illinois, further shifted the nation's spiritual center toward the West. New shrines meant a new commemorative topography. Maurice Halbwachs believed that sacred memories are secured by localization—the marking of important events where they are believed to have occurred ([1950] 1980, 128–57). The relationship of these markers to one another as well as to their respective historical referents, however, determines their significance. Spatial contrasts, thus, express historical and cultural contrasts. Lincoln shrines in the West stand in the same relation to Washington shrines in the East as egalitarianism stands in relation to hierarchy. Whether the Hodgenville shrine is considered separately or in relation to the ones in Washington, the same dualism appeared.

"The Glory of a Home Like Thine"

Shortly after Lincoln's birthplace was dedicated, construction of the Lincoln Memorial began. Tension between egalitarian and hierarchical themes were as evident in the making of this monument as they were of Hodgenville's. The Lincoln Memorial's location and massive scale, however, transcended this tension in a way that did not happen in Kentucky. This was not inevitable. In hindsight, the Memorial's final design may seem natural and proper, but for many years the two Lincolns—the folk hero and the epic hero—figured prominently in debates about what form the Lincoln Memorial should take.

Planning for the Lincoln Memorial had begun during the heady years following the Spanish-American War. The time had come to make Washington, D.C., a great world capital, and ideas for enlargements and improvements were in the air. Coincident to all such schemes was the enlargement and improvement of Lincoln.

Appointed by Congress to conceive a monument plan, the original Lincoln Memorial (McMillan) Commission consisted of four members, all of whom were strong Union supporters in their youth. Since they wished to make Lincoln's monument as imposing as possible, they selected a site (Potomac Park) that put it in direct relation with the Washington Monument and Capitol Building without causing it to fall under their shadows. The commission's recommendation, however, was preliminary; in fact, it authorized one of its members, James T. McLeary, to survey European monuments for later consideration. After a long delay, corresponding, perhaps, to behind-the-scenes bickering and planning, McLeary submitted his report. He had been impressed by the Appian Way leading into Rome and recommended a seventy-two-mile American Appian Way connecting Washington, D.C., and Gettysburg, Pennsylvania. McLeary had good reasons for this plan. Since the road would run through parts of Virginia, it would constitute a "wedding ring" unifying North and South. It would also suit Lincoln's fame, which was rising so rapidly that traditional monuments would be unable to keep up with it. A highway could be embellished with future monuments to Lincoln. Congressmen also recognized the practical value of a new highway in a country exploding with automobiles, for it would stand for "a fight against idle sentimentalism by sensible utilitarianism of which there was no nobler exemplar than Lincoln" (U.S. House of Representatives, 1913, 2229). This reasoning, based as it was on solid progressive ideals, appealed widely. In 1910, the highway bill passed the Senate but failed in the House, possibly on suspicion that a major act of commemoration would be tainted by special highway and real-estate interests (which turned out to have been warranted [*New York Times,* January 20, 1913]).

The highway plan was still alive in Congress even after the Lincoln Memorial Commission voted to place a traditional monument to Lincoln at the edge of the Mall in Potomac Park. Soon, however, the traditional monument and Potomac Park site captured the imagination of most congressmen. "The place of honor," as secretary of state and former Lincoln secretary John Hay put it, "is on the main axis," and Lincoln of all Americans deserved it (U.S. House of Representatives, 1913, 22). The main axis's shrines, Representative William Sharp believed, would amplify each other's effects. He imagined the patriotic tourist, newly inspired by his visit to the Capitol and the Washington Monument, as "he pursues his way to Lincoln's memorial, rising with its lines of strength and beauty before him" (2240). Architect Henry Bacon, formally invited by the Commission to execute his memorial design, could imagine the glorious connection from another vantage point: "From the hills of the District and Virginia the constantly recurring views of a great Lincoln memorial, seen in association with the Washington Monument and the dome of the Capitol, will be impressive in the highest degree" (22).

Not everyone wanting to see the memorial in Washington favored the Potomac Park location. Some preferred a shrine near Union Station, the city's busiest location, or the Capitol Building, its most famous landmark. Their recommendations were based on the assumption that existing population and legislative centers dignify whatever is placed near them. Some wanted a living memorial—a national vocational school for children; some preferred to save the capital city from "unrestrained and unregulated individualism" (*Outlook*, August 12, 1911, 811) by a column-lined boulevard connecting the Capitol Building and Washington Monument. William H. Davis, speaking for America's black people, wished to see a monument containing an alcove for each state dominated by a statue commemorating Lincoln's role as emancipator, a theme that had been studiously avoided during the debates in order to preserve the spirit of regional reconciliation (Stephenson 1993, 99). John Hay explained why the originally recommended Potomac Park site, located two miles from the Capitol and train station and one mile from the Washington Monument, was the most appropriate. "Lincoln," he said, "was of the immortals. You must not approach too close to the immortals. His monument should stand alone, remote from the common habitations of man, apart from the business and turmoil of the city; isolated, distinguished, and serene" (U.S. House of Representatives 1913, 22).

As a sacred being, Lincoln had to be isolated geographically and defended against profane contact. For this reason, Henry Bacon dismissed the idea of a heroic-size statue of Lincoln placed in an open portico and invoked the ancient Greek practice of placing statues of gods in enclosed temples to secure their separation from the mortal world. "The power of impression by an object of reverence and honor," he said, "is greatest when it is secluded and isolated" (Thomas 1991, 477). The memorial's seclusion and isolation was enhanced by its elevation: to reach it one must ascend its many steps, looking upward as if approaching a supernal deity.

If the Lincoln Memorial's distance from existing monuments weakens its connection to them, its size compensates. The more Henry Bacon contemplated remote Grecian temples, the larger the memorial became. His finished building was a temple with thirty-six columns—one for each state in the Union at the time of Lincoln's presidency. Two urns placed outside the temple contained no eternal flames but signified the presence of a god. Daniel Chester French's statue of Lincoln, patterned after Zeus on his throne, completed the classical parallel. French's first version was larger than life, but the massiveness of the temple forced him to double his original dimensions. Thus, Lincoln's memorial continued the tradition of raising the man of the people above the people.

The Lincoln Memorial's ostentation, although appropriate to America's new power, was mitigated by tradition. Just as antique gods look eastward through their temples' entrances and see the rising sun, Lincoln looks eastward and sees the Washington Monument. He perpetuates Washington's glory in the twentieth century by perpetually gazing at his shrine, just as early 1860s prints (fig. 7.11) show him gazing at Washington's bust.

Fixing Lincoln's gaze on George Washington's monument is only one part of an originally ambivalent pattern. Lincoln's shrine was designed to complement the Washington Monument architecturally and ideologically. Given the Monument's extraordinary height and strong vertical lines, the U.S. Commission of Fine Arts, which was established during the design debate, determined that the Lincoln

Figure 7.11. *A. Lincoln*, 1863, print. Photograph courtesy of Harold Holzer.

Memorial's height could be only moderate; its strong lines, only horizontal (*Outlook,* February 10, 1912, 297). Coincidentally, the vertical is to the horizontal everywhere what remoteness is to intimacy,
dignity to plainness, hierarchy to equality (Schwartz 1981). "Although its isolation . . . adds prominence and dignity," the editor of
the socialist *Call* noticed, the Memorial is classic in its "sheer simplicity." The *Call* underscored this interpretation with a cartoon depicting French's statue from the side, which makes Lincoln look more
like a man of sorrows than a man of power. The cartoon's heading
suggests an alternate, yet consistent image: "Memorial to Honest
Abe" (*Call,* May 30, 1922, 2). Monumental architecture thus contrasts Washington, the genteel man, to Lincoln, the common man.
Many people gave the Lincoln Memorial precisely this interpretation.
Many did not.

The American Institute of Architects' Illinois chapter condemned
Bacon's design because it "has no connection historically, nor from
the standpoint of democracy with the work of Abraham Lincoln."
It failed to capture Lincoln's supreme "Americanism" (*Independent,*
February 6, 1913, 281). The editors of *Independent* cited the institute's resolution because they agreed with it. "What is there about
such a monument to remind one of Lincoln even though it enshrines
a gigantic statue of him in gilded bronze. . . ." An unveiled expression
of class resentment followed: "Why should the Great Liberator be
commemorated by an edifice characteristic of a people whose wisest
men upheld the institution of slavery as natural, indispensable and
eternal? If Lincoln had been trained for five years in Greek ideals as
college students still are, very likely he would not have ventured to
assail an institution so ancient and respectable" (281). *Independent*'s
editor, assaulting the same elitism that Barnard's admirers attributed
to his critics, seemed to be reenacting the Barnard/Saint-Gaudens
controversy—fighting the same culture war, mobilizing the same constituencies.

Gutzon Borglum, the most eminent critic of Bacon's neoclassical
design, sided with the *Independent*. In 1912 he wrote to the editor
of the *Baltimore Sun:* "Washington is Roman, but that is not old
enough. We are informed Lincoln must be Greek. I suppose he'll sit,
or stand, plug hat and all, garlanded as was the custom." Two years
later, he wrote to Representative William Borland of Missouri: "I
have no intention of letting up on the Greek Temple." To understanding audiences he said: "In heaven's name, in Abraham Lincoln's
name, don't ask the American people even to associate a Greek tem-

ple with the first great American." Borglum recalled the twentieth
century's Great Commoner to make his point more emphatic: "What
would you think of taking Mr. Lincoln or Mr. [William Jennings]
Bryan over to the Acropolis and putting them there in bronze?" (Borglum 1914). Borglum had a personal interest in the memorial because, even after Congress had committed itself to Bacon, he wanted
to participate in its construction. Borglum's criticism is important,
however, for its content, not its motive. He couched his criticism in
populist discourse, invoking repeatedly the opposition between
"American" and "foreign," a polarity that resonated strongly with
overheated postwar nationalism. Influences from "foreign ports," he
explained in a speech titled "When the People Spoke," "threaten to
dehumanize this one great, unbroken soul we have ourselves reared.
They are going to build in memorial a husk of a Greek temple. . . .
This is not the people's wish; it is not even known to the people
and it will never become sacred nor be understood by the people."
Borglum then moved on to one of his favorite activities: immigrant-
baiting. Listeners recognized this as the point where he would thank
God that "all of America is not as near the graves of Greece and
Egypt as New York . . . " (Borglum n.d.). Borglum was suspicious
of the city of Washington, too. Lincoln's national memorial, he felt,
should be erected in Springfield, Illinois, near his "old haunts." Borglum wanted to see a middle American, not European, monument to
Lincoln.

Critic Ralph Adams Cram was one of many who agreed with
Borglum. When Cram looked upon the Lincoln Memorial he saw "a
pale simulacrum out of a dead past" that does not, and cannot, capture Lincoln's essence as a man (Thomas 1991, 650). Lewis Mumford
expressed the same view: "In the Lincoln Memorial . . . one feels
not the living beauty of our American past, but the mortuary air of
archeology. The America that Lincoln was bred in, the homespun
and humane and humorous America that he wished to preserve, has
nothing in common with the sedulously classic monument that was
erected to his memory" (652).

Bacon was sensitive to these criticisms. He referred to his design
usually as a "memorial hall" and "colonnade," rarely as a "temple."
On one occasion he defined it awkwardly "to a degree a temple"
(Thomas 1991, 456–77). Bacon's admirers, however, were less defensive. They doubted that Lincoln was as ordinary and homespun as
his traditional image suggested. Representative Borland of Missouri
explained:

Some gentlemen say that we ought to build something practical—utilitarian—because Lincoln was a "practical man," and then they refer to his having been a railsplitter.

We do not seek to honor Abraham Lincoln because he split rails. Ten million men in this country can split rails, but where is there another man who could have done what Lincoln did in the wild storm that threatened to wreck the Republic? (U.S. House of Representatives 1913, 2190)

Another defender of the memorial design, an architect, asserted: "The temple does not express the externals of the man, nor his humor and manners, but the qualities that made him great" (Bullard 1952, 336). Lincoln, in Alma Wiley's view, deserved his new temple:

Kings have for queens built spire and monument—
　　Still gleams the jeweled Taj in moonlit pool;
In Buddha's bronze a woman's grief is pent;
　　Once Rome's grim warriors carved in stone their rule;
But what is Orient dome or royal shrine
　　Or crumbling arch's half-forgotten fame
Before the glory of a home like thine,
　　Erected in a grateful people's name? (1925, 27)

The Lincoln Memorial debates were less intense than the Saint-Gaudens/Barnard debates, but their theme was the same—the tension between democracy's conflicting need for leaders with whom the masses can identify and leaders whom they can revere.[6]

Equality and Hierarchy

The American people have long celebrated what they have in common with Lincoln, but they have also recognized that common men can, in some mysterious way, be great men. The late-nineteenth-century Lincoln was a great man, but only for those who were committed to the direction in which he chose to take the nation. Most Southerners and, in the North, antiwar Democrats and disillusioned Republicans failed to see the greatness of his deeds. For most early-twentieth-century Americans, on the other hand, Lincoln's war to preserve the Union and to free the slaves was no mistake. Each generation had a one-sided view of Lincoln, bringing out elements in his makeup that other generations would perceive less clearly and appreciate less fully.

Because Alexis de Tocqueville arrived in the United States in 1832, his conception of American culture reflected an egalitarian strain prominent while Abraham Lincoln came of age. Tocqueville's *Democracy in America* was a study of Jacksonian democracy, a coherent but temporary blend of egalitarianism and individualism— manifested in attacks against rank and privilege, on the one hand, and celebration of competition and money-making on the other. The weaker strain of America's political culture was institutionalized in the Whig party, to which Lincoln, then twenty-three years old, belonged. Whigs disdained Jacksonian democracy. They knew intuitively what sociologist Nelson N. Foote later made explicit: that "the dialectical theme of American history has been a counterpoint of the principles of hierarchy and equality" (1953, 325–26). Hierarchy placed constraints on the egalitarian forms that Abraham Lincoln's shrines and monuments, and, accordingly, the memory of Abraham Lincoln, could credibly take.

The word "hierarchy" derives from the Greek *hieros* (sacred) + *archia* (rule) and refers to the ranking of individuals and actions within a central value system. Because it refers to central, that is, ultimate, values, hierarchy is a condition for communicating and maintaining consensus and stability. Hierarchy, in Louis Dumont's words, requires "a classification of beings, according to their degree of dignity" (1974, 65). Equality, on the other hand, is concerned with the declassification of beings and the diffusion, rather than concentration, of dignity. But if equality and hierarchy are distinctly different ordering principles, one cannot exist without the other. Hierarchy ennobles equality by distilling from mediocrity, commonness, and inferiority (which Tocqueville believed to be democracy's characteristic features) the essential elements of moral and political greatness. Equality, in turn, energizes hierarchy, humanizes it, fuses it with a sense of justice and makes it worthy of devotion. Hence the paradox of a passionately egalitarian people singling out one of its members and elevating him above all others. Expressed through hero worship, hierarchy enables equality to realize and become conscious of itself.

At issue is whether American democracy is to be a haven for the common people, whether it can accommodate inequality in refinement and taste, whether a nation dominated by the tendencies of the mass can ever succeed in great undertakings. Most Americans would have answered these questions affirmatively. Plenty of room existed for symbols of both ordinary people and the elite; the only problem was to locate them meaningfully. Almost everyone loved the side of

Lincoln that George Grey Barnard portrayed, but few wanted to see it representing the United States in a foreign capital. Almost everyone regarded Lincoln's birthplace log cabin a sacred shrine, but as it toured the country (at the very time that plans for Lincoln's national memorial were being discussed), it never occurred to anyone to place it in Washington, D.C.—with or without a marble enclosure. The log cabin, like Barnard's statue, symbolized the dignity of the people, and its appropriate place was in the nation's heartland. Because the Lincoln Memorial, like Augustus Saint-Gaudens's statue, symbolized the dignity of the state, its proper place was in the nation's capital.

Lincoln statues and monuments, however, failed to achieve everything their designers and admirers expected. Immigrants who gazed at Barnard's Lincoln were Americanized no faster than those who did not; Saint-Gaudens's Lincoln neither increased nor decreased England's willingness to defend democracy. Americans were no more patriotic after their visit to Hodgenville than they were before, and the Lincoln Memorial never made its visitors as ecstatic as early planners anticipated. At most, Lincoln's statues and shrines— his *lieux de mémoire,* as Pierre Nora (1996) calls them—provided ways of thinking about democracy, ways of reading the egalitarian and hierarchical features of American life. Like other commemorative devices, they were less effective in the production of practical effects than as articulators of political meaning and identity. These monuments were part of a dual symbolic structure delineating and explaining the dualism of the nation's political culture.

The New Face of Collective Memory: Refining the Discussion

Representative Fred Schwengel of Iowa addressed the Lincoln Memorial University graduating class on June 3, 1963, two months after Martin Luther King Jr. announced the Children's March on Birmingham, Alabama. President John Kennedy supported the marchers' goals, but the first president to realize that segregation was wrong, Schwengel told his Tennessee audience, had been Abraham Lincoln, whose spirit presided over the occasion:

The authoritative position of the government of the United States is the position this Nation inherited from the restatement you left us of the meaning of free government; that is government of the people, by the people, for the people—as originally stated by the Founding Fathers.

Not some people—all people. . . . It began from the hour you issued the Proclamation of Emancipation. (Schwengel 1963, 10173)

The civil rights crisis, as Schwengel describes it, appears as part of a narrative beginning with the American Revolution, running through the Civil War, and moving toward a climax in 1963.

Since Schwengel was a Democrat speaking on behalf of the Kennedy administration's civil rights policy, party leaders may have rewarded him by funding his district's pet projects. But this view, even if true, hardly captures the full meaning of Schwengel's words. Serving political interest is one of commemoration's functions, but Schwengel's Lincoln Memorial University address also realizes a ritual process first described by Emile Durkheim: "The officiant [of commemorative ritual] is one with the ancestor from whom he is descended and whom he reincarnates. The gestures he makes are those which this ancestor made in the same circumstances. Speaking exactly, of course he does not play the part of the ancestral personage as an actor might do it; he is this personage himself" ([1915] 1965, 448). Not merely recalling the past but becoming part of it—identifying with it and being identified by it—such is the heart of the matter of collective memory. Abraham Lincoln had realized this intuitively.

No one thought more often or fervently than Lincoln about his nation's past. He considered America's national heritage as an absolute, transcending interests and reason. His old friend, Alexander Stephens of Georgia, said that for Lincoln the nation's unity "in sentiment, rose to the sublimity of a religious mysticism, while his ideas of its structure and formation in logic, rested upon nothing but the subtleties of a sophism" (Howe 1979, 296). Stephens was partly right, but he did not know how profoundly Lincoln felt about union or understand its relation to the way Lincoln pressed the war. Lincoln saw secession as a heresy—the violation of a sacred trust inherited from the Founders. He was dead serious when he told Stephens before the war started that all issues, except union, were negotiable, including slavery.

Common remembrance, Lincoln felt, is the stuff of which national union is made. As he pleaded for reconciliation in his First Inaugural Address, he appealed to "the mystic chords of memory, stretching from every battle-field, and patriot grave, to every living heart and hearthstone, all over this broad land" to "swell the chorus of union." Abraham Lincoln himself figures centrally in the narrative he so earnestly defended. In 1918, English playwright John Drinkwater observed: "[T]he necessity of forming some opinion about the man is a necessary part in the growth of every American mind" (1920, 5). How, precisely, have these opinions been formed?

Politics of Memory

Considering the commemoration of Lincoln as a symbol of political order makes the ups and downs of his reputation easier to understand. We know that Abraham Lincoln was the nation's preeminent historical figure at the end of World War I, but his status had not always been so elevated. Even during the emotional days of his funeral procession, Lincoln's place in the American consciousness was uncertain. Supported at first by the waves of sympathy his assassination set in motion, Lincoln's image remained stable through the last third of the nineteenth century, then it rose abruptly during the first two decades of the twentieth.

That John Wilkes Booth's bullet killed Lincoln rather than grazed or missed him was a matter of chance, but it transformed Lincoln's reputation. Assassination did not immediately make him a national idol, for the ardor attending his death cooled down after his elaborate funeral, and for the next three to four decades he was revered less and by far fewer people than he would be afterward. Lincoln's historical reputation was established at his death, but its growth was sparked by the Progressive era.

Lincoln was not elevated in the Progressive era because the people had discovered new facts about him but because they had discovered new facts about themselves and regarded him as the perfect vehicle for giving these tangible expression. The "they" who discovered these facts is the problematic element in the theory of the politics of memory. Making the connection between national identity and national memory takes money and time. Reputational entrepreneurs sometimes make this connection with a view to promoting and protecting their own interests; sometimes, with a view to promoting and protecting the interests of society at large. The consequence differs. An audience manipulated into associating its interests with a particular conception of the past will withdraw its commitment as soon as the manipulation ends; but if entrepreneurs and their audience share the same values, then reputational enterprise will sustain rather than create collective memory. At the beginning of the twentieth century, agreements among citizens on basic questions about national history and identity outweighed disagreements. The more privileged may or may not have profited more by this consensus than the less privileged, but political profit hardly exhausts its significance.

A nation, according to nineteenth-century historian Ernest Renan, is more than a collection of individuals or institutions. "A nation is a soul, a spiritual principle constituted by two things: one is the common possession of a rich legacy of memories; the other, the continued will to develop this undivided inheritance" ([1887] 1947, 903). By the end of the Great War, Lincoln had become part of the substance and continuity of the American soul. Possessing in common his "rich legacy of memories," America could retain its identity while its political structures re-formed.

No legacy, however, is equally appealing to all parts of American society. Some Americans question or disparage national memories rather than embrace them; others wish to modify or replace the existing legacy, in part or whole, with another. The nation, then, is not a common legacy of memories fixed once and for all; it is a common movement, a common quest whereby communities seek their own understanding of the past, cherish it, come to grips with it, or deliberately use it in their own way. Memories of Abraham Lincoln are cases in point. Native-born and immigrants, men and women, liberals and conservatives, whites and blacks, Northerners and Southerners, found Lincoln mirroring and modeling different aspects of the cultural heritage. Trends, however, were converging. From the time of Lincoln's death, African American affection remained constant while white affection—especially white women, liberals, Northerners, and immigrants—increased. White Southerners came to terms with Lincoln, too, after the pro-Confederate Lost Cause generation died out. The ascent of Southern recognition started slowly, manifesting itself unmistakably in celebrations of the Lincoln Centennial and mobilization for World War I. Differences in the perception of Lincoln were narrower after World War I than ever before.

According to Peter Karsten (1978), America's increasingly centralized and powerful state is the primary reason for the growth of Lincoln's reputation. Arguing on the basis of contrasting political cultures, Karsten regards George Washington as America's paramount "anti-statist" symbol; Lincoln, the personification of "statism." That Lincoln's reputation grew so rapidly during the Progressive era, a time of significant expansion of governmental power, makes Karsten's argument plausible; however, two problems detract from it. First, Karsten underestimates Washington's symbolic role, which, in its celebration of liberty—an anti-statist ideal—remained a salient aspect of American political tradition both during and after the Progressive era. Secondly, Karsten simplifies what Lincoln stood for. Lincoln did represent the power of the twentieth-century state, but he was not commemorated for that reason alone. Embodying the concerns of the common person—a link that transcends the statist/anti-statist dichotomy—was a necessary element in his twentieth-century reputation. Different men of the past and present, including Alexander Hamilton and Theodore Roosevelt, symbolized different aspects of America's new industrial democracy. Lincoln stood above them in the popular imagination not because his life lent itself to becoming a symbol of the majesty of the state but because it had already become a symbol of the majesty of the people. In a society where fear of expanding state power was sustained by a strong libertarian tradition, the man personifying the priority of the state and its elites would not be revered if he did not also personify the entitlements of the masses.

Although Lincoln's reputation surged during the early years of the twentieth century, it expressed more than the conditions of the time. No strict correspondence exists between the conditions of any era and the objects of its memory. Memory-making requires effort: before any one individual can be regarded as worth remembering, other individuals, like colleagues and family members, political and religious leaders, biographers and artists, editors and writers, must deem that person commemorable and must be able to persuade their audiences to agree. Of the many facts stemming from the recent studies of reputation and fame, this fact—the dependence of reputation and fame on successful promotion by admirers—is best established. However, the most prominent of these studies, including Fine (1996, Forthcoming) on Warren Harding and John Brown, Lang and Lang (1990) on the British etchers, Tuchman and Fortin (1989) on women novelists, Connelly (1977) on Robert E. Lee, and Tucker (1973) on Stalin, focus on only tightly organized, highly visible, or state-sponsored reputational enterprise. The commemorative activities organized for Lincoln between 1865 and 1922 were, however, decentralized and locally sponsored, organized by no unifying let alone hegemonic influence. To reduce Lincoln's swelling reputation to elite manipulation would be to distort what was most essential about it.

The centennial anniversary of Lincoln's birth, the critical point in his canonization, would have been celebrated regardless of contemporary circumstances. Lincoln's admirers were too numerous, and the entrepreneurs of his reputation, working independently of one another, had made his place in America's collective memory too visible not to be celebrated. The centennial's intensity and scope, on the other hand, were enlarged by the circumstances in which it took place. Had Lincoln's assumed character and achievements not echoed the concerns of a new society—a stronger and more democratic society—he would have never been recalled so vividly. Thus, it makes sense to assert, with Charles Horton Cooley, that "fame exists for present use and not to perpetuate a dead past" (1918, 116). "Present use," in the present case, meant not to preserve but to undermine the industrial revolution's plutocracy. The progressive politics of memory was opposed to the interests of the dominant class.

Cooley's observation is important not only because it highlights the situated character of collective memory but also because it reveals collective memory in its positive aspect. The social conditions of the Progressive era drew attention to aspects of Lincoln's life that were less relevant in previous decades. Study of this new connection is not to be understood as a new form of relativism but as a positive research program—one that conceives different social conditions as standpoints from which different aspects of the past become more visible and, when synthesized, yield understandings of Lincoln not otherwise possible. Some might say that Progressive era entrepreneurs "constructed" a new Lincoln or "reconstructed" an old one, but it would be more precise to say that this era accentuated aspects of Lincoln's life no previous or subsequent era could see as vividly.

Memory as a Cultural System

Cooley's formulation of the past's dependence on the present makes sense, but he makes no less sense in suggesting that "personal fames are the most active part of the social tradition," and that the famous name must appeal "not one time only, but again and again, and to many persons, until it has become a tradition" (1918, 112). Cooley never wrote about commemoration and tradition as succinctly as Durkheim, or as richly as Shils and Schudson. He never understood how, through commemorative symbols and ritual, the relevance of the past is solidified. Yet in his commentary titled "Fame" (the "extended leadership," as he called it), Cooley displayed great sensitivity to the tension organizing the commemorative process. He recognized society's dual need to sustain appreciation of past heroes by keeping their images intact and by revising them to match changing conditions and tastes. Thus, Cooley spoke directly to our need to distinguish features of the Lincoln image that are hostage to the concerns of the present from features indifferent to these concerns and resistant to change.

The Progressive generation was conscious of its connection to the past and sought deliberately to commemorate it. Later generations, including the present, have had less interest in the past, but there is a limit to how far collective memory can diminish, and the progressive generation makes this limit evident.

To sustain reverence for Lincoln, his image had to be revised, since the situations in which his earlier image made sense no longer existed. The resulting discontinuity, if we may speculate, results less from conscious design than from what James M. Fields and Howard Schuman call "looking glass perceptions"—the powerful tendency to see our own thoughts and values in others (1976–77, 435–42; see also Schuman 1995). Applied to predecessors, looking-glass perceptions revise old conceptions of the past while creating the perception that no change has occurred. Most Americans of the Progressive era found it difficult to imagine Abraham Lincoln as a man of genteel pretensions looking upon the masses suspiciously, and found it easier to think of him as a man of superior intelligence, moral strength, and political skill yet reared among people like themselves and similar to themselves in values and tastes. Progressive Americans found it easier to think this way because their sense of who they were as a nation presupposed a sense of who he was as a person. The progressive Lincoln, however, cannot be dismissed as a fiction. Remaking Lincoln into a symbol for industrial democracy and global power was based on some invention and much exaggeration, but the historical record made this view credible. Lincoln may have lived most of his adult life as an ambitious lawyer seeking a place for himself in respectable society, but his commonness may be inferred from the circumstances of his early life. Americans made Lincoln a symbol of the common man because Lincoln was born into a society of such men, knew what they were like, and how to be like them when necessary. Progressive commemoration made an egalitarian out of a self-conscious Whig because that Whig did something—acted often enough in non-Whiggish ways—to make the transformation plausible. The materials of the "constructed" past, after all, include facts as well as biases and interests. In democratic societies, where historical interpretations are open to criticism, constructions of the past must be undertaken within the limits of reality—obdurate limits that no one can ignore without cost (Fine 1991; Schudson 1992, 205–21). Since Lincoln's image legitimates changing social realities by retaining its original identity as it adapts to new conditions, twentieth-century Americans came to know the Lincoln known in the late nineteenth century while pressing him selectively to their own service.

Discontinuous Continuities

The early-twentieth-century conception of Lincoln as a symbol of equal opportunity and dignity must not be confused with later conceptions of Lincoln as a symbol of racial and economic equality. Few progressive reformers brooded over the justice of racial segregation, and while many Americans were concerned with equal opportunity and limiting corporate power, no federal relief efforts existed for Lincoln to symbolize. Within this limit, the people's respect for "the great Lincoln"—"Lincoln Triumphant"—never seriously weakened their belief in his being one of their own. That Lincoln was the ultimate Man of the People, likewise, never denied his being a Man above the People. By the early twentieth century, the original egalitarian dimension of Lincoln had ceased to dominate the collective understanding, but it limited the distance he could stand from his admirers.

In hindsight, the Abraham Lincoln of the 1865 funeral eulogies was immediately recognizable in early-twentieth-century newspaper and magazine commentaries, but this identity resulted not from a frozen permanence but an identity of core elements overlaid by constantly changing peripheral ones. In the nineteenth century, Lincoln was promoted largely by men who had known him—men who had tried hard but failed to enhance his historical reputation. In the early twentieth century, his entrepreneurs were more diversified, drawn from a larger segment of the white native-born population, and, in the context of a new social order and new political aspirations, their efforts succeeded. The egalitarian values Lincoln embodied during the Progressive era differed from those he represented in the nineteenth century because the meaning of equality had changed. During Lincoln's childhood equality meant equivalence in the sight of God; in the mid-nineteenth century, equal opportunity in "the race of life." In the early twentieth century, equality was linked with material outcomes through the tremendous expansion of electoral democracy and entitlement of the weak to support from the state in their dealings with the powerful. Thus, the nineteenth-century Lincoln symbolized rural virtues and the dignity of the ordinary person; the twentieth-century Lincoln symbolized anti-corporate, pro-labor and "leveling" sentiments that were incompletely developed during his own lifetime.

Lincoln's symbolizing the aspirations of immigrants would have been foreign to his own generation, as would nineteenth-century Northerners' imagining Southerners embracing him. However, Lincoln's twentieth-century entrepreneurs courted the South by emphasizing his role as savior of the Union rather than emancipator of the slave. Even the grounds for judging Lincoln's handling of the war had changed. Contemporaries found his entry into and management of the war problematic; his twentieth-century successors, including

Southerners, saw the war over which he presided to be worth fighting. Whether he was too harsh or too slow, decisive or indecisive, good or bad at picking competent officers, ceased to be relevant. As the twentieth century turned, the Civil War had become the Good War.

Lincoln highlighted the continuity of past and present because his identity had changed enough to accommodate new concerns and preoccupations but not enough to negate what it previously represented. Many students of memory, however, believe that all aspects of the past lose relevance when social conditions change. This belief is neither unprecedented nor confined to adherents of one perspective. Maurice Halbwachs asked: "How can currents of collective thought whose impetus lies in the past be re-created, when we can grasp only the present[?]" ([1950] 1980, 80). The radical element in this formulation, prefiguring those of present-day constructionists, is not only its focus on present relevance as a condition for remembering but also the assumption that the past endures only if society remains unchanged; different generations entertaining different conceptions of the past must be alien to one another, "like two tree stumps," as Halbwachs put it, "that touch at their extremities but do not form one plant because they are not otherwise connected" (80). Halbwachs assumes that social changes altering perception of the past are reconstructive changes. When these changes occur, the past is replaced rather than built upon or modified. Thus, collective memory undergoes basic revision as new values and social structures replace the old. Theorists of the politics of memory believe, with Lowenthal (1985), that under such conditions "the past is a foreign country."

Understanding social change as a cumulative process, one superimposing new social and symbolic structures on old ones, explains how structural transformation occurs without altering basic values (Lipset 1979). This cumulative process makes it easier to go beyond the politics of memory and understand how early conceptions of the past are sustained across time. Commemoration of Abraham Lincoln may have had a logic and force of its own, accumulating over the years a "self-perpetuating rhetorical power" (Schudson 1989a, 109), but the momentum was certainly sustained by a hospitable social context. The primary condition for the endurance of traditional constructions is always the endurance of the social realities they symbolize. Urban-industrial America was vastly different from the America in which Lincoln lived and died. It consisted of a different economy and class system, a different political order, and a different territory; but it was not a different society. It was the same society because it sustained, in the context of change and dissensus, a stable sense of identity based partly, but firmly, on the egalitarian values Tocqueville had described a century earlier. For this reason, the new image of Lincoln the great man could be superimposed upon the old image of Lincoln the common man but could never replace it.

In collective memory's change and continuity inheres the broader question of how culture's need for stability and revision reconcile themselves to one another and to society. Alfred North Whitehead spoke to this question many years ago when he noted that

[t]he art of free society consists in the maintenance of the symbolic code; and secondly in fearlessness of revision, to secure that the code serves those purposes which satisfy an enlightened reason. Those societies which cannot combine reverence to their symbols with freedom of revision must ultimately decay either from anarchy, or from the slow atrophy of a life stifled by useless shadows. (Peterson 1962, 332)

Society's memory of its great people is one part of this "symbolic code." Emphasizing its revisions and discontinuities, constructionists Bodnar, Alonzo, and Hobsbawm make this code seem more precarious than it actually is. Stressing the continuities of collective memory, essentialists like Durkheim and Shils—who believe in society as an entity *sui generis* (self-generating and self-maintaining)—underestimate the extent to which the code adapts to society's changing needs and tendencies.

The commemoration of Abraham Lincoln is a vehicle for correcting these misunderstandings. Since permanent and changing visions of the past are part of one another, separate theories of collective memory—one to explain variation in what is remembered; another to explain persistence in what is remembered—are unfeasible. Facts of Lincoln's case do not warrant the incorporation of persistence and innovation of memory into a third reconciliatory theory, for the presence of inherited memories in the midst of invented memories requires no reconciliation. The present is constituted by the past, but the past's retention, as well as its reconstruction, must be anchored in the present. As each generation modifies the beliefs presented by previous generations, an assemblage of old beliefs coexists with the new, including old beliefs about the past itself (Shils 1981, 39).

The theory of the politics of memory properly anchors collective memory in the present. Its error is to underestimate the present's carrying power by failing to recognize that the same present can sustain different memories and that different presents can sustain the same memory. Once this error is corrected, collective memory's role in human experience appears with greater clarity. Present evidence, at least, shows that the original, egalitarian image of Lincoln was preserved along with the newer, great man image created by the same society. These contrasting images coexisted because society continued to embrace aspects of its hierarchical past while rejecting the exploitive aspects of its democratic present. Lincoln's changing and enduring images legitimated and sustained one another and were reinforced as Americans framed their present experiences in terms of them.

How we go about remembering Lincoln is no different from how we remember other important figures in American history. Projecting ourselves backward and forward in that historical field, we find significant changes in the perception of most public persons, including Lincoln's political predecessors—George Washington and Alexander Hamilton. Yet we rarely mistake such people for others, since the continuities in their images are more distinctive than the vicissitudes. Exceptions are easy to find. Many original biographies and historical accounts, like the canonization of John Brown, have been revised so extensively as to be almost unrecognizable; others, like John Wilkes Booth, remain unchanged over long periods of time. Although common, these instances are not paradigmatic of collective memory. In most cases, as in the contemplation of Lincoln, we find the past to be neither totally precarious nor immutable, but a stable image upon which new elements are intermittently superimposed. The past, then, is a familiar rather than a foreign country; its people different, but not strangers to the present.

Emulation as a Cultural Pattern

Reflecting the continuities and discontinuities in collective memory, Lincoln's reconstruction can be acknowledged without denying the real Lincoln—the mid-nineteenth-century president whose existence transcends the changing standpoints from which he has been known. Whenever we think of the past, we selectively imitate or simulate some of its aspects and ignore others—a process consisting of imperfect emulations, as Stephen Turner (1999) would call it, which take the form of imperfect role taking. Although a significant dimension of enculturation, this process fails to explain why images of Lincoln are important enough to be sustained in the first place. The analytic framework needed to develop this aspect of Lincoln's symbolic role, so far from the concerns and the mentality of the late twentieth century, is difficult to formulate.

Calls for "the Lincolnizing of America" by inserting year-long Lincoln courses into the curriculum, efforts to make Lincoln "the exemplar of the nation," and cartoon drawings of people looking up at pictures of Lincoln were common in the early twentieth century. Throughout the Progressive era and the Great War, as we have seen, Lincoln's life story was, for its readers, a manual on how to live—a veritable model *for* society. In making their claims about Lincoln, however, admirers were saying something about themselves and their world.

Lincoln's cultural role in the early twentieth century was similar to George Washington's in the early nineteenth. Americans emulated Washington from the day he died in 1799 through the Civil War. Young Walt Whitman wrote in one of his stories about Washington: "Do not suppose, young man, that it is by sermons and oft-repeated precepts we form a disposition great or good. The model of one pure, upright character, living as a beacon in history, does more benefit than the lumbering tomes of a thousand theorists" (Forgie 1979, 26). "A beacon in history" is how Whitman remembered George Washington, and that is how Lincoln's admirers remembered him.

A particular kind of environment made images of Lincoln into models for character-building. We can think about these models by considering a continuum, bounded at one pole by a "culture of deference," at the other by a "culture of equality." Cultures of deference exist when role relations and social classes are demarcated and vertical mobility is limited. "Gentlemen" are obligated to protect the interests of the common people while the latter generally recognize the former's achievements and monopoly of privilege. In this quintessentially hierarchical world, history, in Thomas Carlyle's words, appears as "a succession of biographies of great men," and we socialize children by teaching them about the feats and characters of such men. Thus, Mason Locke Weems' *Life of Washington,* first published in 1801, socialized a generation of Americans. The pride and joy of their class, great men were held up as models for the upbringing of all.

Cultures of equality, on the other hand, exist where role relations and class divisions are unclear, vertical mobility widespread and normative, inequalities impermanent. Historiography, shaped by egalitarian social structures, describes past events as collective rather than individual achievements. In the process, certain people stand out, but they are soon "humanized," remembered for their faults as well as their virtues and assigned a smaller place in the scheme of things. Socialization, also shaped by egalitarian structures, requires "role models," but these are guides for the performance of specific tasks like throwing baseballs, basketballs, and footballs, or specific achievements in business or the professions rather than models of moral character. As their relevance is limited, no year-long study of their life stories is needed.

Erosion of character models, according to Alexis de Tocqueville, is attributable to the rise of democracy. In aristocratic ages, he believed, scholars refer historical events to the will and character of leaders; in democratic ages, they are more likely to see historical events resulting from general tendencies to which all individuals are equally subject (1945, 90–93). If eighteenth-century America was a culture of hierarchy and deference, and late-twentieth-century America is a culture of equality, then early-twentieth-century America—the era of progressive reform and expanding global power—was a transitional society containing elements of both deference and equality. Its culture was no longer deferential in the sense of legitimating a distinguished upper class, but its adults (all of whom were born under nineteenth-century Victorian influence) still admired men of achievement and endeavored to make young people emulate them.

There is a close parallel between Abraham Lincoln in the turn-of-the-century children's literature, produced with a view to promoting emulation (for detail see Miller 1992), and the great emphasis placed on emulation in the social science and education literature. The most renowned social psychologist of the day, Charles Horton Cooley, found emulation to be central to the socialization process. Cooley devoted considerable space to this topic in his classic treatise on *Human Nature and the Social Order*. "All autobiographies which deal with youth show that the early development of character is through a series of admirations and enthusiasms, which pass away, to be sure, but leave character the richer for their existence" ([1902] 1964, 313). Of all such "admirations" and "enthusiasms," hero worship was the highest form. A perceptive and sophisticated observer, Cooley knew the perception of heroes was affected by the needs of their admirers. "Fame," he observed, "may or may not represent what men were; but it always represents what humanity needs them to have been" (1918, 113). Cooley, however, never dismissed the hero as a mere construction. He freely identified his own heroes (which included Abraham Lincoln) in his writings, considered them essential to his own achievements, and generalized his feelings about them: "As hero-worship becomes more imaginative, it merges insensibly into that devotion to ideal persons that is called religious. . . . Hero-worship is a kind of religion, and religion, in so far as it conceives persons, is a kind of hero-worship" ([1902] 1964, 313–14). The relevance of Cooley's analysis for the civil religion and nationalism of his time is straightforward:

The idea of country is a rich and various one and has connected with it many sensuous symbols—such as flags, music, and the rhythm of patriotic poetry—that are not directly personal; but it is chiefly an idea of personal traits that we share and like, as set over against others that are different and repugnant. We think of America as the land of freedom, simplicity, cordiality, equality, and so on, in antithesis to other countries which we suppose to be otherwise—and we think of these traits by imagining the people that embody them (113).

"Freedom, simplicity, cordiality, equality"—no one embodied this combination of traits more perfectly for Cooley's generation than Abraham Lincoln.

Collective memory derives its meaning from the entire realm of its use. Cooley believed that collective memory is at once a mirror and lamp, reflector and template, for society; yet he never articulated fully the relationship between the two. He never distinguished between external experience, which historiography and biography encompass and communicate, and subjective feelings—pride, hatred, grief, joy—which commemoration alone can represent. Commemoration, however, does more than express feelings about the past; it organizes them, makes the past conceivable, intelligible, communicable, and public. The primary power of commemoration is the power of "formulating experience, and presenting it objectively for contemplation" (Langer 1957, 133; 1962, 54–65, 82–94). In other words, commemoration is a way of forming its object in the process of representing it.

The foreground of Lincoln admirers forming and representing him occurred against the background of a rapidly industrializing society, but the alignment of foreground and background was imperfect. Everyone emulating Lincoln recognized his imperfections. Libertarian conservatives admired him even though his presidential conduct violated their belief in states rights and weak central government. Socialists recognized he was a staunch capitalist but esteemed him nonetheless. Racial equality activists invoked his name despite their knowledge of his desire to deport every free black person and every slave he emancipated.

However, if Americans could admire, even adore, Lincoln without making him into a copy of themselves, they were nonetheless determined to demonstrate that his feelings about major issues of the day would be consistent with theirs. Hence the abundance of early-twentieth-century articles asking "What would Lincoln do if he were alive today?" Two aspects of this question warrant attention. First, the question itself shows Lincoln was an ambiguous model. His greatest admirers had to be convinced that contemplation of his character and conduct could enhance their understanding of the contemporary situation. Second, the people asking the question always assumed Lincoln's familiarity with the conditions of their own society—an impossibility; therefore, they must have been generalizing from what Lincoln did in his environment to what he would have done in theirs. Asking "What would Lincoln do if he were alive today?" thus shows how the problems of a new century were rooted in tradition and precedent. If Lincoln were only a "reflection" of the present, a way of studying the contemporary mind, then generalizations based on his conduct would have been unnecessary. The mid-nineteenth-century attitudes ascribed to him would resemble projective tests through which people tell stories revealing their own personalities. The Lincoln stories would not have been written so often and read so widely, however, if they arbitrarily "constructed" a "usable" man that bore no resemblance to the historical record of what the real man had said and done.

Progressive era speculation over "What would Abraham Lincoln do if he were alive today?" presupposed a certain moral bent of mind. In Cooley's words:

There is, I think, no possibility of being good without living, imaginatively of course, in good company; and those who uphold the moral power of personal example as against that of abstract thought are certainly in the right. A mental crisis, by its very difficulty, is likely to call up the thought of some person we have been used to look to as a guide, and the confronting of the two ideas, that of the person and that of the problem, compels us to answer the question, What would he have thought of it? ([1902] 1964, 386)

Viewed in this light, moral examples liberate. Without the "vanished persons" whom we invoke to achieve justice, Cooley explains, we are "prisoners of the immediate environment and of the suggestions of the lower organism" (389). In the more recent words of one of Cooley's greatest admirers: "In culture it is always the example that survives; the person is the immortal idea" (Rieff 1966, 31).

Cooley's kind of emulation generates a moral template out of the facts of Lincoln's life. The template, however, was not evident in the facts. Lincoln's progressivism had to be established by comparing his personal traits and opinions with the traits and positions of contemporary reformers. Transposability gave the Lincoln myth its double aspect of mirror and lamp. To transpose something is to change its position in a system or sequence without altering it essentially. Just as a musical composition can be moved upward or downward in pitch without changing its internal structure, so images of Abraham Lincoln's presidential policies may be moved forward or backward in time without altering their basic meaning. If wage labor is "the new slavery," then chattel slavery must have been contemporary labor's forerunner. Lincoln's emancipating the slave and affirming the rights of labor became two parts of the same liberation narrative.

Lincoln's life becomes a model—that is to say, transposable—by providing metaphors for present conduct, the choice of metaphor being determined by the intentions of the user. That Theodore Roosevelt's supporters were more likely than his opponents to see progressive values in Lincoln does not mean they were merely projecting their own views onto him; it means they were selectively emphasizing attitudes Lincoln actually held. The distinction between twentieth-century situations *illuminated* by Lincoln and twentieth-century values *reflected* in him was largely a matter of which aspect of the man one wished at a given moment to emphasize.

The "fictions" of Lincoln's image, then, were based on real historical accomplishments that made the greatest impression on the country's moral imagination. Lincoln's determination to save the Union, his hatred of slavery, and his belief in equal opportunity for all white men, regardless of their birth, affected posterity. Generalizations of this effect were often unwarranted in their breadth, but they were based on facts and sustained the moral values that made those facts worth remembering. Lincoln endures as a lamp for American consciousness, then, because his accomplishments adapt him to it.

This is only part of the truth, however. If Lincoln's example did not somehow contrast with the present (as an ideal contrasts with reality), then it could not edify the present and its invocation would be pointless. If beliefs about him failed to survive societal change, then by the turn of the century he would have already ceased to be recognizable. Abraham Lincoln was the perfect model for the new century's young and the wayward, native and immigrant, because he was politically complex, standing for the permanence of tradition and the impermanence of class boundaries and invidious ethnic divisions. This is why his remaining a symbol of the common people enhanced rather than diminished his postwar reputation. Great monuments might be dedicated to his memory, his portraits might become holy pictures, but people never forgot what and who he was:

> The little towns, the country roads,
> The woods, the prairies, the abodes
> Of humble men . . .
> These are the shrines that still enfold
> The heart of Lincoln as of old,
> Whose living legend runneth thus:
> We loved him; he was one of us. (Laughlin 1924)

If Lincoln could come back, everyone would know what to expect (Philips 1924). He would prefer simplicity to fanciness; action to words; he would oppose red tape, formalism, and ceremony; he would sit as easily with townspeople as with public men. The temples built for him would never turn his head or cause his admirers to forget what they shared with him.

From the initial conception of these two Lincolns—the man of the people and the man above the people, the folk hero and the epic hero—later generations changed little; they only gave that conception new twists. Americans made Lincoln into what he was by assimilating him to their own egalitarian tradition. Representing the continuity of America's heritage, Lincoln comes into view as "the symbol of an age" because he embodied a cultural legacy built up over generations. He remained a timeless symbol by changing on one level, remaining constant on another, being emulated on both.

Memorial Tangles

The realities of Lincoln in American memory resist easy theorizing. It is impossible for memories to persist unless they change, for events to be commemorated unless they are historically known, for enterprise to succeed without receptiveness, for conflicting accounts of the past to make sense without consensus, for the past to be constructed unless retrieved, or be a model *for* society unless it is also a model *of* it. Lincoln's case, however, shows us how the several contradictions of collective memory are resolved, and this resolution defines where our analysis leads. We began with the politics of memory theory because it clarified the way commemorative elites construe the past according to their own interests. Such a theory seems inapplicable to democratic societies but is a powerful theory capturing much of what we have seen in the changing image of Lincoln.

Between 1865 and 1922 men and women, engineering one of the most drastic political, economic, and social transformations in American history, invoked Lincoln consciously to explicate what they had accomplished. Reducing this invocation to the politics of memory cannot explain it, however, because the theory discounts not only the structural continuities on which political changes were superimposed but also their deep cultural continuities. Commemorative spectacles organized by programmers seeking to preserve the status quo contributed to Lincoln's rising prestige, but their efforts initially failed. Lincoln's image depended on the people's readiness to accept entrepreneurs' representations, and this readiness included the people's interpreting reputational enterprise in terms of their own experience. Those who wrote biographies and reminisced about Lincoln were not the ones who organized commemorative festivals. What is more, the content of these biographies and reminiscences enhanced the power of the spectacles, which in turn limited what writers could plausibly say about him critically. Lincoln's cultural significance involved different people invoking him to endow their different experiences with a common sense of identity.

Cultural Diversity and Collective Memory

No gospel is permanent but some are longstanding. Can we expect of Lincoln what Jesus's disciples expected of Him: to "remain the same yesterday and today and for ever"? It all depends on how much distinction we can tolerate. Generations, like our own, that celebrate "cultural diversity" are not attracted to national heroes. Elevating representatives of society's "dominant culture," their members believe, diminishes the esteem of everyone else. The elevation of Lincoln, in particular, marginalizes all who are not the white Anglo-Saxon Protestant male he was. Instead of admiring Lincoln, America's ethnic communities should appreciate their own heroes, document their own accomplishments, and insist on their rightful place in American history—such is the multiculturalist argument. Multiculturalism is hostile to national heroes because it distinguishes so sharply the identity of the nation from its constituent communities and assumes that the latter see historical actors like Lincoln as strangers with whom they would have nothing to do were it not for the dominant culture's influence. The multicultural perspective defines the state's assertion of national ideals as ethnic genocide.

The multiculturalist perspective inadequately describes the reality of the late nineteenth and early twentieth centuries because the nation's threat to ethnic and regional communities resided then, as it does now, not in its oppressiveness but in its appeal—its corrosive effect on tribalism and the unifying of otherwise separate peoples into an increasingly free, open, and congenial society. Lincoln, in this connection, was a multivocal, not univocal, symbol. True, he arose from a part of society populated mainly by white Protestants, but no one except the most resentful defenders and descendants of slaveholders believed his elevation came at the expense of their provincial heritage. The most oppressed of all American people, the African Americans, never found Lincoln's fame burdensome; it always symbolized their dignity and entitlements (Schwartz 1997).

Whether Lincoln deserved his honors, whether his stature concealed the greater achievements of other men, warrants inquiry. But one thing is certain. Ignoring Lincoln or replacing him by vernacular heroes, as John Bodnar would call them, could not restore an ethnic identity that had already disappeared or provide a sense of self-esteem missing on other grounds. Let us not forget how high Lincoln's pedestal stood during the Progressive era. If he were capable of symbolizing no more than Anglo-Saxon Protestantism, he could not have meant to the American people what he did.

What we have said about Lincoln can be said about the representative symbols of all democratic societies. In his 1883 commencement address to the lycée at Sens, France, Emile Durkheim lectured on the social role of the great man. The purpose of greatness, he said, is to enable humanity to distinguish evil from goodness, falsehood from truth, mediocrity from excellence. Great men are venerated to make what they symbolize visible and understandable. If great men are ignored, the result can only be a sterile equality that immobilizes society and negates its ennobling distinctions. The true function of veneration (even in its attenuated form of mere respect) is not to reward extraordinary individuals but to give to their admirers, humble as well as privileged, a way of thinking about and judging themselves.

If, therefore, there are those among them who do not deign to look down upon the rest of their fellowmen, who busy themselves exclusively with the contemplation of their own grandeur, or who isolate themselves in the enjoyment of their superiority, let us condemn them without a second thought. But for the others—and this is the greater number—for those who give themselves entirely to the masses, for those whose sole concern is for sharing with them their minds and their hearts, for those who, in whatever century they may have lived, whether they were once the servants of the great king or are now citizens of our free republic . . . for those, I beg of you, may we have only words of admiration and love. Let us respectfully proclaim them the benefactors of humanity. (32–33)

What Emile Durkheim said about the heroes of France in 1883 has been said time and again, and with supreme conviction, about Abraham Lincoln during the early twentieth century. Lincoln, symbolizing Durkheim's benefactors, became America's universal man: changing and remaining the same; standing beside the people and above the people; a reflection of and model for them—at once behind, above, and within them.

Notes

Introduction

1. For details on how Lincoln became a symbol of racial equality, see Schwartz 1997.

2. Lincoln drafted the Emancipation Proclamation reluctantly, after all other policies to pacify the South had failed. The proclamation expressly retained slavery not only in the border states but also in the areas occupied by Union troops. Lincoln showed his sympathy for slavery, Secretary of State William Seward complained, by emancipating the "slaves where we cannot reach them and holding them in bondage where we can set them free" (Hofstadter [1948] 1974, 169). Seward's remark explains why his party passed over his own presidential candidacy in favor of Lincoln. Almost all Republicans opposed slavery's extension, but with secession a possibility, they wanted a conservative, not a radical, to execute their policy.

3. The most elaborate case for Lincoln as a prophet of racial equality is presented by LaWanda Cox (1981). She believes there was "considerable consistency" between Lincoln's pre-presidential and presidential attitudes, which included "an active commitment to equality beyond freedom from bondage" (20, 22). The most widely held pro-Lincoln view, however, is that he did not outgrow his prejudice until he became president. See also Lightner 1982; and Cain 1964.

4. For an experimental study of collective inhibition of memory, see Weldon and Bellinger 1997.

5. Personal communication, May 2, 1998.

6. For a preliminary analysis of the relation between images of Abraham Lincoln derived from commemorative patterns and a national survey of what individuals think of Lincoln, see Schwartz and Schuman forthcoming, 1–3.

7. Nora is a cultural conservative, and his analysis is to be understood as a lament rather than celebration of deconstructive history. For detail, see Englund 1992.

8. For parallel discussions in cognitive psychology, see James Fentress and Chris Wickham's application of semantic and episodic memory (1992, 20–21) to social science.

9. Amos Funkenstein (1993) introduced the concept of "historical consciousness" to lessen the distinction between history and commemoration (memory, as he called it). He argued that historiography reflects the suppo-

sitions of commemoration, while commemoration is rooted in a mode of consciousness informed by historical facts. Paul Connerton (1989) made a similar point in his effort to relate "social memory" to "historical reconstruction." In a somewhat different vein, Michael Schudson (1997) defines "non-commemorative forms of effective public memory," such as Watergate and other negative events recorded in history books, as events that are remembered without being expressly commemorated.

10. For detail on the empirical study of narrative frameworks and historical understanding, see Yael Zerubavel's concept of "plot structures" (1995).

11. Linking conceptions of the past to the techniques and practices of power rather than Mannheim's "locations," "interests," and "standpoints," the politics of memory is subsumable under the "new sociology of knowledge" (Swidler and Arditi 1994; see especially 308-17).

12. In the same vein but a different setting, Ana Maria Alonso (1988) shows the hegemonic ideology of the Mexican government, which affirms its own version of the national past at the expense of local memories. "National re-presentations of the past feed on local and regional histories; official history gets fat on the pasts it appropriates and subordinates. State cannibalism is a transformative process. Subordinated histories are treated as 'raw facts,' cooked according to hegemonic recipes and served up as national cuisine" (44). See also Fentress and Wickham's account (1992, 87-143) of local memories.

13. Three overlapping perspectives—multiculturalism, postmodernism, and hegemony theory—constitute leading responses to the contemporary memory crisis. Not everyone conducting collective memory research identifies with these perspectives; many scholars reject them, but all find themselves addressing the issues they raise. Multiculturalists, conceiving Middle America's historical understandings as supports for its cultural dominance and contempt for minorities (Kaye 1991), believe that resistance to conventional history enhances racial and ethnic pride (Rhea 1997). Postmodernists feed the multicultural program by celebrating the "petit narratives" of minorities deleted from official history and by deconstructing the "grand narratives" that address ultimate questions about the dominant·culture's origin, purpose, and fate (Lyotard [1979] 1984, xxiv, 14, 37). Hegemony scholars, too, recognize contending historical constructions of differently empowered communities but focus on the way ruling constructions reconcile the masses to elite claims (Abercrombie, Hill, and Turner 1980, 7-29). As multiculturalism, postmodernism, and hegemony theory influence the late-twentieth-century intellectual environment, they shape the terms in which we debate collective memory. Many scholars, however, have tried to assess these terms—to determine whether collective memory is faithful to historical reality or to present interests. Nachman Ben-Yehuda's (1995) "contextual constructionism," a method that seeks to chart and explain deviations from objective description of past events (pp. 20-22), is a prominent example.

14. Whatever metaphors are used to capture collective memory's reflecting and shaping processes must be arbitrary. M. H. Abrams's *The Mirror and the Lamp: Romantic Theory and the Critical Tradition* (1953) and

Don Handelman's *Models and Mirrors: Towards an Anthropology of Public Events* (1990), for example, differ in purpose and content, but their emphasis on reflection and modeling are equally appropriate as metaphors for collective memory's functions.

15. Experimental evidence on the "reminding" capacities of news accounts also demonstrates how history and memory affect the interpretation of present experience (Strange and Leung 1998).

16. David Lowenthal's *Possessed by the Past* (1996), a study of the societal role of heritage, is the most recent effort to deal with memory's modeling functions. "The cult of heritage," Lowenthal writes, is both "creative art and act of faith. By means of it we tell ourselves who we are, where we come from, and to what we belong" (viii). Yet the heritage cult is not innocent: resting on "fraud as well as truth," it distorts history, popularizes and commoditizes the past, promotes bigotry, xenophobia, even genocide. Lowenthal's emphasis on the negative side of heritage, without the benefit of systematic evidence, leaves many questions unanswered, the most important of which is how heritage, as a source of both mischief and nourishing tradition, works.

17. In this connection, Jonathan Rieder's caveat (1994) is useful, as all such caveats are, but casually reckoned. Speeches suggesting a "civil religion" or similar political consensus in America, he suggests, might be read as expressions not of shared values but of concrete rhetorical and political situations that encouraged certain types of linguistic selections. In other words, some oratory is more like a personal crutch, employed for self-interested reasons, than an expression of an important worldview. Reider cannot be wrong, but he cannot possibly be altogether right; otherwise, all political (and commemorative) statements would be meaningless. To distinguish meaningful from meaningless representations is always an empirical problem to be addressed through the reactions of listeners, viewers, and readers.

One

1. For an instance in which the informational function of the ritual outweighed the emotional, see Barry Schwartz and Lori Holyfield's analysis (1998) of President Richard Nixon's funeral.

2. In mid-August 1864, Lincoln's closest friends and political advisors believed he would lose to any Democrat who ran in the November election. To an acquaintance Lincoln wrote: "You think I don't know I am going to be beaten *but I do* and unless some great change takes place *badly beaten*" (italics in original). The great change to which Lincoln referred was a military victory (Donald 1995, 529).

3. For a convenient summary of these and other critical reactions to Lincoln's Second Inaugural Address, see *Detroit Free Press,* March 11, 1865, 4. (Vice-President Andrew Johnson added weight to the Democrats' scornful appraisal of Lincoln's speech by presenting himself drunk at the inauguration.)

4. A useful summary discussion of the South's reaction to Lincoln's assassination is provided by Michael Davis (1971, 98–104). Accounts of this re-

action, to be described in chapter 2, appeared in every Northern newspaper but played a minor role in determining how Northerners interpreted Lincoln's death.

5. Correspondingly, in a nation emphasizing orderly transition of political power, the preservation of symbolic continuity through traditional commemorative practices is characteristic of both new and old elites. Successive Democratic as well as Republican postwar administrations conformed to these practices, although Democrats would not promote Lincoln's reputation enthusiastically or successfully until the twentieth century.

6. Newspapers serving as sources for this discussion but not directly cited include *The Liberator,* the *Boston Daily Advertiser,* the *Saint Louis Daily Missouri Republican,* and the *Louisville Daily Journal.* One black publication, *The Elevator,* was also consulted.

7. For an excellent collection of poetic responses to Lincoln's death, see *Poetical Tributes* 1865.

8. This analysis is based on the reading of thirty-one eulogies, of which only half are directly cited. The geographical distribution of churches and other public places in which the thirty-one eulogies were delivered does not significantly differ from the distribution of the 346 eulogies listed in the *Lincoln Bibliography* (Monaghan 1943). These two regional distributions correlate closely with urban population size. The Mid-Atlantic and New England states, for example, contained 64 percent of the nation's urban population in 1860 and produced 65 percent of the Lincoln eulogies from 1865 listed in the *Bibliography.* The Midwestern states had 18 percent of the urban population in 1860 and accounted for 16 percent of the eulogies from 1865. Correspondingly, 68 percent of the present sample of thirty-one eulogies was produced in the Mid-Atlantic and New England states; 13 percent in the Midwestern states.

9. Death and martyrdom were not "new themes," contrary to what Bellah (1970, 177–78) suggests. They were sacred to American nationhood long before Lincoln took office. Lincoln drew upon them himself at his 1861 inauguration, invoking the memory of "every battlefield and patriot grave" in order to "swell the chorus of Union."

10. Six weeks earlier, in his funeral-day sermon, Reverend Gordon Hall had declared: "Oh, a God of righteousness and equity must be incensed at seeing us execute the poor ignorant deserter, while we excuse the clearheaded, deliberate arch-traitor" (1865, 16).

11. Fifteen years later, a correspondent made a similar point as he remembered the Civil War: "The stirring events of that struggle passing under our very eyes, and in which most of us had some share, rendered the distant revolution tame. Having made history ourselves, we naturally had less reverence for historic characters of a remote past" (*New York Times,* March 13, 1880, 7).

12. Journalists reported public "alarm and consternation" at the news that President Garfield had been shot, yet the people went about their usual business. As the president's condition deteriorated, they prepared for his death, but when it came the press said relatively little about their reaction,

reporting instead on the state funeral preparations (*New York Times,* July 3–September 19, 1881). Likewise, the shooting of President McKinley provoked sincere "awe and grief," but the crowds were "philosophical and stoical" in their emotional response (*New York Times,* September 7, 1901, 1).

13. In foreign affairs, Kennedy's failures (the Bay of Pigs, his inability to prevent construction of the Berlin Wall) seem to have been offset by his successes (the Cuban missile crisis). In domestic affairs, however, his achievements, mainly in civil rights enforcement, added to his troubles on the economy and other issues. Most white people throughout the country believed that he was moving too fast on racial matters, that he was concerned about the well-being of blacks but indifferent to the interests of the white working class (Gallup 1972, 3:1789; *U.S. News and World Report,* July 8, 1963, 38–40; July 15, 1963, 29–30). Many liberals, in turn, felt that Kennedy was not doing enough on any count. "The Kennedy performance," as one commentator complained, "is less impressive than the Kennedy style" (*New Republic,* June 1, 1963; see also Gallup 1972, 3:1800, 1850; and *U.S. News and World Report,* September 9, 1963, 36–37).

14. The shock of Kennedy's death was magnified by modern communications. Four days of uninterrupted television coverage brought the assassination and funeral into the home, where it engaged many families almost continuously (Greenberg and Parker 1965, 1–146). Television broadened participation in the Kennedy rites, just as the funeral train and display of the open presidential coffin had broadened participation in the Lincoln funeral. The result in both cases was a sense of national communion that would be remembered for many years.

15. Personal communication from Alan Woolfolk, July 15, 1998. Woolfolk emphasizes Nelson W. Aldrich's (1988) application of the distinction to Kennedy. Aristocrats, according to Aldrich, are defined by their claims of stylistic superiority; patricians, by claims of moral superiority.

16. An example of this emphasis is the *Washington Star*'s editorial of November 23, 1963: "He brought gaiety, glamour and grace to the American political scene in a measure never known before. That lightsome tread, that debonair touch, that shock of chestnut hair, that beguiling grin, that shattering understatement—these are what we shall remember." In contrast, the religious eulogies delivered in churches throughout the country focused on what the assassination revealed and what moral lessons the people should draw from it (Fine 1965).

17. "Personal charisma" is itself a concept of the television age, having little directly to do with Max Weber's initial formulation (1968, 1:241–42, 266–72; 2:1111–15). For Weber, the charismatic leader is always the radical who performs extraordinary feats in the service of a social movement. The common misuse of Weber's term reflects the need for a concept that brings personal magnetism into the analysis of political symbols.

Two

1. For a discussion of the failed plot to steal Abraham Lincoln's remains, see *New York Times,* November 11, 1876, 5; and *Chicago Daily Tribune,*

November 22, 1876, 3. The would-be thieves hoped to exchange the president's body for the release of a counterfeiter imprisoned in Joliet penitentiary. The two perpetrators were apprehended and sentenced to one year in prison.

2. Lincoln's image probably lost its emotional edge within a week or two of his entombment. After John Kennedy was shot, the National Opinion Research Corporation surveyed a nationwide sample to determine reactions to his death and funeral. Surveyors were especially interested in physical reactions: heart rate, perspiration, nausea, drinking, smoking, sleeping. The symptoms of emotional distress, although more intense and long-lasting among Kennedy's supporters, were found among a substantial portion of every sector of the population during the four days between his death and his burial. Within a week or two of his burial, however, they had subsided for everyone (Sheatsley and Feldman 1965). We do not possess such information for Lincoln, but we may assume that the same pattern of effects occurred among his contemporaries.

3. Ratios are based on *New York Times* citation counts estimated at five-year intervals between 1870 and 1900, then summed. No citations on James Madison appeared in this sample. The ratios of Lincoln counts to Benjamin Franklin and Alexander Hamilton counts are 3.9 and 6.9, respectively.

4. *Louisville Journal,* April 17, 1865. This story and others favorable to Lincoln were reprinted throughout the South (see, for example, *Macon Telegraph,* May 13, 1865, 1).

Three

1. Earlier hostility to Lincoln is evident in William Herndon's admission that there had been a great deal of prejudice and bitterness toward Lincoln, "but these were *beginning* to fade" (Herndon and Weik 1889, 1:vii; italics are mine). At about the same time, Rabbi Simon Wolf, speaking of national opinion, observed that Lincoln's fame and glory were incomplete ([1888] 1927, 187).

2. Lincoln's death and his birth centennial were both occasions for oratory, parades, religious services, public gatherings, and private meetings. The parallel was highlighted during the centennial by frequent references to Lincoln as "The Martyr" and by the presence of "living relics"—people who had participated in his funeral. Survivors of the Germania Mannerchoir sang in 1909 the very hymns they had sung at Lincoln's funeral. Two women who had placed flowers on his coffin were present to observe his centennial. Henry Rathbone, whose father had been sitting beside the president when he was shot, visited Chicago expressly to honor Lincoln's memory. Perhaps one hundred thousand or more Chicagoans remembered Lincoln's funeral as they witnessed his centennial.

3. The newspapers also reflected upon themselves. The *Chicago Daily Tribune,* for example, congratulated itself on the two-hundred-page special Lincoln issue distributed on Sunday, February 7—the day before the beginning of Lincoln Week. Staff writers explained how much time and money

it had taken to acquire so many photographs and to assemble so many authentic stories. The demand for the Lincoln supplement was so great that the edition in which it appeared vanished as soon as it hit the streets, and new copies had to be printed. Later in the week, Chicago's mayor called the special issue a "civic triumph"; another city official said it was "the greatest paper I ever saw," while a third declared, "It was overpowering to me." An aged couple that had died by accidental asphyxiation left behind the most poignant testimonial: "Both victims were lying side by side dressed in their night clothes, and on the stand nearby lay copies of the daily papers displaying the Lincoln stories which they had been reading before they went to bed" (February 13, 1909, 9).

4. Albion Small, organizer of the world's first department of sociology, at the University of Chicago, was a great admirer of Lincoln. Concerned to exploit the methods of science to promote ethics, Small was especially moved by Lincoln's dedication to a conception of justice that he himself also embraced. In his address "Abraham Lincoln—The Prophet of Democracy," to Temple Aduth Israel congregation of Louisville, Kentucky, in 1907, Small declared: "[H]e has exhibited himself to posterity as a man standing, as it were, between the upper and nether mill stone of conflicting interests, saying, from his heart of hearts, daily and hourly to Almighty God: 'Show me what justice is and where it is, and by thy grace, so far as it is in me it shall be done'" (Dibble 1975, 247).

5. For detail on how this liminal period led into progressive reform, see Noble 1970.

6. The institutionalization of sociology as a separate academic discipline, reflecting the era's distinctiveness, arose out of the need for rational decision-making and planning founded on reliable knowledge of society. American sociology was, in this sense, a product of progressivism.

7. For a treatment of the complexity of progressivism at the level of political parties, see Reiter 1998.

8. By 1917, three-quarters of the nation's counties and two-thirds of its states had prohibited alcohol. During the war years, native-born Americans associated drunkenness with immigrants' vices and want of patriotism.

9. The number of Lincoln articles published by each magazine between 1890 and 1921 are: *Century*, 78; *Outlook*, 55; *Harper's Weekly*, 32; *Independent*, 31; *Nation*, 29; *Literary Digest*, 26; *Review of Reviews*, 22; and *Collier's*, 16.

10. The progressive labor movement, following on the heels of the 1890s patriotic boom, was tightly integrated into the culture of nationalism. Andrew Neather distinguished between the "labor republicanism" of the nineteenth century, which was militant and dedicated to promoting workers' interests at employers' expense, and the "labor patriotism" of the Progressive era—a counterfeit movement, as Heather conceives it, whose celebrations, framed in flags and patriotic symbols (including images of Lincoln), disguised its recognition of capitalist hegemony. "In its American context at least, even for socialists, patriotism was and is a peculiarly coercive ideology. . . . Business Americanism forced organized labor to direct more energy

into a patriotism that emphasized loyalty at the expense of the radical anti-capitalist currents of republicanism, a shift toward the '100 percent Americanism' of the 1920s" (1996, 101). Such is the dominant-ideology account of one phase of the history of the labor movement. Whatever truth there might be in Neather's statement, it is clear that Lincoln's symbolizing the "labor patriotism" of the early twentieth century was more than a capitalist defense mechanism.

Four

1. Bryan named his newspaper *The Commoner.*

2. That the family background of Jefferson Davis, symbol of aristocracy, was so similar to Lincoln's, his democratic counterpart, shows how common it was. Davis's grandfather, a Welshman, emigrated to Georgia in the mid-eighteenth century, but it remained for his son, Samuel, to acquire property (in compensation for commanding a troop of irregular cavalry during the Revolution). Selling what he owned, Samuel joined the tide of westward immigration and established a home in Kentucky, where he fared poorly; shortly after the birth of his tenth and last child, he moved to Mississippi. Although Jefferson's father never succeeded in lifting his family above its middle-class status, one of his older sons prospered and sent his younger brother Jefferson to a Dominican seminary in Kentucky. Only beyond this point do the careers of Lincoln and Davis diverge: Davis moved on to higher education; Lincoln, to work and politics.

3. Michael Burlingame makes this claim in his psychobiography *The Inner World of Abraham Lincoln* (1994). According to Burlingame, Lincoln's hatred of slavery went back to his childhood recollection of his father's having exploited him as a source of farm labor—which is ironic, given Thomas's public opposition to slavery.

4. The product of the Lincoln Legal Papers project amounts to more than 250,000 pages of material and is now available on CD-ROM.

5. In their busiest year together (1853), Lincoln and his partners handled one-third of all cases brought before the Sangamon Circuit Court, surpassing by far the practices of the other forty lawyers serving the area.

6. That Abraham named his second son Thomas (Tad), after his father, suggests that his feeling for his father may have been ambivalent rather than hostile.

7. Lincoln's adulthood reflects both the aristocratic and the patrician dimensions of gentility. His aristocratic penchant is evident in his concern for high achievement and refinement of appearance and manner; his patrician side is evident in his paternalistic belief in the moral superiority of his class and political position. (For detail on the aristocratic and patrician elements of gentility, see Aldrich 1988.)

8. Herndon was ahead of his time, for naturalism did not mature until the twentieth century.

9. "It was the spring of 1865. Father was coming up the hill, mother and I were watching for him. Usually he walked with a brisk step, head up, but now his step was slow, his head dropped. Mother ran to meet him crying,

'Frank, Frank, what is it?' I did not hear the answer; but I shall always see my mother turning at his words, burying her face in her apron, running into her room sobbing as if her heart would break. And then the house was shut up and crape was put on all the doors, and I was told that Lincoln was dead. From that time the name spelt tragedy and mystery. Why all this sorrow over a man we had never seen, who did not belong to our world—*my* world? Was there something beyond the circle of hills within which I lived that concerned me? Why, and in what way, did this mysterious outside concern me?" (Tarbell 1939, 11).

10. The church, too, required reform. Wilson, the son of a Presbyterian minister, observed in 1910 that while the Catholic Church would allow the peasant to become Pope (1966, 21, 180), Protestant churches were serving the classes, not the masses, and had "more regard for pew rents than for men's souls" (20, 367).

11. Such egalitarian ideals showed up in pictorial as well as written accounts of Lincoln's demeanor. An advertisement for the 1917 film *Son of Democracy* provides an example:

YOUR FRIEND, "ABE" LINCOLN

"Abe" Lincoln would have been your friend, mighty glad to come to your house for Sunday dinner, and all afternoon he would have entertained the folks—had them laughing and crying in turns—with stories of his dramatic life.

You can't invite Lincoln to dinner now. But you can do better, you can *see* enacted on the screen in the new Paramount photoplay "The Son of Democracy" these stories that he told. You can *see* the boy in his log home, his strange, sometimes humorous, often pathetic adventures. You can *see* him as President. . . . In "The Son of Democracy" each feature is a complete drama. There are stirring fights, amusing complications and the funniest little pickaninny you ever saw steals a white hen; and Abe, the boy, is the attorney for his defense before a most peculiar judge. . . . "The Son of Democracy" will show you all this.

That young Lincoln was no different from the average boy at study or at work or in uniform, that he would grow into a president who would remain a common man, was central to *Son of Democracy*'s plot. With its childhood pranks, rough-house, and prophetic court cases, the film was part of a larger body of portrayals that celebrated Lincoln's humble origins and conveyed the message that people should not forget that the greatest of all men was a common man.

12. Popular songs of the day made a similar point:
Teddy went to Harvard; Bill [Taft] went to Yale;
Here's to them! Long years to them! and hearts that never fail;
But ere your feast is ended, before the night is spent, won't you
Drink to the old red schoolhouse, boys? For that's where Lincoln
          went. (Hardy 1910)

13. Lincoln's demeanor on the campaign trail prefigured not only his accessibility as president, but also his inclination to seek out the people. As a stark exception to Firth's "principle of energy conservation," Lincoln's

gregariousness proved an egalitarian rapture. C. B. Edwards of Raleigh, North Carolina, for example, recalled for his readers the Southerner who planned to attend one of Lincoln's inauguration affairs but decided not to shake hands with him as he passed through the reception line. This man carried out his plan: he passed the president without greeting him. Lincoln, however, left his own place to confront the sullen visitor. "No man who is taller and handsomer than I am," he said, "can pass by me today without shaking hands with me." At this point, the ardent Southerner's hostility vanished. "Who could refuse to shake hands with a man who would leave his position and put his hand in front of you and use such complimentary language as Mr. Lincoln did?" (1906, 637).

14. Clemency scenes were expressed in poetry as well as in prose and painting, but the emphasis on the terror-stricken family remains. Usually the family is represented by the mother, sometimes by the father. In Henry Tyrell's poem "Lincoln's Way," the father is the narrator:

> Now a father, poor and aged, bowed alike with years and wo,
> Crushed by all the pain and sorrow that a parent's heart can know,
> Brought, despairing, his petition; he would plead in Lincoln's ear;
> And he prayed to heaven for mercy, that through God's love, man
>   might hear. . . .

> "My two sons, my only children, to the Union's cause I gave,
> One lies buried in Virginia in an unknown soldier's grave.
> And the other, last and dearest—for what error I know not—
> Is condemned as a deserter, and is sentenced to be shot."

> "My old friend," said Lincoln, kindly, "there has inquiry been made,
> And the execution, meanwhile, I have caused to be delayed
> Until further orders from me. This one fact at least, I know:
> Your young man can serve us better here above ground than below."

> "God be thanked!" the old man, trembling, cried, "and blessings on
>   your name!
> But—but—what if they should execute him when your orders
>   came?"

> "Never fear! before I order that," said Lincoln, grim and sage—
> "Well, your son will beat Methuselah, or die of sheer old age!"
>   (Wright-Davis 1919, 350)

Such was "Lincoln's way." He delayed the execution pending the outcome of an investigation but had no intention of approving a death sentence, no matter what the facts revealed.

15. Lincoln's compassion did not seem to be limited to Northern casualties. At least it did not seem that way in the twentieth century. John Wise, son of Henry Wise, Virginia's governor at the time of John Brown's raid, was in Richmond during the last days of the war and witnessed Lincoln entering the city: "Did he enter in triumph and with threatening mien, as Goth and Hun swept down on Rome? No. In his own simple, gentle way Abraham Lincoln was standing at the deserted door of the Confederacy, and

with tears of sympathy in his eyes rather than any smile of triumph on his face" (*Saint Louis Post Dispatch*, February 12, 1918, 2).

Five

1. The young woman portraying Liberty is Golda Meier, future prime minister of Israel.

2. Jenken Lloyd Jones was a close associate of Jane Addams, whose views on Lincoln also verged on adoration. For detail, see Rice 1993, 134–97.

3. The making of the 1909 centennial began in earnest in 1908, when the governor of Illinois proposed that cities and towns throughout the state plan elaborate celebrations. These will "make Illinois a Mecca for patriotic pilgrims on the occasion of the Lincoln centenary" (*Chicago Daily Tribune*, February 22, 1908, 8). The majority of businessmen who endorsed the plan probably expected economic benefits from it, and some may have endorsed it for this reason alone. The centennial's significance, however, cannot be reduced to the short-term profit motive or even the long-term benefits that go along with making the state a "center of patriotism." Chicago's Association of Commerce director was, in fact, repelled by the very thought of making money from the memory of Lincoln's centennial. "There is nothing selfish about it," he said, "though the country now is saturated with selfishness" (2). Evidence for his sincerity is no less credible than speculation about his insincerity.

4. Since progressive and socialist goals overlapped so considerably, they were often confounded. Thus, critics of Herbert Croly, the first and greatest progressive ideologue, condemned him for being a socialist stalking horse.

5. These statements, taken from a congressional entry (*Congressional Record*, February 12, 1908, HR 2282), were well known within the socialist community. Marx himself regarded Lincoln the ultimate pragmatist but never underestimated the historical significance of his actions.

6. For a fascinating study of one metaphorical variation on this theme, see Fine and Christoforides (1991) on "Dirty Birds, Filthy Immigrants, and the English Sparrow War."

7. Extensive coverage of Lincoln Day observances began during the second decade of the twentieth century. From 1885 to 1905, the *New York Age*, like other black newspapers, reported few Lincoln Day festivities; from 1905 to 1909, however, the *Age* published thirty-six entries, mostly on the 1909 centennial of Lincoln's birth, then fifty-four entries between 1910 and 1914, and seventy-three entries between 1915 and 1920.

8. "Pairing," according to Alfred Schutz (1970, 321), occurs when an object's appearance is associated with another object that does not appear but without which one is unable to understand the first object's significance. That this second, "appresented" object is Booker T. Washington is evident not only from common knowledge of his self-help and black enterprise philosophy, but also from the reprinting of his speech on the same page as the cartoon.

9. The 1909 centennial permanently increased Lincoln's visibility in the larger Southern newspapers. The volume of articles was slim, but the trend was significant and consistent, with the *New Orleans Times, Savannah Morning News,* and *Charleston News and Courier* all publishing more articles about Lincoln after the centennial than before.

Six

1. The notion of animate and inanimate objects being "good to think with" was introduced by Claude Lévi-Strauss (1963, 89) and is now so much a part of the social science vocabulary as to require no text reference.

2. For details on Adolph Weinman's seated Lincoln, see Bullard 1952.

3. To say that Americans recognized the evil of slavery is not to say they were ready to accept full responsibility for its presence in their country. According to one rationalization, slavery was established by foreigners, the Dutch West India Company in 1626; and a British monarch, James II (*Los Angeles Times,* February 12, 1918, pt. 2, p. 4).

4. The Bixby letter reflected Lincoln's sentiments, but it was actually written by his secretary John Hay. It was sent by mistake. Mrs. Bixby, a brothel keeper, was a Confederate sympathizer who lost two, not five, sons. One of her surviving sons received an honorable discharge; the other two deserted. She apparently lied about their deaths in order to make herself eligible for war benefits. (For detail, see Burlingame 1999.)

5. See also "Lincoln's College Flag," a song keyed to the tune of a football marching song: "I fought the fight I thought was right / A southern gray the uniform I wore / But strife is stilled and God has willed / That we are more united than before. / Now the East, West, North and South know just one rule / To love that flag that waved from Lincoln's school" (Heelen and Helf 1912).

6. This six-phase keying process is often related to collective action frames. Action frames, as William Gamson (1992) defines them, are beliefs that promote reform and stimulate participation in social movements. Action frames define present injustices and induce victims or indignant observers to see themselves as remedial agents. Analysis of the keying of problematic presents to the past shows contemporary action frames to be deeply embedded in collective memory.

7. If even the most excellent distortion studies—such as those appearing in Daniel Schacter's *Memory Distortion* (1995; see especially Michael Schudson's "Dynamics of Distortion in Collective Memory")—are not placed in the context of such a biographical reality, then that reality will appear to be a specter, freely invocable by anyone wishing to be advanced by it.

Seven

1. These remarks appear in a Halo & Company 1918 advertising brochure.

2. Lincoln statues symbolized the majesty of the state, but, as was then the case for all statues of American heroes, few were produced by the state. Between 1865 and 1899, ten of the fourteen Lincoln statues erected through-

out the United States (including replicas) were paid for by private individuals; three by private organizations, including veterans' organizations and schools collecting contributions from their students or the public at large; one by the United States government. Between 1900 and 1919, private sponsorship continued to be the rule. Fifteen, or almost half of the thirty-two statues erected (including replicas) were paid for by individuals, fifteen by private organizations collecting donations from the public, and two by state governments.

3. In contrast, David Donald noted in his essay "The Folklore Lincoln" that these two conceptions of Lincoln—as mythological demigod and as legendary frontier hero—"began to blend" (1947, 162), which may be taken to mean "became indistinguishable." More recently, Richard Morris (1997) distinguishes three images: the "rail-splitter," the man who rose from log cabin to White House, and "the American Christ/Moses"—entertained by three "cultural groups": romanticists, heroists, and religionists respectively. When the (heavily eulogistic) evidence underlying this trichotomy is laid out, however, the rail-splitter and social climber are difficult to distinguish, and the heroists and religionists seem to entertain similar points of view. In turn, Donald's claim that the folk and epic lineaments of Lincoln's image became blurred after the turn of the century is plainly wrong, for we have seen in this chapter that commentators discussed the folk/epic balance explicitly, noting the increasing conspicuousness of Lincoln's epic traits.

4. Lincoln's closeness to the soil symbolized the poverty and manual labor Barnard's critics openly despised. "It is amazing," observes Ida Tarbell, "to see this old dislike to leanness and poverty and rough clothes . . . expressing itself in an organized campaign against an interpretation of Abraham Lincoln which not only admits the poverty and meagerness of his early life but glories in it." The critics, Tarbell adds, are saying that "democracy exists in no class below their own" (1917, 225, 227). On this same point Edwin Markham brings his weight to bear: "Do we speak in song and story of the dignity of labor? This statue is an eloquent expression of that great idea, and if that idea is a mistake, then . . . the democratic ideal is a hollow bubble" (1917, 228).

5. So fateful was this matter that some believed the original Lincoln and Washington statues (by Saint-Gaudens and Houdon), not mere replicas, should be sent abroad (*Art World,* August 1917, 416). And at a Lincoln Memorial University meeting, someone proposed that the school's chancellor, Reverend Doctor John Wesley Hill, be appointed as "national censor and custodian of the plans, lines, proper figures, postures, etc., showing how Lincoln should be presented to the people of Europe or any other country" (*New York Times,* November 25, 1917, sec. 9, p. 5).

6. Tension between egalitarianism and hierarchy was evident in the Lincoln Memorial's dedication. President Harding announced that he spoke "as a reverent and grateful American rather than one in official responsibility," for "the true measure of Lincoln's place is in the heart of American citizenship." Edwin Markham then read his poem "Lincoln: Man of the People," reinforcing the president's remarks. Both statements, in consequence if not

intent, undermined appreciation of the Lincoln Memorial's architectural grandeur. Harding's speech, on the other hand, was much less than a ringing endorsement of equality, just as Markham's poem was more than a portrayal of an ordinary country man. Harding used the occasion to explain that majority rule had to be "properly checked," while minority views must not be "hurried into the majority expressions of the republic." And if Markham saw in Lincoln "the tried clay of the common road," he also saw him as the "lordly cedar" falling with great echo (*Chicago Daily Tribune,* May 31, 1922, 1).

References

Abbott, Lyman. 1909. "Lincoln as a Labor Leader." *Outlook* 91:499–505.
———. 1916. "A Lesson from History." *Outlook* 113:219–22.
Abercrombie, Nicholas, Stephen Hill, and Bryan Turner. 1980. *The Dominant Ideology Thesis*. London: Allen and Unwin.
Abrams, M. H. 1953. *The Mirror and the Lamp: Romantic Theory and the Critical Tradition*. New York: Oxford University Press.
Abrams, Richard. 1964. *Conservatism in a Progressive Era: Massachusetts Politics, 1900–1912*. Cambridge: Harvard University Press.
Adair, Douglass. 1974. *Fame and the Founding Fathers: Essays by Douglass Adair*. New York: W. W. Norton.
Adams, Charles Francis. 1890. *Richard Henry Dana: A Biography*. 2 vols. Boston: Houghton Mifflin.
Adams, John Coleman. 1894. "Lincoln's Place in History." *Century* 47: 590–96.
Addams, Jane. 1910. *Twenty Years at Hull-House*. New York: Macmillan.
Albelda, Randy, and Chris Tilly. 1996. "Once upon a Time: A Brief History of Welfare." *Dollars and Sense* (November/December): 20–21.
Aldrich, Nelson W. Jr. 1988. *Old Money: The Mythology of America's Upper Class*. New York: Knopf.
Alexander, Jeffrey, ed. 1988. *Durkheimian Sociology: Cultural Studies*. Cambridge: Cambridge University Press.
Alexander, Jeffrey. 1982. *Theoretical Logic in Sociology*. Berkeley: University of California Press.
Allen, Ethan. 1865. *A Discourse Prepared for the National Fast Day*. Baltimore, MD: William K. Doyle.
Alonso, Ana Maria. 1988. "The Effects of Truth: Re-Presentations of the Past and the Imagining of Community." *Journal of Historical Sociology* 1:33–57.
American Association of Colleges of Teacher Education. 1973. "No One Model American: A Statement on Multicultural Education." *Journal of Teacher Education* 24:264–65.
Ames, Kenneth. 1993. "Afterword: History Pictures Past, Present, and Future." Pp. 221–31 in *Picturing History: American Painting, 1770–1930*, edited by William Ayres. New York: Rizzoli.
Anderson, Benedict. 1983. *Imagined Communities*. London: Verso/NLB.

Anderson, Dwight. 1982. *Abraham Lincoln: The Quest for Immortality*. New York: Knopf.

Andrews, Mary Raymond. 1907. *The Perfect Tribute*. New York: Charles Scribner's Sons.

Arnold, Isaac N. 1885. *Life of Abraham Lincoln*. Chicago: Jensen and McClurg.

———. 1886. *History of Abraham Lincoln and the Overthrow of Slavery*. Chicago: Clarke and Co.

Bacon, Henry. [1912] 1913. Lincoln Memorial Commission. *Report of the Architect on the Final Design for the Lincoln Memorial*. December 5, 62nd Cong., 2nd sess., S. Doc. 965.

Baigell, Matthew. 1993. "On the Margins of American History." Pp. 201–20 in *Picturing History: American Painting, 1770–1930*, edited by William Ayres. New York: Rizzoli.

Bancroft, George. 1866. *Memorial Address on the Life and Character of Abraham Lincoln*. U.S. Congress, February 12. Washington, DC: Government Printing Office.

Bancroft, T. B. 1909. "An Audience with Abraham Lincoln." *McClure* 32: 447–50.

Barnes, Earl. 1900. "Children's Ideals." *Pedagogical Seminary* 7:3–12.

Barr, Thomas Hughes. 1865. *A Discourse Delivered . . . on the Occasion of the Funeral . . . of Our Late President, Abraham Lincoln*. Wooster, OH: Republican Steam Power Press.

Barthel, Diane. 1996. *Historic Preservation: Representing the Past in Great Britain and the United States*. New Brunswick: Rutgers University Press.

Basler, Roy P. 1935. *The Lincoln Legend*. New York: Octogon Books.

Beard, Charles A., and Mary R. Beard. 1921. *History of the United States*. New York: Macmillan.

Becker, Carl. 1935. *Everyman His Own Historian: Essays on History and Politics*. New York: F. S. Crofts and Co.

Bellah, Robert N. 1970. "Civil Religion in America." Pp. l68–92 in *Beyond Belief*. New York: Harper and Row.

———. 1975. *The Broken Covenant*. Chicago: University of Chicago Press.

Bellah, Robert N., Richard Madsen, William M. Sullivan, Ann Swidler, and Steven M. Tipton. 1985. *Habits of the Heart*. New York: Harper and Row.

Bensel, Richard F. 1990. *Yankee Leviathan: The Origins of the Central State Authority in America, 1859–1877*. Cambridge: Cambridge University Press.

Ben-Yehuda, Nachman. 1995. *The Masada Myth: Collective Memory and Mythmaking in Israel*. Madison: University of Wisconsin Press.

Berezin, Mabel. 1997. *Making the Fascist Self: The Political Culture of Interwar Italy*. Ithaca, NY: Cornell University Press.

Berger, Peter. 1963. *Invitation to Sociology*. Garden City, NY: Doubleday.

Berger, Peter, Brigitte Berger, and Manfred Kellner. 1973. *The Homeless Mind: Modernization and Consciousness*. New York: Vintage.

Bernstorff, Ambassador Count J. 1913. *Abraham Lincoln as the Germans Regarded Him*. Springfield, IL: Lincoln Day Address.

Bingham, J. C. 1865. *The Spoiler Spoiled.* New York: Office of the Whig and Dispatch.

Blacknall, O. W. 1915. *Lincoln as the South Should Know Him.* Raleigh, NC: Manley's Battery Chapter of the Children of the Confederacy.

Bland, William T. 1920. *Congressional Record,* March 17, 66th Cong., 2nd sess., 4479–80.

Bledsoe, Albert. 1873. "Lamon's Life of Lincoln." *Southern Review* (April): 328–64.

Block, Fred L. 1996. *The Vampire State: And Other Myths and Fallacies about the U.S. Economy.* New York: New Press.

Blum, John Martin. 1980. *The Progressive Presidents.* New York: W. W. Norton.

Boardman, George. 1865. *The Death of President Lincoln.* Binghampton, NY: F. N. Chase.

Bodnar, John. 1992. *Remaking America: Public Memory, Commemoration, and Patriotism in the Twentieth Century.* Princeton: Princeton University Press.

———. 1996. "The Attractions of Patriotism." Pp. 3–17 in *Bonds of Affection: Americans Define Their Patriotism,* edited by John Bodnar. Princeton, NJ: Princeton University Press.

Borglum, Gutzon. 1910. "The Beauty of Lincoln." *Everybody Magazine* (February): 219.

———. 1914. Letter from Borglum to Borland. February 24. Washington, DC, Library of Congress, Manuscript Division, box 73. Typescript.

———. n.d.(a) Letter to Editor of the *Baltimore Sun.* Washington, DC, Library of Congress, Manuscript Division, box 99. Typescript published January 15, 1912.

———. n.d.(b) "Public Address." Washington, DC, Library of Congress, Manuscript Division, box 99. Typescript.

———. n.d.(c) "When the People Spoke." Speech. Washington, DC, Library of Congress, Manuscript Division, box 99. Typescript.

Boritt, Gabor S. 1978. *Lincoln and the Economics of the American Dream.* Memphis, TN: Memphis State University Press.

Borland, William. 1913. "Lincoln Memorial." *Congressional Record,* January 29, 62nd Cong., 3rd sess., 2229–52.

Boyarin, Jonathan, ed. 1994. *Remapping Memory: The Politics of Time and Space.* Minneapolis: University of Minnesota Press.

Braden, Waldo. 1988. "Any Poor Man's Son: The Public Image of Lincoln." Pp. 4–14 in *Abraham Lincoln: Public Speaker.* Baton Rouge: Louisiana State University Press.

Briggs, George W. 1865. *Eulogy on Abraham Lincoln.* Salem, MA: City Council.

Brint, Steven. 1994. "Sociological Analysis of Political Culture." Pp. 3–44 in *Research on Democracy and Society,* vol. 2, edited by Frederick D. Weil. Greenwich, CT: JAI Press.

Brown, Neil. 1912. *Abraham Lincoln.* Milwaukee: Loyal Legion of Wisconsin.

Browne, William Hand. 1872. "Lamon's Lincoln." *Southern Magazine* (Baltimore, MD) 11:370–79.

Bryan, Alfred, and Harry Tierney. 1917. "It's Time for Every Boy to Be a Soldier." New York: Jerome H. Remick and Co. Sheet music.

Bryan, William Jennings. 1898. *Lincoln vs. Hamilton*. Lincoln, NE: Women's Bimetallic League.

Bullard, Frederic L. 1952. *Lincoln in Marble and Bronze*. New Brunswick: Rutgers University Press.

Burlingame, Michael. 1994. *The Inner World of Abraham Lincoln*. Bloomington: Indiana University Press.

———. 1999. "The Trouble with the Bixby Letter." *American Heritage* (July/August):64–67.

Busbey, Hamilton. 1911. "Recollections of Abraham Lincoln and the Civil War." *Forum* 45:282–40.

Cain, Marvin R. 1964. "Lincoln's Views on Slavery and the Negro." *Historian* 26:502–20.

Callahan, North. 1970. *Carl Sandburg: Lincoln of Our Literature*. New York: New York University Press.

Campbell, Joseph. 1973. *The Hero with a Thousand Faces*. Princeton: Princeton University Press.

Capers, Gerald M. 1965. *Occupied City*. Lexington: University of Kentucky Press.

Carlyle, Thomas. 1966. *On Heroes, Hero-Worship, and the Heroic in History*. Lincoln: University of Nebraska Press.

Carpenter, Francis Bicknell. 1867. *Six Months at the White House*. New York: Hurd and Houghton.

Carr, Clark E. 1907. "Why Lincoln Was Not Renominated by Acclamation." *Century* 73:503–6.

Carson, Mina Julia. 1990. *Settlement Folk: Social Thought and the American Settlement Movement, 1885–1930*. Chicago: University of Chicago Press.

Cerulo, Karen. 1995. *Identity Designs: The Sights and Sounds of a Nation*. New Brunswick: Rutgers University Press.

Chalmers, David M. 1986. *Neither Socialism nor Monopoly: Theodore Roosevelt and the Decision to Regulate the Railroads*. Malabar, FL: R. E. Krieger.

Chambers, Will Grant. 1903. "The Evolution of Ideals." *Pedagogical Seminary* 10:101–43.

Chase, Thomas. 1865. *An Address on the Character and Example of President Lincoln*. Philadelphia: Sherman and Co.

Cheney, John Vance. 1909. "Lincoln." *Atlantic* 103:277–78.

Chittenden, A. E. 1891. "The Faith of President Lincoln." *Harper's Magazine* 82:385–91.

———. [1891] 1909. *Lincoln and the Sleeping Sentinel: The True Story*. New York: Harper and Brothers.

Cho, Erin. 1993. "Lincoln Logs: Toying with the Frontier Myth." *History Today* (April): 31–34.

Cmiel, Kenneth. 1993. "Destiny and Amnesia: The Vision of Modernity in Robert Wiebe's The Search for Order." *Reviews in American History* 21: 352–68.

Coddington, David. 1865. *Eulogy on President Lincoln*. New York: Baker and Godwin.

Cohen, Lizabeth. 1990. *Making a New Deal: Industrial Workers in Chicago, 1919–1939*. Cambridge: Cambridge University Press.

Commager, Henry Steele. 1950. *The American Mind: An Interpretation of American Thought and Character since 1880*. New Haven: Yale University Press.

Connelly, Thomas L. 1977. *The Marble Man: Robert E. Lee and His Image in American Society*. New York: Knopf.

Connerton, Paul. 1989. *How Societies Remember*. Cambridge: Cambridge University Press.

Cooley, Charles Horton [1902] 1964. *Human Nature and the Social Order*. New York: Schocken.

———. [1909] 1962. *Social Organization*. New York: Schocken.

———. 1918. "Fame." Pp. 112–24 in *Social Process*. New York: Charles Scribner's Sons.

Cooper, Harry. 1918. *Abraham Lincoln: A Pattern for Our Times*. London: Everybody's Booklets.

Coser, Lewis, ed. 1992. *Maurice Halbwachs on Collective Memory*. Chicago: University of Chicago Press.

Cousins, Robert G. 1900. *Abraham Lincoln*. New York: Republican Club of the City of New York.

Cox, LaWanda. 1981. *Lincoln and Black Freedom*. Columbia: University of South Carolina Press.

Crèvecoeur, J. Hector St. John. [1782] 1963. *Letters from an American Farmer*. New York: Dolphin.

Crocker, Ruth Hutchinson. 1992. *Social Work and Social Order: The Settlement Movement in Two Industrial Cities, 1889–1930*. Urbana: University of Illinois Press.

Croly, Herbert. 1909. *The Promise of American Life*. New York: Macmillan.

———. 1920. "The Paradox of Lincoln." *New Republic* 21:350–53.

Cunliffe, Marcus. 1988. *The Doubled Images of Lincoln and Washington*. Robert Fortenbaugh Memorial Lecture. Gettysburg, PA: Gettysburg College.

Cunningham, Noble E. Jr. 1991. *Popular Images of the Presidency: From Washington to Lincoln*. Columbia: University of Missouri Press.

Current, Richard N. 1958. *The Lincoln Nobody Knows*. New York: Hill and Wang.

———. 1983a. "Bancroft's Lincoln." Pp. 172–86 in *Speaking of Abraham Lincoln: The Man and His Meaning for Our Times*. Urbana: University of Illinois Press.

———. 1983b. "Unity, Ethnicity, and Abraham Lincoln." Pp. 105–25 in *Speaking of Abraham Lincoln*. Urbana: University of Illinois Press.

————. 1987. *American History: A Survey.* New York: Knopf.

Cutter, Edward F. 1865. *Eulogy on Abraham Lincoln.* Boston: Coles-
worthy.

Czarnowski, Stefan [1919] 1975. *Le Culte des heros et ses conditions so-
ciales.* New York: Arno Press.

Dallinger, Frederick. 1925. "Anniversary of the Birth of Washington." *Congressional Record,* February 23, 68th Cong., 2nd sess., 4443–45.

Dalton, Kathleen. 1979. "Why America Loved Teddy Roosevelt." *Psycho-
history Review* 8:16–26.

Danbom, David B. 1987. *"The World of Hope": Progressives and the Struggle for an Ethical Public Life.* Philadelphia: Temple University Press.

Davis, Benjamin H. 1949a. *Report of Research on the Traditional Abraham
Lincoln Birthplace Cabin.* Hodgenville, KY: Abraham Lincoln National
Historical Park.

————. 1949b. *Revised Report on the Original Thomas Lincoln Nolin
Creek Farm.* Hodgenville, KY: Abraham Lincoln Birthplace National Historic Park.

Davis, Michael. 1971. *The Image of Lincoln in the South.* Knoxville: University of Tennessee Press.

Davis, William C. 1999. *Lincoln's Men: How President Lincoln Became
Father to an Army and a Nation.* New York: Free Press.

Decker, Joe F. 1986. "The Progressive Era and the World War I Draft."
Magazine of History (Winter/Spring): 15–18.

Degler, Carl N. 1992. "One among Many: The United States and National
Unification." Pp. 89–119 in *Lincoln: The War President,* edited by Gabor
S. Boritt. New York: Oxford University Press.

Dibble, Vernon. 1975. *The Legacy of Albion Small.* Chicago: University of
Chicago Press.

Dixon, Thomas. 1905. *The Clansman: An Historical Romance of the Ku
Klux Klan.* New York: Doubleday.

————. 1913. *The Southerner: A Romance of the Real Lincoln.* New York:
D. Appleton and Co.

————. 1920. *A Man of the People: A Drama of Abraham Lincoln.* New
York: D. Appleton and Co.

Domhoff, William G. 1996. *State Autonomy or Class Dominance? Case
Studies on Policy-Making in America.* New York: Aldine de Gruyter.

Donald, David Herbert. [1947] 1989. *Lincoln Reconsidered.* New York:
Vintage.

————. 1948. *Lincoln's Herndon.* New York: Knopf.

————. 1995. *Lincoln.* New York: Simon and Schuster.

Douglas, Charles Noel, and Karl L. Hoschna. 1906. "Lincoln, Oh! Lincoln,
We Honor You Today." New York: Crest Action and Dialog Songs. Sheet
music.

Douglas, Mary. 1966. "Abominations of Leviticus." Pp. 39–57 in *Purity
and Danger: An Analysis of Concepts of Pollution and Taboo.* London:
Routledge and Kegan Paul.

————. 1975. "Self-Evidence." Pp. 276–318 in *Implicit Meanings.* London:
Routledge and Kegan Paul.

Douglass, Frederick. [1861–63] 1969. *Douglass's Monthly*. Vols. 4–5. New York: Negro Universities Press.

———. 1962. "Oration . . . Delivered on the Occasion of the Unveiling of the Freedmen's Monument." Pp. 481–93 in *Life and Times of Frederick Douglass*. New York: Collier.

Drinkwater, John. 1920. "In Lincoln's America." *Collier's* 65:5–6.

Ducharme, Lori J., and Gary A. Fine. 1995. "The Construction of Nonpersonhood and Demonization: Commemorating the Traitorous Reputation of Benedict Arnold." *Social Forces* 73:1309–31.

Dumont, Louis. 1974. *Homo Hierarchicus*. Chicago: University of Chicago Press.

Durden, Robert F. 1965. "Ambiguities in the Antislavery Crusade of the Republican Party." Pp. 362–94 in *The Antislavery Vanguard*, edited by Martin Duserman. Princeton: Princeton University Press.

Durkheim, Emile. [1883] 1973. "Address to the lycéens of Sens." Pp. 25–33 in *Emile Durkheim on Morality and Society*, edited by Robert N. Bellah. Chicago: University of Chicago Press.

———. [1889] 1964. *The Division of Labor in Society*. New York: Free Press.

———. [1890] 1973. "The Principles of 1789 and Sociology." Pp. 34–42 in *Emile Durkheim on Morality and Society*, edited by Robert N. Bellah. Chicago: University of Chicago Press.

———. [1911] 1974. "Value Judgements and Judgements of Reality." Pp. 80–97 in *Sociology and Philosophy by Emile Durkheim*, edited by Talcott Parsons. New York: Free Press.

———. [1915] 1965. *The Elementary Forms of the Religious Life*. Free Press.

———. [1925] 1973. *Moral Education*. New York: Free Press.

Durkheim, Emile, and Marcel Mauss. 1963. *Primitive Classification*. Chicago: University of Chicago Press.

Eddy, Frederick B. 1919. "On Saint-Gaudens' Statue of Lincoln." P. 226 in *The Book of Lincoln*, edited by Mary Wright-Davis. New York: George H. Doran.

Edmonds, George. 1904. *Facts and Falsehoods concerning the War in the South, 1861–1865*. Memphis: A. R. Taylor and Co.

Edwards, C. B. 1906. "An Incident of Lincoln's First White House Reception." *Century* 72:636–37.

Egar, John H. 1865. *The Martyr-President*. Leavenworth, KS: Bulletin Job Printing Establishment.

Eisenach, Eldon J. 1994. *The Lost Promise of Progressivism*. Lawrence: University Press of Kansas.

Eliot, Charles W. 1906. *Four American Leaders*. Boston: American Unitarian Association.

Ellis, Richard J. 1993. *American Political Cultures*. New York: Oxford University Press.

Ellis, Richard J., and Aaron Wildavsky. 1988. *Dilemmas of Presidential Leadership: From Washington through Lincoln*. New Brunswick: Transaction.

Elmore, Harry. 1917. "A Parallel in Statesmanship: Lincoln and Asquith." *Contemporary Review* 111:11–18.

Emerson, Ralph W. [1850] 1900. *Representative Men.* New York: P. F. Collier and Son.

———. [1865] 1990. "Abraham Lincoln." Pp. 30–34 in *Building the Myth: Selective Speeches Memorializing Abraham Lincoln,* edited by Waldo W. Braden. Urbana: University of Illinois Press.

Englund, Steven. 1992. "The Ghost of Nation Past." *Journal of Modern History* 64:299–320.

Falasca-Zimponi, Simonetta. 1997. *Fascist Spectacle: The Aesthetics of Power in Mussolini's Italy.* Berkeley: University of California Press.

Fehrenbacher, Don E. 1987. *Lincoln in Text and Context: Collected Essays.* Stanford: Stanford University Press.

Fenichel, Otto. 1953. "The Scoptophilic Instinct and Identification." Pp. 373–97 in *Collected Papers,* vol. 1. New York: W. W. Norton.

Fentress, James, and Chris Wickham. 1992. *Social Memory.* Oxford: Blackwell.

Fess, Simeon D. 1914. *Congressional Record,* February 12, 63rd Cong., 2nd sess., 3391–97.

Fields, James M., and Howard Schuman. 1976–77. "Public Beliefs about the Beliefs of the Public." *Public Opinion Quarterly* 40:427–48.

Filene, Peter G. 1993. "Narrating Progressivism: Unitarians v. Pluralists v. Students." *Journal of American History* 79:1546–62.

Fine, Gary. 1991. "On the Macrofoundations of Microsociology." *Sociological Quarterly* 32:161–77.

———. 1996. "Reputational Entrepreneurs and the Memory of Incompetence: Melting Supporters, Partisan Warriors, and Images of President Harding." *American Journal of Sociology* 101:1159–93.

———. 1998. *Difficult Reputations.* Manuscript.

———. 1999. "John Brown's Body: Elites, Heroic Embodiment, and Legitimation of Political Violence." *Social Problems.* 46:225–49.

Fine, Gary, and Lazaros Christoforides. 1991. "Dirty Birds, Filthy Immigrants, and the English Sparrow War: Metaphorical Linkage in Constructing Social Problems." *Symbolic Interaction* 14:375–93.

Fine, William M. 1965. *That Day with God.* New York: McGraw-Hill.

Fink, Leon. 1997. *Progressive Intellectuals and the Dilemmas of Democratic Commitment.* Cambridge: Harvard University Press.

Firth, Raymond. 1973. *Symbols: Public and Private.* Ithaca: Cornell University Press.

Fischer, David Hackett. 1989. *Albion's Seed: Four British Folkways in America.* New York: Oxford University Press.

Fischer, Roger. 1988. *Tippacanoe and Trinkets Too: The Material Culture of American Presidential Campaigns, 1828–1984.* Urbana: University of Illinois Press.

Fitzgerald, Frances. 1979. *America Revised.* Boston: Little, Brown.

Focht, Benjamin K. 1920. "Abraham Lincoln." *Congressional Record,* February 26, 66th Cong., 2nd sess., app., 8849–51.

Foote, Nelson N. 1953. "Destratification and Restratification." *American Journal of Sociology* 63:325–26.

Forgie, George. 1979. *Patricide in the House Divided.* New York: W. W. Norton.

Foster, Gaines M. 1987. *Ghosts of the Confederacy.* New York: Oxford University Press.

Fowler, John Jr. 1865. *An Address on the Death of President Lincoln.* New York: John A. Gray and Green.

Fraser, Walter J. 1989. *Charleston! Charleston!* Columbia: University of South Carolina Press.

Frederickson, George. 1975. "A Man but Not a Brother: Abraham Lincoln and Racial Equality." *Journal of Southern History* 61:39–58.

Freud, Sigmund. [1913] 1950. *Totem and Taboo.* New York: W. W. Norton.

———. [1921] 1960. *Group Psychology and the Analysis of the Ego.* New York: Bantam.

———. [1939] 1970. *Moses and Monotheism.* New York: Vintage.

Friedlander, Saul, ed. 1992. *Probing the Limits of Representation: Nazism and the "Final Solution."* Cambridge: Harvard University Press.

Friedman, Reena Sigman. 1994. *These Are Our Children: Jewish Orphanages in the United States, 1880–1925.* Hanover: Brandeis University Press.

Frisch, Michael. 1989. "American History and the Structures of Collective Memory: A Modest Exercise in Empirical Iconography." *Journal of American History* 75:1130–56.

Funkenstein, Amos. 1993. *Perceptions of Jewish History.* Los Angeles: University of California Press.

Gallup, George. 1972. *The Gallup Poll: Public Opinion, 1935–1971.* 3 vols. New York: Random House.

Gamson, William A. 1992. *Talking Politics.* Cambridge: Cambridge University Press.

Garfinkel, Harold. 1956. "Conditions of Successful Degradation Ceremonies." *American Journal of Sociology* 61:420–24.

Geertz, Clifford. 1973a. "After the Revolution: The Fate of Nationalism in the New States." Pp. 234–54 in *Interpretation of Cultures.* New York: Basic Books.

———. 1973b. "Ideology as a Cultural System." Pp. 193–233 in *The Interpretation of Cultures.* New York: Basic Books.

———. 1973c. "Religion as aCultural System." Pp. 87–125 in *The Interpretation of Cultures.* New York: Basic Books.

———. 1973d. "Thick Description." Pp. 3–32 in *The Interpretation of Cultures.* New York: Basic Books.

———. 1983a. "Art as a Cultural System." Pp. 94–120 in *Local Knowledge.* New York: Basic Books.

———. 1983b. "Centers, Kings, and Charisma: Reflections on the Symbolics of Power." Pp. 121–46 in *Local Knowledge.* New York: Basic Books.

———. 1983c. "Common Sense as a Cultural System." Pp. 72–94 in *Local Knowledge.* New York: Basic Books.

———. 1983d. "From the Native's Point of View: On the Nature of Anthropological Understanding." Pp. 55–70 in *Local Knowledge*. New York: Basic Books.

Gellner, Ernest. 1983. *Nations and Nationalism*. Ithaca: Cornell University Press.

George, David Lloyd. 1917. "The Case for War for Democracy." *Survey* 37:564–65.

Gilder, Richard. 1909a. *Lincoln the Leader*. Boston: Houghton Mifflin.

———. 1909b. "Lincoln the Leader." *Century* 77:481–507.

Gillis, John R., ed. 1994. *Commemorations: The Politics of National Identity*. Princeton: Princeton University Press.

Glassberg, David. 1990. *American Historical Pageantry: The Uses of Tradition in the Early Twentieth Century*. Chapel Hill: University of North Carolina Press.

Goffman, Erving. 1974. *Frame Analysis: An Essay on the Organization of Experience*. New York: Harper and Row.

Goldman, Eric F. 1956. *Rendezvous with Destiny*. New York: Random House.

Goldstein, Robert J. 1995. *Saving Old Glory: The History of the American Flag Desecration Controversy*. Boulder, CO: Westview Press.

Goodman, J. T. [1911] 1970. "Abraham Lincoln." Pp. 59–61 in *The Praise of Lincoln*, edited by A. Dallas Williams. Freeport, NY: Books for Libraries Press.

Gould, Billy. 1917. "Answer Mr. Wilson's Call." New York: A. J. Stasny Music Co. Sheet music.

Gould, Lewis L. 1991. *The Presidency of Theodore Roosevelt*. Lawrence: University Press of Kansas.

Gramsci, Antonio. 1971. *The Prison Notebooks*. New York: International Publishers.

Greeley, Horace. [1868] 1891. "Estimate of Lincoln: An Unpublished Address." *Century* 42:371–82.

Greenberg, Bradley S., and Edwin B. Parker, eds. 1965. *The Kennedy Assassination and the American Public*. Stanford: Stanford University Press.

Greenfeld, Liah. 1992. *Nationalism: Five Roads to Modernity*. Cambridge: Harvard University Press.

Gregory, Stanford W., and Jerry M. Lewis. 1988. "Symbols of Collective Memory: The Social Process of Memorializing May 4, 1970, at Kent State University." *Symbolic Interaction* 11:213–33.

Griswold, Wendy. 1987. "A Methodological Framework for the Sociology of Culture." Pp. 1–35 in *Sociological Methodology*, vol. 17, edited by Clifford Clogg. Washington, DC: American Sociological Association.

Guitteau, William Backus. 1919. *Our United States: A History*. New York: Silver, Burdett, and Co.

Gurley, P. D. 1865. *The Voice of the Rod*. Washington, DC: William Ballantyne.

Habermas, Jurgen. 1975. *Legitimation Crisis*. Boston: Beacon Press.

Halbwachs, Maurice. [1925] 1952. *Les Cadres sociaux de la mémoire*. Paris: Presses Universitaires de France.
————. 1941. *La Topographie légendaire des évangiles en Sainte Terre*. Paris: Presses Universitaires de France.
————. [1950] 1980. *Collective Memory*. New York: Harper and Row.
————. 1991. *Maurice Halbwachs on Collective Memory*, edited and translated by Lewis A. Coser. Chicago: University of Chicago Press.
Hall, Gordon. 1865. *President Lincoln's Death: Its Voice to the People*. Northampton, MA: Trumbull and Gere.
Hamilton, J. G. 1909. "Lincoln and the South." *Sewanee Review* 17:128–38.
Handelman, Don. 1990. *Models and Mirrors: Towards an Anthropology of Public Events*. Cambridge: Cambridge University Press.
Handler, Richard, and J. Linnekin. 1984. "Tradition: Genuine or Spurious." *Journal of American Folklore* 97:273–90.
Hanna, William F. 1992. "Theodore Roosevelt and the Lincoln Image." *Lincoln Herald* 94:7–11.
Hapgood, Norman. 1919. "Washington and Lincoln." *Dial* 67:92–93.
Harbaugh, H. 1865. *Treason and Law*. Philadelphia: J. B. Rogers.
Hardy, Will. 1910. "The School Where Lincoln Went." Boston: Bostonia Publishing Co. Sheet music.
Harris, Joel Chandler. 1900. "The Kidnapping of President Lincoln." In *On the Wing of Occasions*. New York: Doubleday.
Hauerwas, Stanley, and L. Gregory Jones, eds. 1988. *Why Narrative? Readings in Narrative Theology*. Grand Rapids, MI: Eerdmans.
Hay, Robert P. 1969a. "George Washington: American Moses." *American Quarterly* 21:780–91.
————. 1969b. "Providence and the American Past." *Indiana Magazine of History* 65:79–101.
Hays, Samuel P. 1995. *The Response to Industrialism, 1885–1914*. Chicago: University of Chicago Press.
Hayward, Steven. 1991. "The Children of Abraham." *Reason* 23:25–31.
Heelen, Will A., and J. Fred Helf. 1912. "Lincoln's College Song." New York: J. Fred Helf. Sheet music.
Heilman, Samuel. 1982. *People of the Book*. Chicago: University of Chicago Press.
Hepworth, George H. 1865. Sermon, in *Sermons Preached in Boston*. Boston: J. E. Tilton and Co.
Herndon, William H., and Jesse W. Weik. 1889. *Herndon's Lincoln: The True Story of a Great Life*. 3 vols. Springfield, IL: Herndon's Lincoln Publishing Co.
Hertz, Robert. [1910] 1960. *Death and the Left Hand*. Trans. Rodney and Claudia Needham. Aberdeen, UK: Cohen and West.
Higham, John. 1969. *Strangers in the Land: Patterns of American Nativism, 1860–1925*. New York: Atheneum.
Hill, John Wesley. 1925. *Congressional Record*, February 23, 4448–449.

Hinckley, Frederic A. 1897. *The Summons of Washington and Lincoln to the American of Today.* Philadelphia: Spring Garden Unitarian Society.

Hirsch, Carol. 1918. "Abraham Lincoln, What Would You Do?" Milwaukee: Metropolitan Music Publishing Co. Sheet music.

Hirsch, Emil G. [1892] 1927. "Abraham Lincoln." Pp. 191–207 in *The Tribute of the Synagogue,* edited by Emanuel Hertz. New York: Block Publishing Co.

Hitchcock, Henry. 1865. *God Acknowledged, in the Nation's Bereavement.* Cleveland: Fairbanks, Benedict and Co.

Hobsbawm, Eric, and Terence Ranger. 1983. *The Invention of Tradition.* Cambridge: Cambridge University Press.

Hobson, Jonathan T. 1913. *The Master and His Servant: Comparative Outline Sketches of the Redeemer of Mankind, and the Emancipator of a Race.* Dayton, OH: United Brethren Publishing House.

Hochschild, Arlie R. 1979. "Emotion Work, Feeling Rules, and Social Structure." *American Journal of Sociology* 85:551–75.

Hoffman, Eugene A. 1865. *The Martyr President.* New York: C. A. Alvord.

Hofstadter, Richard. [1948] 1974. "Abraham Lincoln and the Self-Made Myth." Pp. 118–74 in *The American Political Tradition.* New York: Knopf.

———. 1955. *The Age of Reform: From Bryan to F. D. R.* New York: Knopf.

———. 1969. *The Progressive Historians.* New York: Knopf.

———, ed. 1963. *The Progressive Movement.* Englewood Cliffs, NJ: Prentice Hall.

Holland, Josiah G. 1866. *Life of Abraham Lincoln.* Springfield, MA: Gurdon Bill.

Holzer, Harold. 1993. *Washington and Lincoln Portrayed: National Icons in Popular Prints.* Jefferson, NC: McFarland and Co.

Hosmer, Charles B. Jr. 1965. *Presence of the Past.* New York: G. P. Putnam's Sons.

Howe, David Walker. 1979. *The Political Culture of the American Whigs.* Chicago: University of Chicago Press.

———. 1997. *Making the American Self: From Jonathan Edwards to Abraham Lincoln.* Cambridge: Harvard University Press.

Howlett, T. R. 1865. *Dealings of God with Our Nation: A Discourse . . . on the Day of Humiliation and Prayer.* Washington, DC: Gibson Brothers.

Huget, James Percival. 1918. *What Would Lincoln Say to This Generation?* Brooklyn, NY: Tompkins Avenue Congregational Church.

Humphrey, Grace. 1917. "Lincoln and the Immigrant." *Outlook* 115:237–38.

Hunter, James. 1991. *Culture Wars: The Struggle to Define America.* New York: Basic Books.

Irwin-Zarecka, Iwona. 1994. *Frames of Remembrance.* New Brunswick: Transaction.

Jameson, Frederic R. 1983. "Postmodernism and Consumer Society." Pp. 111–25 in *The Anti-Aesthetic: Essays on Postmodern Culture,* edited by Hal Foster. Port Townsend, WA: Bay Press.

———. 1984. "Postmodernism, Or, The Cultural Logic of Late Capitalism." *New Left Review* 146:53–92.

Jerome, William, and J. F. Mahoney. 1924. "We'll Link His Name to Lincoln." New York: F. B. Haviland. Sheet music.

Jerome, William, Joe Young, and Jean Schwartz. 1914. "I Love You Like Lincoln Loved the Old Red, White & Blue." New York: Harry Williams Music Co. Sheet music.

Johns, Bethany. 1984. "Visual Metaphor: Lost and Found." *Semiotica* 52 (3/4): 291–333.

Johnson, Howard, Irving Bibo, and Lou Klein. 1925. "(Don't Be Ashamed of) The Name of Abraham." New York: Ager, Yellen, and Bornstein. Sheet music.

Jones, Richard Lloyd. 1906. "Lincoln's Birthplace." *Collier's* 36:18–20.

Kaestle, Carl F., et al. 1991. *Literacy in the United States.* New Haven: Yale University Press.

Kaine, John Langdon. 1913. "Lincoln as a Boy Knew Him." *Century* 85: 555–59.

Kammen, Michael. 1978. *A Season of Youth.* New York: Knopf.

———. 1986. *Spheres of Liberty: Changing Perceptions of Liberty in American Culture.* Madison: University of Wisconsin Press.

———. 1987. *A Machine That Ran of Itself.* New York: Knopf.

———. 1991. *Mystic Chords of Memory.* New York: Basic Books.

Karsten, Peter. 1978. *Patriot Heroes in England and America.* Madison: University of Wisconsin Press.

Kaye, Harvey. 1991. *The Powers of the Past: Reflections on the Crisis and the Promise of History.* Minneapolis: University of Minnesota Press.

Kearl, Michael C., and Anoel Rinaldi. 1983. "The Political Uses of the Dead in Contemporary Civil Religions." *Social Forces* 61:693–708.

Kertzer, David. 1988. *Ritual, Politics, and Power.* Yale University Press.

Kip, William I. 1865. *Address Delivered on the Day of Humiliation and Prayer.* Frankfurt: C. Naumann's Druckerei.

Kiser, Samuel. 1911. "Lincoln." Pp. 10–11 in *The Praise of Lincoln,* edited by A. Dallas Williams. Freeport, NY: Books for Libraries Press.

Knapp, G. L. 1909. "Some New Views of Lincoln." *Review of Reviews* 39: 241–42.

Kolko, Gabriel. 1963. *The Triumph of Conservatism: A Reinterpretation of American History, 1900–1916.* New York: Free Press.

Koonz, Claudia. 1994. "Between Memory and Oblivion: Concentration Camps in German Memory." Pp. 258–80 in *Commemorations: The Politics of National Identity,* edited by John R. Gillis. Princeton: Princeton University Press.

Krauskopf, Rabbi Joseph. 1899. *Ninetieth Birthday of Lincoln and Darwin: A Sunday Lecture.* Philadelphia: Press of Samuel Goodman.

———. 1927. "Could a Lincoln Be President in Our Day?" Pp. 263–79 in *The Tribute of the Synagogue,* edited by Emanuel Hertz. New York: Block Publishing Co.

Kroeber, Alfred. [1923] 1963. *Anthropology: Cultural Patterns and Processes.* New York: Harcourt, Brace, and World.

Kunhardt, Dorothy. 1965. *Twenty Days.* New York: Harper and Row.

de Lamartine, Alphonse. 1946. "Declaration of Principles." Pp. 328–33 in *Introduction to Contemporary Civilization in the West: A Source Book,* vol. 2. New York: Columbia University Press.

Lambert, William H. 1909. "The Gettysburg Address: When Written, How Received, Its True Form." *Pennsylvania Magazine* 33:385–408.

Lamon, Ward Hill. 1872. *The Life of Abraham Lincoln: From His Birth to His Inauguration as President.* Boston: James R. Osgood and Co.

Lang, Gladys, and Kurt Lang. 1990. *Etched in Memory: The Building and Survival of Artistic Reputation.* Chapel Hill: University of North Carolina Press.

Langer, Suzanne. 1957. "The Art Symbol and the Symbol in Art." Pp. 124–40 in *Problems of Art.* New York: Charles Scribner's Sons.

———. 1962. *Philosophical Sketches.* Baltimore, MD: Johns Hopkins University Press.

Laughlin, E. O. 1924. "The Lincoln Circuit." *Ladies Home Journal* 41:26.

Lawrence, Alexander A. 1961. *A Present for Mr. Lincoln.* Macon, GA: Ardivan Press.

Lee, Henry. 1800. *A Funeral Oration Prepared and Delivered at the Request of Congress.* Brooklyn, NY: Thomas Kirk.

Lee, James W. 1909. *Abraham Lincoln: A Tribute.* Atlanta, GA: Trinity Methodist Episcopalian Church.

Lemmon, George T. 1909. "The Feminine Element in Lincoln." *Delineator* 73:403–6.

Lévi-Strauss, Claude. 1955. "The Structural Study of Myth." *Journal of American Folklore* 68:428–44.

———. 1963. *Totemism.* Boston: Beacon Press.

Levy, Leonard. 1927. "The Message of Lincoln." Pp. 318–32 in *The Tribute of the Synagogue,* edited by Emanuel Hertz. New York: Block Publishing Co.

Lewis, Edward R. 1915. "Was Lincoln a Murderer?" *Outlook* 110:524–26.

Lewis, Lloyd. 1929. *Myths after Lincoln.* New York: Press of the Readers Club.

Lewis, Thomas Hamilton. 1918. "Anniversary of the Birthday of Abraham Lincoln." *Congressional Record,* February 12, 65th Cong., 2nd sess., 1984–85.

Lichtman, Allan J. 1998. "The Rise of Big Government: Not as Simple as It Seems." *Reviews in American History* 26:445–51.

Lightner, David. 1982. "Abraham Lincoln and the Ideal of Equality." *Journal of the Illinois State Historical Society* 75:289–308.

Lincoln, Abraham. 1953–1955. *The Collected Works of Abraham Lincoln,* edited by Roy Basler. 9 vols. New Brunswick: Rutgers University Press.

Lincoln on the Liquor Question. 1920. Indianapolis: Art Press.

"Lincoln's Old Program." 1920. Letter to the Editor, *New York Herald Tribune,* Washington DC, Library of Congress, Manuscript Division, Letitia B. Martin Papers, box 4.

Lindenmeyer, Kriste. 1995. "The U.S. Children's Bureau and Infant Mortality in the Progressive Era." *Journal of Education* 177:57–69.

Lindsay, Vachel. 1945. "Abraham Lincoln Walks at Midnight." Pp. 53–54 in *Vachel Lindsay: Collected Poems.* New York: Macmillan.

Link, Arthur S. 1954. *Woodrow Wilson and the Progressive Era, 1910–1917.* New York: Harper and Row.

Link, Arthur S., and Richard L. McCormick. 1983. *Progressivism.* Arlington Heights, IL: Harlan Davidson.

Linthicum, Richard. [1911] 1970. "Lincoln." P. 155 in *The Praise of Lincoln,* edited by A. Dallas Williams. Freeport, NY: Books for Libraries Press.

Lipset, Seymour Martin. 1979. *The First New Nation: The United States in Historical and Comparative Perspective.* New York: W. W. Norton.

———. 1996. *American Exceptionalism: A Double-Edged Sword.* New York: W. W. Norton.

Litwack, Leon F. 1961. *North of Slavery: The Negro in the Free States.* Chicago: University of Chicago Press.

———. 1979. *Been in the Storm So Long: The Aftermath of Slavery.* New York: Vintage.

Locke, David R. 1890. "President Lincoln's Humor." *Magazine of American History* 24:52–53.

Loewen James. 1995. *Lies My Teacher Told Me: Everything Your American History Textbook Got Wrong.* New York: New Press.

Lossing, Benson J. 1865. *Common School History of the United States.* New York: Mason Brothers.

Love, Robertus. [1911] 1970. "At Lincoln's Tomb." Pp. 21–23 in *The Praise of Lincoln,* edited by A. Dallas Williams. Freeport, NY: Books for Libraries Press.

Lovejoy, Arthur. [1936] 1964. *The Great Chain of Being: A Study of the History of an Idea.* Cambridge: Harvard University Press.

Loveland, Anne. 1971. *Emblem of Liberty: The Image of Lafayette in the American Mind.* Baton Rouge: Louisiana State University Press.

Lowden, Governor Frank O. 1919. *Lincoln the American.* Lincoln Day Address. Springfield: Illinois State Journal Co., State Printers.

Lowell, James Russell. 1978. *The Poetical Works of James Russell Lowell.* Boston: Houghton Mifflin.

Lowenthal, David. 1985. *The Past Is a Foreign Country.* Cambridge: Cambridge University Press.

———. 1996. *Possessed by the Past: The Heritage Crusade and the Spoils of History.* New York: Free Press.

Lukacs, John. 1994. *Historical Consciousness: The Remembered Past.* New Brunswick: Transaction.

Luthin, Reinhard. 1960. *The Real Abraham Lincoln.* Englewood Press: Prentice-Hall.

Lyotard, Jean-François. [1979] 1984. *The Postmodern Condition.* Minneapolis: University of Minnesota Press.

Macdonell, A. 1917. "America Then and Now: Recollections of Lincoln." *Contemporary Review* 111:562–69.

MacIntyre, Alasdair. 1981. *After Virtue: A Study in Moral Theory.* London: Duckworth.

Maier, Charles S. 1993. "A Surfeit of Memory? Reflections on History, Melancholy, and Denial." *History and Memory* 5:136–51.

Maines, David R., Noreen M. Sugrue, and Michael A. Katovich. 1983. "G. H. Mead's Theory of the Past." *American Sociological Review* 48: 161–73.

de Maistre, Joseph. 1971. *The Works of Joseph de Maistre.* Edited by Jack Lively. New York: Schocken.

Manchester, William. 1967. *The Death of a President.* New York: Harper and Row.

Mann, Arthur. 1962. "The Progressive Tradition." Pp. 157–79 in *The Reconstruction of American History,* edited by John Higham. New York: Harper and Row.

Mannheim, Karl. [1928] 1952. "The Problem of Generations." Pp. 276–320 in *Essays on the Sociology of Knowledge,* edited by Paul Kecskemeti. London: Routledge and Kegan Paul.

———. 1936. *Ideology and Utopia.* New York: Harcourt, Brace and World.

Markham, Edwin. [1911] 1970. "Lincoln, The Man of the People." Pp. 13–15 in *The Praise of Lincoln,* edited by A. Dallas Williams. Freeport, NY: Books for Libraries Press.

McCleary, James T. 1908. "What Shall the Lincoln Memorial Be?" *Review of Reviews* 38:339.

McClintock, John. 1865. *Discourse Delivered on the Day of the Funeral of President Lincoln.* New York: J. M. Bradstreet, and Son.

McConnell, Stuart. 1992. *Glorious Contentment: The Grand Army of the Republic, 1865–1900.* Chapel Hill: University of North Carolina Press.

———. 1996. "Reading the Flag: A Reconsideration of the Patriotic Cults of the 1890s." Pp. 102–19 in *Bonds of Affection: Americans Define Their Patriotism,* edited by John Bodnar. Princeton: Princeton University Press.

McCraw, Thomas. 1975. "Regulation in America: A Review Article." *Business History Review* 49:159–83.

McDonagh, Eileen L. 1989. "Issues and Constituencies in the Progressive Era: House Roll Call Voting on the Nineteenth Amendment, 1913–1919." *Journal of Politics* 51:119–36.

———. 1992. "Representative Democracy and State Building in the Progressive Era." *American Political Science Review* 86:938–50.

McDougall, William. 1920. *The Group Mind.* New York: London: G. P. Putnam's Sons.

McPherson, James M. 1991. *Abraham Lincoln and the Second American Revolution.* New York: Oxford University Press.

———. 1994a. "Liberating Lincoln." *New York Review of Books* (April 21): 7–10.

———. 1994b. *What They Fought For: 1861–1865.* Baton Rouge: Louisiana State University Press.

Mead, George Herbert. 1929. "The Nature of the Past." Pp. 235–42 in *Essays in Honor of John Dewey,* edited by J. Coss. New York: Henry Holt.

———. 1932. *The Philosophy of the Present.* LaSalle, IL: Open Court.

———. 1934. *Mind, Self, and Society.* Chicago: University of Chicago Press.

———. 1938. *The Philosophy of the Act.* Chicago: University of Chicago Press.

Mechling, Jay. 1987. "Dress Right, Dress: The Boy Scout Uniform as a Folk Costume." *Semiotica* 64 (3/4): 319–33.

Meier, August. 1963. *Negro Thought in America. 1880–1915.* Ann Arbor: University of Michigan Press.

Meigs, Mark. 1994. "Crash-Course Americanism: The A.E.F. University, 1919." *History Today* (August): 36–43.

Mencken, Henry L. [1918] 1920. "Pater Patriae." *Smart Set* 141:220–23.

Merton, Robert K. 1957. "The Sociology of Knowledge." Pp. 456–88 in *Social Theory and Social Structure.* Glencoe, IL: Free Press.

Metcalf, Peter, and Richard Huntington. 1991. *Celebrations of Death: The Anthropology of Mortuary Ritual.* Cambridge: Cambridge University Press.

Miller, Carolyn Pishny. 1992. "Biographies about Abraham Lincoln for Children (1865–1969): Portrayals of His Parents." Ph.D. diss., Department of Education, University of Illinois.

Miller, Eugene F. 1998. "Democratic Statecraft and Technological Advance: Abraham Lincoln's Reflections on Discoveries and Inventions.'" Manuscript.

Miller, Eugene F., and Barry Schwartz. 1985. "The Icon of the American Republic: A Study in Political Symbolism." *Review of Politics* 47:516–43.

Miller, Paul W., ed. 1949. *Atlanta: Capital of the South.* New York: Oliver Durrell.

Mitchell, S. Weir. [1911] 1970. "Lincoln." P. 70 in *The Praise of Lincoln,* edited by A. Dallas Williams. Freeport, NY: Books for Libraries Press.

Monaghan, Jay, comp. 1943–45. *Lincoln Bibliography, 1839–1939.* 2 vols. Springfield: Illinois State Historical Library Collections.

Moore, Herbert, and W. R. Williams. 1917. "America Today." Chicago: Rossiter. Sheet music.

Moore, Rayburn S. 1982. *A Man of Letters in the Nineteenth Century South: Selected Letters of Paul Hamilton Hayne.* Baton Rouge: Louisiana State University Press.

Morgan, Sarah. 1991. *The Civil War Diary of a Southern Woman.* Athens: University of Georgia Press.

Morris, Richard. 1997. *Sinners, Lovers, and Heroes: An Essay on Memorial-*

izing in Three American Cultures. Albany: State University of New York Press.

Mosse, George L. 1990. *Fallen Soldiers: Shaping the Memory of the World Wars.* New York: Oxford University Press.

Mott, Frank Luther. 1957. *A History of American Magazines.* 4 vols. Cambridge: Harvard University Press.

Mowry, George E. 1958. *The Era of Theodore Roosevelt, 1900–1912.* New York: Harper.

Munch, Richard. 1985. "Commentary." Pp. 225–37 in *Neofunctionalism,* edited by Jeffrey C. Alexander. Beverly Hills, CA: Sage.

Murphy, Con. T. 1898. "Old Glory, the Blue, and the Gray." Chicago: Meyer and Brother. Sheet music.

Murray, Henry. 1962. "Definition of Myth." Pp. 7–37 in *The Making of Myth,* edited by Richard M. Ohmann. New York: G. P. Putnam's Sons.

Nadel, Ehrman S. [1917] 1965. *A Virginian Village.* Freeport, NY: Books for Libraries Press.

Nagel, Paul C. 1971. *This Sacred Trust.* New York: Oxford University Press.

National Industrial Conference Board. 1920. "A Lincoln Day Message." Boston: National Industrial Conference Board. Abraham Lincoln Museum, Harrogate, TN. Brochure.

Naveh, Eyal. 1991. "The Transformation of the 'Rags to Riches' Stories: Business Biographies of Success in the Progressive Era and the 1920s." *American Studies International* 29:60–80.

Neather, Andrew. 1996. "Labor Republicanism, Race, and Popular Patriotism in the Era of Empire, 1890–1914." Pp. 82–101 in *Bonds of Affection: Americans Define Their Patriotism,* edited by John Bodnar. Princeton: Princeton University Press.

Neely, Mark E., Jr. 1982. *The Abraham Lincoln Encyclopedia.* New York: Da Capo Press.

Newkirk, Garrett. 1921. "A Boy at Lincoln's Feet: A Reminiscence of a Lincoln-Douglas Debate." *Outlook* 127:216–17.

"A New Portrait of Abraham Lincoln." c. 1918. Arthur H. Hahlo and Co., New York. Advertisement.

Nicolay, Helen. 1912. "Characteristic Anecdotes of Lincoln: From Unpublished Notes of His Private Secretary, John G. Nicolay." *Century* 84:697–703.

Nicolay, John G. 1891. "Lincoln's Personal Appearance." *Century* 42:932–38.

Nicolay, John G., and John Hay. [1890] 1914. *Abraham Lincoln.* 10 vols. New York: Century Co.

———. 1894. *Complete Works of Abraham Lincoln.* 2 vols. New York: Century Co.

Nisbet, Robert A. 1966. *The Sociological Tradition.* New York: Basic Books.

Noble, David W. 1958. *The Paradox of Progressive Thought.* Minneapolis: University of Minnesota Press.

———. 1970. *The Progressive Mind.* New York: Oxford University Press.

Nora, Pierre. 1996. *Realms of Memory*. New York: Columbia University Press.

Oates, Stephen B. 1977. *With Malice toward None*. New York: Harper and Row.

Olick, Jeffrey K. 1994. "Collective Memory as a Discursive Process: The Nazi Past in West German Politics, 1949–1989." Paper presented at the Annual Meeting of the American Sociological Association, Los Angeles.

———. 1999. "Genre Memories and Memory Genres: A Dialogical Analysis of May 8th, 1945, Commemorations in the Federal Republic of Germany." *American Sociological Review* 64:381–402.

Olick, Jeffrey K., and Daniel Levy. 1997. "Collective Memory and Cultural Constraint: Holocaust Myth and Rationality in German Politics." *American Sociological Review* 62:921–36.

Olick, Jeffrey K., and Joyce Robbins. 1998. "Social Memory Studies: From Collective Memory to the Historical Sociology of Mnemonic Practices." *Annual Review of Sociology* 24:105–40.

O'Neill, Edward H. 1935. *A History of American Biography: 1800–1835*. Philadelphia: University of Pennsylvania Press.

Oppenheim, James. [1911] 1970. "The Lincoln Child." Pp. 196–202 in *The Praise of Lincoln*, edited by A. Dallas Williams. Freeport, NY: Books for Libraries Press.

Ozouf, Mona. 1976. *Festivals and the French Revolution,* trans. Alan Sheridan. Cambridge: Harvard University Press.

Parry, Gwyn A. 1961. "An Amazing Lincoln Death 'Celebration.'" *Northern Neck of Virginia Historical Magazine* 11:1036–39.

Parsons, Talcott. 1951. *The Social System*. New York: Free Press.

Pelikan, Jaroslav. 1985. *Jesus through the Centuries*. New York: Harper and Row.

Persons, Stow. 1973. *The Decline of American Gentility*. New York: Columbia University Press.

Peskin, Allen. 1977. "Putting the Baboon to Rest: Observations of a Radical Republican on Lincoln's Funeral Train." *Lincoln Herald* 79:26–28.

Pessen, Edward. 1984. *The Log Cabin Myth*. New Haven: Yale University Press.

Peterson, Gloria. 1968. *An Administrative History of the Abraham Lincoln Birthplace National Historic Site*. Hodgenville, KY: National Park Service.

Peterson, Merrill D. 1962. *The Jefferson Image in the American Mind*. New York: Oxford University Press.

———. 1994. *Abraham Lincoln in American Memory*. New York: Oxford University Press.

Peterson, Richard A., ed. 1976. *The Production of Culture*. Beverly Hills, CA: Sage.

Pettegrew, John. 1996. "'The Soldier's Faith': Turn-of-the-Century Memory of the Civil War and the Emergence of Modern American Nationalism." *Journal of Contemporary History* 31:49–73.

Philippe, Robert. 1980. *Political Graphics*. New York: Abbeville Press.

Philips, Charles. 1924. "If Abe Came Back." *Catholic World* 119:349–57.

Pickering, W. S. F. 1984. *Durkheim's Sociology of Religion: Themes and Theories.* London: Routledge and Kegan Paul.

Pitcaithley, Dwight. n.d. "A Splendid Hoax: The Strange Case of Abraham Lincoln's Birthplace Cabin." National Park Service. Manuscript.

Plumb, John H. 1970. *The Death of the Past.* Boston: Houghton Mifflin.

Poetical Tributes to the Memory of Abraham Lincoln. 1865. Philadelphia: J. B. Lippincott.

Potter, David M. 1948. *The Lincoln Theme and American National Historiography.* Oxford: Clarendon Press.

———. 1962. "The Quest for the National Character." Pp. 197–220 in *The Reconstruction of American History,* edited by John Higham. New York: Harper and Row.

Powell, Lyman. 1901. "Washington and Lincoln: A Comparative Study." *Review of Reviews* 23:191–96.

Radcliffe-Brown, A. R. [1952] 1968. *Structure and Function in Primitive Society.* New York: Free Press.

Randall, J. G. 1947. *Lincoln: The Liberal Statesman.* New York: Dodd, Mead.

———. 1957. *Mr. Lincoln.* New York: Dodd, Mead.

Rawick, George P., ed. 1977. *The American Slave.* 17 vols. Prepared by the Federal Writers Project of the Works Progress Administration. Westport, CT: Greenwood Press.

Reiter, Howard L. 1998. "The Bases of Progressivism within the Major Parties." *Social Science History* 22:83–116.

Remensnyder, Junius B. 1918. "President Lincoln's Address at Gettysburg." *Outlook* 118:243–44.

Renan, Ernest. [1887] 1947. "Qu'est-ce qu'une nation?" *Oeuvre complète.* 2 vols. Paris: Calman-Levy.

Rhea, Joseph T. 1997. *Race Pride and the American Identity.* Cambridge: Harvard University Press.

Rice, Judith A. 1993. "Abraham Lincoln and Progressive Reform, 1890–1920." Ph.D. diss., Department of History, University of Illinois.

Rieder, Jonathan. 1994. "Doing Political Culture: Interpretive Practice and the Earnest Heuristic." Pp. 117–51 in *Research on Democracy and Society,* vol. 2, edited by Frederick D. Weil. Greenwich, CT: JAI Press.

Rieff, Philip. 1966. *Triumph of the Therapeutic.* New York: Harper and Row.

Robbins, Frank L. 1865. *A Discourse on the Death of Abraham Lincoln.* Philadelphia: Henry B. Ashmead.

Roberts, Mary Fanton. 1917. "Lincoln, Soul and Body of Democracy—As Shown in the Barnard Statue." *Touchstone* 2:54–63.

Roosevelt, Theodore. 1904. *Presidential Addresses and State Papers,* 2 vols. New York: Review of Reviews Co.

———. 1913. *Lincoln Day Speech.* Progressive Service Documents, D-2, New York: Progressive National Committee.

———. 1919. "Lincoln." *Review of Reviews* 59:161–62.

———. 1961. *The New Nationalism*. Introduction by William E. Leuchtenburg. Englewood Cliffs, NJ: Prentice-Hall.

Rusen, Jorn. 1989. "The Development of Narrative Competence in Historical Learning." *History and Memory* 1:35–59.

Rusnack, Robert J. 1982. *Walter Hines Page and the World's Work, 1900–1913*. Washington, DC: University Press of America.

Rutledge, Archibald. 1928. "A Southerner Views Lincoln." *Scribner's Magazine* 83:209–13.

Ryan, Mary. 1989. "The American Parade: Representations of the Nineteenth-Century Social Order." Pp. 131–53 in *The New Cultural History*, edited by Lyn Hunt. Berkeley: University of California Press.

Sanders, Elizabeth. 1990. "State Theory and American Political Development." *Studies in Law, Politics, and Society* 10:93–99.

Sapir, Edward. 1930. "Symbols." Pp. 492–95 in *Encyclopedia of the Social Sciences*, vol. 14. New York: McGraw-Hill.

Saussure, Ferdinand de. [1915] 1966. *Course in General Linguistics*. New York: McGraw-Hill.

Schacter, Daniel L., ed. 1995. *Memory Distortion: How Minds, Brains, and Societies Reconstruct the Past*. Cambridge, MA: Harvard University Press.

Schilder, Paul. 1950. *The Image and Appearance of the Human Body*. New York: International Universities Press.

Schluter, Herman. [1913] 1965. *Lincoln, Labor, and Slavery: A Chapter from the Social History of America*. New York: Russell and Russell.

Schneirov, Matthew. 1994. *The Dream of a New Social Order: Popular Magazines in America, 1893–1914*. New York: Columbia University Press.

Schudson, Michael. 1982. "The Politics of Narrative Form: The Emergence of News Conventions in Print and Television." *Daedalus* 111:97–112.

———. 1989a. "How Culture Works." *Theory and Society* 18:153–80.

———. 1989b. "The Present in the Past versus the Past in the Present." *Communication* 11:105–13.

———. 1992. *Watergate in American Memory*. New York: Basic Books.

———. 1995. "Dynamics of Distortion in Collective Memory." In *How Minds, Brains, and Societies Remember the Past*, edited by Daniel L. Schacter. Cambridge: Harvard University Press.

———. 1997. "Lives, Laws, and Language: Commemorative versus Non-Commemorative Forms of Effective Public Memory." *Communication Review* 2:3–18.

Schuman, Howard. 1995. "Attitudes, Beliefs, and Behavior." Pp. 68–89 in *Sociological Perspectives in Social Psychology*, edited by Karen S. Cook, Gary Alan Fine, and James A. House. New York: Simon and Schuster.

Schuman, Howard, and Amy Corning. 2000. "Collective Knowledge of Public Events: The Soviet Era from the Great Purge to Glastnost." *American Journal of Sociology* 105:913–56.

Schuman, Howard, and Cheryl Rieger. 1992. "Historical Analogies, Generational Effects, and Attitudes toward War." *American Sociological Review* 57:315–26.

Schuman, Howard, and Jacqueline Scott. 1989. "Generations and Collective Memories." *American Sociological Review* 54:359–81.

Schurz, Carl. 1891. "Abraham Lincoln." *Atlantic Monthly* 67:721–50.

Schutz, Alfred. 1970. *On Phenomenology and Social Relations,* edited by Helmut R. Wagner. Chicago: University of Chicago Press.

Schwartz, Barry. 1981. *Vertical Classification.* Chicago: University of Chicago Press.

———. 1982. "The Social Context of Commemoration: A Study in Collective Memory." *Social Forces* 61:374–402.

———. 1983. "George Washington and the Whig Conception of Heroic Leadership." *American Sociological Review* 48:18–33.

———. 1985. "Emerson, Cooley, and the American Heroic Vision." *Symbolic Interaction* 8:103–20.

———. 1987. *George Washington: The Making of an American Symbol.* New York: Free Press.

———. 1991a. "Iconography and Collective Memory: Lincoln's Image in the American Mind." *Sociological Quarterly* 32:301–19.

———. 1991b. "Social Change and Collective Memory: The Democratization of George Washington." *American Sociological Review* 56:221–36.

———. 1993. "Picturing Lincoln." Pp. 135–56 in *Picturing History: American Painting, 1730–1930,* edited by William Ayres. New York: Rizzoli.

———. 1995. "Newark's Seated Washington." *New Jersey History* 113: 23–59.

———. 1996a. "Lincoln at Gettysburg: Social Change and Collective Memory." *Qualitative Sociology* 19:908–27.

———. 1996b. "Memory as a Cultural System: Abraham Lincoln in World War II." *American Sociological Review* 61:908–27.

———. 1997. "History and Collective Memory: How Abraham Lincoln Became a Symbol of Racial Equality." *Sociological Quarterly* 38: 469–96.

———. 1998a. "Frame Images: Toward a Semiotics of Collective Memory." *Semiotica* 121:1–38.

———. 1998b. "Postmodernity and Historical Reputation: Abraham Lincoln in the Late Twentieth Century." *Social Forces* 77:63–103.

Schwartz, Barry, and Lori Holyfield. 1998. "Nixon Postmortem." *Annals of the American Academy of Political and Social Science* 560:96–110.

Schwartz, Barry, and Eugene F. Miller. 1986. "The Icon and the Word: A Study in the Visual Depiction of Moral Character." *Semiotica* 61 (1/2): 69–99.

Schwartz, Barry, and Howard Schuman. 2000. "The Two Meanings of Collective Memory." *Newsletter of the Sociology of Culture Section of the American Sociological Association.* 14:1–3.

Schwengel, Fred. 1963. "A Report to Mr. Lincoln." *Congressional Record,* June 8, 88th Cong., 1st sess., 10172–73.

Shalin, Dmitri. 1988. "G. H. Mead, Socialism, and the Progressive Agenda." *American Journal of Sociology* 93:913–51.

Sheatsley, Paul B., and Jacob J. Feldman. 1965. "A National Survey on Public Reactions and Behavior." Pp. 149–77 in *The Kennedy Assassination and the American Public*, edited by Bradley S. Greenberg and Edwin B. Parker. Stanford: Stanford University Press.

Sherman, Daniel J. 1994. "Art, Commerce, and the Production of Memory in France after World War I." Pp. 186–214 in *Commemorations: The Politics of National Identity*, edited by John R. Gillis. Princeton: Princeton University Press.

Sherwood, Isaac R. 1913. "Lincoln Memorial." *Congressional Record*, January 29, 62nd Cong., 3rd sess., 2233–34.

Shils, Edward A. 1975a. "Charisma, Order, and Status." Pp. 256–75 in *Center and Periphery: Essays in Macrosociology*. Chicago: University of Chicago Press.

———. 1975b. "Ritual and Crisis." Pp. 153–63 in *Center and Periphery: Essays in Macrosociology*. Chicago: University of Chicago Press.

———. 1975c. "Theory of Mass Society." Pp. 91–110 in *Center and Periphery: Essays in Macrosociology*. Chicago: University of Chicago Press.

———. 1981. *Tradition*. Chicago: University of Chicago Press.

Shils, Edward, and Michael Young. 1975. "The Meaning of the Coronation." Pp. 135–52 in *Center and Periphery: Essays in Macrosociology*. Chicago: University of Chicago Press.

Silver, Abba Hillel. 1927. "A Saint of Democracy." Pp. 643–49 in *The Tribute of the Synagogue*, edited by Emanuel Hertz. New York: Block Publishing Co.

Sinclair, Upton. 1906. *The Jungle*. New York: Doubleday, Page, and Co.

Sinkler, George. 1971. *The Racial Attitudes of American Presidents*. Garden City: Doubleday.

Sklar, Kathryn Kish. 1988. "Organized Womanhood: Archival Sources on Women and Progressive Reform." *Journal of American History* 75:176–83.

Smith, Philip. 1991. "Codes and Conflict: Toward a Theory of War as Ritual." *Theory and Society* 20:103–38.

Spillman, Lyn. 1997. *Nation and Commemoration*. Cambridge: Cambridge University Press.

Steiner, Edward A. 1918. *Uncle Joe's Lincoln*. New York: Fleming H. Revell Co.

Stephenson, Charles Todd. 1993. "Celebrating American Heroes: The Commemoration of George Washington, Abraham Lincoln, Theodore Roosevelt, and Thomas Jefferson, 1832–1943." Ph.D. diss., Department of History, Brown University.

Stephenson, Nathaniel W. 1919. "Lincoln and the Progress of Nationality in the North." *Annual Report of the American Historical Association* 1:351–63.

———. 1922. *Lincoln: An Account of His Personal Life, Especially of Its Springs of Action as Revealed and Deepened by the Ordeal of War*. Indianapolis: Bobbs-Merrill.

Stewart, Judd. 1912. *Abraham Lincoln on Present-Day and Abraham Lincoln as Represented by Theodore Roosevelt*. Letter to Members of the

State Constitutional Convention, Columbus, Ohio. Plainfield, NJ: np. Illinois State Historical Society, box 31. Pamphlet.

Stoddard, W. O. 1885. *Abraham Lincoln: True Story of a Great Life.* New York: Fords, Howard, and Hulbert.

Stone, Andrew L. 1865. "A Discourse Occasioned by the Death of Abraham Lincoln." Pp. 337–58 in *Sermons Preached in Boston.* Boston: J. E. Tilton.

Strange, Jeffrey J., and Cynthia C. Leung. 1999. "How Anecdotal Accounts in News and in Fiction Can Influence Judgements of a Social Problem's Urgency, Causes, and Cures." *Personality and Social Psychology Bulletin.* 25:436–49.

Strong, George Templeton. [1865] 1952. *Diary of George Templeton Strong,* edited by Allan Nevins and Milton H. Thomas. 3 vols. New York: Macmillan.

Strong, Sydney. 1920. *Jesus and Lincoln.* Seattle, WA: Queen Anne Congregational Church.

Sumner, Charles. [1900] 1969. *His Complete Works,* 20 vols. New York: Negro Universities Press.

Swidler, Ann, and J. Arditi. 1994. "The New Sociology of Knowledge." Pp. 305–29 in *Annual Review of Sociology,* edited by John Hagan. Palo Alto, CA: Annual Reviews.

Swidler, Ann. 1986. "Culture in Action: Symbols and Strategies." *American Sociological Review* 51:273–86.

Tarbell, Ida M. 1895. *The Life of Abraham Lincoln.* 2 vols. New York: Doubleday and McClure.

———. 1923. "Abraham Lincoln's Money Sense." *American Magazine* 99:13–15+.

———. 1924. *In the Footsteps of Lincoln.* New York: Harper and Brothers.

———. 1939. *All in the Day's Work: An Autobiography.* New York: McMillan.

Tariello, Frank. 1981. *The Reconstruction of American Political Ideology, 1865–1917.* Charlottesville: University Press of Virginia.

Teller, Morris. 1927. "Washington and Lincoln." Pp. 679–81 in *The Tribute of the Synagogue,* edited by Emmanuel Hertz. New York: Block Publishing Co.

Terdiman, Richard. 1993. *Present Past: Modernity and the Memory Crisis.* Ithaca: Cornell University Press.

Thayer, Mrs. Charles M. 1922. "My Interview with Robert Lincoln, September 1922." Washington, DC, Library of Congress, Manuscript Division, Gutzon Borglum Papers, box 73. Typescript.

Thistlethwaite, Mark 1988. "The Most Important Themes: History Painting and Its Place in American Art." Pp. 7–58 in *Grand Illusions: History Painting in America,* edited by William H. Gerdts and Mark Thistlethwaite. Fort Worth, TX: Amon Carter Museum.

———. 1979. *The Image of George Washington.* New York: Garland.

Thomas, Benjamin P. 1947. *Portrait for Posterity: Lincoln and His Biographers.* New Brunswick: Rutgers University Press.

Thomas, Christopher A. 1991. "The Lincoln Memorial and Its Architect, Henry Bacon." Ph.D. diss., Dept. of History of Art, Yale University.

Thrall, William F., Addison Hibbard, and C. Hugh Holman. 1960. *A Handbook to Literature*. New York: Odyssey Press.

de Tocqueville, Alexis. [1840] 1945. *Democracy in America*. Vol. 2. New York: Knopf.

Towne, Laura M. 1969. *Letters and Diary of Laura M. Towne*. New York: Negro Universities Press.

Tuchman, Gaye, and Nina Fortin. 1989. *Edging Women Out: Victorian Novelists, Publishers, and Social Change*. New Haven: Yale University Press.

Tucker, Robert C. 1973. *Stalin as Revolutionary, 1879–1929: A Study in History and Personality*. New York: W. W. Norton.

Turner, Ralph. 1976. "The Real Self: From Institution to Impulse." *American Journal of Sociology* 81:989–1016.

Turner, Stephen. 1999. "Imitation or the Internalization of Norms: Is Twentieth-Century Social Theory Based on the Wrong Choice?" Paper presented at the Annual Meeting of the American Sociological Association, Chicago, IL, August.

Twain, Mark. n.d. *A Birthplace Worth Saving*. Circular.

Tylor, Lyon G. 1921. *Propaganda in History*. Richmond, VA: Richmond Press.

United States. n.d. *The Civil War in Motion Pictures: A Bibliography of Films Produced in the United States since 1897*. Washington, DC: Library of Congress.

U.S. Department of Commerce. 1920. *Census of the United States*. Washington, DC: Bureau of the Census.

———. 1975. *Historical Statistics of the United States, Colonial Times to 1970*. Part 1. Washington, DC: Bureau of the Census.

U.S. House of Representatives. 1913. *Congressional Record*, February 12, 62nd Cong., 3rd sess.

———. 1914. *Congressional Record*, February 12, 63rd Cong., 3rd sess.

———. 1915. *Congressional Record*, March 4, 63rd Cong., 3rd sess.

———. 1918. *Congressional Record*, February 12, 65th Cong., 2nd sess.

———. 1920. *Congressional Record*, February 13, 66th Cong., 2nd sess., 8783–85.

———. 1925. *Congressional Record*, "Address by Dr. John Wesley Hill on Abraham Lincoln." February 23, 68th Cong., 2nd sess., 4447–49.

Verba, Sidney. 1965. "The Kennedy Assassination and the Nature of Political Commitment." Pp. 348–60 in *The Kennedy Assassination and the American Public*, edited by Bradley S. Greenberg and Edwin B. Parker. Stanford: Stanford University Press.

Walzer, Michael. 1967. "On the Role of Symbolism in Political Thought." *Political Science Quarterly* 82:191–205.

Ward, John W. 1955. *Andrew Jackson: Symbol for an Age*. New York: Oxford University Press.

Warner, Lloyd. 1959. *The Living and the Dead*. New Haven: Yale University Press.

Warren, Louis A. 1950. "The Traditional Birthplace Cabin." Abraham Lincoln National Historical Park, Hodgenville, KY. Manuscript.

Watterson, Henry. 1909. "Lincoln from the Southern Standpoint." *Cosmopolitan* 46:363–75.

Weber, Max. 1947. *The Theory of Social and Economic Organization*, edited by Talcott Parsons. New York: Oxford University Press.

———. 1949. *Methodology of the Social Sciences*, trans. Edward A. Shils and Henry A. Finch. Glencoe, IL: Free Press.

———. 1968. *Economy and Society*. Vols. 1–2. Berkeley: University of California Press.

Weik, Jesse W. 1909. "Personal Recollections." *Outlook* 91:345–48.

Webster, J. Stanley. 1916. *Abraham Lincoln*. Speech to Young Men's Republican Club, February 11. Seattle, WA.

Weisberger, Bernard A. 1994. *The La Follettes of Wisconsin: Love and Politics in Progressive America*. Madison: University of Wisconsin Press.

Weldon, Mary Susan, and Krystal D. Bellinger. 1997. "Collective Memory: Collaborative and Individual Processes in Remembering." *Journal of Experimental Psychology: Learning, Memory, and Cognition* 23:1160–75.

Welles, Gideon. 1909. "The Diary of Gideon Welles: The Death of Lincoln" *Atlantic* 54:590–92.

West, Willis Mason. 1913. *American History and Government*. Boston: Allyn and Bacon.

"What I Have Learned from Abe Lincoln." 1918. *American Magazine* 85: 17–19.

Wheeler, Marjorie S. 1993. *The New Women of the South: The Leaders of the Woman Suffrage Movement in the Southern States*. New York: Oxford University Press.

White, Ethel Bowen. 1919. *Harry's Hero*. Springfield: Collections of the Illinois State Historical Library.

White, William Allen. 1910. *The Old Order Changeth: A View of American Democracy*. New York: Macmillan.

Wiebe, Robert H. 1967. *The Search for Order, 1877–1920*. New York: Hill and Wang.

Wiggins, William H. 1987. *O Freedom! Afro-American Emancipation Celebrations*. Knoxville: University of Tennessee Press.

Wiley, Alma Adams. 1925. "The Lincoln Memorial." *Ladies Home Journal* 42:27.

Williams, Raymond. 1987. *Marxism and Literature*. New York: Oxford University Press.

Williams, Wayne C. 1922. "Abraham Lincoln and Nicolai Lenine—A Contrast." *Current Opinion* 72:320–23.

Wills, Garry. 1992. *Lincoln at Gettysburg: The Words That Remade America*. New York: Simon and Schuster.

Wilson, Douglas L. 1998a. "Lincoln's Affair of Honor." *Atlantic Monthly* 281:64–71.

———. 1998b. *Honor's Voice: The Transformation of Abraham Lincoln*. New York: Knopf.

Wilson, James Grant. 1904. "Washington, Lincoln, and Grant." *Cornhill* 90:456–61.

Wilson, Richard G., Dianne H. Pilgrim, and Richard N. Murray. 1979. *The American Renaissance, 1876–1917.* New York: Pantheon.

Wilson, Samuel. 1910. *Abraham Lincoln: An Apostle of Temperance and Prohibition.* Westerville, OH: American Issue Publishing Co.

Wilson, Woodrow. 1889. *The State: Elements of Historical and Practical Politics.* Boston: D. C. Heath and Co.

Wilson, Woodrow. 1917. *A Compilation of the Messages and Papers of the Presidents.* 20 vols. Prepared under the direction of the Joint Committee of Printing of the House and Senate. New York: Bureau of National Literature.

———. 1966. *Papers.* Edited by Arthur S. Link, et al. 69 vols. Princeton: Princeton University Press.

de Witt, Benjamin Parke. [1915] 1968. *The Progressive Movement.* Seattle, WA: University of Washington Press.

Wolf, Simon. [1888] 1927. "Abraham Lincoln." Pp. 187–90 in *Tribute of the Synagogue,* edited by Emanuel Hertz. New York: Block Publishing Co.

Wood, Nancy. 1994. "Memories' Remains: Les Lieux de Mémoire." *History and Memory* 6:123–49.

Woodward, C. Vann. 1957. *The Strange Career of Jim Crow.* New York: Oxford University Press.

———. 1971. *Origins of the New South: 1877–1913.* Baton Rouge: Louisiana State University Press.

Wright-Davis, Mary. 1919. *The Book of Lincoln.* New York: George H. Doran, Co.

Yerushalmi, Josef H. 1982. *Zakhor: Jewish History and Jewish Memory.* Seattle: University of Washington Press.

Yetman, Norman R. 1970. *Life under the Peculiar Institution: Selections from the Slave Narrative Collection.* New York: Holt, Rinehart and Winston.

Zangwill, Israel. 1914. *The Melting Pot.* London: W. Heinemann.

Zelinsky, Wilbur. 1988. *Nation into State: The Shifting Symbolic Foundations of American Nationalism.* Chapel Hill: University of North Carolina Press.

Zelizer, Barbie. 1995. "Reading the Past against the Grain: The Shape of Memory Studies." *Critical Studies in Mass Communication* 12:214–39.

Zerubavel, Eviatar. 1997. *Social Mindscapes: An Invitation to Cognitive Sociology.* Cambridge: Harvard University Press.

Zerubavel, Yael. 1995. *Recovered Roots.* Chicago: University of Chicago Press.

Zilversmit, Arthur, ed. 1971. *Lincoln on Black and White: A Documentary History.* Belmont, CA: Wadsworth.

Zinn, Howard. 1980. *A People's History of the United States.* New York: Harper.

Zmora, Nurit. 1994. *Orphanages Reconsidered: Child Care Institutions in Progressive Era Baltimore.* Philadelphia: Temple University Press.

Index